The Gospel and Henry VIII

During the last decade of Henry VIII's life, his Protestant subjects struggled to reconcile two loyalties: to their Gospel and to their king. This book tells the story of that struggle and describes how a radicalised English Protestantism emerged from it.

Focusing on the critical but neglected period 1539–47, Dr Ryrie argues that these years were not the 'conservative reaction' of conventional historiography, but a time of political fluidity and ambiguity. Most evangelicals continued to hope that the king would favour their cause, and remained doctrinally moderate and politically conformist. The author examines this moderate reformism in a range of settings – in the book trade, in the universities, at court and in underground congregations. He also describes its gradual eclipse, as shifting royal policy and the dynamics of the evangelical movement itself pushed reformers towards the more radical, confrontational Protestantism which was to shape the English identity for centuries.

ALEC RYRIE is Lecturer in Modern History at the University of Birmingham.

Cambridge Studies in Early Modern British History

Series editors

ANTHONY FLETCHER
Professor of Social History, Institute of Historical Research, University of London

JOHN GUY
Visiting Research Fellow, Clare College, Cambridge

JOHN MORRILL
*Professor of British and Irish History, University of Cambridge,
and Vice-Master of Selwyn College*

This is a series of monographs and studies covering many aspects of the history of the British Isles between the late fifteenth century and the early eighteenth century. It includes the work of established scholars and pioneering work by a new generation of scholars. It includes both reviews and revisions of major topics and books, which open up new historical terrain or which reveal startling new perspectives on familiar subjects. All the volumes set detailed research into our broader perspectives and the books are intended for the use of students as well as of their teachers.

For a list of titles in the series, see end of book.

THE GOSPEL AND HENRY VIII
Evangelicals in the Early English Reformation

ALEC RYRIE
University of Birmingham

CAMBRIDGE UNIVERSITY PRESS
Cambridge, New York, Melbourne, Madrid, Cape Town, Singapore, São Paulo

Cambridge University Press
The Edinburgh Building, Cambridge CB2 8RU, UK

Published in the United States of America by Cambridge University Press, New York

www.cambridge.org
Information on this title: www.cambridge.org/9780521823432

© Alec Ryrie 2003

This publication is in copyright. Subject to statutory exception
and to the provisions of relevant collective licensing agreements,
no reproduction of any part may take place without the written
permission of Cambridge University Press.

First published 2003
This digitally printed version 2007

A catalogue record for this publication is available from the British Library

Library of Congress Cataloguing in Publication data
Ryrie, Alec.
The Gospel and Henry VIII : evangelicals in the early English Reformation / Alec Ryrie
p. cm. – (Cambridge Studies in Early Modern British History)
Includes bibliographical references and index.
ISBN 0 521 82343 9
1. Reformation – England. 2. Protestantism – England – History – 16th century.
3. Henry VIII, King of England, 1491–1547. 4. Great Britain – History – Henry VIII,
1509–1547.
I. Title. II. Series.
BR377.R97   2003
274.2′06 – dc21   2003046118

ISBN 978-0-521-82343-2 hardback
ISBN 978-0-521-03665-8 paperback

For Victoria

*No man can serue two masters. For ether he shall hate the one and love the other,
or elles leane to the one, and despise the other.*
Matthew 6:24

Feare God. Honoure the kynge.
I Peter 2:17

CONTENTS

List of figures	page xi
List of tables	xii
Acknowledgements	xiii
Notes on the text	xv
List of abbreviations	xviii
Introduction	1
The woman on the rock	1
The nature of the problem	5

Part I: The regime and the reformers

1	A Counter-Reformation?	13
	Interpreting the 'Henrician reaction'	13
	The whip with six strings	23
	Religious policy in the 1540s	39
2	Fearing God and honouring the king	58
	The obedience of a Christian man	58
	'Walke soberly': defiance, dishonesty and discretion	69

Part II: The faces of reform

3	The exiles	93
4	Pulpit and printshop	113
	A loyal opposition	113
	Polemicists and their audiences	121
	Justification and the Mass	134
	The commonwealth	145
5	The universities	157
	Godliness and good learning	157

	'The corruption of the realme'	170
	Pronunciation and authority	183
6	The court	194
	In the shadow of the king	194
	'A madding tyme': poets and reformers	205
	The road back to Rome	213
7	The evangelical underground	223
	The unacceptable face of reformism	223
	Radical conventicles and respectable patrons	237
	Conclusion	248

Appendixes 259

Appendix I: Reformers executed or exiled between the passage of the Act of Six Articles and the death of Henry VIII — 261

Appendix II: Controversial religious printing in English, 1541–6 — 271

Bibliography 274
Index 293

FIGURES

A1 Controversial religious imprints in English, 1541–6   *page* 271
A2 English-language imprints by type, 1541–6   273

TABLES

5.1	Works by Protestant authors owned by Cambridge testators, 1535–47	page 172
7.1	Accusations of heresy against Kentish clergy, 1543	224
7.2	Accusations of heresy against Kentish laity, 1543	225
7.3	Accusations of heresy against London laity, July 1540	225

ACKNOWLEDGEMENTS

A book may have one name on the cover, but behind it stands a cast of thousands. My debt to my teachers is lasting, especially Gardiner Thompson, Sandra Raban and Jonathan Steinberg. Andrew Pettegree introduced me to Reformation studies, and he continues to remind me that the Reformation's proper stage is Europe as a whole. I am particularly grateful to John Jackson, for his scholarship as well as for his and his family's unfailing hospitality and friendship. Craig D'Alton's uncanny understanding of the Bodleian Library, and Chris Chapman's principle of photocopying everything, saved me a great deal of time; both of them also helped me to waste time very agreeably. Tom Freeman initiated me into the mysteries of John Foxe; Michael Riordan allowed me to use his invaluable register of court reformers. I am also indebted to the late John Fines for giving me a copy of his register of early English Protestants. Helen Parish and Tim Watson helped me to understand a few of Oxford's foibles, and Vicky Leat showed me that the research process is survivable. Richard Hall and everyone from Saltford, Corston and Newton St Loe supported me more than they know.

Since I began the work on which this book is based in 1996, a great many long-suffering friends and colleagues have heard or read more than they might ever have wished to about 1540s evangelicalism. The European Reformation Research Group's conferences have been a valuable source of intellectual and other refreshment. The book has benefited in numerous ways from Peter Marshall's shrewd insights, as I have from his friendship. In particular, he read portions of the text and made valuable comments, as did Craig D'Alton, Tom Freeman, Felicity Heal and Michael Riordan. Susan Brigden and Ralph Houlbrooke, who examined the doctoral thesis on which this book is based, were generous in their support and perceptive in their criticism; I am grateful to them for both. I have also benefited from conversations with – among others – Caroline Campbell, Louise Campbell, Eric Carlson, Catharine Davies, Martin Dotterweich, Eamon Duffy, Carrie Euler, Christopher Haigh, Elisabeth Leedham-Green, Caroline Litzenberger, Graeme Murdock, Judith Pollmann, Richard Rex, Ethan Shagan, Brett

Usher, Alexandra Walsham, Bill Wizeman and Margaret Yates. None of these people will agree with everything I have said; nor should they be blamed for the errors which have survived despite them.

One of the greatest debts which the researcher incurs is to the patience, courtesy and efficiency of librarians and archivists. I am grateful to the staff of the following institutions for their assistance, as I am to the institutions for allowing me the use of their collections: the Bodleian Library in Oxford; in Cambridge, the University Library, and the libraries of Corpus Christi, Emmanuel and Trinity Colleges; the British Library; the Public Record Office; the Corporation of London Records Office; the Guildhall Library; Lambeth Palace Library; the Library of the Honourable Society of the Inner Temple; the Wellcome Institute for the History of Medicine; the Folger Shakespeare Library; the county record offices of Devon, Gloucestershire, Norfolk, Northamptonshire, Wiltshire and Worcestershire; the Library of Shrewsbury School; St. Andrews University Library; Birmingham University Library; and perhaps most of all, Bristol University Library. During 1996–9 I held a postgraduate studentship from the Humanities Research Board of the British Academy, and the text of the book was completed during a period of study leave granted by the University of Birmingham in 2002: I am grateful for both. The benefits I have derived from belonging to the scholarly communities at Birmingham and at St Cross College, Oxford are less tangible but no less important.

Three thanks in particular need to be underlined. To Diarmaid MacCulloch, who was a model doctoral supervisor; much of what merit this book may have is due to him. It has been a privilege and a pleasure to work with him. To my parents, who first sparked my love for history, and who supported me throughout the process even to the extent of reading the entire text; but in truth my debt to them both cannot be calculated. And finally, to Victoria, who makes it worthwhile.

NOTES ON THE TEXT

A PROBLEM OF TERMINOLOGY

This book is about the religious conflicts in England in the last decade or so of Henry VIII's life (c. 1538–47). Those conflicts were bitter, but they were also ill-defined. The religious controversialists of the Reformation had not yet sorted themselves out into clear parties. This was true across Europe, but sharp divisions were particularly slow to form in England. The religious confusion and fluidity which resulted is one of the central themes of this book. It also gives rise to a problem of terminology, for by the 1540s, no generally accepted terms had as yet been coined for the emerging religious factions.

The obvious labels – 'Catholic' and 'Protestant' – are problematic. All sides claimed to be Catholic Christians. The claim was made with particular energy by those (like Henry VIII) who rejected the papacy but remained opposed to further doctrinal change. From Rome's perspective, however, these people were no more Catholic than Martin Luther.[1] The least inadequate description of these people is as 'conservative' or 'traditionalist', and these are the usages I have adopted. However, they come with a health warning, since many of these people were in their own terms energetic reformers. Their 'conservatism' consists of their rejection of the doctrinal claims of Protestantism – and some 'conservatives' were open to a degree of compromise even on this.

To speak of 'Protestantism', however, is to imply a much more firmly defined identity than as yet existed. When the word was used at all in 1540s England, it referred to the German states which had embraced Luther's doctrines and had formed a military alliance against the Holy Roman Emperor, Charles V. Only after Henry VIII's death in 1547 do we find it being applied to religious reformers in England. In this book, 'Protestant' is used – with

---

[1] Peter Marshall, 'Is the Pope a Catholic? Henry VIII and the semantics of schism', in *Catholics and the Protestant Nation: English Catholicism in Context 1534–1640*, ed. M. Sena and Ethan Shagan (Manchester, forthcoming 2004).

only mild anachronism – to refer to the theologies of Luther, Zwingli and other leading Continental reformers (as well as to the broader Protestant movement as it was later to become established in England). Several recent studies have described the English reformers who were influenced by those theologies as 'evangelicals' or 'gospellers', and I have followed this usage.[2] These were at least terms which contemporaries would have recognised, although they are not without difficulties. The reformers' claim that the Gospel was their exclusive property is as questionable as their opponents' claim to be the only Catholic Christians. Moreover, 'evangelical' suggests an experiential and emotional form of Christianity which belongs more to the eighteenth century than the sixteenth.

Other terms are more straightforward. I have used 'reformer' and 'reformist' to refer to all those who wished for a thorough reform of Christian doctrine – principally evangelicals, but also those influenced by the indigenous English tradition of Lollardy. Terms such as 'Lutheran' and 'Reformed'[3] are intended to carry at least a degree of doctrinal precision, although those positions were themselves very loosely defined in this period. The contemporary terms 'sacramentary' and 'sacramentarian' refer to those who *denied* that Christ was really, objectively and bodily present in the bread and wine of the Eucharist. Reformed Protestants were sacramentaries; Lutherans, however, were not, and affirmed Christ's bodily presence without embracing the full-blown Catholic doctrine of transubstantiation. This issue was a key fault line in 1540s English evangelicalism.

Such vague terminology is regrettable, and an annoyance both to writer and reader. But it is not an accident. It reflects the reality that religious divisions and religious communities were themselves vague and ill-defined during this early period of the Reformation. If ambiguous terminology reminds us that the religious conflicts of this period were beset with ambiguity, it has served its purpose.

SOURCES AND CONVENTIONS

In quoting from contemporary texts all abbreviations have been silently expanded. Some punctuation and capitalisation has been amended for clarity. All translations are my own unless otherwise noted. All Biblical quotations

---

[2] Peter Marshall and Alec Ryrie, 'Protestantisms and their beginnings', in *The Beginnings of English Protestantism*, ed. Marshall and Ryrie (Cambridge, 2002), 5; Diarmaid MacCulloch, *Thomas Cranmer: A Life* (New Haven and London, 1996), 2–3. For a different approach to the same question, see Catharine Davies, *A Religion of the Word: The Defence of the Reformation in the Reign of Edward VI* (Manchester, 2002), xx.

[3] 'Reformed' Protestantism is the tradition arising from Switzerland and the Rhineland, whose founding father was Huldrych Zwingli but which was later identified with Jean Calvin.

are taken from the Great Bible of 1539. The year is reckoned to begin on 1 January throughout.

Much of chapter 4, and sections of chapter 7 and of the conclusion, draw on my article 'The strange death of Lutheran England', *Journal of Ecclesiastical History* 53 (2002), 64–92.

ABBREVIATIONS

AM	John Foxe, *Actes and monuments of matters most speciall in the church* (RSTC 11225: 1583)
AM (1563)	John Foxe, *Actes and Monuments of these latter and perillous dayes* (RSTC 11222: 1563)
APC	*Acts of the Privy Council of England*, ed. John R. Dasent, vol. I (1890)
BL	British Library
Bonner Register	Guildhall Library, London, MS 9531/12
CCCC	Corpus Christi College, Cambridge
CLRO	Corporation of London Record Office
DNB	*Dictionary of National Biography*
ECL	Emmanuel College Library, Cambridge
Emden	A. B. Emden, *A Biographical Register of the University of Oxford A.D. 1501 to 1540* (Oxford, 1974)
ET	*Epistolae Tigurinae de rebus potissimum ad ecclesiae Anglicanae reformationem* (Cambridge: Parker Society, 1848)
HJ	*The Historical Journal*
HPT	*The House of Commons 1509–58*, ed. S. T. Bindoff, 3 vols. (History of Parliament Trust, 1982)
JEH	*Journal of Ecclesiastical History*
LJ	*Journals of the House of Lords*, vol. I
LP	*Letters & Papers, Foreign & Domestic, of the Reign of Henry VIII*, ed. James Gairdner and R. H. Brodie, 21 vols. (1862–1932)
OL	*Original Letters relative to the English Reformation*, ed. Hastings Robinson (Cambridge: Parker Society, 1846)
P&O	*Proceedings and Ordinances of the Privy Council of England*, ed. Harris Nicolas, vol. VII (1837)
PRO	Public Record Office

RSTC	W. A. Jackson, F. J. Ferguson and K. F. Pantzer, *A Short-Title Catalogue of Books Printed . . . 1475–1640 . . . revised* (1986)
TCC	Trinity College, Cambridge
TRP	*Tudor Royal Proclamations 1485–1553*, ed. Paul L. Hughes and James F. Larkin (New Haven and London, 1964)
WCRO	Worcestershire County Record Office
Wriothesley	Charles Wriothesley, *A Chronicle of England during the Reigns of the Tudors*, ed. William D. Hamilton, vol. I, Camden Society new series 11 (1875)

The place of publication for all works is London unless otherwise noted.

Introduction

THE WOMAN ON THE ROCK

In 1537 the vicar of Yoxford in Suffolk, a man named Thomas Wylley, wrote to Henry VIII's chief minister Thomas Cromwell. The ostensible purpose of the letter was to complain about his parishioners and neighbours, who had responded with open hostility to the reformist Gospel which he was preaching. Despite that Gospel's official backing, Wylley protested, 'the most part of the prystes of Suffolk wyll not reseyve me yn to ther Chyrchys to preche'. Instead, he was reputed to be 'a gret lyar'. And so he appealed for Cromwell to support him against these local obscurantists: 'The Lorde make you the Instrument of my helpe Lorde Cromewell, that I may have the lyberty to preche the trewthe.'

The bulk of the letter, however, was given over to demonstrating exactly how Wylley had been preaching the truth. He was an aspiring playwright, and had been using the stage as a propaganda tool. At least one of his plays had already been performed. He enclosed the text of a second, 'a Reverent Recyvyng of the sacrament', with his letter, emphasising that he had dedicated it to Cromwell. Clearly, his hope was less for the liberty to preach in and around Yoxford than for the liberty to leave Suffolk altogether and enter Cromwell's service. His feelings for his flock can perhaps be guessed from the title of one of his plays: 'a Rude Commynawlte'.[1]

We know nothing more about the ambitious vicar of Yoxford. His story could be retold almost endlessly from the state papers of the late 1530s, and scholars of the English Reformation since the mid-1970s have done just that. This is a story of evangelical reformers, the forerunners of English Protestantism, struggling to make themselves heard in a country where loyalty to traditional religion ran deep, and where the new Gospel which they preached met with widespread hostility – not least because of its very novelty. It is a story of a new religion being forced on an unwilling people by the power of

---

[1] PRO SP 1/116 fo. 158ʳ (*LP* XII (i) 529).

the Tudor state; a story whose moral, in J. J. Scarisbrick's words, is that 'on the whole, English men and women did not want the Reformation and most of them were slow to accept it when it came'.[2]

However, this is not the only story which Thomas Wylley's letter tells. He informed Cromwell that he was composing yet another play, 'caulyd, The Woman on the Rokke, yn the fyer of faythe affynyng, & a purgyng yn the trewe purgatory'. No text survives for this, or any of Wylley's plays, but we may guess at its theme. The woman on the rock presumably represents the true Church, the bride of Christ. Wylley seems to be drawing on the symbolism of the Book of Revelation, in which the woman with child who symbolises either the Virgin Mary or the Church is persecuted by the devil, and carried away to safety. In Wylley's version, however, the woman is not in the wilderness, but on the Rock, that is, grounded in Christ himself. Despite her travails, she has a firm footing. More interestingly, the persecution she faces is described as the fire of faith, refining and purging her. Rather than being troubled by the devil, she is burning in a refiner's fire, a biblical symbol for God. This fire is both caused by her faith and a means of purifying that faith.[3] This play seems to have been telling a story far older than that told by the 'revisionist' historians of the Reformation. Here we have, apparently, the classic Protestant tale of the true Church under persecution. It is a precursor of the story told so vividly a generation later, in John Foxe's huge and hugely influential history of the English Church and its martyrs, the *Actes and Monuments*.

The central assumption of this Protestant view of the Reformation was that the religious conflicts in sixteenth-century Europe were a reflection of the eternal, cosmic confrontation between Christ and Antichrist. Foxe maintained that the division between papist and Protestant was no chance alignment, the result of the contingencies of religious politics. It was a worldly reflection of a spiritual chasm.

> There is no neutrality, nor mediation of peace, nor exhortation to agrement that will serue betwene these two contrary doctrines, but either the Popes errors must geue place to Gods word, or els the veritye of God must geue place vnto them.[4]

On this view the religious divide was both eternal and unbridgeable. And this basic dualism was affirmed across Europe by polemicists on both sides. Catholics merely reversed the colours. The eventual formalisation of the divide and the creation of entrenched religious identities defined over against one another lent apparent support to Foxe's view. Until recently, it was common practice for historians tacitly to affirm this interpretation by using the

---

[2] J. J. Scarisbrick, *The Reformation and the English People* (Oxford, 1984), 1.
[3] Psalm 40:2; Malachi 3:2; Matthew 7:24–27; Hebrews 12:29; I Peter 1:7; Revelation 12.
[4] *AM*, 1234.

terms 'Catholic' and 'Protestant' as party labels from the very beginning of the Reformation controversies. The terminological problems arising from the realisation that this is untenable have not yet been resolved satisfactorily.[5] This book, however, argues that Foxe was wrong. The religious divide which Foxe celebrated, and which he did so much to perpetuate, need not have taken the shape which it eventually did. There was both mediation of peace and exhortation to agreement, nor did the two doctrines always appear so contrary. In the early years of the Reformation, religious reform had many faces, and not all of them fit into the later portraits of the Reformation as it should have been.

Foxe's depiction of an unbridgeable religious divide has proved to be remarkably enduring. Partisan Catholic and Protestant historians have long shared an interest in maintaining it, and some recent scholarship emphasising the vitality of traditional religion has also reinforced it. However, the new interest in traditional religion has also allowed the wide variations in English religious belief and practice in the first two generations of the Reformation to come to light. Some other recent work has argued that the opposing religious parties were less sharply separated from one another and from mass culture than they would have liked to believe.[6] This book examines an old subject – early English Protestantism – in the light of our new-found awareness of the many-headed nature of religious culture in this period. It traces the more important strands of reformist thought and behaviour, and connects them to their broader political and social context. It follows their development over one critical period of the English Reformation, the last years of Henry VIII's life; from the closing period of Cromwell's Reformation in 1538–40, marked by a perceived official rejection of further religious change, to the death of the old king in January 1547, which – as things turned out – opened the way for an aggressively Protestant regime under his young son Edward VI. And it argues that the fate of evangelicalism during those years was dominated by the tension between the reformers' two loyalties, to their king and to their faith.

In this early period of the Reformation, evangelicals hoped that that tension could be resolved. The divisions of which Foxe later wrote were far from watertight. Thomas Wylley's play might serve as a symbol of this ambiguity. The woman on the rock may be a symbol of Protestantism under persecution, but the description of her suffering is lifted from traditional Catholic theology. She is 'a purgyng yn the trewe purgatory'. We may be sure that the play was polemical, but its polemic borrowed from the vocabulary of

---

[5] See above, pp. xv–xvi.
[6] See, for example, Christopher Marsh, *Popular Religion in Sixteenth-Century England* (Basingstoke, Hants., 1998); Alexandra Walsham, *Providence in Early Modern England* (Oxford, 1999).

its opponents. There was no room for the traditional doctrine of purgatory in the kind of evangelicalism which Wylley preached. Purgatory was not mentioned in Scripture. Evangelicals roundly rejected the idea that penitential suffering after death could be part of the scheme of salvation, arguing that this made Christ's sacrifice meaningless. Wylley's reference to the 'trewe' purgatory makes it clear that he shared these reservations. His 'purgatory' appears to be a metaphor for suffering for the sake of Christ in this world. However, by using the idea of purgatory rather than simply denouncing it, he ventured onto his opponents' doctrinal ground. Most religious polemic of the Reformation era was a dialogue of the deaf, with polemicists more concerned to shore up the faith of the converted than to persuade their opponents. In this case, however, both the medium of drama and the use of an opponent's vocabulary suggest a genuine attempt to reach out to the unconverted. Wylley's unmistakably evangelical ideas are deliberately framed so as to be accessible to a traditionalist audience. Moreover, this is more than a canny technique of proselytisation. His use of purgatory as an image unavoidably implies that traditional religion might have something to contribute towards the right understanding of the faith. There was a true purgatory even if purgatory as his audience understood it was false.

The years after Cromwell's fall in 1540 were troubled times for reformers. The fire of faith claimed its victims, and others, like the woman in Revelation, were carried to the cruel safety of exile. But most of them remained 'affynyng, & a purgyng yn the trewe purgatory'. Many were like Thomas Wylley, whose opposition to traditional religion was not so absolute that he would not borrow ideas from it. They were ready to dress their reformism in conservative clothes. For some, this was grounded in a genuine wish to convert their opponents, rather than merely to exchange polemical shellfire. For others, it was because religious identities were as yet unformed. We find many reformers expressing exotic opinions and doing so in idiosyncratic terms. Others still hoped to use their evangelical insights, not to separate the true Church from the false, but to reforge England's disintegrating religious unity. Most importantly, like the Suffolk playwright, almost all English evangelicals had their hopes centred on the regime, and in particular on the person of Henry VIII. Their reluctance to disobey their lawful sovereign and their fear of persecution combined with the regime's continued (if ambiguous) sponsorship of limited reform to produce an evangelicalism which was both non-confrontational and remarkably diverse.

The 'trewe purgatory', however, was not a state but a process. Political events, as well as the internal dynamics of the reformist movement itself, ensured that by the time of the old king's death English reformism was no longer as scattered, doctrinally ill-defined and politically open to compromise as it had been. Reformers became increasingly alienated from the state, not least because of the regular bouts of persecution which they faced. In particular, a political crisis in the spring of 1543 left many previously moderate reformers thoroughly alienated from the regime. If the fictional woman on the rock can be taken as a symbol of English evangelicals at the beginning of this period, at the end the obvious symbol is, appropriately, more tangible: Anne Askew or Ayscough, an outspoken gentlewoman executed for heresy in 1546. Partly because of the vivid account of her interrogations which she wrote, Askew became the most memorable reformist martyr of the 1540s. Despite intense pressure to recant, she maintained her radical doctrines and refused to betray her associates. So, notoriously and in gross violation of the law, she was stretched on the rack so severely that by the time she was burned she could no longer stand. She could not have been more different from Thomas Wylley. By 1546, as a symbol of England's evangelicals, the compromises and ambiguity of the woman on the rock had been overtaken by the demonstrative steadfastness of the woman on the rack.

THE NATURE OF THE PROBLEM

Politics and Protestants, Christopher Haigh argued in 1987, are subjects which have had 'at least their due' from scholars of the English Reformation.[7] And it is clearly true that an overemphasis on evangelicalism can distort our view of religious culture in the early sixteenth century. It obscures the mass of the people who left their traditional religion only with great reluctance. More seriously, perhaps, to concentrate on evangelicals is to risk accepting a neat polarisation between Catholic and Protestant, which tends to homogenise the 'multiple manifestations of the new religion' and the equally varied shades of loyalty to the old, while the confused, disconnected and sceptical are written out of the picture altogether.[8] These concerns have driven a good deal of recent scholarship.[9] Given this historiographical context, the appearance of another book which focuses on religious reformers with an emphasis on their political context perhaps requires some explanation.

Part of the justification is familiar. Early evangelicals, like all minorities, remain of intrinsic interest and it is appropriate that they should attract historiographical attention disproportionate to their numbers. As a minority which came to political dominance within a generation and to a kind

---

[7] Christopher Haigh, 'Introduction', in *The English Reformation Revised*, ed. Haigh (Cambridge, 1987), ix.
[8] Caroline Litzenberger, *The English Reformation and the Laity: Gloucestershire 1540–1580* (Cambridge, 1997), 7.
[9] See, for example, Robert Whiting, *The Blind Devotion of the People: popular devotion and the English Reformation* (Cambridge, 1989); Marsh, *Popular Religion*; Susan Brigden, *London and the Reformation* (Oxford, 1989), 378–422.

of social dominance within two, they are doubly important. Moreover, to the extent that this minority had its political and religious identity formed at an early stage, its history is of vital importance for understanding the English Protestant identity which was to have such a profound impact on the centuries which followed.

Granted that the early development of English evangelicalism is a subject of lasting importance, the historiographical advances of the past two decades have nevertheless profoundly changed our view of this subject. Those very advances, however, require that our understanding of evangelicalism should be reassessed. Just as an overemphasis on Protestantism can distort our view of other parts of the religious landscape, so the new attention which traditional religion has received has implications for our view of reformist movements. This book aims to explore some of those implications for one critical and neglected period of the early Reformation, namely the last eight or so years of Henry VIII's reign. The period is particularly important in light of the central question posed for Reformation scholarship by 'revisionism' – the so-called 'compliance conundrum'.[10] If most English and Welsh men and women were hostile to religious change, how were the successive Tudor regimes able successfully to impose the dramatic changes which took place in the years after 1534? This question is at its sharpest in the reign of Edward VI, when changes which transformed parish religion more profoundly than anything which Henry VIII had done were forced through by unstable regency regimes in six years, and when serious resistance was limited to one rising in two English counties. In the 1960s A. G. Dickens was clear as to how this was possible: the 'quiet advances of Protestantism during Henry's last years account for the ease with which Somerset established it as the official religion from the beginning of the new reign'.[11] The implication is that during the period after Cromwell's fall the evangelical movement gathered so much support that by 1547 it commanded the allegiance of a critical mass of the English people, if not an actual majority.

More recent scholarship has made this difficult to accept. It is true that by the time of Edward VI's accession, the evangelical minority amongst his subjects was an exceptionally important group. It included a disproportionate number of the wealthy and powerful, it was geographically concentrated in such a way as to magnify its influence, and beyond its hard core of committed adherents stood a much larger number of the interested and the confused. Its numbers were growing rapidly, and its conservative opponents were

---

[10] The term is Christopher Marsh's: *Popular Religion*, 197. The recent work of Ethan Shagan suggests, usefully, that 'collaboration' may be a more useful concept than mere 'compliance'. Ethan Shagan, *Popular Politics and the English Reformation* (Cambridge, 2002).
[11] A. G. Dickens, *The English Reformation* (1964), 329.

divided and politically vulnerable. Nevertheless, it remained a small minority.[12] However, if we reject Dickens' portrait of a Reformation driven by a large evangelical mass movement, the problem remains. Where did the Edwardian Reformation come from, and how did it succeed? And although much of the answer must, of course, lie in Edward's reign itself, we are driven, like Dickens, to look back to the last years of Henry's reign. These were the years in which Edwardian Protestantism was forged: the evangelicals' true purgatory. A major purpose of this book is to explore how English evangelicalism changed during this period, both socially and theologically. The results of the exploration will, I hope, shed some light on the later evangelicalism that emerged from these years, and the Reformations which it drove.

A final oddity is that while this book's scope is localised in time, it takes England and Wales in their entirety as its stage. This may seem perverse. After all, the grip which Foxe's interpretation maintained over Reformation historiography has been challenged most effectively in the past forty years by a series of studies which have gone beyond Foxe's material and the State Papers to the local archives of England and Wales. Local studies of this kind enabled Dickens to cast Foxe's account in a new light, and Christopher Haigh to challenge that account head-on. Margaret Bowker's studies of the diocese of Lincoln undermined received truths about the weaknesses of late medieval Catholicism. Other local studies have helped to nuance our account of the Reformation process and to move on from the 'revisionist' agenda.[13] To attempt a national overview, traipsing once again through the crowded field of Tudor high politics, might appear to be pointlessly repetitive. I would suggest, however, that the golden age of the local study in English Reformation history is passing. It is not merely that the map is nearing completion, for some significant gaps remain. Rather, these studies at their best have not simply been attempts to complete a jigsaw puzzle, but have raised questions and introduced methodologies which have had far-reaching implications. Without such fresh approaches, a comprehensive study of the early Reformation in, say, Dorset or Staffordshire is unlikely to reveal significant new trends with which we are not already familiar.

---

[12] Alec Ryrie, 'Counting sheep, counting shepherds: the problem of numerical allegiance in the English Reformation', in *The Beginnings of English Protestantism*, ed. Peter Marshall and Alec Ryrie (Cambridge, 2002).

[13] A. G. Dickens, *Lollards and Protestants in the Diocese of York 1509–58* (Oxford, 1959); Christopher Haigh, *Reformation and Resistance in Tudor Lancashire* (Cambridge, 1975); Ralph Houlbrooke, *Church Courts and People during the English Reformation* (Oxford, 1979); Margaret Bowker, *The Henrician Reformation: The Diocese of Lincoln under John Longland 1521–47* (Cambridge, 1981); Diarmaid MacCulloch, *Suffolk and the Tudors: Politics and Religion in an English County 1500–1600* (Oxford, 1986); Brigden, *London*; Litzenberger, *English Reformation and the Laity*.

Moreover, despite the huge contribution which they have made, local studies are not necessarily the ideal means of analysing the processes of religious change. In a state as powerfully centralised as Tudor England, the role of the central government cannot be ignored. That government's wishes were of course mediated to the localities through local elites, yet even the indirect impact of such policies could be enormous. The steady flow of rumours about national politics, and the regime's concern to control such rumours, demonstrate that central politics mattered locally.[14] A study of the Reformation which is grounded purely in a local archive is as likely to be unbalanced as one which never ventures beyond the state papers. This is particularly so when dealing with early evangelicals. Patrick Collinson reminds us that such people 'were local in the sense of having had a location, but they were not necessarily localised'.[15] Men and women were converted to reformist views by hearing visiting preachers from outside their region, or, especially in the earliest days, through evangelical books printed on the Continent or in London. They themselves were highly mobile and maintained informal networks of communication across the country. Local studies of evangelicalism stumble over the fact that many evangelicals refused to stay put in one locality. They looked for earthly authority not to the justice of the peace, the local magnate or the bishop, but to the king. They saw themselves in a national (or international) context; and it is in that context that they demand to be studied.

Part I of this book, therefore, examines the national political situation and the evangelical responses to it. Chapter 1 considers the religious politics of the last decade of Henry VIII's reign. It contests the common view of this period as one of conservative reaction, arguing that this interpretation derives largely from a later, partisan historiography. It suggests instead that the regime's religious policies in these years were profoundly ambiguous; sets the limited persecution of these years in context; and examines the undercurrents of continued reform which were just as influential as the eye-catching conservative successes. Chapter 2 examines the ways in which evangelicals dealt with this confused political situation. It surveys the faltering development of evangelical political thought, arguing that the majority of reformers in these years went out of their way to avoid or defuse confrontations with the regime, and continued to exalt royal authority. The test of such theoretical positions came, of course, when the regime chose to enforce the heresy laws or otherwise place individual evangelicals under pressure. I argue that under such circumstances, most reformers were more inclined to dissimulation,

---

[14] G. R. Elton, *Policy and Police: The Enforcement of the Reformation in the Age of Thomas Cromwell* (Cambridge, 1972), 46–82.

[15] Patrick Collinson, 'England', in *The Reformation in National Context*, ed. Bob Scribner, Roy Porter and Mikuláš Teich (Cambridge, 1994), 84.

Introduction

recantation and pragmatic compromises than to defiance and martyrdom. The last years of Henry's reign have been described as a Counter-Reformation, comparable to that under Mary Tudor in the 1550s.[16] Yet this was a period when both the regime and the reformers were, on the whole, acting so as to lower the temperature of their disagreements.

Part II considers the range of faces which evangelicalism presented under these circumstances. Chapter 3 examines perhaps the most prominent and well-known group of evangelicals from the 1540s: those who fled to exile on the Continent. These exiles included some very prominent evangelical publicists, most of whom held decidedly radical views. I argue, however, that their impact on events and attitudes in England at the time was extremely limited, and that they cannot be taken as representative of the broader evangelical movement. Chapter 4 examines the other public face of reformism: the work of those evangelical preachers and authors who remained in England during this period. It suggests that their work reveals a coherent set of doctrinal and political priorities strikingly different from those of the exiles. As well as being non-confrontational towards the regime, these evangelicals were willing to engage with religious conservatives on their own ground. Their theology was moderate in flavour, owing more to Lutheran ideas than to the radical Swiss and southern German tradition drawn on by many of the exiles. Yet this movement should not be seen simply as toothless. For all their doctrinal moderation, these reformers held forthright views on questions of social morality and the reform of the commonwealth, views which they shared with their more radical brethren and which brought them into conflict with the regime.

Chapter 5 examines the arena in which this conflict became most apparent: education. Education was a central value for reformers, but over the course of this period it became uncomfortably clear that the regime had little interest in supporting schools and the universities, and indeed was more inclined to plunder them. Evangelicals defended the universities as a matter of principle, but also from self-interest. By 1540 an evangelical minority was firmly, and to a degree securely, established at Oxford and especially at Cambridge. The university reformers were no firebrands, but they defended their comparatively moderate doctrines with some determination. During this period they were fighting and winning intellectual battles which were programmatic for a more assertive evangelicalism to come.

University reformism overlapped into the precarious world of evangelicals at court and in royal service, which is examined in chapter 6. Court reformers' proximity to the centres of power gave them an influence and a (sometimes mistaken) sense of security which their lowlier brethren did

---

[16] Christopher Haigh, *English Reformations* (Oxford, 1993), 14.

not share. Their position also helped to efface the (often substantial) doctrinal differences between them, as personal, political and patronage links cut across such barriers. One particular reformist coterie, the circle of young bloods around the poets Sir Thomas Wyatt and Henry Howard, the earl of Surrey, was characterised by an easy assumption of evangelical language and ideas without much in the way of deep religious commitment. Such fashionable reformism was never going to sweep the world before it, but it did do a great deal to smooth the way for the new learning. However, court circles also reveal another, easily neglected facet of late Henrician evangelicalism: the apparently principled retreat of some who had been partisans of reform in the 1530s into more conformist or even conservative views. The choice between king and Gospel was difficult for reformers in positions of power to evade, and some of them chose the former.

Chapter 7 examines the hidden face of evangelicalism: the world of conventicles and underground groupings of all kinds. Although there is no reason to believe that formal underground congregations existed in this period, the scattered evidence which survives suggests a range of informal evangelical activity from simple gatherings of friends, through evangelical discussion groups to more organised conventicles. The full range of doctrinal and political views can be found amongst these groups, but I argue that they tended towards more confrontational stances, especially when they were dominated by lay people. Such groups also show a limited but clear influence from the old Lollard conventicles on which, in some cases, they were overlaid. Yet the members of these groups were also in contact with more respectable reformers, and the chapter concludes with an analysis of the links of patronage and friendship that tied the reformist movement together, often cutting across doctrinal lines.

Finally, a conclusion returns to politics, considering how the events of the mid-1540s affected this kaleidoscope of reformist opinion. Political shifts interacted with the internal dynamics of evangelicalism, I argue, to undermine the moderate reformism of the printers and preachers and to drive the movement as a whole towards the radicalism of the exiles and those in England who shared their views. As such, on the old king's death, his son's minority government fell into the hands not merely of evangelicals, but of evangelicals with a startlingly radical, Swiss-inspired agenda. By 1547, the struggle for the soul of English evangelicalism had been won decisively by radicals linked to the continental Reformed tradition. It was a victory whose effects were to be felt for centuries; and it was not unopposed.

PART I

The regime and the reformers

1

A Counter-Reformation?

The heauen is hye, the earth is depe, and the kynges herte is vnsearcheable.
Proverbs 25:3.

INTERPRETING THE 'HENRICIAN REACTION'

Historians aspire to follow our evidence impartially and fearlessly, over whatever terrain it may lead us; but in practice we often find ourselves being drawn along the paths beaten by our predecessors. This is particularly so when negotiating a landscape as scarred by passage as the English Reformation. Christopher Haigh, for example, judged that A. G. Dickens' influential account of the English Reformation had followed the deepest of these channels, cut by John Foxe in the sixteenth century.[1] The period 1539–47, however, contains its own distinct set of historiographical tiger traps. Dickens' view is best summed up by the title of the relevant chapter in his survey: 'A balance of forces'.[2] On this interpretation, the forward march of Protestantism was hindered in the early 1540s, as religious conservatives vied with evangelicals for the ear of the king, and scored some successes. However, the most striking aspect of the treatment of this period by the whole 'Whig-Protestant' tradition was the extent to which it was ignored altogether. Patrick Collinson has suggested that the approach taken by Dickens and his contemporaries

confined the essential history of the English Reformation to the thirty years from 1529 to 1559, a manageable three-course meal preceded by a few late medieval apéritifs and rounded off with a small cup of Elizabethan coffee.[3]

---

[1] 'Introduction', *English Reformation Revised*, ed. Haigh, 1.
[2] Dickens, *English Reformation*, 167.
[3] Patrick Collinson, 'Comment on Eamon Duffy's Neale Lecture and the Colloquium', in *England's Long Reformation 1500–1800*, ed. Nicholas Tyacke (1998), 71.

On this analogy, the 1540s were treated as a *pause digestif*, of the kind that can sometimes be necessary when a heavy and somewhat unusual appetiser is to be followed by bolting down a conventional main course. Perhaps understandably, a historiography which was interested chiefly in the advancing tide of Protestantism, and the failure of attempts to stem it, skipped over the early 1540s as an interlude in which little of lasting significance appeared to be happening. The late Henrician period has received much less scholarly attention than the rest of that thirty-year crisis.

One of the many valuable services which Dickens' work performed for English Reformation scholarship was to serve as a lightning-rod for the attacks of his 'revisionist'[4] successors. Like so many other parts of his thesis, Dickens' view of Henry VIII's last years has been disputed. The revisionists, however, disagree as to which of the forces that Dickens believed to be balanced was actually in the ascendant. Eamon Duffy has described this period as one phase of an ongoing attack on traditional religion. He does identify a 'resurgence of traditionalism' in the period, but he emphasises that the reformers continued to inflict serious damage on central aspects of traditional piety, such as the cult of the saints and prayer for the dead.[5] Haigh, by contrast, sees this period as the first of England's official Counter-Reformations, asserting that in late 1538 'Henry VIII stopped the Reformation dead'. On this view, the last eight years of his life were a period of almost unmitigated gloom for the reformers.[6]

This has more or less become the new consensus.[7] The case for this view is clear enough. The late 1530s had been heady days for the evangelical minority in England. Following the break with Rome in 1534, Thomas Cromwell held the office of vice-gerent in spirituals, effectively exercising the newly established royal supremacy over the English Church on Henry VIII's behalf. He was supported by his fellow-evangelical Thomas Cranmer, the archbishop of Canterbury, and by several other highly placed reformist sympathisers. Their activities were permitted and to a degree encouraged by the king himself. During this period, official statements cast doubt on a range

---

[4] A term which is contentious amongst those it has been applied to: Haigh uses it enthusiastically of himself, while Eamon Duffy argues that all competent historians are revisionists by definition. Like much of the terminology surrounding the study of the English Reformation, it is used here with a due sense of unease, and without an intention to prejudice the issues involved.
[5] Eamon Duffy, *The Stripping of the Altars* (New Haven and London, 1992), 424–47.
[6] Haigh, *English Reformations*, 152.
[7] See, for example, Litzenberger, *English Reformation and the Laity*, 33, 44; Andrew Pettegree, *Marian Protestantism: Six Studies* (Aldershot, Hants., 1996), 86; Glyn Redworth, 'A study in the formulation of policy: the genesis and evolution of the Act of Six Articles', *JEH* 37 (1986), 45, 51; Richard Rex, *Henry VIII and the English Reformation* (Basingstoke, 1993), 144–5; Martha C. Skeeters, *Community and Clergy: Bristol and the Reformation c. 1530–c. 1570* (Oxford, 1993); 'Introduction', in *Long Reformation*, ed. Tyacke, 8.

of traditional doctrines and practices, most notably purgatory and prayer for the dead. Royal injunctions and proclamations drastically restricted the use of images and the veneration of saints, and effectively ended the practice of pilgrimage. The English Bible, so long prohibited, was not merely legalised but ordered to be placed in every parish church in the realm. Most dramatically of all, monasticism, a way of life which represented all that evangelicals most deplored in the old Church, was entirely exterminated, through an astonishing exercise of royal power. At the end of 1538, however, the first signs appeared that the king wished to apply the brakes. A proclamation reasserted that certain heretics were going to remain unacceptable: notably Anabaptists, who profaned baptism, and sacramentaries, who denied Christ's corporal presence in the Eucharist. To reinforce the point, the king himself presided over the trial and execution of one outspoken sacramentary, John Lambert. In 1539, this new mood was given statutory backing. Under close royal supervision, Parliament passed 'An acte abolishing diversity in Opynions', which reasserted six key points of traditional doctrine and which was commonly known, at the time and ever since, as the Act of Six Articles. It laid down fearsome penalties for those who denied the articles. A year later, in July 1540, Thomas Cromwell was executed for treason and heresy, along with three prominent evangelical preachers. Sporadic persecution of reformers continued for the remainder of the reign, driving some into exile and forcing others to lie low. The new direction of policy was underlined in 1543, when another statute, the 'acte for thadvauncement of true Religion', restricted access to the English Bible. The long-awaited comprehensive statement of the Henrician Church's doctrines which was published the same year, the so-called *King's Book*, also gave little comfort to the reformers. In particular, it robustly rejected the evangelical conviction that Christians are saved by faith alone and not by works. This conservative reaction continued, albeit in fits and starts, to the very end of the reign. In the last summer of Henry VIII's life, in 1546, a further bout of heresy prosecutions claimed several prominent victims, and even Henry's last queen, Katherine Parr, only narrowly escaped arrest.[8]

This interpretation, however, has a dubious intellectual pedigree. By emphasising the conservatism of the 1540s, Haigh and others have, ironically enough, brought their interpretation back into line with the views of John Foxe and of the other, earlier English reformers on whose writings and opinions he drew. In his massive martyrological history, the *Actes and Monuments*, Foxe wrote that 'after the taking a way of the sayd Cromwel...

---

[8] Most surveys of the period summarise these events: see, for example, Haigh, *English Reformations*, 152–67. For a less polemical view, see Peter Marshall, *Reformation England 1480–1642* (2003), chapter 2.

the state of Religion more and more decayed, during all the residue of the raygne of king Henry'. Such an unlikely alliance between Foxe and the modern revisionists might indicate that they must both be right. However, by following Foxe's interpretation, the revisionists have made themselves heirs to a narrative which is seriously flawed.

Foxe's account began with Henry VIII's disastrous fourth marriage, to Anne of Cleves, which collapsed in recriminations almost before it had begun. Foxe believed that underlying this debacle was a factional conflict between Thomas Cromwell and Stephen Gardiner, the conservative bishop of Winchester. Foxe then went on to describe how 'in the yeare next folowing, which was of the Lorde [1]540 . . . [the king] summoned a solemne Parliament to be holden at Westminster the 28. day of Aprill'. It is in this parliament that Foxe placed the Act of Six Articles, which he described, borrowing Richard Grafton's phrases, as 'the whip with 6 stringes', 'the bloudy act'. In fact, the parliament which enacted the Six Articles had opened on 28 April 1539, not 1540. Foxe was misled by the peculiar dating system in the chronicle which he used as his source for this account. He did, however, correctly date Cromwell's fall from power to 1540, and this convenient chronological error served to make his account much more compelling. Misdating the Six Articles by a year allowed him to write that 'after the Parliament was finished . . . the Lord Cromwell . . . within few dayes after was apprehended'.[9] On this reading, the passage of the Six Articles and Cromwell's arrest – events a year apart between which there was no direct connection – become two halves of a papalist *coup* led by Bishop Gardiner.[10]

Foxe's narrative moved on to depict a gathering storm of persecution. He noted that on 29 January 1541, a commission was issued under the Act of Six Articles for the arrest of suspected heretics. This commission was responsible for the prosecution and execution of a young Londoner called Richard Mekins, a story which Foxe told in some detail. However, this firmly dated event served as a peg upon which a series of more significant and more dubious tales of persecution could be hung. The prosecutions under the Six Articles, Foxe wrote, 'extended . . . to Salisbury, Northfolke, Lincolne,

[9] *AM*, 1134–6. Much of Foxe's account was drawn from Edward Hall and Richard Grafton, *The vnion of the two noble and illustrate famelies of Lancastre & Yorke* (RSTC 12721: 1548), which used mayoral years rather than regnal years for dating – hence Foxe's confusion. In the first English edition of his book (*AM* (1563), 586–9), Foxe also followed Hall and Grafton for Cromwell's fall, which he therefore dated to 1541. However, while he corrected the latter date in subsequent editions, he did not amend the date of the Six Articles. This is clearly error rather than conspiracy, from a historian with little interest in chronology, but it was an error which fitted neatly into Foxe's preconceptions. I am grateful to Tom Freeman for his assistance with this point.

[10] Gardiner was a consistent villain to Foxe and other early Protestant writers. On this, see Michael Riordan and Alec Ryrie, 'Stephen Gardiner and the making of a Protestant villain', *Sixteenth Century Journal* (forthcoming).

and through all other Shyres and quarters of the realme; so that whereas any popish Prelate most bare stroke, there most persecution encreased'. His examples were three burnings from Salisbury (these can tentatively be dated to 1541–2, but it seems there were in fact only two executions); and seven recantations and two burnings in Lincoln diocese. These last two victims underline the slapdash nature of Foxe's chronology. Their crimes were pre-Reformation Lollard offences (the use of English prayers and Scripture), and Foxe elsewhere recorded them as having been executed in 1521.[11]

The centrepiece of Foxe's evidence for the impact of the Six Articles, however, is an impressive list of some 200 Londoners arrested under the Act during the spring of 1541. This list, while invaluable, is again dogged by chronological problems. At the end of the list we find the cases of several prominent reformers – Alexander Seton, John Porter, Thomas Becon, Robert Wisdom and others – which in fact were scattered through the early 1540s. Foxe made no distinction between these and the others, probably because his research assistants compiled the list carelessly. The main list itself is also misdated; these arrests can be shown to have taken place in July 1540 – that is, shortly before Cromwell's execution.[12]

These scattered cases, fused together by Foxe's chronology to suggest sustained, nationwide persecution, set the tone for his account of the remainder of the reign. Throughout that account, Foxe argued that Henry VIII was little more than a reluctant accomplice to crimes committed by court conservatives, in particular Gardiner. This was a most useful fiction. Foxe could scarcely have ignored Henry's persecution of evangelicals, even if he had wished to do so. But nor could he condemn the old king outright; it would have meant rejecting Henry's real contributions to the evangelical cause, and undermining the legitimacy of the Elizabethan Church. By portraying Henry as his councillors' puppet, Foxe solved several problems at once. He managed to incorporate the testimonies he had received from informants such as Ralph Morice and the earl of Bedford, both of whom described late Henrician politics in these terms; he was able implicitly to chide his own queen for listening to evil counsellors; and he more or less succeeded in strapping Henry VIII's religious ambiguities into a confessional straitjacket.[13] As such, he could fit some measures of real reform into his story. In particular, he

---

[11] *AM*, 774, 838.
[12] *AM*, 1201–7. The London arrests can be dated from a packet of twenty indictments dated 17 July 1540 and endorsed by the mayor. All but two of these name persons from Foxe's list and include details of the same offences Foxe records. Richard Hilles' testimony confirms that these twenty indictments represent only some of the arrests at that time; he wrote that before the general pardon of 15 July 'a number of people from everywhere in England were imprisoned, in particular the preachers of the Gospel'. PRO SP 1/243 fos. 61–80 (*LP Addenda* 1463); *ET*, 138 (*OL*, 208). Cf. Brigden, *London*, 320, n. 127.
[13] I am grateful to Tom Freeman for discussions on this point.

praised Henry for his orders of 1541 restraining the use of images, for his relaxation of the Lenten fast and for the statute of 1544 which moderated the penal code of the Act of Six Articles.[14] Somewhat surprisingly, however, Foxe did not mention any swing towards the evangelical party in the last months of the king's life. Indeed, while Foxe claimed that in 1545 Henry was coming to distrust Gardiner, 'wherby he was the more forward to incline somewhat in furthering the desolate cause of religion', by the following year little trace of this inclination remains. Foxe did include Archbishop Cranmer's somewhat dubious claim that in August 1546 Henry was considering the abolition of the Mass. However, he emphasised that Henry's last public religious statement was a draconian proclamation against heretical books of the same month. That proclamation, Foxe commented darkly, would have

> done much hurt in the church among the godly sort, bringing them either into great daunger, or els keeping them in much blindnes, had not the shortnes of the kinges dayes stopped the malignant purposes of the foresayd Prelates, causing the king to leave that by death vnto the people, which by his life he would not graunt.

Thus Henry's death almost becomes a divine judgement on the proclamation. In the first edition of the *Actes and Monuments*, this was reinforced by a tale that Gardiner had presented the king with a list of evangelicals' names, 'the execution of whome shoulde shortly haue folowed' if Henry had lived.[15]

In other words, Foxe's account of the early 1540s, for all its subsequent influence, is highly problematic. Chronology was never Foxe's strongest point, and in this section of his book that problem was compounded by the haste with which he and his researchers were working, the tendentious nature of many of his sources and his sometimes inept attempts to resolve the contradictions which these problems threw up. The result is a thoroughly chaotic account. Foxe could be tempted to include some peculiar tales, such as Gardiner's list of wanted evangelicals. He gave only the scantiest attention to some key events: the 1543 Act for the Advancement of True Religion is only mentioned once, in passing, when it is (again) misdated to 1544 and presented as if its purpose was to permit the nobility and gentry access to the Bible in English rather than to forbid it to their social inferiors.[16] This disarray meant that Foxe's account was more than usually susceptible to being moulded by his biases and preconceptions. His view of the king as a puppet, his account of the Six Articles and other aspects of this section of his book all show this pervasive influence. His interpretation does not, of course, depend exclusively on his errors; but those errors are serious enough to call the interpretation into question.

---

[14] *AM*, 1210, 1230–1. Cf. *Statutes of the Realm, printed by command of his majesty King George III*, vol. III (1817), 960–1 (35° Henry VIII c. 5); *TRP*, 261, 309.
[15] *AM*, 1231, 1245, 1259; *AM* (1563), 673–4. [16] *AM*, 1230.

Moreover, this skewed interpretation can be traced back into Foxe's sources themselves. The most striking forerunner of Foxe's view of the early 1540s is Edward Hall's *Chronicle*, published in 1548. The sections of this piece dealing with the last years of Henry's reign were in fact written by Hall's publisher, Richard Grafton, whose sometimes incautious combination of reformist commitment and commercial activity made him one of the most eye-catching evangelicals of the period. For Grafton, as for Foxe, the tone for the last years of Henry's reign was set by the Act of Six Articles, which he reviled in a much-quoted passage.

> Among the common people it was called the act of sixe articles, & of some it was named the whip withe sixe strynges, and of some other and that of the moste parte, it was named the bloudy statute, for of truth it so in shorte time after skourged a great nombre in the citie of London. . . . In fourtene daies space there was not a preacher nor other persone in the citie of name, whiche hod spoken against the supremacie of the bishop of Rome, but he was wrapped in the sixe articles, insomuche as thei indicted and presented of suspicion to the nombre of fiue hundred persones and above.

Grafton not only used many of the terms which Foxe would later adopt, but also made a similar chronological error. This ferocious purge, which he claims took place 'in shorte time after' the passage of the Act in 1539, is in fact clearly that of July 1540 (the purge which Foxe was to misdate in the other direction).[17] It is rather harder to explain Grafton's chronological confusion than Foxe's. Grafton was describing a recent event which we may be sure he would have found memorable, since he himself was one of those arrested.[18] However, this mistake, if mistake it was, powerfully reinforced Grafton's contention that the passage of the Act of Six Articles marked a decisive change in the tenor of the regime's religious policy. He concluded his description of the first commission's cruelties by generalising the event:

> In the tyme that these six Articles indured whiche was eight yeres and more, thei [the commissioners] brought many an honest and simple persone to there deathes, for suche was the rigour of that lawe, that if two witnesses false or true, had accused any and auouched that thei had spoken agaynst the sacrament, ther was then no way but death.[19]

Although modern accounts are usually couched in more subtle terms, this description of the 1540s as the age of the Six Articles is distinctly reminiscent of the current historiographical consensus.

---

[17] Any doubt that Grafton is describing the same quest recorded by Foxe, Hilles and the mayoral indictments is removed by his statement that those arrested were released through the intervention of Lord Chancellor Audley. Foxe's account is identical, and Hilles' differs only in that he believed that it was Edward Crome's intercession which had moved the king to mercy. *AM*, 1206; *ET*, 138 (*OL*, 208).

[18] *AM*, 1203.   [19] Hall, *The vnion of . . . Lancastre & Yorke*, fo. 234^v.

However, it is only in Edward VI's reign that we find reformers writing of 'their whip of correction . . . hanged [with] .vi. stringes'.[20] The consensus becomes less clear-cut if we consider the opinions of those evangelicals who were writing while the Six Articles were actually in force. Few reformers would have agreed that they were living through a time of unbridled persecution. It is true that they abhorred the Six Articles. Foxe's mentor John Bale wrote in 1544 that they were 'enacted and establyshed with more tyrannie than euer vndre the Romishe Pope, Mahomete or anye other tyraunt afore'.[21] The London radical Henry Brinklow joined many others in deploring the ferocity of the rules of evidence which the Act laid down: 'Whan so euer .ij. false knaues shal secretly accuse a man, althoughe he were as ignorant as a chyld of .ii. dayes old, yet must he eyther dye, beare a fagot, or recant. . . . Death, death, euyn for tryfyls, so that thei folow the high prystys in crucyfyeng Christ.'[22] These writers did not, however, see the passage of the Act as a decisive turning-point or a defining moment in the way that Grafton, Foxe and their modern successors do. Indeed, the closer we come to 1539, the more low-key the Act's opponents become. William Jerome, burned as a heretic in 1540, denounced the House of Commons as 'Butterflies and knaues with other wordes of reprofe' for passing the Act – which is certainly impolite, but on the scale of Reformation polemic it hardly registers.[23] Even those inclined to use stronger language found themselves in some difficulties when attacking the Act. In 1544, Bale wrote that the aim of the Six Articles was

to repare the broken walles of youre ryall Rome agayne, as in dede they wold do euen to the verie cloudes yf they were wele folowed. . . . Were they ones receyued, graunted, and executed vndre peyne of deathe, the Pope shulde neuer dye in Englande.[24]

In other words, Bale was forced to admit that the Act's threats had not been fully implemented, and that its dangers remained largely potential.

Even these more nuanced attacks on the Six Articles do not represent the mainstream of contemporary evangelical opinion. Grafton and Foxe, with the help of some chronological shuffling, portrayed the Six Articles as the inauguration of a period of more or less steady persecution, but this was not how matters appeared at the time. Thomas Cromwell survived the passage of the Six Articles by a year, and as continental visitors reported with surprise, for much of that year the prospects for reform seemed bright.[25] In February

---

[20] Peter Moone, *A short treatise of certayne thinges abused* (RSTC 18056: 1548), sig. A3ᵛ.
[21] John Bale (ps. Henry Stalbrydge), *The epistle exhortatorye of an Englyshe Christiane unto his derely beloued contraye of Englande* (RSTC 1291: Antwerp, 1544), fo. 6ʳ.
[22] Henry Brinklow (ps. Roderick Mors), *The complaynt of Roderyck Mors . . . vnto the parliament howse of Ingland* (RSTC 3759.5: Strassburg, 1542), sigs. D1ᵛ–2ʳ.
[23] PRO SP 1/158 fo. 120ᵛ (*LP* XV 411.2).
[24] Bale, *Epistle exhortatorye*, fo. 6ᵛ.   [25] MacCulloch, *Cranmer*, 257.

1540, a well-connected young evangelical named Nicholas Partridge wrote to Heinrich Bullinger, the chief minister of Zurich and European Protestantism's most energetic networker. Partridge's news was good. With a modest whiff of patriotism, he stated that the reformers' advances in England were 'perhaps not to be despised'. By this he meant the completion of the dissolution of the monasteries, and the executions of three conservative abbots some months before. But he was also concerned to allay Bullinger's fears regarding the impact of the Six Articles.

> Good pastors are freely preaching the truth, nor has punishment been visited on them on account of the articles of which you write. The most merciful king would willingly desire the promotion of the very truth; and to this end he has willed several bishops to consult about the selection of twelve monasteries, where boys might be brought up in all kinds of good learning with piety and holiness.

Partridge's friend John Butler, another correspondent of Bullinger's, drew attention to the outspoken preaching of Robert Barnes, a stalwart of the evangelical movement who was to be executed in the wake of Cromwell's fall. Butler also drew some comfort from the fact that 'books of every kind may safely be offered for sale'.[26] Bullinger, we may assume, met these assurances with a measure of scepticism. Certainly, Martin Luther and his right-hand man Philip Melanchthon saw the Six Articles as a disaster.[27] At least one distinguished Continental Protestant, however, refused to write off Henry VIII after the Six Articles. The Strassburg reformer Martin Bucer wrote to Thomas Cranmer in October 1539 stating his belief that the king's apparent lurch towards conservatism was purely a by-product of his foreign policy. If the implementation of the Six Articles could be delayed, Bucer hoped, 'the disguises of Antichrist being detected, the king would at length see Christ's truth'.[28] Despite the 'bloudy Act', in early 1540 informed evangelicals could justifiably remain optimistic.

However, this Indian summer of the Cromwellian Reformation came to a sudden and brutal end when, just under a year after the passage of Six Articles, Cromwell himself was arrested. He was executed in July 1540, as were Barnes, Jerome and Thomas Garrett, and as we have seen, large numbers of other reformers were rounded up. It was certainly the worst crisis which English evangelicals had faced since they had first scented royal favour. Yet they were not wholly dismayed. Indeed, within weeks of Cromwell's death evangelicals could be found hoping that the world might turn again in

---

[26] *ET*, 398, 406 (my translations); cf. *OL*, 614, 627.
[27] Philip Melanchthon, *The epistle of the famous and great Clerke Philip Melancton made vnto oure late Souereyne Lorde Kynge Henry the eight, for the reuokinge and abolishing of the six articles* (RSTC 17789: Antwerp, 1547); Martin Luther, *Luther's Works vol. 53: Letters III*, ed. and tr. Gottfried G. Krodel (Philadelphia, 1975), 204–6.
[28] *ET*, 345 (*OL*, 528).

their favour. After all, if this was the worst crisis, it was not the only one. The king's supposed commitment to the evangelical cause had survived the fall of Anne Boleyn in 1536 and the passage of the Six Articles in 1539, and it might plausibly enough survive this disaster as well. In the months and years after Cromwell's fall, most reformers still pinned their hopes for the future on the king. In May 1541, the Salisbury evangelical John Erley wrote to two of his contacts in London, asking optimistically for news from the capital:

> You be not onely assosiat And in compenye dayly with suche maner of men as be fauourable to the worde of gode, But also with suche as can partely delate whethr that it be of any lichod [likelihood] that godes worde shall haue free pasage or no.[29]

Those who were closer to the centre of power could do more than simply wait. On 15 September 1540, four evangelical members of the royal households fell to talking politics in the king's great chamber. All agreed that the evangelical cause was opposed, not by the king himself, but by Stephen Gardiner and the duke of Norfolk. One of this group, a sewer in the queen's privy chamber called William Smethwick, was more forthright than the others, and John Lassells, who held the same post in the king's chamber, felt the need to offer a word of advice. As Lassells wrote shortly afterwards:

> I did perswad master smythwyke not to be to rashe or quike in maynrenyng the scrypture, for yff we wolde lete them [Gardiner and Norfolk] a lone and suffer a lettell tyme they wolde (I doubte not) ower throwe them selves, standyng manyfestlye a nenst god and theyr prynce.

As evidence for this sanguine view, Lassells told his friends a story of how Norfolk had confronted a man who was rumoured to have married a former nun. According to Lassells, the man replied,

> My lorde, I knowe no nonnes nor religious folke in thys realme nor no suche bondage seyng god and the kyng haue made them free. To the same worde the Duke sayd, by godes body sacred it wyll never owt of my harte as longe as I lyue.[30]

Norfolk's easy way with words would plant his destruction, and the evangelicals need only wait; or so Lassells believed. This was not simply a case of a timid courtier urging caution, for Lassells was no quietist. Six years later, he was to boast abroad his desire to be called before the Privy Council to be examined for his sacramentarian convictions, and to go to the stake without wavering. In 1540, however, his optimism rested partly on his underestimate of the duke of Norfolk – a common mistake amongst both contemporaries and historians – but much more on his certainty that the king was ultimately on the side of the angels. Unlike Grafton and Foxe, and unlike the authors of

---

[29] PRO STAC 2/34/28 fo. 6^r.
[30] PRO SP 1/163 fo. 46^r (*LP* XVI 101). Smethwick was foolish enough to disregard Lassells' advice and to accuse Norfolk of treason – hence Lassells' record of the conversation.

the modern consensus, Lassells and those like him did not believe that there had been a fundamental change in the regime's attitude to reform with the passage of the Six Articles, or even with the fall of Cromwell. Those events were of course disturbing, but more evident was the continuity represented by the king himself. For the time being, most reformers continued to be confident that while the storms of faction might blow him from his course, his destination was set. Henry had publicly and deliberately assumed the mantle of the great reforming kings of the Old Testament, and his evangelical subjects believed him. He was Josiah, and Hezekiah, and David, and the reformation for which they looked would come from him. This conviction was itself an important political fact. It remains to be seen to what extent it was an exercise in wishful thinking.

THE WHIP WITH SIX STRINGS

The greatest obstacle to evangelical trust in the king was, of course, the periodic execution of evangelicals in the king's name. Yet this was not quite so severe a problem as it might appear. Behind Foxe's carefully constructed picture of generalised persecution lies a more complex reality. Records survive of at most thirty-nine evangelicals who died at the hands of the regime for religious offences between the passage of the Act of Six Articles and Henry's death.[31] Three of these – 'Henry' and his servant, and Oliver Richardine – are recorded only by Foxe, and dated sufficiently vaguely that it would be unwise to date their deaths firmly to this period. Two more – Andrew Hewet and Nicholas Belenian – appear to have been listed by Foxe in error, as other sources name other men in their places. Of the remainder, three were executed for treason rather than heresy; and three died in custody, the three deaths being, it seems, one accident, one suicide and one murder. Twenty-eight persons remain as almost certainly having been burned for heresy in the period. Most of them died during two short bursts of persecution: nine in 1540, around the time of Cromwell's fall, and ten more in the summer of 1546. Moreover, these victims have a distinctive doctrinal profile. It is possible to guess at the offences for which twenty-four of the twenty-eight died. Of these, twenty were apparently executed wholly or principally for sacramentarian beliefs, which as we shall see, marks them out from the common run of English heretics.

Records are, of course, patchy. For example, the case of Thomas Capper, executed in Cardiff in 1542, is known only through a note in the Cardiff bailiffs' accounts recording the expenses of his imprisonment and burning.[32] There were certainly more victims from across the country of whom we will never know. Nevertheless, these figures are strikingly low. Compared to the

---

[31] See Appendix I. [32] Glanmor Williams, *Wales and the Reformation* (Cardiff 1997), 143.

scale of the persecution under Queen Mary, when around 300 reformers died in a shorter period, this was negligible. More telling, perhaps, are comparisons with the contemporary situation on the Continent. In the Netherlands, between 1539 and 1545, some 105 persons were burned for heresy in the province of Holland alone. Another twenty-seven suffered in Flanders, and comparable numbers also died in Brabant and other provinces. During this period, several Dutch reformers sought the comparative safety of exile in England. The records of the prosecution of reformers in France are not so complete, but in Paris alone, the *Chambre ardente* burned thirty-nine reformers in three years shortly after this date, and in Provence, hundreds of Waldensians were massacred in 1543.[33] The situation in England in Henry's last years seems more comparable to the clampdown on Lollardy in 1520–2, during which some eleven heretics died in Coventry and the Chilterns.[34] It is also worth remembering that during the same period, 1539–47, at least fourteen people were executed for their allegiance to the papacy. Although well aware of the executions that took place, for most of this period evangelicals were conscious that the full power of the state was not being brought to bear on them.[35] Given the fearsome threats of the 'bloudy statute', remarkably little blood was actually shed.

This comparative lenity may be attributed, in part, to the weaknesses of the regime. The legal process was never entirely under the control of the state, and convictions could not always be secured. When Bishop Bonner prosecuted the London teenager Richard Mekins in 1541, he found himself in unexpected difficulties. Mekins' heresy was not particularly extreme, and he was apparently willing to recant in order to avoid the flames. While the Act of Six Articles gave him no legal right to do this, it seems to have affected the jurors' opinions, for they refused to reach a verdict. Bonner had to face the embarrassment of empanelling a second jury, which he put under considerable pressure to secure a conviction. Mekins burned, but it was a Pyrrhic victory for Bonner: the case became notorious, and he was not foolish enough to attempt such a prosecution again.[36] Foxe claimed that Bonner remarked of the first jury, 'In London they euer finde nothyng'; if this is true,

---

[33] Alastair Duke, *Reformation and Revolt in the Low Countries* (1990), 71, 92, 99; Andrew Pettegree, *Foreign Protestant Communities in Sixteenth-Century London* (Oxford, 1986), 81; Mark Greengrass, *The French Reformation* (Oxford, 1987), 36–8.

[34] John A. F. Thomson, *The Later Lollards 1414–1520* (Oxford, 1965), 238.

[35] John Bale, *A brefe chronycle concernynge the Examinacyon and death of the blessed martyr of Christ syr Iohan Oldecastell the lorde Cobham* (RSTC 1276: Antwerp, 1544), fo. 10^r. Some reformers were willing to put a sinister interpretation on this lenity: see below, pp. 82–3.

[36] *AM*, 1202. This case is referred to by, amongst others, John Bale in his *Epistle exhortatorye*, fo. 8^v; Hall, *The vnion of... Lancastre & Yorke*, fo. 244^r; Wriothesley, 126; TCC MS R3.33 fo. 127^{r-v}; George Joye (ps. James Sawtry), *The defence of the mariage of preistes: agenst Steuen Gardiner* (RSTC 21804: Antwerp, 1541), sig. D3^v.

it suggests that the difficulties of prosecuting heretics ran deeper than this one case. Fear of such complications may have been behind the decision in 1540 to convict Robert Barnes and his two companions of heresy by attainder, so bypassing the judicial process. The regular general pardons that accompanied parliamentary sessions complicated prosecutions; jurisdictional clashes might protect suspects; and even the creation of Six Articles commissions could be a cumbersome process.[37] Moreover, law enforcement was an expensive business, and impoverished bodies such as the newly erected dioceses sometimes found that their ambitions outran their pockets.[38]

Such obstacles aside, authorities were sometimes unwilling to use their powers against heresy, dragging their feet over technicalities.[39] Muriel McClendon's recent study of Norwich, England's second city, suggests that concerns about civic autonomy and authority could override religious fears. Although any principled toleration is most unlikely, the Norwich magistrates do seem to have seen 'a measure of spiritual diversity' as a lesser evil than the intrusion of royal or ecclesiastical authority into the city's affairs.[40] The mayor of Canterbury went so far as to allege that if the king was Supreme Head of the Church in England, he was supreme head of the Church in Canterbury, and would govern matters there as he chose – although this comment landed him in court.[41] Even in London, according to Bishop Gardiner, some aldermen tolerated evil-doers and made light of royal and parliamentary commands – regarding them either as ungodly, or as unrealistic. The bishops themselves were often willing to go well out of their way to avoid executions where law and policy made it possible to do so. Gardiner stated that he had no wish to be 'over curious' in searching out offenders who had concealed their heresy, aiming merely to punish those who had broadcast their allegiance to proscribed doctrines.[42] And everywhere, the rules were bent in the favour of wealthy or well-connected offenders.[43]

---

[37] Muriel St Clare Byrne (ed.), *The Lisle Letters* (Chicago, 1981), vol. V, 539, 546, 569, 586; Elton, *Policy and Police*, 300–1; PRO SP 1/158 fo. 72^r (*LP* XV 362).
[38] For example, the planned visitation of Gloucester diocese in 1542 quickly petered out: Gloucester Record Office GDR 2, pp. 11–43.
[39] CLRO Repertory 10 fo. 214^v.
[40] Muriel McClendon, *The Quiet Reformation: Magistrates and the Emergence of Protestantism in Tudor Norwich* (Stanford, 1999), 14–15.
[41] PRO STAC 2/20/3.
[42] Stephen Gardiner, *The Letters of Stephen Gardiner*, ed. James Arthur Muller (Cambridge, 1933), 134, 160; and see below, pp. 81–4.
[43] For example, London livery companies such as the Skinners and Drapers were regularly able to secure preferential treatment for members accused of heresy. Even Bonner emphasised to Anne Askew that she had been treated with more gentleness than usual because she was 'come of a worshypfull stocke'. CLRO Repertory 11 fo. 158^v; *AM*, 2060; Anne Askew, *The first examinacyon of Anne Askew, latelye martyred in Smythfelde*, ed. John Bale (RSTC 848: Wesel, 1546), fo. 37^v.

Even apparently well-founded cases could unravel if witnesses were thought to have been bribed or to be malicious.[44] The ferocious penalties for misprision might also persuade witnesses to withdraw evidence or remain silent, for merely to be slow in coming forward was potentially a grave offence.[45] Sometimes, however, the prosecuting authorities were unable to find witnesses at all, even when the offence was a public event. When arrested for expounding the Bible in St Paul's Cathedral – hardly a surreptitious offence – John Porter reportedly boasted that the charge would never be proved against him.[46] Growing public opposition to heresy executions was already a feature of prosecutions on the Continent, and evangelicals alleged that in England, too, executions sometimes took place before dawn to avoid crowds gathering.[47] Conservatives were certainly uncomfortably aware of an unease with persecution which was far more widespread than actual sympathy with heretical ideas. In 1546 Richard Smith, the regius professor of divinity at Oxford and a leading conservative, denounced 'that clemencie & lenitie, which our delicate gentilmen do require & looke to be shewed, euen to manifest & notable heretiques in our time'.[48] Even a state as centralised as Tudor England could not prosecute heresy systematically against the wishes of a large section of the population.

These problems, however, can be only a partial explanation for the regime's comparative lack of prosecution. Ultimately, the restrained nature of the late Henrician persecutions must be ascribed to the deliberate policy of the regime. There were bouts of persecution tied to political events: notably in 1540 and 1546, and to a lesser extent in 1543. Those in traditionally Lollard areas such as Colchester and Ipswich also continued to be vulnerable, as they had been for nearly a century and a half. Otherwise, a heretic had to be exceptionally notorious or exceptionally unlucky to be brought to the stake. Despite what Grafton, Foxe and many of their successors believed, the Act of Six Articles was not used as the legal basis for a general purge of evangelicals. Indeed, many even of those who were troubled were not prosecuted under the Act. On closer examination, the legend of the 'whip with six strings' proves somewhat ill-founded. Reformers tended to assess the Act according to where it fell on a one-dimensional spectrum between Rome and their own particular brand of evangelicalism, and their historians

---

[44] In 1542 heresy charges against a group of Coventry reformers collapsed after they argued that the mayor of Coventry was simply pursuing a grudge; likewise, in 1545, the only witness who came forward when Anne Askew was first prosecuted was dismissed as malicious. PRO STAC 2/3 fo. 61^r; PRO KB 9/129; Wriothesley, 155; and see below, pp. 228–9.
[45] PRO SP 1/164 fo. 197^v (*LP* XVI 518.1).
[46] *AM*, 1207. Cf. Dickens, *Lollards and Protestants*, 243.
[47] Pettegree, *Marian Protestantism*, 160–1; Bale, *Epistle exhortatorye*, fos. 14^v–15^r.
[48] Richard Smith, *The assertion and defence of the sacramente of the aulter* (RSTC 22815: 1546), fo. 7^v.

A Counter-Reformation?   27

have largely followed this lead. However, much of the Henrician settlement does not fit neatly onto such a spectrum, and the Six Articles need to be assessed on their own terms.

There was plenty in the Act to cause reformist disquiet. Its penal code was draconian and was open to considerable abuse. As the contents of the Act became known, there was an unseemly scramble of evangelicals trying to ensure their safety. On 15 July 1539, three days after the Act came into force, Cromwell's chaplain Henry Malet was desperately trying to recall a contentious biblical commentary from the printer. Malet had authorised the book for publication before he had seen the Act, but he was now backpedalling. 'I dare not be so bold over such statutes', he explained, 'as I can with doctors vpon scriptuer.'[49] A few weeks earlier, Cromwell had received a letter from a priest called John Foster, which makes pathetic reading. Foster had recently been hoping for a place at court, but he had also been rash enough to marry. The Six Articles' prohibition of clerical marriage therefore left him badly exposed. His letter briefly stated his belief that clerical marriage ought to have been permitted, but he then proceeded to try to undo as much of the damage as he could.

> By the noyse of the peopull I perseyue I haue dunne amysce: which saythe that the kyngys erudyte yugementt, with all hys cowncell temperall & spyrytuall hathe stableschyd a contrary order; that all prestys shalbe separat by a day: with which order I haue contentyd my selfe. And as sone as I herde yt to be tru, I sentt [her – deleted] the woman to her frendys iij score mylys from me, and spedely and with all celeryte I haue resortyd hether to desyre the kynges hyghtnes of hys fauor and absolucyon for my amysce doyng.[50]

The humdrum tragedy behind this meek obedience, suggested eloquently by Foster's alteration of the word 'her' to 'the woman', must have been repeated in dozens of ways across the country. It is this bleak pragmatism, rather than the eye-catching heroism of the few who fled into exile, which shows us the reality of the change in atmosphere brought about by the Act.

Important as the penal code was, however, the heart of the Act was the schedule of six articles which gave it its common name. These articles first appeared as a list of leading questions put to the House of Lords by the duke of Norfolk on 16 May 1539,[51] and in their final form in the statute they were framed as follows.

> I. First, that in the most blessed Sacrament of the Aulter, by the streng[t]he and efficacy of Christes myghtie worde, it beinge spoken by the prest, is present really, under the forme of bread and wyne, the naturall bodye and bloode of our Saviour

---

[49] PRO SP 1/152 fo. 164ʳ (*LP* XIV (i) 1272). The book was published the following year, once it had become clear that the Act was not going to be rigorously enforced (RSTC 21038).
[50] BL Cotton MS Cleopatra E.iv. fo. 140ʳ (*LP* XIV (i) 1125).   [51] *LJ*, 109.

Jesu Criste, conceyved of the Virgin Marie, and that after the consecracion there remayneth noe substance of breade or wyne, nor any other substance but the substance of Criste, God and man;

II. Secondly, that Comunion in bothe kindes is not necessarie ad salutem by the lawe of God to all persons; . . .
III. Thirdly, that Preestes . . . may not marye by the lawe of God;
IV. Fourthlye, that vowes of Chastitye or Wydowhood by Man or Woman made to God advisedly ought to be observed by the lawe of God . . . ;
V. Fyftly, that it is mete and necessarie that private masses be contynued and admytted in this the Kinges English Churche and Congregacion as wherby good Cristen people orderinge them selfes accordingly doe receyve bothe godly and goodly consolacions and benefyttes, and it is agreable also to Gods lawe;
VI. Sixtly, that auriculer confession is expedient and necessarie to be retayned and contynued used and frequented in the Churche of God.[52]

It is easy enough to see how the Act came by its reputation as 'a comprehensive, statutory, and penal definition of the six essential points of Catholic doctrine'.[53]

There is, however, more to this list than meets the eye. If this was intended as a general restatement of a conservative orthodoxy, it was a distinctly peculiar one. Vast areas of doctrinal controversy were passed over in silence. One evangelical petitioner against the Act drew attention to this, arguing that there were other issues which would cause 'asmuche variaunce in your graces realme as any of them treated of' – naming purgatory; prayer to saints; the question of whether the authority of the Bible was supplemented by so-called 'vnwriten verities'; free will versus predestination; the use of images; and justification.[54] The king's emphatic rejection of the evangelical view of that last subject in particular was well known, yet the Act only touched on the issue in the most indirect way. Most surprisingly of all, there was no attempt in the Act to regulate access to the English Bible. In April 1539 a proclamation had been drafted, reiterating the need to use the Bible with due respect for authority. The king heavily amended the draft, so that in its final form it laid down that no one

> shall openly read the Bible or New Testament in the English tongue in any churches or chapels *or elsewhere* with any loud or high voices *and specially* during the time of divine service . . . *Notwithstanding*, his highness is pleased and contented that such as can *and will* read in the English tongue shall and may quietly and reverently read the Bible and New Testament *quietly and with silence* by themselves *secretly* at all times.[55]

---

[52] *Statutes*, 739–40 (31° Henry VIII c. 14).
[53] Redworth, 'Genesis . . . of the Act of Six Articles', 51.
[54] BL Cotton MS Cleopatra E.v. fo. 53ᵛ (*LP* XIV (i) 971).
[55] *TRP*, 285. Royal emendations are italicised.

Despite the extreme nature of these proposed restrictions, however, the proclamation was never issued. There was no mention of the matter in the Six Articles, and indeed no action was taken until 1543.

What was included in the Act was as odd as what was omitted. The demand for communion in both kinds – that is, that the laity should receive both bread and wine in communion – was never a key point of contention in England as it was on the Continent, perhaps in part because Lollardy had never had much concern with this issue.[56] A few cases of evangelical clergy attempting to give their congregations communion in both kinds can be found during this period, and a few polemicists had words to say on the subject, but it was a dispute with little energy in it.[57] Following the proposition of the six questions, the bishops and mitred abbots debated them, and some records of their deliberations survive. On this question, only two bishops – Cranmer, and Barlow, the bishop of St David's – registered opposition to the proposed clause. All the other evangelical bishops apparently acceded to it – even Hugh Latimer and Nicholas Shaxton, who were to be forced to resign for their opposition to the Act as a whole.[58] Even if English evangelicals would have preferred communion in both kinds, few were willing to argue that it was necessary for salvation, or to disobey a king who wished to forbid the practice. Equally odd is the use of the phrase 'private Masses' in the fifth article. This was a derogatory term which orthodox conservatives would not normally have used and which probably derived from the vocabulary of continental Lutheranism.[59] In other words, the Act's doctrinal priorities were thoroughly peculiar.

This much has always been apparent, but an explanation has only recently begun to emerge, thanks to the work of Rory McEntegart. He has analysed the linked religious and military negotiations between England and the alliance of German Lutheran princes known as the Schmalkaldic League. McEntegart shows that five of the Act's six clauses arose directly from those negotiations. The first article, on the Eucharistic presence, was conceived separately from the others, and, as we shall see, it was also perceived as separate in England. The remaining five derived precisely from the five issues identified as the key disputed points when negotiations between English and

---

[56] Anne Hudson, *The Premature Reformation* (Oxford, 1988), 289. By contrast, for the Hussite tradition in Central Europe, communion in both kinds was a central demand.

[57] See, for example, John Bale (ps. John Harryson), *A dysclosynge or openynge of the Manne of synne* (RSTC 1309: Antwerp, 1543), fos. 85ᵛ–6ʳ; William Turner (ps. William Wraghton), *The rescuynge of the romishe fox . . . The seconde course of the hunter at the romishe fox* (RSTC 24355: Bonn, 1545), sigs. I4ʳ–6ᵛ; Bowker, *Henrician Reformation*, 168–9; Elton, *Policy and Police*, 38–9.

[58] PRO SP 1/152 fo. 19ᵛ (*LP* XIV (i) 1065).

[59] An observation which I owe to Richard Rex.

Lutheran diplomats broke off inconclusively in 1538. The arguments advanced in favour of those five articles in Parliament in 1539 were the same as had been put forward by the English during the negotiations of 1538.[60]

The process by which these diplomatic disputes led to domestic anti-heresy legislation remains somewhat unclear. The possibility of a parliamentary act against heresy was first floated early in 1539 by a (somewhat unreliable) friend of the evangelicals, Lord Chancellor Audley. At much the same time, Thomas Cromwell was also planning 'a device . . . for the unity in religion'.[61] McEntegart suggests, plausibly, that these plans were moving towards an 'act of one article', which would affirm the Real Presence of Christ in the Eucharist. That doctrine was still widely accepted in English evangelical circles (as well as by the Lutherans). Against this background, a fresh German delegation arrived in England. McEntegart has shown that at this stage the king was willing to continue negotiating on the theological questions, and that the Lutherans refused to do so, instead proposing thoroughly unrealistic military terms for an alliance. During April and May 1539 several attempts to break this deadlock failed (a failure for which McEntegart squarely blames the Germans). It was during this process that Norfolk formally put to Parliament the six questions which eventually formed the core of the Act.[62]

However, while McEntegart is surely right to insist that the Act should be seen in the context of these diplomatic events, there is no direct evidence as to how it was connected. He does not explore this beyond suggesting that the Lutheran delegates' refusal to engage in further theological discussions prompted the king to send the disputed questions to Parliament for discussion.[63] It seems clear, however, that the questions were framed so as to elicit conservative answers, and the involvement of so prominent a conservative as Norfolk confirms this. Parliament was being asked to confirm doctrinal decisions already taken. A more plausible explanation would be that the king was using Parliament itself as a negotiating tool. On the same day as Norfolk put the questions to the Lords, a further delegation was sent to the Lutheran ambassadors demanding that they soften their stance. The threat of legislation to enforce a conservative settlement of all of the issues that had been left outstanding may have been a piece of brinkmanship, intended to shock the Lutherans into negotiation; for while Norfolk's questions invited conservative answers, their form held open the possibility of backing down without losing face. If this was so, the bluff was called. The Lutheran negotiations collapsed, the bill progressed through Parliament with a few amendments, and England was left with an anti-heresy statute which froze

---

[60] Rory McEntegart, *Henry VIII, the League of Schmalkalden and the English Reformation* (Woodbridge, Suffolk, 2002), 108–27, 150–63, esp. 159.
[61] *Ibid.*, 150; *LP* XIV (i) 655.
[62] McEntegart, *Henry VIII*, 135–7, 150–63.   [62] *Ibid.*, 157–8, 162–3, 166.

into legislation the issues at the centre of a passing diplomatic dispute. As a result, the Act reflected neither the king's central concerns about domestic heresy nor the realities of the English situation.

Indeed, despite its title, the Act, as it eventually emerged, dealt with only three issues: auricular confession, clerical and monastic celibacy, and the Mass. Even on these three points, it has long been recognised that the Act did not actually roll back any of the official reforms of the 1530s. It certainly dashed the hopes of those who had looked for further change, but none of Cromwell's achievements were undone. Moreover, on one of the three issues, the reformers managed to modify the text of the original bill sufficiently to make it acceptable. When the bishops debated the subject of confession, the core group of evangelicals – Cranmer, Latimer, Shaxton, Barlow, Goodricke of Ely and Hilsey of Rochester – were joined by Salcot of Bangor, Holgate of Llandaff, Warton of St Asaph and Reppes of Norwich, as well as the abbots of Westminster and Gloucester, in denying that confession was 'necessary by the lawe of god'. Instead, they claimed, 'thei canne not fynde expresly by the worde of god that Auriculare confession is necessary by the same, but thei doone saie and affirme that yt is very requysyte and expedient to be obserued and vsed'. Their view still only commanded the support of a minority, but this was not a democratic process. When the bill returned to Parliament, Henry himself let it be known that he was on the reformers' side – although for very different reasons.[64] The leading conservative bishops – Gardiner, Tunstall of Durham and Archbishop Lee of York – were forced to accept defeat, although not with grace. Tunstall tried to reopen the issue, but only succeeded in infuriating the king.

A year later, the scars left by this defeat were still visible. In April 1540, a committee of bishops and senior clergy was established by the king to work towards an official statement of the Henrician Church's doctrine. At some stage early in its deliberations a series of questions on the seven sacraments was put to it, and the various committee members' responses to each question were conflated to give collective answers. In some cases one or two dissenters refused to subscribe to this collective response. One of the questions was: 'Whither a man be bounde ... to confesse his secrete deddly synnes to a preiste?' All but Archbishop Cranmer agreed that a Christian conscious of guilt of deadly sin must confess to a priest 'if he will obteyne the benefyte of absolucyon ministred by the preste'. However, the committee then split, apparently irreconcilably, between nine evangelicals and fellow-travellers who

---

[64] The success of a minority in the Lords in persuading the king to change his mind, and thus in changing the legislation, underlines the fact that Norfolk's questions were to be answered by the king himself and not by parliamentary process. PRO SP 1/152 fo. 19ʳ (*LP* XIV (i) 1065); BL Cotton MS Cleopatra E.v fo. 131ʳ (*LP* XIV (ii) Appendix 29); Alec Ryrie, 'Divine kingship and royal theology in Henry VIII's Reformation', *Reformation* 7 (2002), 64–5, 71.

believed that 'absolution by a preste is the surest waye, if he maye be convenyently had', and ten conservatives, including Lee, Tunstall and Gardiner, who insisted that 'absolucyon to be ministred by a preste, if a convenient preste may be had, is necessarie'. It was the only question on which there was no consensus, and the importance which conservatives attached to it is underlined by Gardiner's presence on the list. He was not a member of the committee and played no other recorded part in its deliberations. It seems likely he was brought in to provide a casting vote on this critical issue. Yet the difference between these two statements is if anything slenderer than the difference between the two statements at issue in 1539. The subject still clearly touched a raw nerve.[65]

For many moderate evangelicals, the clause eventually enacted in the Six Articles was an entirely satisfactory statement, rather than a compromise which they could bring themselves to swallow. Reformers were certainly suspicious of auricular confession, but most of them wished to reform the practice rather than to abolish it.[66] Even a radical such as John Bale, who saw confession as having been invented by the clergy to conceal their treasons and to detract from the work of Christ, hastened to affirm the value of confession to 'prestes of godlye knowlege'.[67] Thomas Becon went so far as to write of 'the holye sacrament of Penaunce', and while he deprecated unlearned confessors, he added, 'why auriculare Confession shuld be condemned & exiled from the boundes of christianite I se no cause, but that it shoulde be approued, retayned, maynteyned & vsed, I fynd causes many.' The causes he gave were impeccably evangelical. Confession encourages humility and self-knowledge, allays doubt and provides a forum in which the priest may teach his flock. Becon valued even the absolution, understanding it as 'a free deliuerauuce [*sic*] from all youre synnes thorow Christes bloud', and arguing that the penitent should hear the priest's words and believe them 'as though God him selfe had spoken them'.[68] From this point of view, the sixth of the Six Articles was entirely unexceptionable.

Reformist attempts to amend the other two sets of articles, dealing with the Mass and with celibacy, failed. There is no denying that these clauses were a serious blow to the evangelical cause. Nevertheless, the picture is less

---

[65] BL Cotton MS Cleopatra E.v fo. 43^{r-v} (*LP* XV 826).
[66] Davies, *Religion of the Word*, 100–1.
[67] John Bale, *John Bale's King Johan*, ed. Barry B. Adams (San Marino, CA, 1969), lines 2500–2; Bale, *A dysclosynge or openynge of the Manne of synne*, fos. 22^v–23^r, 30^{r-v}, 67^v; Anne Askew, *The lattre examinacyon of Anne Askewe, latelye martyred in Smythfelde*, ed. John Bale (RSTC 850: Wesel, 1547), fo. 32^v.
[68] Thomas Becon (ps. Theodore Basille), *A new yeares gyfte more precious than golde, worthy to be embrased no lesse ioyfully than thankfully* (RSTC 1738: 1543), sig. L6^v; Thomas Becon (ps. Theodore Basille), *A Potacion or drinkynge for this holi time of lent* (RSTC 1749: 1542), sigs. E2^r–4^v, 6^v; cf. PRO SP 6/9 no. 3, p. 69 (*LP* XVIII (i) 611.6).

clear than it at first appears. Of the three clauses touching the Mass, two were of the second order of importance to evangelicals. The article denying communion in both kinds, as we have seen, owed much to the priorities of German Lutheranism and little to those of English evangelicalism. The article upholding private Masses is also more ambiguous than at first appears. Private Masses were used principally because of their efficacy as a sacrifice. In particular, if a private Mass were celebrated in remembrance of a dead person (as in a chantry), it could hasten that person's passage through purgatory. All evangelicals deplored this doctrine, and we might therefore expect that this clause would be opposed most fiercely of all. Indeed, when the German reformer Philip Melanchthon wrote a short treatise against the Act, it was this clause which he singled out first as needing to be refuted. The Eucharist, he argued in some detail, was not a sacrifice.[69] However, the record of the debates amongst the bishops shows that, of the four clauses for which opinions are recorded, this was the only one to be passed unopposed. Not even Latimer and Shaxton, who were to oppose the whole bill openly in Parliament and to lose their bishoprics as a consequence, registered any disquiet.[70]

There is no firm evidence as to why the bishops were so willing to let this clause pass, but the answer appears to lie in the ambiguity of its wording. The sacrifice of the Mass and intercession for the dead are implied but not explicitly asserted. The original question put by Norfolk and debated by the bishops simply asked whether private Masses were conformable to scripture. During the process of drafting the Act proper, the king rewrote the clause entirely, and its eventual form was his personal composition. It praised the 'godly and goodly consolacions and benefyttes' which Christians might derive from such Masses, but nowhere did it specify what those consolations and benefits might be.[71] To Melanchthon, this was contemptible sophistry:

Where they say that the people myght receyue thereby rytches comfortes and benifites, why adde they not what comfortes, and what benifites? The byshoppes name not to what ende the merites of the priuie masses shoulde be applied, bycause they know that it can not be defended. And so they play and mocke wyth wordes that they maye slippe out of the application if it be dispraysed, and yet wil they haue the application of the priuie masses vnderstand of the people.[72]

For English evangelicals, however, anxious to obey their king and to paper over doctrinal cracks as far as they could, this ambiguity was a positive relief. 'Godly and goodly consolacions and benefyttes' could, after all, be taken to

---

[69] Melanchthon, *Epistle*, sigs. A8^v–B3^r.
[70] PRO SP 1/152 fo. 19^r (*LP* XIV (i) 1065). No opinions are recorded for the clause on transubstantiation (on which see below, pp. 34–6) or for that on vows, where the issues were essentially the same as for clerical celibacy.
[71] BL Cotton MS Cleopatra E.v fos. 328^r, 330^r (*LP* XIV (i) 868.9).
[72] Melanchthon, *Epistle*, sig. A5^{r-v}.

refer to something innocuous, such as the remembrance of Christ's passion. This line of attack was pursued by the preacher who was England's master of ambiguity, Edward Crome. Despite his repeated equivocations and recantations, Crome was no coward. In the autumn of 1540, immediately after the fall of Cromwell, 'because he saw the more need ... he preached with more fervour than for some time before' (or so it appeared to the young Richard Hilles, an admirer of Crome's whose own zeal is more striking than his accuracy). Crome and the leading conservative Nicholas Wilson spent much of the autumn in a running pulpit debate, of which one of the main themes was Masses for the dead. Crome opposed them, arguing that the destruction of the monasteries demonstrated that the regime had in fact abandoned the use of Masses for the dead.[73] However, he was careful throughout not to argue that private Masses were to be rejected altogether. As the London reformer Richard Forsett described the matter:

The variance bitwen Crome and Wilson was not whether priuate masses be profitable and necessary or not but whether they profited the soules departed or not ... for they did both agree that masses were profitable to men lyvyng.[74]

In the event, this particular piece of sophistry failed, and Crome was forced to recant his views.[75] Nevertheless, in 1539 the ambiguity of this clause in the Six Articles meant that the question was still open. The evangelical bishops could read the signs of the times well enough not to force a conflict which could be postponed to a more propitious date.

The first of the articles, dealing with the presence of Christ in the Eucharist, is another matter entirely. This was the central, critical clause of the Act, and was qualitatively different from the other five articles. The full ferocity of the penal code, including the denial of a chance to recant, applied only to those offenders who contravened this first article. It was the matter about which the king felt most passionately, and most conservatives agreed with him. There were some heresies which Henry mistrusted or saw as destabilising, but it appears that he saw the denial of Christ's presence in the Eucharist – 'sacramentarianism' – simply as loathsome. Royal proclamations during the late 1530s repeatedly bracketed together Anabaptists and sacramentaries as equally evil and dangerous, the two groups who destroyed the right use of the two holiest sacraments, and who in so doing tore up the whole fabric of the society which Henry so wished to keep united.[76] The political momentum behind this clause was set moving in November 1538 by the trial of the sacramentary John Lambert, and was built up in the spring of 1539 by reports of sacramentaries in Calais. The correspondence of Lord Lisle, the king's

---

[73] *ET*, 140–1 (*OL*, 211–12). [74] PRO STAC 2/34/28, fo. 5ʳ.
[75] Bonner Register fo. 26ᵛ. [76] See, for example, *TRP*, 227, 270–3, 280.

deputy in Calais, demonstrates that, from the moment that rumours began to circulate about a statute to enforce religious unity to the final passage of the Act, the attack on sacramentaries was assumed to be its dominant if not its only theme. On 20 May 1539, four days after Norfolk put the six questions to the Lords, Lisle's man in London, John Husee, wrote to him:

> I think verily there will be such a discreet order taken concerning the Blessed Sacrament of the Altar ere this Parliament be prorogued, that some . . . will hereafter tremble in mentioning that Blessed Sacrament which they not long since hath most unreverently, against all Christian faith and religion, misused and ill spoken of.

Writing to Lady Lisle the following day, Husee described the proposed statute as 'an act . . . concerning the blessed Sacrament of the Altar'. Nor was this only Husee's slant on events, for on 23 May Lord Sandys wrote to Lisle, describing the bill as one intended to settle 'such arguments and doubts as were in controversy concerning the blessed Sacrament of the Altar'. On 13 June, Husee was able to send a more complete account of the Act.

> The Act concerning the Sacrament is passed . . . the sum whereof is, that whatsoever hereafter be reasoned and spoken of the same, after the consecration, otherwise than hath been in time past; that is, the very body of God to be there in flesh and blood, realiter et essentialiter; the offenders thereof to be taken as traitors and heretics.

He also mentioned the enforcement of clerical celibacy and vows of chastity, but only referred in passing to 'the other articles'. Finally, eight days later, Lisle was sent another, somewhat belated summary of the Act by Thomas Bois, one of the Calais MPs:

> There is such an act past, the which shall set every true Christian man in a good quietness as concerning the blessed sacrament of the altar, and for shrift, and housel, and for the calling in of all such erroneous books as do object against any part or point in the said act.[77]

All of these men, close to the centre of power as they were, agreed that the Act was essentially an attack on sacramentarianism, with its other clauses subordinate if they were mentioned at all. They were afterthoughts added to a bill which was at heart a defence of the Real Presence. It is no coincidence that the document summarising the bishops' opinions of the articles lists only their reactions to the other five. Glyn Redworth has suggested that another page, containing the division of opinions on the first article, is missing, but this seems unlikely. A simple listing of votes of the kind recorded for the other articles would not take an entire folio page, and there is no evidence to suggest that such a page existed.[78] It is more likely that the king made it

---

[77] Byrne, *Lisle Letters*, vol. V, 483, 486, 492, 533–4, 540.
[78] Redworth, 'Genesis . . . of the Act of Six Articles', 59; cf. PRO SP 1/152 fos. 15–22 (*LP* XIV (i) 1065).

clear that the first of the Six Articles was simply not up for discussion. It was the centrepiece of the Act. A line was being drawn (not a moment too soon, Husee and Bois evidently believed), and the bishops would not be allowed to interfere.

Nevertheless, one change was made to the wording of this clause before the bill reached the statute book. Throughout the drafting process, the clause referred simply to 'transubstantiation'. At some stage before the king amended the final draft of the bill, however, the word was dropped, and the lengthier affirmation included in the final Act was substituted. The alteration was essentially cosmetic, since that affirmation was virtually a dictionary definition of transubstantiation; in Redworth's phrase, 'the accidents of the definition may have altered but its substance remained the same'.[79] Yet accidents are not without their importance. The word 'transubstantiation' was strongly associated with the papacy, and it was non-scriptural. The regime's rejection of it, like its willingness to abandon the word 'purgatory', spoke of a deep-seated hostility to anything tainted with papalism and of a firm commitment to biblical authority. Perhaps more importantly, the rejection of a traditional term also implies the questioning of the traditions of interpretation that went with it. Lucy Wooding has described how, later in the century, conservative authors tried to defend the traditional doctrine of the Mass by appeal to Scripture alone, unsupported by medieval precedent or ecclesiastical authority.[80] The removal of the term 'transubstantiation' from the Six Articles had a similar effect. The implication of the clause as it was eventually enacted was that the regime was no longer holding to a long-established truth hallowed by tradition, but trying to arrive at that same definition *de novo*. As a result, the complex tradition underpinning established Eucharistic doctrine was being left behind. If traditional forms of doctrinal authority were being questioned, then every scrap of doctrinal territory had to be fought for. This was a profoundly radical process, even if in this case it led to a conservative conclusion. Those evangelicals who explored alternatives to transubstantiation (at times retaining a belief in the Real Presence) were of course anathematised by the Act.[81] In another sense, however, they were following its example.

For all these faint comforts, the proposed Act remained a body blow to evangelicals' hopes for future reformation. They struggled to avert it. One petition submitted to Convocation from an evangelical source survives; there may well have been more. That petition called on the king to decide matters

---

[79] Redworth, 'Genesis ... of the Act of Six Articles', 64. McEntegart's comment that the revised clause was 'acceptable to all parties' is altogether too optimistic: McEntegart, *Henry VIII*, 159.
[80] Lucy Wooding, *Rethinking Catholicism in Reformation England* (Oxford, 2000), 106–7.
[81] For examples of this, see below, pp. 142–3.

of such great moment only after 'long, great, and mature delyberacion'. It suggested that he consult internationally before deciding finally, and warned darkly that some radicals might be driven to treason by a conservative settlement (a sentiment unlikely to have had the desired effect on the king). However, the only doctrinal issue with which the petition engaged was clerical marriage. Having pointed out that clerical marriage was not held even by papists actually to be forbidden by scripture, the petitioners begged the king to suspend that part of the Act, or, failing that, to hold formal disputations on the subject in both universities. The arrangements they suggested for these disputations amount to rigging, and they were evidently confident of this, as they volunteered to be put to death if the judges declared against them.[82] There was, however, no mention of any of the other articles. The Eucharistic issue which was so central to the regime's purpose is passed by.

Clerical marriage was a subject about which the king felt strongly, but it was not the heart of the Act. Nevertheless, for a remarkable number of evangelicals, the ban on clergy and former religious marrying was the provision which provoked the most comment. George Constantine, an evangelical priest who was a veteran of the illegal book trade of the late 1520s, and a graduate of Thomas More's prisons, was so disheartened by this clause that he felt there was little point in continuing as a priest. As he said,

I was a surgyon in Brabant a whoale yere, and in good fayth, seinge that coniugium sacerdotum [priests' marriage] is concluded agenst Gods worde, I entende to studie the same facultie agayne. I will loke over myne olde bokes. I am glad that I haue them yet.[83]

Some Continental commentators also saw the bar on clerical marriage as the gravest of the Act's provisions. Bucer, describing the Act as 'most exceedingly bitter', singled out clerical celibacy for particular consideration (he also mentioned private Masses in passing). Melanchthon's treatise against the Six Articles also paid particular attention to this issue.[84]

By its nature, however, clerical marriage was an issue which was of interest to a limited audience. Although plenty was written on the subject by reformist polemicists, it was not likely to arouse mass support. Indeed, some lay reformers close to the regime were content to accept continued clerical celibacy. Christopher Mont, the evangelical sent as the English envoy to the German Lutherans in early 1539, played down the importance of clerical celibacy to his hosts. It was maintained, he apparently argued, because 'the common people as yet weake in the knowlege of the worde',

---

[82] BL Cotton MS Cleopatra E.v fos. 53^r–4^v (*LP* XIV (i) 971).
[83] George Constantine, 'A memorial from George Constantine to Thomas Lord Cromwell', *Archaeologia* 23 (1831), 76–7.
[84] *ET*, 344–6 (*OL* 527–30); Melanchthon, *Epistle*, sigs. A5^v–6^r, B3^r–5^r.

faced with married clergy, 'myght therby conceyve an opinion of concupiscence in them, and by reason thereof contempne their preachinges'.[85] The concentration on clerical celibacy as the main evil of the Six Articles is significant, not because clerical celibacy was an overwhelming concern of English evangelicals – it was not; but because it draws attention to the remarkable silence from reformers in response to the central thrust of the Act, the clause on the Eucharistic presence. English conservatives loudly celebrated the firm establishment of transubstantiation. English evangelicals seem to have done their best to ignore it.

As a piece of penal legislation, the Act of Six Articles was not a success. Its doctrinal scope was too narrow to underpin a general drive against heresy. The commissioners who organised the heresy purge in London in July 1540 are said to have been driven to the dubious expedient of adding 'branches' to the Six Articles to embrace a more comprehensive range of offences. It is certainly true that a great many of those arrested in that purge were held for offences not covered by the Act, such as despising established ceremonies or failing to attend church.[86] The Act's purpose, however, was not to provide a legal basis for the extermination of heresy but to proclaim the Henrician orthodoxy of the moment, both for domestic and foreign consumption. Above all, it was meant to indicate unmistakably that sacramentarianism had no place in Henry's realms. That first article, indeed, went beyond merely condemning sacramentarian views. By insisting on the full-blown doctrine of transubstantiation, it also anathematised the Lutheran view that Christ was corporally present in the Eucharist but that the substance of bread and wine remained. There was never any doubt, however, that the real fire of the king's anger was directed at the sacramentaries. The compliment was, in due course, returned. By the time they wrote, Bale, Grafton, Foxe and the other architects of the legend of the whip with six strings were sacramentaries themselves. For those who continued to accept the Real Presence, the central clause of the Act of Six Articles was not nearly so difficult to swallow. Even Melanchthon's treatise on the Act did not mention that clause, and he at least faced no political pressure to remain silent.

Why was the reformist reaction to the Six Articles so low-key? Because the Act was first and last directed at sacramentarian doctrines, and in 1539 only a small minority of English reformers were drawn to such doctrines. The king's continued bracketing of Anabaptists and sacramentaries was not an accident. In England in 1539, both were extremist minorities.[87] When John Lambert was condemned as a sacramentary in November 1538,

---

[85] BL Cotton MS Cleopatra E.v fo. 185ʳ (*LP* XIV (i) 844).
[86] Hall, *The vnion of . . . Lancastre & Yorke*, fo. 234ᵛ; *AM*, 1202–5. The twenty persons who were indicted had all been accused of heresies which fell within the scope of the Act: PRO SP 1/243 fos. 61–80 (*LP* Addenda 1463).
[87] See below, pp. 138–43.

establishment evangelicals such as Cranmer and Barnes did not merely accept his prosecution but actively participated in it. Despite the rhetoric of Foxe and his predecessors, we should not be surprised that the Act of Six Articles did not herald a general persecution. There is no evidence that it was ever intended to. It was a signal to observers at home and (especially) abroad that some areas were going to remain off-limits for Henry's Reformation. Supremely, it was a signal that the regime was going to work to ensure that sacramentarianism, a marginal belief in England at the time, would remain so. Evangelicals did not like it, but the bulk of them could live with it. If it had been the unambiguous assertion of orthodoxy which Foxe described, no such coexistence would have been possible. However, if it asserted an orthodoxy at all, it was Henry VIII's own, and his orthodoxy did not map neatly onto the sharp division between Catholic and Protestant which later generations knew.

RELIGIOUS POLICY IN THE 1540S

In one sense, however, the Six Articles did set the tone for religious policy throughout the remainder of the reign: the pattern of an apparent return to conservatism masking more complex and ambiguous policies remains.

I have argued elsewhere that the driving force behind Henry VIII's religious policies during the last decade of his life was the Royal Supremacy and his insistence on maintaining it. Most of the doctrinal directions taken by his regime derived directly or indirectly from the new role to which he believed God had called him.[88] As a consequence, the political environment which English evangelicals faced during these years was neither consistently hostile nor consistently favourable. The familiar narrative of conservatism in Henry's last years conceals a more complex story. What follows argues that the stubborn political optimism of many evangelicals was not as deluded as it may seem. This is not to deny the real and savage setbacks which their cause endured during the early 1540s, including but not limited to a degree of persecution. However, those setbacks are not the whole story. There was no steady conservative advance. Rather, during the last seven years of Henry's reign, the political messages for evangelicals were bewilderingly mixed. Most recent scholarship on this has focused on the causes of this political switchback. A well-established view argues that policy was driven by faction-fighting at court, and that its direction shifted in accordance with the political fortunes of the players around the king.[89] More recently, others

---

[88] Ryrie, 'Divine kingship'.
[89] Eric Ives, *Faction in Tudor England* (Historical Association: Appreciations in History 6, 1979); G. R. Elton, 'Tudor government: the points of contact. III: the court', *Transactions of the Royal Historical Society*, series v. 26 (1976), 211–28; Robert Shephard, 'Court factions in early modern England', *Journal of Modern History* 64 (1992), 721–45.

have grown suspicious of the explanatory power of faction, and have suggested that the king's own priorities were the hub around which his regime's policies turned. The apparent twists and turns of those policies might reflect the consistent views of a king who subscribed neither to evangelical nor to conservative orthodoxies.[90] Whatever the roots of the regime's policies were, however, it was their impact that evangelicals in the country had to face.

In the immediate wake of the Six Articles, as we have seen, evangelicals were genuinely optimistic that the Act would be left behind as the Gospel's advance continued. And with some reason: no commissions were issued under the Act's terms, and no arrests made. The suppression of the remaining monasteries continued. In November a new proclamation urged the preparation of a new English translation of the Bible, reaffirming the regime's intention to provide the people with 'the free and liberal use of the Bible in our own maternal tongue'.[91] Stephen Gardiner was ejected from the Privy Council for labelling Robert Barnes a heretic, fuelling excited rumours. In Lent 1540, Barnes was emboldened, or goaded, openly to attack the bishop in a sermon at Paul's Cross.[92] Meanwhile Cromwell was created earl of Essex. The fragility of the evangelical triumph was only exposed when, with bewildering suddenness, Cromwell was arrested. He was executed on 28 July; Barnes and his two associates were burned two days later. And now the Six Articles were finally put into effect, leading to the arrest of hundreds of Londoners for heresy.

However, in a pattern that was to become familiar, the disaster was less complete than it appeared. The purge ended almost as soon as it had begun, and all of those arrested were swiftly released. A number of suspected heretics from Calais were released at the same time. In both cases Lord Chancellor Audley, one of Cromwell's protégés, may have had a role in persuading the king to call off the heresy-hunters; but if so, Audley's action was as much a recognition of the impossibility of the task as an expression of any evangelical solidarity. Not since the days of Thomas More and Bishop Stokesley's campaigns in the early 1530s had there been an attempt comprehensively to stamp out heresy in London, and since then the problem had grown too large for such techniques to work. There were not enough prisons in London to hold everyone who had been tainted with heterodoxy. Moreover, the accusations ranged beyond the kind of renegade priests and artisan Lollards with which English heresy-hunters had long been familiar. Some of London's

---

[90] Greg Walker, *Persuasive Fictions: Faction, Faith and Popular Culture in the Reign of Henry VIII* (Aldershot, Hants., 1996), 2–23; Richard Rex, 'The crisis of obedience: God's Word and Henry's Reformation', *HJ* 39 (1996), 863–94; Ryrie, 'Divine kingship'.
[91] *TRP*, 286.
[92] PRO SP 1/155 fo. 190r (*LP* XIV (ii) 750.1); Stephen Gardiner, *A declaration of such true articles as George Ioye hath gone about to confute as false* (RSTC 11588: 1546), fo. 6^{r-v}.

most respectable and substantial citizens were arrested in July 1540. These included men such as John Blage, a wealthy grocer who was Archbishop Cranmer's London business agent; John Starkey, a prosperous fishmonger who was not only a former mayor of Canterbury but also a sitting MP; and Giles Harrison, the king's beer-brewer.[93] Harrison's case is particularly telling. His offence, as described by Foxe, took place when he and some friends were in a tavern.

> Some of them sayd let us go to Masse: I say, Tarye, sayd hee: and so takyng a peece of bread in his handes, lift it up ouer his head: And likewise takyng a cuppe of wyne, and bowyng down his head, made therewith a crosse ouer the cuppe, and so takyng the said cup in both his handes, lift it ouer his head, saying these woordes: haue ye not heard Masse now?[94]

It is easy to see how this crass parody led to Harrison's arrest, but it is almost impossible to see how the case might have ended in a heresy trial. Harrison was no gospeller. Nothing else in his career indicates any interest in religion at all. This made his bar-room performance all the more disturbing. Its clear message was that popular reverence for the sacrament had been so far eroded that a respectable brewer (albeit one fortified by his own wares) might think that his drinking companions would find such a performance funny. By the summer of 1540, heresy in London was beyond the reach of the law. Riot or massacre might have stamped it out; due legal process could not. This purge, so critical to Grafton and Foxe's depiction of a general persecution after the Six Articles, was in reality an isolated event.

During the autumn of 1540, then, as the temperature of the religious confrontation fell back, evangelicals began to explore the boundaries of the new dispensation. While they were not going to be exterminated, it was not clear how much room for manoeuvre they would have. The early signals were not particularly encouraging. In October, Bishop Bonner issued a general injunction to his clergy against unlicensed preaching, singling out the Scottish reformer John Willock. That winter, the irrepressible Edward Crome engaged in a very public argument about the value of private Masses.[95] The matter caused sufficient contention that by Christmas 1540 he was forbidden to preach further, pending the king's judgement. When that judgement was delivered, on 18 January 1541, it went wholly against Crome. Crome was forced to make a thorough recantation, in which the ambiguities of the Six

---

[93] Brigden, *London*, 412, 419; *AM*, 1228; *DNB* (Robert Blagge); Peter Clark, *English Provincial Society from the Reformation to the Revolution: Religion, Politics and Society in Kent 1500–1640* (Hassocks, Surrey, 1977), 39–41. On this purge, see above, p. 17, and Susan Brigden, 'Popular disturbance and the fall of Thomas Cromwell and the reformers, 1539–40', *HJ* 24 (1981) 257–78.

[94] *AM*, 1205. Cf. PRO SP 1/243 fo. 72^r (*LP* Addenda 1463).

[95] Bonner Register fo. 18^v; see above, pp. 34–45.

Articles were replaced by a clarity thoroughly unpalatable to evangelicals. The text prepared for him emphasised that private Masses were an effectual sacrifice on behalf of both the living and the dead; although it added, in keeping with the royal orthodoxy, that no one could specify how much, for how long or for whom such Masses were profitable. In a backhanded compliment to the force of Crome's argument, the recantation also insisted that the value of Masses for the dead in no way impugned the king's justice in suppressing the monasteries, and that those who preached the sacrifice of the Mass 'do not thereby as fer forth as I knowe goe aboute . . . to bring in agayne the bysshop of Rome'.[96]

This was an unequivocal defeat. It signalled that from now on, any outspoken advocate of evangelical doctrine risked a heresy accusation, and plenty of such accusations followed for the remainder of the king's reign. Most were defused in some way, often but not always by the accused's willingness to recant. This new climate might seem simply to demonstrate that reformist hopes were mere moonshine, although it is clear that from the regime's point of view, Crome's worst offence was that he had fomented public disagreement and disorder.[97] Nor was the Crome case isolated. The day before Crome's fate was judged, Sir Thomas Wyatt and Sir Ralph Sadler were arrested and sent to the Tower: both were clients of Cromwell's, and most observers assumed that the fate of men arrested in such a fashion was already sealed. A general purge of evangelical sympathisers threatened.[98] This was seemingly reinforced on 29 January, when a Six Articles commission was issued for London.[99] However, these threats both fizzled out. Remarkably, Wyatt and Sadler were both released and more or less rehabilitated. And the heresy commissioners, having pursued Richard Mekins and broken their teeth on him, adopted a more cautious approach thereafter.[100] Reformism remained a dangerous pastime. However, the threatened serious assault again failed to materialise.

Instead, as the days lengthened, the political winds began to blow in the other direction. The king was perhaps becoming discontent with his conservative councillors. In March the French ambassador Marillac (admittedly a strikingly unreliable witness) claimed that Henry was reproaching them with procuring Cromwell's death and so causing him to put to death 'the most faithful servant he had ever had'.[101] For whatever reason, the reformers felt the benefit of the king's change of mood in a matter close to their hearts: the English Bible. The royal injunctions of 1538 – which were still in

---

[96] Bonner Register fo. 26ᵛ; *ET*, 140–3 (*OL*, 211–15).
[97] Bonner Register fo. 26ᵛ. [98] *LP* XVI 461, 534.
[99] Bonner Register fo. 18ᵛ. [100] See above, pp. 24–5.
[101] Jean Kaulek (ed.), *Correspondance Politique de MM. de Castillon et de Marillac* (Paris, 1885), 274 (*LP* XVI 590).

force – required all parish churches to acquire a copy of the Bible, but progress had been slow. On 6 May 1541, a royal proclamation required all parishes which had not yet done so to acquire a copy of the authorised 'Great Bible' (a reference to the physical size of the volume) by the beginning of November. Non-compliant parishes were now threatened with a fine rather greater than the cost of the book, and this seems to have done the trick. Churchwardens' accounts show that rates of Bible acquisition picked up sharply after the proclamation. In the diocese of London, at least, the proclamation was – unusually – ordered to be posted on the door of every parish church.[102]

Further royal actions and pronouncements in the same year maintained this new mood. During the early spring of 1541, the king gave a fresh impetus to the ongoing process of refounding those cathedrals which had been monasteries, and refounding a few other ex-monasteries as cathedrals. The new foundations now began to be stripped of dedications to traditional saints such as Swithun and Frideswide, and instead to be dedicated to biblical saints, or simply to Christ or the Trinity. More substantially, preaching was to be a far more important part of the life of the new foundations. These changes were hardly evangelical in themselves, but they did draw on ideas put forward by evangelicals and were thoroughly in tune with their hopes for reform of the Church.[103] By the summer, the king seemed to be openly embracing parts of the evangelical agenda once again. A royal letter to justices of the peace was concerned with partisans of Rome rather than with heretics, demanding that 'the pryve maynteinors of that papistical factyon may be tryed out and brought to iustiyce'.[104] In July, the king issued a proclamation on feast days which had been drafted by Archbishop Cranmer. This stripped further unbiblical material from the ecclesiastical calendar and abolished the mid-winter festivals of inversion, such as boy-bishops.[105] Most dramatically, the king's experiences on his great northern progress that summer renewed his zeal against the abuse of images in worship. In the 1530s he had become convinced of the dangers of idolatry, and he remained so.[106] In September, Archbishop Lee of York was ordered to cause all shrines throughout the northern province to be razed. Two weeks later, a rather more enthusiastic Archbishop Cranmer was likewise commanded to ensure that searches be made across the southern province for shrines or their appurtenances, and

---

[102] *TRP*, 297; Ronald Hutton, 'The local impact of the Tudor Reformations', in *The English Reformation Revised*, ed. Christopher Haigh (Cambridge, 1987), 118; *LP* XVI 819.
[103] Richard Rex and C. D. C. Armstrong, 'Henry VIII's ecclesiastical and collegiate foundations', *Historical Research* 75 (2002), 401–5.
[104] PRO SP 1/166 fo. 81^v (*LP* XVI 945).   [105] *TRP*, 301–2; MacCulloch, *Cranmer*, 283–4.
[106] For a late example, see BL, C.25.b.4 (*The psalter of Dauid in English* (1544?), tr. George Joye – Henry VIII's copy), fo. 35^v.

that if any such thing was found, it should be destroyed 'so as there remayne noe Memorye of it'.[107] This was the kind of reformation for which evangelicals had been hoping; and this is why, during this so-called conservative reaction, reformers can be found whose chief complaint is that the clergy are slack in implementing royal commands.[108]

The English Bible remained the centre of religious controversy. In February 1542, the licensed translation was questioned in Convocation. This debate threatened to slip dangerously out of the reformers' control, for only three of the English and Welsh bishops – Cranmer, Goodricke of Ely and Barlow of St David's – were now reliable evangelical partisans, and the reformers lost several minor battles in Convocation that year. Bishop Gardiner promptly came forward with a list of a hundred Latin words which he suggested had been misleadingly translated in the existing version – although he did not, as is sometimes asserted, suggest that they should not be translated into English at all. Cranmer saved the situation by appealing to the king, who agreed to refer the matter of the translation to the universities.[109] Although this transparently political manoeuvre was strongly opposed by the other bishops, they continued to accept the validity of the Great Bible. Bishop Bonner refused to restrict access to the Bibles in St. Paul's Cathedral, despite considerable provocation from evangelicals.[110] He also, in injunctions issued to his clergy in 1542, required them to engage in a regular programme of Bible study, and stated his intention to enforce this.[111] The next Convocation, in February 1543, even ordered that all parish clergy should read from the English Bible to their congregations, at the rate of a chapter a week. This order built upon a decision apparently taken the previous year to issue set homilies to be used by preachers. No texts for these survive, but in Edward VI's reign Cranmer apparently remembered them as having been worthwhile, so they can be presumed to have leaned towards reformist ideas. However, both the homilies and, apparently, the reading programme were overtaken by the events of 1543.[112]

Most of the evidence for describing Henry's last years as a conservative reaction comes from the year 1543. During that year, English evangelicals faced significant attacks on three fronts: on their doctrines, their books and

---

[107] *P&O*, 247; Lambeth Palace Library, Register of Thomas Cranmer fo. 18^{r-v}. For enforcement of these orders, see Bonner Register fo. 252^r; Margaret Spufford, *Contrasting Communities: English Villagers in the Sixteenth and Seventeenth Centuries* (Cambridge, 1974), 242.

[108] For example, BL Royal MS 17.B.xxxv fo. 8^v.

[109] David Wilkins (ed.), *Concilia Magnae Brittaniae et Hiberniae*, vol. III (1737), 860–2; MacCulloch, *Cranmer*, 290–1. The myth that Gardiner intended what would have amounted to a bilingual Bible is exploded by Glyn Redworth, *In Defence of the Church Catholic: The Life of Stephen Gardiner* (Oxford, 1990), 162–3.

[110] See below, pp. 220–21.   [111] Bonner Register fos. 26^v–7^r, 39^v.

[112] Wilkins, *Concilia*, vol. III, 863; Gardiner, *Letters*, 296.

their persons. Together, these attacks make 1543 the high watermark of Henrician conservatism. If the evangelical advance had been stalled by the events of 1538–40, it is only in 1543 that it can be seen to be rolled back.

The origins of the doctrinal attack reach back to 1537, when, under Cromwell's leadership, the bishops had produced a substantive statement of doctrine intended to be adopted as authoritative for the English Church, entitled *The institution of a Christen man*. As befits a book written by committee, its doctrinal stance was unclear, and neither conservatives nor evangelicals were fully satisfied with it. It was published by the king's printer, Thomas Berthelet, but the king refused to give it his personal approval, and it became known as the *Bishops' Book*. It retained a degree of authority – as late as 1542, Bonner was requiring all his clergy to obtain a copy[113] – but the process of revising it began almost immediately. The king himself took a close interest. Two copies of the *Bishops' Book* annotated by him survive. Another leading participant was Archbishop Cranmer, whose comments on the king's annotations include some remarkably brusque put-downs of his royal master.[114] The revision effort was given a statutory basis in 1540, and committees to work on different aspects of it were established in the same year.[115] Yet most of these early efforts at revision were eventually discarded, and some of the most significant issues remained unresolved. When the final text came before Convocation in March 1543, Cranmer was still fighting to have the book reflect an evangelical understanding of justification. In this he failed completely.[116] *A necessary doctrine and erudition for any christen man* was published on 29 May, with the full royal approval that gave it the nickname of the *King's Book*. It decisively rejected the notion that justification comes through faith alone. Drawing on the theology of John Fisher, it argued that although scripture spoke of justification by faith,

> men may not thynke, that we be iustified by faith, as it is a seuerall vertue, separated from hope and charitie, feare of god and repentaunce, but by it is ment Faith, neither onely ne alone, but with the forsaid vertues coupled togyther.[117]

The new book presented a more conservative face than its predecessor in a number of areas, but this was the decisive shift. As Gardiner put it, 'If such as travaile in the doctrine of fayth only brought their water pott to the Kinges

---

[113] Bonner Register fo. 39ᵛ.
[114] BL Royal MS 17.C.xxx; Bodleian Library, 4° Rawlinson 245; Thomas Cranmer, *Miscellaneous Writings and Letters of Thomas Cranmer*, ed. John Edmund Cox (Cambridge: Parker Society, 1846), 83–114.
[115] *Statutes of the realm*, 783–4 (32° Henry VIII c. 26); BL Cotton MS Cleopatra E.v fos. 39–47, 56–9 (*LP* XV 826); MacCulloch, *Cranmer*, 268, 276.
[116] Wilkins, *Concilia*, vol. III, 868; Gardiner, *Letters*, 336–7.
[117] *A necessary doctrine and erudition for any christen man, sette furthe by the kynges maiestie* [the 'King's Book'] (RSTC 5168: 1543), fo. 2ʳ⁻ᵛ.

booke, they were lyke to go thence with out lycquour.'[118] The evangelicals' central doctrine, which had been left almost untouched by the Six Articles, was now unambiguously rebuffed.

Indeed, it was also proscribed. On 8 May 1543, three days after the completed text of the *King's Book* was presented to the House of Lords, the Lords read a bill 'for the Abolishment of erroneous Books'.[119] This eventually issued as the Act for the Advancement of True Religion, a grandiose title for what was essentially a penal statute enforcing the *King's Book*. The Act did not refer to the book directly, but it prohibited any writing, preaching or other promulgation of any material which contradicted the doctrine set forth by the king since – significantly – 1540. A hefty fine was imposed for the possession of openly heretical books, to be effective almost immediately on the Act's coming in to force. After a further three months, such fines were to be imposed for any books which questioned any aspect of the new doctrinal settlement, even in passing. The Act also explicitly reaffirmed the Six Articles. Until 1543, evangelicals had had significant room for doctrinal manoeuvre, within the law – room which they exploited to the full, as we shall see. After 1543, this was drastically restricted.[120]

The Act's clampdown on the trade in evangelical books gave statutory force to a campaign that had already begun. In February, a treaty had been concluded with the Emperor, Charles V. This not only provided Henry VIII with a strong incentive to prove his orthodox credentials,[121] but also included a clause promising imperial help in controlling the cross-channel trade in heretical books.[122] In the spring, the regime's attention turned to the domestic evangelical press. On 8 April, seven London printers and a bookseller were imprisoned by the Privy Council 'for printing off suche bokes as wer thowght to be unlawfull'. These included three of the four most prominent reformers in the London trade. The fourth, John Gough, was interrogated by the Council later in the month, and a bookseller who may have worked for Gough was then imprisoned. Twenty-five other booksellers were also questioned. In other words, most of London's active printers and a fair quorum of its booksellers were hauled before the Council. All were required to provide details of all books which they had bought and sold in the past three years, and to give any information they might have regarding the traffic in imported heretical books. In truth, many even of those who were imprisoned had had only the faintest connection with reformist books.

---

[118] Gardiner, *Letters*, 338.   [119] *LJ*, 230, 232; *APC*, 127.
[120] *Statutes of the realm*, 894–7 (34º & 35º Henry VIII. c. 1); see below, pp. 117–19.
[121] The *King's Book* was certainly used for this purpose, although it cannot be written off as diplomatic posturing: if its principal audience had been foreign, it would have been published in Latin immediately, rather than a year later. *LP* XIX (i) 168.
[122] PRO SP 1/176 fo. 17^{r-v} (*LP* XVIII (i) 144.5).

Moreover, those who had been imprisoned were released after two weeks, apart from two of the most partisan reformers, who were held for a further ten days.[123] This was not a targeted police operation. It was a warning shot, and it worked. The printing of evangelical books within England virtually ceased.[124]

However, the most notorious clause of the 1543 Act was directed not at evangelical books in general, but at the Bible. The well-established and quixotic ban on Tyndale's translation was reiterated, and Bibles with 'any annotacions or preambles' were banned. Only licensed clergy were now permitted to read from the Bible publicly. Nobles and gentry were permitted to read it aloud only within their own households. Merchants, noblewomen and gentlewomen might read it only privately. The whole of the rest of the population was now banned from reading the English Bible at all, although the Act empowered the king to suspend this clause if he wished to do so.[125] The king had long shown a propensity to rewrite Scripture to fit his own views.[126] Now he had replaced it altogether, with the *King's Book*. Writing four years later, the evangelical courtier William Palmer claimed that the bill first introduced into Parliament had laid down that 'no man ought to rede the bible / Onles that he were a lernyde man' – meaning, apparently, only clergy. If so, a Parliament composed of nobles, gentry and merchants won an exception for themselves and their wives.[127] Even so, this was a grievous blow to evangelical hopes.[128]

Along with the revision of doctrine, and the attack on publishing and Bible-reading, evangelicals in 1543 faced a renewed threat of arrest, imprisonment and possible execution. The most significant conservative victory in this area concerned two of the most vocal reformers of the early 1540s, Thomas Becon and Robert Wisdom. Becon was a remarkably prolific and popular author; his friend Wisdom had become one of London's most prominent evangelical preachers. Around Easter 1543 both men were arrested. In May they signed formal recantations, and in July were made to recant publicly and abjectly at Paul's Cross in London. Becon, in particular, was made to destroy copies of each of his books before the crowd, denouncing the heresies which had been found in each one. After this, and once sureties had been found, both men were released. However, neither of them made any further public contribution to the cause until the new reign. Both withdrew to the Midlands and lived in something like seclusion. In 1546 Wisdom, fearing

---

[123] *APC*, 107, 115, 117, 120–1, 125, 129; Bodleian Library, Jesus College MS 74 fo. 258^r.
[124] For further discussion of this move and its effects, see below, pp. 117–19.
[125] *Statutes of the realm*, 895–6 (34º & 35º Henry VIII. c. 1).
[126] As Cranmer pointed out to him repeatedly: Cranmer, *Letters*, 83–114.
[127] TCC, MS R3.33 fos. 139^v–40^r, 146^v–7^r.
[128] For evangelical responses to this, see below, pp. 252–4.

arrest, fled into exile at Bremen. Writers and preachers, as well as printers, were being silenced.[129]

However, the conservative plotters of 1543 were aiming higher: at no less a target than the archbishop of Canterbury. The drawn-out plots hatched by conservatives in Kent, at Windsor and at court to tar Cranmer and his allies with heresy have been described in detail by Diarmaid MacCulloch.[130] For our purposes, the significance of these plots is their failure. Although Cranmer's position seemed precarious, he and his household emerged unscathed, and MacCulloch suggests that his survival may have been assured very early on in the process.[131] The only evangelical casualties were Anthony Pearsone, an incautious sacramentarian priest with connections in both Windsor and Kent, and a churchwarden and a singing man from Windsor. All three were burned at Windsor in July. While evangelicals remembered them as martyrs, they were hardly first-rank figures. Significantly, two other men who should have joined them at the stake, Robert Benett and John Marbeck, were spared. Benett was ill at one stage of the proceedings, and so was simply left in prison when the others were moved; he was eventually released. Once the point had been made by the other executions, further bloodshed was apparently not thought necessary.

The case of the other man to be reprieved at the last moment, Marbeck, is more revealing. A gifted musician who also compiled the first English concordance, Marbeck was spared partly because his accusers hoped to use him to catch more valuable prey. Marbeck was close to Simon Heynes, the dean of Exeter and one of the most well-connected evangelicals of the period. Partly on Marbeck's evidence, Heynes spent some months in custody. Marbeck was also in contact with Philip Hoby, a gentleman usher in the king's privy chamber. Conservatives suspected – rightly – that the privy chamber was abuzz with heretics, and hoped to use Marbeck's evidence to smoke them out. Hoby and nine other courtiers were arrested on charges of having supported Pearsone. John Foxe's account of these events includes a dramatic narrative of how the courier bearing the evidence against these courtiers was 'pulled in by the sleeue' by evangelicals concerned to protect their friends, but the survival and eventual release of the privy chamber evangelicals seems actually to have been down to the king. The synthetic outrage which John Bale expressed on Henry's behalf apparently reflected his real feelings: 'They haue not feared to entre the kynges owne house to hunte theyr game ... couetynge so to haue murthered his most trustye fryndes and faythfull seruauntes.'[132] Executing courtiers was a privilege Henry reserved for himself. Indeed, his

---

[129] Bonner Register fos. 44^r–5^v; Wriothesley, 142–3; Thomas Becon, *The iewell of ioye* (RSTC 1763: 1550), sigs. B4^v–D4^r; PRO SP 1/223 fo. 152^r (*LP* XXI (i) 1491).
[130] MacCulloch, *Cranmer*, 297–322.   [131] *Ibid.*, 310.
[132] Bale, *Epistle exhortatorye*, fo. 9^r.

decision both to pardon the privy chamber reformers and to defend Cranmer ensured that the conservatives' plots did not merely fail: they backfired. Having claimed three rank-and-file victims, they themselves lost two figures of some significance. The zealous heresy-hunter John London died in prison in 1544, awaiting trial for perjury committed while investigating the Windsor heretics. And Bishop Gardiner's nephew and secretary, Germain Gardiner, was executed for treason on 7 March 1544. The formal charge was treasonable contact with Cardinal Pole, but the execution was widely understood as a shot across the bishop's bows.[133]

These events are symptomatic of a broader conservative failure to implement the victories of 1543. This is not to minimise those victories: the silencing of the evangelical presses was a lasting achievement, and doctrinal statements such as those in the *King's Book* were important whether acted on or not. Nevertheless, it remains significant that there is very little evidence of any attempts to enforce the ban on Bible-reading, or the other provisions of the Act for the Advancement of True Religion. There is the well-known example of the Gloucestershire shepherd, Robert Wyllyams, who in 1546 inscribed a copy of a treatise of Polydore Vergil's with the words: 'I bout thys boke when the testament was obberagatyd that shepe herdys myght not red hit. I prey god amende that blyndnes.'[134] This suggests that Bibles were no longer widely available, although as far as it goes this is evidence simply of wariness of the law, not of its enforcement. Likewise, one evangelical believed that the law had driven the English Bible out of use across the country – although he admitted that this was not the case in London, the only area of which he seems to have had first-hand knowledge.[135] I am aware of only one record of actual enforcement of the law. In the spring of 1546, one Edward Bretton, a shoemaker of East Bergholt, Norfolk, was arrested in Norwich. He had 'redde openly vpon the bible' to two of his friends in Norwich Cathedral, 'contrary to an acte theroff made'.[136] Even this is hardly clear-cut, despite the reference to the statute. Reading aloud in church was always controversial, as it carried the potential for disrupting worship. Moreover, it is odd that these men should have chosen to do so, given the blatantly illegal nature of the act. It is unlikely that this was a deliberate protest, as they recanted with unseemly haste. It is more likely

---

[133] *AM*, 1210–23; *LP* XVIII (ii) 241.6; *APC*, 97–8, 117–18, 126, 150–1; MacCulloch, *Cranmer*, 310. For one (strikingly cruel) evangelical reading of Germain Gardiner's death, see Turner, *Rescuynge of the romishe fox*, sigs. B8ᵛ–C1ʳ.

[134] The book is now lost: the inscription is recorded in Thomas Hearne's preface to his edition of William Camden, *Annales rerum Anglicarum et Hibernicarum regnante Elizabetha*, 3 vols. (1717), vol. I, xxix–xxx.

[135] BL Royal MS 17.B.xxxv fo. 8ᵛ.

[136] Norfolk Record Office NCR 16a/5 p. 323, cited in McClendon, *The Quiet Reformation*, 83.

that the law had lapsed to the point at which they did not believe that they were taking a serious risk. Most likely of all, they chose to hold their reading group in the cathedral because they did not own a Bible themselves. The case strongly implies that the cathedral's copy was still open for consultation by churchgoers. This is remarkable, given that almost all of those churchgoers were theoretically banned from reading the Bible at all. If the cathedral of England's second city was openly assisting those who wished to flout the law, the ban on Bible-reading cannot have been enforced too vigorously.[137] Nor, indeed, was there much effort to enforce the heresy laws at all in the wake of the events of 1543. During 1544, as the regime turned to concentrate all its efforts on the French war, there are very few records of prosecutions for any kind of reformist activity.[138]

Moreover, even the *King's Book* was not an unmitigated disaster for evangelicals. In one significant section it is famously more outspoken than the *Bishops' Book*. Its treatment of that mainstay of medieval piety, purgatory and prayer for the dead, was uncompromising. Citing II Maccabees, the formulary conceded that prayer for the dead was praiseworthy and that the dead benefited from prayers or Masses said on their behalf. This having been granted, however, it proceeded to tear the devotional heart out of the doctrine. Although one might pray for the dead in general, it denied that one might pray for a specific dead person. It denied that Christians can know the state in which the dead might be, or how prayers might assist them – specifically anathematising the word 'purgatory'.[139] Nor can this be taken as an isolated statement. It is foreshadowed in a number of earlier official statements, such as the Ten Articles of 1536. More specifically, the king's amendments to the *Bishops' Book* insist that we cannot know the condition

---

[137] One evangelical polemicist lamented the growing inaccessibility of church Bibles: but the worst allegation he could make was that they were being moved to parts of the church where the poor were frightened to come, rather than actually being removed from public display. Henry Brinklow?, *A supplication of the poore Commons* (RSTC 10884: London or Antwerp, 1546), sig. A6^r.

[138] I have been able to find only seven possible cases. Three come from a single act book, in the Suffolk archdeaconry of Sudbury, where a woman was accused of baking on a holy day; a man was found to own Tyndale's New Testament; and a second man refused to make a donation towards a new pyx in terms that *might* imply heresy. In addition, Robert Singleton was executed in March 1544 on a somewhat mysterious charge of treason; Anne Askew had a confrontation of some kind with the clergy of Lincoln Cathedral; John Coyte, a London curate, was charged with refusing to hear confessions or use processions, but apparently defended himself successfully; and Hugh Eton, a London hosier, was convicted of mocking the Mass and did public penance. Suffolk Record Office, Ipswich IC/500/5/1 fos. 16^v, 23^v, 26^r; Brigden, *London*, 371, 400; Askew, *The first examinacyon*, fos. 32^v–3^r; John Fines, *A Biographical Register of Early English Protestants and Others Opposed to the Roman Catholic Church 1525–58* (part I: Sutton Courtenay Press, 1985; part II: unpublished); and see Appendix I.

[139] *King's Book*, fos. 93^v–4^r; cf. II Maccabees 12:39–45.

of souls after death, and warn that works of penance should be done in this life rather than being deferred to the next. This stance was maintained against the protests of conservative bishops such as Richard Sampson, who vehemently opposed any shift in this direction.[140] The statement in the *King's Book* did not have immediate practical consequences, in part because the institutions most closely associated with prayer for the dead, the monasteries, were already gone. To an extent, therefore, this was merely the ratification of a *fait accompli*, proving the protests of Edward Crome and others right after the fact. Prayer for the dead continued (Henry VIII's will made extravagant provision for his own soul), but it continued in an increasingly hostile political climate. The Chantries Act of 1545 empowered the king to dissolve chantries and other institutions at will. It was a measure born from financial expediency rather than evangelical zeal, but it would scarcely have been possible if the doctrine of purgatory had not already been systematically undermined.[141]

While the Chantries Act cannot be counted as a reformist achievement, during 1544–5 evangelicals did win two substantial parliamentary victories. In 1544, while Germain Gardiner and other conservatives were being sent to the block, Parliament was emasculating the penal code of the Act of Six Articles. Claiming that under the old Act 'divers secret and untrue accusacions and presentmentes maie be maliciously conspyred against the Kinges subjectes', a new statute required most accusations to be supported by a dozen witnesses. Even heretical preaching could only be prosecuted if reported within forty days of the offence.[142] Perhaps more significantly, in the next parliament, in late 1545, an attempt to introduce a fresh anti-heresy measure failed. This was a bill against heretical books, and it was sufficiently serious for a heavyweight committee of the Lords to be set up to consider it, under Cranmer's chairmanship. 'It was at the beginning sett earnestly forward', but it eventually failed in the House of Commons. The rumour was that the king had been happy to see it fall; so much so that some later thought that he had vetoed the bill.[143]

For actual reformist advances in 1544–5, however, we must look to the parishes. Archbishop Cranmer's steady liturgical work bore its first substantive fruit in these years: the new English litany, published with royal approval in 1544, and the revised English version of the traditional devotional text known as the primer. A proclamation of 1545 prescribed this as the only

---

[140] BL Royal MS 17.C.xxx fos. 145^v–7^v; BL Royal MS Appendix 78 fo. 23^r.
[141] On the Chantries Act, see below, pp. 164–5.
[142] *Statutes of the realm*, 960–1 (35° Henry VIII. c. 5); *LJ*, 252–6; John Gough Nichols (ed.), *Chronicle of the Grey Friars of London*, Camden Society old series 53 (1852), 46.
[143] *LJ*, 269; PRO SP 1/212 fo. 112^v (*LP* XX (ii) 1030.2); Stanford E. Lehmberg, *The Later Parliaments of Henry VIII 1536–1547* (Cambridge, 1977), 231–2.

primer permitted to be used. The shift from Latin to English was striking enough, but these texts were more than translations. The Latin originals had been infused with the veneration of saints, prayer for the dead and other aspects of Catholic piety. The new versions did not explicitly embrace evangelical theology, but these remnants of traditional religion were pared down to the bone.[144] Contemporaries had no doubt that these new texts reeked of the new learning. In at least one parish, the new litany provoked a demonstration by outraged traditionalists. By contrast, the evangelical polemicist William Turner praised the king for having, 'contrary to the myndes of all Pharises, begone to set out the seruice in englishe'.[145] And the king's commitment to the new texts was undoubted. The litany was published at the end of May 1544. On 11 June, royal orders to the bishops required that it be used in every parish of the realm. The king's primary concern appears to have been that his people should be supporting his military adventures in prayer, but he was insistent that they should pray 'in oure natyve englysshe tonge', and required the clergy to set forth the litany 'by preachinges good exhortacion and otherwayes to the people, in suche sorte as they, fealing the godly taste thereof, may gladly and yoyuslye with thanks receaue embrace and frequent the same.' The following summer, with the war beginning to go sour, the Privy Council ordered that the new litany should also be used in place of the traditional processional, dramatically restricting one of the most demonstrative forms of popular piety. This order was repeated in October 1545, when the English litany was ordered to be used indefinitely, throughout the realm, every day. Earlier the same year, the new primer was published. The proclamation licensing this text again emphasised the merit of making such devotional texts available in English (although English primers were no novelty), and banned all other primers, Latin or English. A further tranche of innovations was almost accomplished in January 1546. With royal approval, Cranmer drew up a list of traditional ceremonies to be prohibited. Most of these, again, centred on the use or abuse of images. Images were no longer to be covered during Lent, and creeping to the cross on Good Friday – a ceremony which evangelicals found particularly hard to stomach – was to have been banned. Gardiner's timely intervention thwarted this plan, but significantly, he did not block it with theological argument but with a warning that it would endanger the unusually delicate diplomatic situation.[146] In

---

[144] This is examined in detail in Charles C. Butterworth, *The English Primers (1529–1545): Their Publication and Connection with the English Bible and the Reformation in England* (Philadelphia, 1953), 256–75; Duffy, *Stripping of the Altars*, 443–7.

[145] PRO SP 1/203 fos. 86–91 (*LP* XX (i) 1118); Turner, *Rescuynge of the romishe fox*, sig. K8^r.

[146] Lambeth Palace Library, Register of Thomas Cranmer, fo. 49^v (*LP* XIX (i) 732); Bonner Register fos. 60^v, 72^{r-v}, 83^r; *TRP*, 349–50; Cranmer, *Letters*, 414–15; MacCulloch, *Cranmer*, 330–2, 351–2.

A Counter-Reformation? 53

early 1546, it seemed as if the reformist cause might have acquired some modest political momentum.

In the spring and summer, however, there was another determined conservative counter-attack. Doctrinal definitions were not at issue this time, but the book trade was, and evangelical blood was shed on a greater scale than in 1543. The crisis was again sparked by Edward Crome, the reformers' perennial lightning-rod. Perhaps misreading the political weather, in April 1546 he preached a sermon denouncing the sacrifice of the Mass. He was quickly arrested and agreed to recant, but when brought to deliver his recantation sermon, he defied his captors and reiterated his original heresy.[147] These events were dramatic enough, but it seems that leading conservatives at court decided to use them as a pretext for a comprehensive assault on evangelicalism. There were good reasons for doing so. The political situation was growing steadily more tense and unpredictable, and the public mood more febrile. Henry VIII's final bid for martial glory had run aground, leaving England diplomatically isolated and militarily vulnerable. One consequence of this was an astonishingly high tax burden. Taxes had risen steadily since Cromwell's fall; London's assessment for parliamentary subsidy had never been higher than £10,000 per annum before 1541, but in 1546 it was £28,406, by far the highest rate paid in the entire sixteenth century. Nearly £200,000 was raised across the country as a whole. Such sums were not exacted without some fairly brutal arm-twisting. Discontent with taxation was becoming proverbial.[148] The Church, too, was struggling to meet the king's incessant financial demands, and evidence of belt-tightening can be found across the country.[149] Perhaps partly because of these demands, food prices were exceptionally high during the spring and summer. Under these circumstances it is hardly surprising that the regime was unusually jumpy about sedition, prophecies and other manifestations of discontent. Yet the court itself was abuzz with rumours and conspiracies. Over it all hung the unmentionable but increasingly obvious fact that the king was not a healthy man.[150]

In this climate, Crome's stand took on a greater significance. The Privy Council rounded up a number of prominent evangelicals who, they believed,

---

[147] This affair and its aftermath are well summarised in Brigden, *London*, 363–77, and in Susan Wabuda, 'Equivocation and recantation during the English Reformation: the "subtle shadows" of Dr. Edward Crome', *JEH* 44 (1993), 224–42.

[148] Ian Archer, 'The burden of taxation in sixteenth-century London', *HJ* 44 (2001), 607–9, 611; Lehmberg, *Later Parliaments*, 220; *An inuectiue ageinst glotony and dronkennes* (RSTC 14126.5: 1545), sig. B3^{r-v}.

[149] For example, Exeter Dean and Chapter Library, Chapter Act Book 3552 fo. 38^r; Bonner Register fos. 113^r, 129^r.

[150] Wriothesley, 163; CLRO Repertory 11 fos. 195^v, 215^{r-v}; *LP* XXI (i) 552; PRO SP 1/220 fos. 60^r–9^r (*LP* XXI (i) 1027); J. J. Scarisbrick, *Henry VIII* (1968), 484–8.

had encouraged him in his defiance. As their enquiries continued through May and into June, the focus shifted from the Crome case to a thorough attack on the evangelical leadership in England. Those arrested included the former bishops Hugh Latimer and Nicholas Shaxton, and Cranmer's right-hand man Rowland Taylor. Robert Wisdom fled abroad before he could be taken. As a police operation, this purge was undoubtedly a success. Crome himself gave in only the day after his defiant second sermon. Most of the others also submitted, some more abjectly than others. Shaxton, initially steadfast, appears to have undergone a genuine conversion; he reverted to conservative views and maintained them for the remainder of his life. These events also provoked some heresy-hunting in the country at large, prompting arrests and a few executions. A new proclamation against prohibited books was introduced, and the imperial authorities were persuaded to clamp down on the activities of the English exiles in the Netherlands. Bonner held a book-burning at Paul's Cross in July and another in September, and this renewed hostility to evangelical books seems to have been a signal for many conservatives to destroy English Bibles, primers and other officially approved texts.[151]

There had been no sustained assault on reformers of this breadth and magnitude since the break with Rome, and they were profoundly dismayed by it. However, from the conservative point of view, it should be counted a failure. The conservatives' objective in 1546 was not merely to silence the evangelical leaders, but to incriminate suspected evangelical sympathisers at court. As spring turned to summer, it became increasingly clear that the purpose of this purge was political. This is why so much attention came to focus on the tough-minded Lincolnshire gentlewoman Anne Askew. Askew's own heresy was not seriously at issue. She had escaped when arrested previously largely because Bishop Bonner had chosen to let her go. Once rearrested in May 1546, she was clearly not going to escape. Her political significance derived from her contacts at court. She had, she eventually admitted, been supported in prison by the wives of Edward Seymour, the earl of Hertford and future Lord Protector, and of Sir Anthony Denny, gentleman of the privy chamber and intimate friend of the king. She also freely conceded her close relationship with John Lassells, a sewer in the privy chamber who had already been examined and declared himself ready to die to defend his faith. Her accusers suspected, no doubt correctly, that her contacts at court went well beyond this. As well as these two, she was specifically questioned about her relationship with the dowager duchess of Suffolk – Katherine Willoughby, a known

---

[151] Wriothesley, 168–9, 175; Bonner Register fo. 92^{r-v}; George Joye, *The refutation of the byshop of Winchesters derke declaration of his false articles, once before confuted* (RSTC 14828.5: London?, 1546), sig. A2^r; PRO SP 1/226 fo. 16^r (*LP* XXI (ii) 321); and see Appendix I.

evangelical firebrand – and with the dowager countess of Sussex. She was also in touch with the rather more boisterous reform-minded clique around the earl of Surrey. Her cousin Thomas Hussey was Surrey's friend, and she appears to have had access to some of Surrey's poetry in prison. Had Askew broken and made a full confession, she might have implicated a number of the reformers' most powerful friends in her heresy. Most significantly of all, behind all these figures stood the queen, Katherine Parr, whose evangelical views were becoming increasingly plain. Many of Askew's known associates belonged to the queen's inner circle. Nicholas Throckmorton, the queen's cousin, was later to walk to the stake with Askew, a very public (and dangerous) statement of loyalty. If Seymour, Denny and the queen could have been separated from the king, it would have been a conservative victory comparable with the toppling of Cromwell.[152] Perhaps it would have been greater, since those who were left standing would take charge of the minority government that was plainly approaching.

These were realistic ambitions, but they failed. The clearest reason for this failure was Askew's steadfast refusal to break under pressure. It was a nervous time for her friends at court. A series of moderate evangelicals pleaded with her to give in, including the queen's brother, William Parr, the earl of Essex. Their hope appears to have been to negotiate a simple recantation which would both spare Askew's life and avert the risk that she might incriminate others. However, she treated these visitors with scarcely less disdain than she did her interrogators. Her determination eventually, and notoriously, led Lord Chancellor Wriothesley and Sir Richard Rich to rack her with their own hands, but this in itself is a sign of how desperate they had become. To rack anyone under such circumstances, let alone a gentlewoman, was quite illegal. The torture was initially carried out by Sir Anthony Knevet, the lieutenant of the Tower; but, according to his own testimony, Knevet eventually released her from the device, concluding that nothing would come of it. When Wriothesley demanded that he continue, he refused. A quarrel ensued, and Knevet hurried to lay the matter before the king while the two courtiers took over the torturer's role themselves. That Knevet should have thus defied them is a sign of how contentious their actions had become.[153]

More importantly, perhaps, Knevet's flight to the court is a reminder that it does not do to leave a live king out of one's calculations. If Askew's courage

---

[152] Susan Brigden, 'Henry Howard, Earl of Surrey, and the "Conjured League"', *HJ* 37 (1994), 508, 525; Askew, *The lattre examinacyon*, fos. 40^{r-v}, 43^{r-v}; Susan E. James, *Kateryn Parr: The Making of a Queen* (Aldershot, Hants., 1999), 271–3.

[153] Askew, *The lattre examinacyon*, fos. 17^v–18^r, 20^v–1^r, 23^v, 38^v, 45^r; BL Harleian MS 419 fo. 2^r. Askew named Wriothesley and Rich as her torturers: in the 1560s, Knevet told John Foxe that Sir John Baker, not Rich, had been the second man.

is the most visible cause of the conservative failure, the king's reluctance to endorse a full-scale purge is perhaps the most important. According to Knevet, Henry was disturbed by news of Askew's racking. He did not intervene in her case, but he did pardon one of those condemned to die with her, George Blage, a member of the privy chamber. Blage's heresy is undoubted, but he was a personal favourite of the king's, and according to Foxe, Henry was 'sore offended . . . that they would come so nere him, & euen into his priuie chamber'.[154] They would come closer to him than that, however. As Askew went to the stake, broken but triumphant, her enemies apparently made a last, desperate attack on the queen. This account we owe entirely to Foxe, who apparently gathered his information from the queen's sister and two of the ladies of her privy chamber. We cannot be certain that it happened at all, much less in the melodramatic form that we have it. Nevertheless, the bare bones of the story are of some importance. As with the Askew case, it seems that Wriothesley, rather than the evangelicals' favourite scapegoat Gardiner, led the assault. The king permitted an investigation into the queen's orthodoxy, but also acted in such a way that she became aware of this and, sensibly, threw herself on his mercy. Perhaps he genuinely changed his mind; perhaps he had never wanted to do more than to teach her a lesson and to remind the conservative plotters who was really in charge. In any case, he both protected her and used the occasion to humiliate her enemies, very much as he had done with Cranmer three years earlier.[155] In the end, the conservative attacks of 1543 and 1546 both came up against the same obstacle: Henry VIII's reluctance to let a heresy-hunt turn into a rout that might alter the balance of political power or, worse, tread on his own toes.

The dramatic summer of 1546 claimed its casualties, and it also, as we shall see, played a part in reshaping English evangelicalism. Yet it was not a disaster for the reformers, and could almost be seen as a defensive victory. It was the conservatives' last throw of the dice, and it failed. The king would permit a degree of movement, but not a wholesale purge. His distrust of his conservative councillors was at least as deep as his distaste for heresy. Nor would he allow his councillors' religious feuds to distract him from his wars, the overwhelming preoccupation of the last years of his life. The political landscape in which the reformers found themselves in 1546 was in its essentials the same one to which they had become accustomed since Cromwell's fall. That landscape was very different from the high road to reformation which they had enjoyed in the 1530s, when each step forward followed with comparative ease and seeming inevitability on the last. After 1540, evangelicals found themselves in bewildering surroundings, their path treacherous

---

[154] *AM*, 1246; *LP* XXI (i) 1383.72.
[155] *AM*, 1242–4; cf. Redworth, *In Defence of the Church Catholic*, 233–4.

and the going difficult. There were dangerous pitfalls to negotiate and they had to fight for each small step. At times it was all they could do not to fall back. Indeed, in 1543, they did fall back some way, although not as far as they feared. Yet progress remained possible. The climate was uncomfortable but not actually hostile. Once they had familiarised themselves with the new situation, there were resting-places and even opportunities to be had. There were also problems to be solved. Perhaps the most pressing of these was how to deal politically with a king whose Reformation remained both much less than they hoped for and also far more than they feared.

2

Fearing God and honouring the king

Let euery soule submit him selfe vnto the auctoryte of the hyer powers.

Romans 13:1

THE OBEDIENCE OF A CHRISTIAN MAN

The idiosyncratic religious policies of Henry VIII's regime created a series of conundrums for English evangelicals. In the 1540s, they had to deal with a political situation which was decidedly more complex than that faced by most of their European co-religionists. As well as having to engage with the Roman Church and those whose instincts remained close to it, they had to handle their king. This was a far more difficult proposition, since he was alternately their supporter and their opponent, and he emphatically could not be ignored. And just as the royal supremacy was at the heart of Henry's religious policy, so the different reformers' responses were centred in their views of the supremacy and in their ethics of obedience.

The strong, Henrician doctrine of the royal supremacy was neither Protestant nor Catholic. But it was certainly easier for reformers to swallow than it was for conservatives. Behind all the doctrinal issues raised by the European Reformation, after all, lay the fundamental issue of authority. Against the traditional view that biblical authority was supplemented or authenticated by the authority of the Church, evangelicals asserted the authority of bare Scripture. Yet in practice the reformers looked to the state and to temporal rulers to enforce that authority. The prince and the magistrate were the reformer's natural allies against the power of Rome. Before evangelical ideas had established more than a toehold in England, the relationship between Lutheranism and the German princes was being worked out in these terms. The problem with this approach, of course, was that not all princes were willing to play the part which the reformers had scripted for them. Henry VIII certainly was not during the 1520s. It was under these uncomfortable circumstances that English evangelicals first worked out how they should relate to the state, the supposed ally which was persecuting them. This was done most famously and influentially in William Tyndale's 1528 treatise *The obedience of a Christen man*.[1]

It is no coincidence that Luther wrote of Christian liberty, and Tyndale of Christian obedience. Henry VIII had not yet attained the dizzying vision of his own authority of his later years, but he nevertheless took himself extremely seriously, and his kingdom was as centralised and as rigorously governed as any in Europe. Tyndale's stated aim in writing was to refute the accusation that the reformers were seditious. Perhaps inevitably, then, this early evangelical orthodoxy was fairly grim. For Tyndale, as for most other evangelical writers, the key texts were the commandment to honour father and mother, glossed so as to embrace obedience to all established authorities; and the section of Romans 13 which affirmed a simple Christian duty of obedience to the secular power. 'The king is in the rowme of God,' Tyndale wrote, 'and his lawe is God's law.' Clergy and laity alike were duty-bound to obey him. 'Whosoeuer therfore resisteth power resisteth God: yee though he be Pope, Bisshope, monke or frere.' Obedience, of course, has its limits, for God's commands are to be obeyed above a king's, but although Christians might in conscience disobey a tyrant, Tyndale would not countenance any form of active resistance.

> Yf [kings] commaunde to doo euell we must then disobey and saye we are otherwise commaundet of God: but not to ryse agenste them. They will kyll vs then sayest thou. Therefore, I saye is a christen called, to sofre euen the bitter deeth for his hopes sake and because he will doo no euyll.

The substance of this uncompromising view of secular authority is fairly close to the authority which Henry VIII would later claim for himself (although Tyndale did not contemplate kings seizing direct control over doctrine). However, Tyndale's strong doctrine of obedience was tempered with a bleak assessment of the reality of monarchy. Despite their God-given authority, he wrote, kings

> be captyues or euer they be kynges, yee all most yer they be borne. No man maye be sofred aboute them but flatterers and soch as are fyrst sworne true vnto oure most holye fathers the Bisshopes.

As a result, they are become mere 'hangmen vnto the Pope'. Moreover, they are not only dupes, but tyrants, 'most comenly mercylesse. . . . Yf they promyse, they are yet men, as vnconstante as are other people and as vntrue.' He compared Henry VIII to Pilate, who had let himself be coerced into

---

[1] John Bale named this as one of four key works in the first wave of English reformist printing. Bale, *Epistle exhortatorye*, fo. 6ʳ. For examples of its circulation see *AM*, 1021–3; Elisabeth Leedham-Green, *Books in Cambridge Inventories*, 2 vols. (Cambridge, 1986); Bowker, *Henrician Reformation*, 145–6. It was repeatedly banned: *AM* (1563), 451, 573–4; Lambeth Palace Library, MS 306 fo. 65ᵛ.

killing the innocent, and added that most kings had killed true prophets and apostles and would therefore be damned. He also emphasised the theologically unexceptionable, but nevertheless tactless point that 'the most despised person in his realme is the kynges brother and . . . equall with him in the kyndome of God'. He was willing to criticise specific kingly actions: 'They haue no soch auctorite of God so to pylle and polle as they doo and to reyse vppe taxes and gaderinges to mayntene their fantasies and to make warre.' Likewise, he asserted that kings have no authority from God to maintain the Church in its splendour, and indeed that kings who grant and maintain the Church's false liberties are damned for so doing. He also argued that ecclesiastical wealth should be used for the common weal, with only a tenth kept back for royal use.[2]

This tough-minded approach fitted the situation in the 1520s, but in the early 1530s, when Henry moved on from enjoying Tyndale's opinion of his office[3] to creating a genuine royal supremacy, reformers found themselves in a situation which was more comfortable but also less clear-cut. Henry's flirtation with evangelicalism offered reformers opportunities (or temptations) which led them to take a more generous view of his authority. While Thomas Cromwell's ascendancy lasted, the alliance between the regime and the evangelicals was firm enough that most reformers were willing to pass over Tyndale's sceptical opinion of kingship. Cromwell himself took a close interest in ensuring that this was so, and under his supervision a quasi-official evangelical view of the supremacy, laden with hyperbole, took shape. His publicist Richard Morison stated simply that 'God wolle all subiectes, peyne of eternall damnation, to obeye their princis', and, arguing that the sin of Adam was a form of treason against God, he described treason as the archetype of all sin.[4] Reformers around the king competed to make ever more extravagant declarations of loyalty, from the claim that Henry fitted the model of true kingship in the Psalter better than any king since David, to the assertion that, as God's 'pryncypall mynister', he had enacted so perfect a reformation that all previous attempts seemed but 'a sommer game'.[5]

Perhaps the most spectacular and cloying example of this genre of flattery came in 1540 from the pen of John Pylbarough, a governor of Lincoln's Inn who was rising moderately in Cromwell's service.[6] In early 1540, he made

---

[2] William Tyndale, *The obedience of a Christen man and how Christen rulers ought to governe* (RSTC 24446: Antwerp, 1528), fos. 21^r, 22^v, 29^v–30^v, 33^r, 51^v, 78^r–81^r, 119^v, 152^r, 153^r.

[3] John Gough Nichols (ed.), *Narratives of the Days of the Reformation*, Camden Society old series 77 (1859), 52–6.

[4] Richard Morison, *An exhortation to styrre all Englyshe men to the defence of theyr countreye* (RSTC 18110: 1539), sigs. A8^v–B1^v; Richard Morison, *An invective ayenste the great and detestable vice, treason* (RSTC 18111: 1539), sig. C5^{r-v}.

[5] BL Royal MS 7.F.xiv fo. 53^r; PRO SP 1/143 fo. 164^r (*LP* XIV (i) 368).

[6] *LP* XIV (ii) 529, Appendix 43; James K. McConica, *English Humanists and Reformation Politics* (Oxford, 1965), 192.

a bid to further his career by producing a pamphlet entitled *A commemoration of the inestimable graces and benefites of God*, dedicated to Cromwell and published by Thomas Berthelet, the king's printer. This tract used a somewhat loose exposition of the *Benedictus* as a peg on which to hang intemperate praise of the king. The tone of the piece is spiritedly reformist, praising Henry for bringing England out of the darkness of the Romish Antichrist into the light of God's Word. Like Morison's work, it is couched in strongly nationalistic terms. As we might expect, Pylbarough did not merely celebrate the king's title but accepted a higher doctrine of the supremacy than Tyndale would have been ready to concede. The king, he wrote, 'hath power ouer your bodyes and goodis, and is your defender and preseruer, and also charged in his spiritual ministery with you under god'. However, this was just the beginning. He described the king as a 'holy prophete of the mooste hyghest god', and as 'thyne holy enoynted, immediate minyster, and vicar ouer vs . . . to whom also we owe only to haue recourse as vnto thy chiefe herdeman'. Then he embarked on a series of increasingly bizarre comparisons between the king and various biblical figures who were his types. Henry thus became David, the righteous king, a parallel often made by Henry himself;[7] David's successor, the promised saviour born of David's line who would free his people from oppression; Josiah, setting forth the book of the Law; John the Baptist, making straight the way of the Lord; St Paul, confronting and confounding St Peter in his errors; and ultimately, the archangel Michael.[8]

It was the king whose pride was being flattered outrageously in this manner, but it was the evangelicals who fell. Within six months of the publication of Pylbarough's tract, Cromwell was dead and the reformers' hopes for the future were in disarray. The discontinuities between their own religious priorities and those of the Supreme Head, which had been smoothed over during the Cromwell years, became harder to ignore. It was unclear whether their alliance with the king could endure. As a result, it was after 1540 that significant divisions in the evangelical attitudes towards royal authority and the royal supremacy became evident for the first time.

Given the current historiographical consensus, and the tone of Foxe's and Grafton's assessments of this period,[9] it should be no surprise that one group of evangelicals became significantly cooler about royal authority after Cromwell's fall. For these reformers, Cromwell's propaganda had papered over too many cracks, and they returned to Tyndale's robust approach. The veteran evangelical George Joye asked in 1543,

---

[7] Pamela Tudor Craig, 'Henry VIII and King David', in *Early Tudor England*, ed. Daniel Williams (Woodbridge, Suffolk, 1989).
[8] John Pylbarough, *A commemoration of the inestimable graces and benefites of God* (RSTC 20521: 1540), sigs. A2^v, A4^v–B1^v, B2^v–3^r, B4^v, C1^v–2^v, D4^v.
[9] See above, pp. 14–20.

Where be now owr flaterer of kinges into the destruccion of their bodies and soules & into the perdicion of their realmes? John called them edders whelpes, Christe called Herode that foxe, we must saye my Lorde & it please your grace, your highe maiesty &c.

John Bale had been a part of Cromwell's propaganda machine, and the portrait of royal authority in his *King Iohan* was well within Henrician orthodoxy. In exile in the 1540s, however, Bale could not resist the occasional ironic crack at a regime which took itself so seriously. In a pamphlet of 1546 he quoted Christ's words:

He that loueth hys father or mother, hys sonne or doughter, hys prynce or gouernour, aboue me, he is not mete for me, Math. 10. I feare me thys wyll be iudged hygh treason. But no matter.

More provocatively, Bale picked up the king's portrayal of himself as David, and emphasised that for all of his victories David was punished by God because of his contempt for marriage – an aspect of the story which Henry had not chosen to emphasise.[10]

Others had more profound objections. William Turner was a botanist, physician and evangelical polemicist whose tracts of 1543 and 1545 were amongst the most influential of the exile publications in this period.[11] He pointedly refused to grant the king the title of Supreme Head of the Church of England, insisting instead on Supreme Governor. This in itself was capital treason. Turner argued that the title Supreme Head was simply a reflection of papal pretensions, and claimed that as a result of it, 'certayn wanton persones . . . therfore call the kyngis hyghenes pope of Englond'. He also rejected the legal basis of the title, arguing that the king's authority should be grounded on the rock of Scripture rather than the sands of English law. He made the effective, and highly inflammatory, point that 'If the kyng be therfor lawfully hede of the chirche of Englonde & ire lande, because the hole realme hathe agreed ther to, then when all the hole realm consented that the pope shuld be called the hede of the chirche of Englonde he was lawfully called the hede of the chirche of englonde.' Most damagingly of all, Turner sought to redefine the king's headship in terms that the regime would have found unacceptable.

I hold as well as ye do that he is supreme hede of the chirche of England and ireland, if ye understande by thys worde chirche an outwarde gatheryng together of men and wymen, in a polytike ordre. But if ye take thys worde chirche in the signification

---

[10] George Joye, *The vnite and Scisme of the olde chirche* (RSTC 14830: Antwerp, 1543), fo. 10ᵛ; Askew, *The lattre examinacyon*, fo. 45ᵛ; Bale, *A dysclosynge or openynge of the Manne of synne*, fo. 75ʳ; Tudor Craig, 'Henry VIII and King David'; Helen Parish, *Clerical Marriage and the English Reformation: Precedent, Policy and Practice* (Aldershot, Hants., 2000), 129–34, 155.

[11] See below, p. 106.

that it is taken in the xvi. of Matthew . . . I deny that the kyng or any erthly man, may be called hede of the chirche saue only Christe. . . . Was kyng herode the virgine Maries mysticall hede, and spirituall hede of the Apostelles and of the rest of Christis chirche? or was the Emperour the spirituall hede of Christies chirche in thos dayes?

This last argument was embarrassingly powerful: so much so that Archbishop Cranmer, the most steadfast advocate of the royal supremacy, was forced in 1555 to concede that Nero had been head of the Church in St Paul's time.[12]

Turner was the only evangelical polemicist who directly disputed the king's title, but others were uneasy about what it represented. Henry Brinklow, a London mercer whose radical pamphlets written under the name of Roderyck Mors infuriated Stephen Gardiner,[13] denied (as Thomas More had) that king and Parliament could bestow the supremacy of the Church.

This is the .xiii. artycle of our crede added of late, that what so euer the parlament doth, must nedys be well done. . . . If this be so . . . then haue ye brought Rome home to your own dores, & geuen the auctoryte to the kyng and the parlament, that the carnal bisshops gaue vnto the pope . . . [and] we be in as euyl case, as whan we were vnder the bisshop of Rome.

The supremacy, in Brinklow's eyes, was largely an excuse for raising taxes, a perception which gave rise to an atrocious pun: under the new dispensation, he wrote, 'all men must so often pay pay, that a man if he toke not good hede wold thynk, that the latyn papa were translated into English'. However, Brinklow also took issue with the spiritual authority to which the king laid claim, and the example he cited was chosen to be as inflammatory as possible.

What kyng or emperor, yee what bisshop or Apostle, can dyspense with godds word, which he eyther biddeth or forbiddeth? Where as Christ saieth, thow shalt not put away thy wyfe but only for adultery, can all the whole world, ye antychrystes, dispense with me to put away my wyfe, but for that cause only?[14]

This was no longer abstract political philosophy, but a personal attack on Henry VIII.

Nor did Brinklow stop there. He was one of the few evangelicals willing to face down the accusation that those who dissented from the official religious settlement were guilty of treason:

Ye wyll saye vnto me, What art thou that callest these thynges dyrtye tradycyons, and popish ceremonyes, seyng the Kinges grace forbyddeth them not, and vseth part of them him self? I answer, that . . . it be so that GOD throughe the Kyng hath cast

---

[12] William Turner (ps. William Wraghton), *The huntyng and fyndyng out of the Romishe fox* (RSTC 24353: Bonn, 1543), sig. A2^r; Turner, *Rescuynge of the romishe fox*, sigs. A2^r, B4^r, C2^r–3^v; MacCulloch, *Cranmer*, 577.
[13] Gardiner, *Letters*, 159–63.
[14] Brinklow, *Complaynt of Roderyck Mors*, sigs. D5^v–6^r, E1^r, G5^v.

oute the deuell oute of this realme, and yet both he and we supp of the broth in which the deuell was sodden, and that God hath not yet opened the eyes of the Kyng to set all thynges in right frame.[15]

Brinklow may also have been the author of the 1546 pamphlet *A supplication of the poore Commons*, which echoes Tyndale's warning that kings who fail to care for their people will be subject to divine judgement. This book sees the king as responsible for all those suffering starvation and poverty in his realm, and warns that 'the bloud of all them that through your negligence shal perysh, shalbe required at your hand'. To this author, Henry was not David but Ahab, deliberately consulting false prophets so as to be told what he wanted to hear.[16]

This, however, was exceptional. Almost all reformers, even the most outspoken, chose to direct their anger at the false prophets rather than at the king. George Joye was as uneasy about the royal supremacy as Brinklow, but in his eyes it was a plot by the clergy to defend the Mass by enlisting the secular authorities on their side.[17] Often this approach of blaming those around the king was little more than an evasion. The reformers directed their fire against the bishops – in particular Gardiner, the bishop of Winchester – simply because they could not bring themselves to attack the king directly.[18] Few can have been taken in by this convention, and Gardiner's exasperation is forgivable:

Suppose ye, the kynges maiestie can not vnderstande, what ye meane by Wynchester? when ye attribute all the fashion of the realme, to Winchester? cal the actes that myslyke you Wynchesters? al statutes Wynchesters? all iuste punishementes (howe so euer ye call them) Wynchesters? and charge all vpon Wynchester, that in so doing ye name Wynchester, in stede of that ye dare not name and speake oute. . . . I am ashamed, that any part of his maiestees glorie, in defense of religion from youre corruption, shulde be deriued vnto me.[19]

Transparent as it was, most evangelical polemicists continued to employ this kind of scapegoating. As Gardiner implied, they did not dare impugn their king directly, for fear of wrecking their credibility with their readers; nor could they easily reconcile direct attacks on Henry VIII with their loyalist consciences.

---

[15] Henry Brinklow (ps. Roderick Mors), *The Lamentacion of a Christian, against the Citie of London* (RSTC 3764: Bonn, 1542), sigs. B2^r, B6^r, D1^r.
[16] Brinklow?, *Supplication of the poore Commons*, sigs. B4^v, B5^r, B7^v.
[17] George Joye, *The exposicion of Daniel the Prophete* (RSTC 14823: Antwerp, 1545), fo. 225^v.
[18] Riordan and Ryrie, 'Stephen Gardiner and the making of a Protestant villain'.
[19] Gardiner, *A declaration of such true articles as George Ioye hath gone about to confute*, fo. 96^v.

However, the distinction between the king and his conservative counsellors was more than wishful thinking. The king's theological instincts did indeed differ from those of Gardiner, Norfolk and other leading conservatives, and evangelicals were well aware of this. This line of thought was developed most carefully by Joye in the commentary on the book of Daniel he compiled in 1545. In his account of how King Darius was duped by his councillors into casting Daniel into a den of lions, Joye was careful to avoid naming the king in question, and it is plain that his subject is Henry as much as Darius. The passage is worth quoting at length.

Here is set forthe an example of a weake faithed king betwixt whose sinne and the sin of the persewers of crystis ministres, we ought diligently to discerne. He is weake faithed which loueth and embraceth the trwe doctrine, wold promoue it, suffreth himself to be enstructed and studieth to profite there in and desyreth the techers to be preserued, and confesseth the trwth in a maner, albeit he dare not defende it openly and frely enoughe nor strongly, nethelesse he nether denieth it nor persecuteth it. . . . Siche weake ons were the apostles at crystis death.

This well-meaning but weak-faithed king was, however,

demented and bewitched with these pestilent perswasions of his wiked rulers as thus saying. Consider (oh king) thou art but one man and ignorant of this mater, thou must geue faith to the lerned doctors. . . . In the newe and soden mutacion of these realmes it is to hard for the[e] to plant any new religion & to abolish the olde customs. It wil gender sedicions and vprores and miche inquitenes in thy realme, put away therfore these new lerned with their new lerning, or tarye tyl a more quiete tyme, tyll it may be beter borne of you commons and lordis.

The analogy here becomes transparent, as the biblical councillors become 'lerned doctors' manipulating a king who is attempting to establish a 'new religion' in his realm, with the consent of his 'commons and lordis'. Like the English bishops, these 'doctors' label the religious changes 'new lerning', a traditionalist code-word for evangelicalism. And like the bishops, they play on the king's fears of sedition. Joye is clear that it is they who bear the brunt of the fault for Daniel's condemnation. The king ought to have resisted their scheming, but

because this king sinned not of a set purpose willingly, therfor anon was he smiten with pitie and repentance. . . . The king repented with so manly a faith that he punisshed these accusers and his counsellers of this perellouse nouite and mutacion put into his head so vngodly. Wold God all emprours and kings wold practize this Darius his example.[20]

---

[20] Joye, *Daniel*, fos. 90ʳ–1ᵛ; Richard Rex, 'The new learning', *JEH* 44 (1993), 26–44. Melanchthon also compared Henry to Darius, whom he called 'the seruaunt of other mennes crueltie and wyckednesse' – which can hardly have mollified Henry. Melanchthon, *Epistle*, sigs. A2ᵛ–3ᵛ.

Even if Joye was here toning down a more unforgiving attitude towards the king so as to avoid offending his evangelical readers' royalist sensibilities, this would merely underline the extent to which most evangelicals wished to see themselves as loyal subjects.

Indeed, although the relatively sceptical attitudes of Joye, Brinklow, Turner and others are eye-catching, they are also misleading. Loyalty to the king ran deep in English evangelicalism. After 1540, the belief that he was still a potential ally kept alive the trust built up during the 1530s. On the question of obedience itself, which so concerned the regime, evangelicals were united in believing themselves to be 'bounde by [t]he commaundement of God to obey our prynce with all humilite . . . and that not onely for fear of the swerde but also for conscience sake'.[21] Likewise, even the most outspoken agreed with Tyndale's old position that conscientious disobedience to established authority must never extend to open resistance.[22] At most, they were willing to remind the king that he, too, was under divine authority.[23] Many more, however, preferred not to contemplate such distasteful questions. Thomas Becon, the most prolific evangelical author of the period, argued for the authority of princes in terms of which Cromwell would have been proud. He used the royal supremacy to minimise ecclesiastical authority, but he also affirmed it for its own sake. Rulers, he wrote, are 'the vicars of God . . . the lyuish Image of God . . . the ministers of God for oure wealth. . . . By them the Gospell of Christ triumpheth, & all sectes & heresies are extyrpted & plucked vp by the rootes.' Becon also stated firmly that the Christian liberty which he preached was 'spirituall & not carnal', and did not excuse believers from paying taxes or obeying the law. He even affirmed the obligation to obey tyrants – while making it quite clear that this question was only of theoretical interest to Henry VIII's subjects.[24] The only even implicit criticism that he was willing to venture was the wish that Henry might continue the work he had begun.[25]

Becon's work was published in London, within the law, and he had to watch his step when dealing with such issues. Others, however, faced no

---

[21] Robert Barnes' words, quoted in John Standish, *A lytle treatise composyd by Iohan Standysshe . . . against the protestacion of Robert Barnes at the tyme of his death* (RSTC 23209: 1540), sig. F1^{r-v}. Cf. Becon, *Potation for lent*, sig. L6^v.

[22] Bale, *A dysclosynge or openynge of the Manne of synne*, fo. 97^r; Brinklow, *Complaynt of Roderyck Mors*, sig. A4^r; George Joye, *A present consolation for the sufferers of persecucion for ryghtwysenes* (RSTC 14828: Antwerp, 1544), sig. B4^v; Standish, *Lytle treatise against the protestacion of Robert Barnes*, sig. F2^r.

[23] ECL MS 261, fos. 125^v–6^r.

[24] Thomas Becon (ps. Theodore Basille), *A pleasaunt newe Nosegay, full of many godly and swete floures* (RSTC 1742: 1542), sigs. I1^r–3^v, K3^r, K6^{r-v}, L1^v.

[25] Thomas Becon (ps. Theodore Basille), *Newes out of heauen* (RSTC 1740: 1541), sig. A6^v; Thomas Becon (ps. Theodore Basille), *A newe pathway vnto praier, ful of much godly frute and christen knowledge* (RSTC 1734: 1542), sig. R6^r.

such pressures. *The Lordis flayle*, a 1540 tract by the former Augustinian canon Thomas Solme, was printed abroad and was openly sacramentarian, but Solme was still happy to call Henry God's 'tru minyster owre supreme hed ymmediately vnder Christ'. Moreover, he argued,

> kyngs truly er his true mynisters yn this cherch mylitante, and ther is non that supplith nexte to Christe but only thei. Al othere powrs that be yn erth, be of them, as dukis, bernes [barons], lordis, knyghtis, apostels, Iugges, & suche lyke, where fore they that resiste there kynge, & them of hym sente, resyst the ordinance of God. . . . A Chrystyn kynge, may not only prouyd gydis for a polytyke order, but also for a spyrytall order.

He described the ideal Christian king's ministry as characterised by truth and humility, but like a true Henrician, he skirted round the awkward question of how to deal with kings who fell short of this ideal.[26]

This willingness to give the king the benefit of any possible doubt was one of the most persistent themes of evangelical attitudes to the regime in this period. Miles Coverdale argued that where there were persecutions, they were carried out against the king's will and behind his back. Coverdale prayed 'that the kynges moost roiall persone might se as farre, as his auctorite extendeth, for I feare the comon prouerbe to be true, that there runneth by the myll much water, which the miller knoweth not of.'[27] Likewise, Robert Wisdom carefully denied that the king was responsible for evil acts committed in his name. John Bale argued, somewhat improbably, that evangelicals were less likely to be persecuted in London than elsewhere in the country, because the proximity of the king would restrain conservatives. He also described William Tolwin, a London evangelical who was forced to recant in 1541, as having preached 'accordynge to the wholsom commaundement of Christ and the kynge'.[28] And even while William Turner denied the king's title, he continued to express a serene confidence that Henry VIII agreed with him.[29]

These writers tried to exonerate the king from responsibility for the regime's darker side, but more moderate evangelicals simply ignored the subject altogether. In 1544 Richard Tracy claimed, with an almost wilful optimism, that 'there was neuer more godly lawes made for the punyshmente

---

[26] Thomas Solme, *Here begynnyth a traetys callyde the Lordis flayle* (RSTC 22897: Antwerp, 1540), sigs. C4^r, C8^r.

[27] Miles Coverdale, *A confutacion of that treatise, which one Iohn Standish made agaynst the protestacion of D. Barnes* (RSTC 5888: Zurich, 1541), sig. D5^r.

[28] ECL MS 261, fo. 117^v; Bale, *Epistle exhortatorye*, fo. 9^r; Bale, *A dysclosynge or openynge of the Manne of synne*, fo. 3^r.

[29] Turner, *Rescuynge of the romishe fox*, sigs. A3^v, K8^r. Later in life, Turner was not so positive about Henry: William Turner, *The huntyng of the romyshe vuolfe* (RSTC 24356: Emden, 1555), sig. D6^{r-v}.

of synne, nor neuer more iuste and godly executyon of lawes admynistred' than at the present.³⁰ Similarly, in 1541, Becon wrote

> O Englond, Englond, God calleth the vnto repentaunce . . . by sendyng the suche a vertuous, mercyful, fatherlyke and puyssant a [sic] Prynce. . . . Neuer was there father, that so greatly watched for ye healthe of his sonne, as he dothe for ours. . . . If this title *Pater patrie* might lawfully at ony time be ascribed vnto ony temporall rulare, certes to our moste victorious Prynce it is moost of all due & conuenient.³¹

The well-established theme of comparing Henry to the great kings of the Old Testament was also taken up with enthusiasm by the reformers: Josiah, the rediscoverer of the Law, and Hezekiah, the iconoclast, were the favourites.³² The analogy was deeply felt, and ideal for the reformers' purposes. The Old Testament kings provided models of reform, in particular of the destruction of idols, which both set the agenda for evangelicals and provided a tool which even the most loyal of writers could use gently to point the king in the direction of further reform.³³ But they also provided scriptural grounds for the obedience which Henrician ideology and the realities of power demanded.

For all their suspicions of the regime, and their vilification of Gardiner and other conservatives, most evangelicals remained deeply reluctant throughout this period to be seen to be disloyal to their king. Nor should their loyalty be seen as superficial. George Constantine's view of the regime was hardly rosy, but in 1539 he was still willing to propose, as a practical possibility, risking his own life to demonstrate the effectiveness of a medical treatment to the king. As he commented, 'what made it any matter for my lyfe or twentye thousande soch for the preservacion of his lyfe?'³⁴ For most evangelicals, this ethic of obedience went beyond Tyndale's stern pessimism. Most of them were eager to put the best possible gloss on the king's actions; to accept as much of the king's vision of his own authority as they could force their consciences to swallow; and to look to Henry and to the young Prince Edward as

---

[30] Richard Tracy, *A supplycacion to our moste soueraigne lorde Kynge Henry the eyght* (RSTC 24165: Antwerp, 1544), sig. A4ᵛ.

[31] Thomas Becon (ps. Theodore Basille), *The new pollecye of warre, wherin is declared not only how ye mooste cruell Tyraunt the great Turke may be ouer come, but also all other enemies of the Christen publique weale* (RSTC 1735: 1542), sigs. D7ʳ, E3ᵛ.

[32] See, for example, Bale, *Epistle exhortatorye*, fo. 7ʳ; Bale, *A dysclosynge or openynge of the Manne of synne*, fo. 11ʳ; Thomas Becon (ps. Theodore Basille), *An Inuectyue agenst the moste wicked & detestable vice of swearing* (RSTC 1731: 1543), fo. 71ᵛ; Richard Taverner, *A Catechisme or institution of the Christen Religion* (RSTC 23709: 1539), sig. A3ᵛ; Arthur Kelton, *A commendacion / Of welshmen* (RSTC 14919: 1546), sig. F8ᵛ–G1ʳ; Solme, *The Lordis flayle*, sigs. B5ᵛ–6ᵛ.

[33] For examples of the subtlety with which Old Testament typology was used, see Christopher Bradshaw, 'David or Josiah? Old Testament kings as exemplars in Edwardian religious polemic', in *Protestant History and Identity in Sixteenth-Century Europe*, ed. Bruce Gordon, vol. II (1996).

[34] Constantine, 'Memorial', 75–6.

their hopes for the future of the evangelical cause.³⁵ This strong undercurrent of loyalty and obedience is vital for understanding the evangelical responses to the regime during these years. Even in the dark days of the autumn of 1546, when the prospects for reform had never looked bleaker and 'the waues of the see are great . . . and doth horryblye rage', John Bale insisted:

> Consydre agayne . . . that the lorde whych dwelleth on hygh . . . is able to change a kynges indignacyon (whych is but deathe) into most peaceable fauer and louynge gentylnesse, Prouerbiorum 16. For the hart of a kynge is euermore in the hande of God, and he maye turne it whych waye he wyll.³⁶

Bale had no illusions about Henry – indeed, his view of English events was probably unnecessarily bleak. Yet he continued to believe that when God restored the true Gospel, he would do it by turning the heart of the king. Evangelicals remembered the apparently miraculous shift in their king's religious outlook in the early 1530s;³⁷ they continued to hope, and to believe, that when the time was right God would turn his heart again. Until that time, all that they could do was proclaim the truth as far as their situation would allow; pray; wait; and, as far as their consciences would allow it, obey.

'WALKE SOBERLY': DEFIANCE, DISHONESTY AND DISCRETION

If evangelical approaches to fairly abstract questions of political theory were so clouded with uncertainty and wishful thinking, the problems were all the more apparent when those questions came to a sharp point. When a king demanded obedience to ungodly laws on pain of death – specifically, when a king such as Henry VIII persecuted the Gospel – how ought Christians to respond? Tyndale had argued that in such circumstances, one should not hesitate to die rather than violate the law of God. This view placed him within the ancient Christian tradition of martyrdom, and aligned him with the mood and example of the European Reformation so far. The choice which was thus placed before evangelicals was thoroughly uncomfortable, but stark in its clarity. As John Bale put it, one must

> eyther suffre most tyrannouse deth, or els with mouthe openlye denye Christes verite which is moche worse than the death. For where as he which mannefullye suffreth, declareth himselfe an able wytnesse of the lorde, he that cowardlye recanteth sheweth himselfe to be but a faynt harted hypocrite, throwyng himselfe whollye vndre Antichristes yoke.³⁸

---

[35] Similarly, early in Elizabeth I's reign, her Catholic subjects were reluctant to believe that she was genuinely opposed to their cause. Wooding, *Rethinking Catholicism*, 195–6.
[36] Askew, *The first examinacyon*, fo. 45ᵛ.
[37] See, for example, Richard Morison's tactless but enthusiastic reference to the fact. Morison, *Invective ayenste . . . treason*, sig. D4ᵛ.
[38] Bale, *Epistle exhortatorye*, fo. 25ʳ.

It is straightforward enough to round up English authors who took a similar, or even stronger line. George Joye wrote in 1545, 'Trewth it is, that it is all one thynge, not to defende the trewth and to denye the trewth. . . . Let men beware how they dissemble with the trewth in this worlde, lest in soche an vngodly securite they pluke the synne of the holy ghost into theyr bosoms.' By dissembling, Joye meant not only recanting in the formal sense, but almost any kind of deceit. He again cited the example of Daniel, who, when prayer was forbidden by King Darius, continued to pray by his window:

> Why Daniel? What nedest thou thus openly to haue put thyself in perell? thou mighst haue worshipt god in spirit or secretely and not by these externe gestures haue declared it: or for that space not to haue praid at all. No, not so did Daniel, for he knewe that the trewe religion and worship must be farre from all colourable dissembling without any lying shyftis of hypocricie.[39]

On this view, the Christian's adherence to the truth should not only be faithful, but ostentatious. And it was in this spirit that Joye issued a stirring summons to martyrdom:

> Let vs therfore (chrysten brethren) be constant in obeyinge god rather then men, although they slay vs for the verite. For our innocent blode shed for the gospell, shall preache it with more frute (as did abelis, steuens etc) than euer did our mouthes and pennes. . . . For what profit, sayth Dauid, comethe of my blode if it be layd downe with my body in graue to be corrupted? Is it not beter spent powered forth onto the lordis felde to be therwyth made fatte fecunde and fertyle?[40]

This admirably lucid position is not far from the view which would eventually become the Protestant orthodoxy.

The power of these arguments has recently been reasserted with some spirit by Brad Gregory. To sixteenth-century Christians of any persuasion, Gregory argues, the willingness to die rather than recant was 'the sober realism of a man with his eyes wide open'. If Christ would disown those who disowned him, then a Christian under persecution would almost be compelled to choose bodily death, as the far lesser evil than damnation. In the face of such logic, Gregory suggests, no evasion was possible: 'Christ's demands were non-negotiable. For people . . . committed to Protestantism in the later years of Henry VIII's reign in England, following them might mean death.'[41] However, a number of late Henrician evangelicals did indeed attempt to negotiate their way out of such demands. In the 1540s there remained significant support for the so-called Nicodemite opinion that it was

---

[39] Joye, *Daniel*, fos. 33^r, 84^v.
[40] Joye, *Present consolation*, sigs. B4^v–5^r. Brad Gregory has pointed out that this book is closely based on Urbanus Rhegius' 1531 *Consolatory Letter to All the Christians of Hildesheim*. Brad S. Gregory, *Salvation at Stake: Christian Martyrdom in Early Modern Europe* (Cambridge, MA, 1999), 155.
[41] Gregory, *Salvation at Stake*, 154–62.

possible to conceal one's faith without compromising it.[42] The uncompromising position of Bale and Joye was controversial. This was not simply a matter of cowardice. The peculiar political context of 1540s England muddied the waters. Joye himself admitted that 'Yet do our bisshops compell men to recant sayinge. That where the head & gouerner professeth Chryst, there can be no persecucion.'[43] This was a genuine dilemma. One should not deny Christ; this was universally accepted. But was obeying Henry VIII tantamount to a denial of Christ? How could this be when the king himself was a Christian? If Henry imposed discipline on the Church of which he was Supreme Head, surely his subjects were bound in conscience to obey him, rather than claiming that their impertinently held theological opinions outweighed their acknowledged duty of obedience to their sovereign? This was an argument which the regime used repeatedly during the 1540s, and whose power evangelicals grudgingly acknowledged.[44] Where there was an unmistakeable division between 'true', Protestant and 'false', papist Churches, the case for embracing martyrdom remained strong. This was the case in contemporary France and the Netherlands, and it was later to be the case in England under Mary's reign. Under these circumstances evangelicals manifested a willingness to die for their cause which alarmed their opponents. Henry VIII's Church, however, could not easily be dismissed as the congregation of Antichrist. The ambiguity of English religious policy ensured that the evangelical response to it was equally ambiguous.

If the starting point for the 'orthodox' viewpoint which Gregory has celebrated was obedience to Christ, the starting point for Nicodemism was obedience to the crown. Most reformers accepted that the king had some spiritual authority, and so could not easily deny that the regime had some authority to enforce orthodoxy as it saw fit. Robert Barnes, for example, argued in 1531 that there were two ways in which temporal power might exercise spiritual authority. It might openly defy Scripture, which, of course, was unacceptable. Alternatively, however, it might lay down commands on so-called *adiaphora*, matters indifferent to salvation, and Barnes held that such commands had to be obeyed. This issue dogged English Protestantism

---

[42] This view took its name from Nicodemus, who was a disciple of Christ's in secret: John 3:1–2, 7:50–2. The Nicodemite arguments are summarised in Pettegree, *Marian Protestantism*, 89–94. Recantation and dissimulation in Henrician England have been discussed most recently in Wabuda, 'Equivocation and recantation' (a valuable case-study of one particularly accomplished Nicodemite, Edward Crome).
[43] Joye, *Present consolation*, sig. A6^r.
[44] For example, Bonner Register fo. 44^r; ECL MS 261 fos. 90^r, 117^v, 119^v; Robert Crowley, *The opening of the woordes of the prophet Ioell, in his* second *and* third chapters, *concerning the signes of the last day. Compiled M.D. XLVI* (RSTC 6089: 1566), sig. A4^r; Coverdale, *Confutacion of . . . Iohn Standish*, sig. D3^r. Cf. Miles Huggarde, *The displaying of the protestantes, with a description of diuers their abuses* (RSTC 13557: 1556), fos. 53^v–4^r.

into Elizabeth I's reign and beyond, as regimes clashed with reformers who questioned their right to settle such 'indifferent' matters as clerical vestments. Even when dealing with an avowedly Protestant regime, later puritans such as Thomas Sampson felt their exclusion from office to be a kind of martyrdom. In Barnes' view, however, if the temporal power chose to curtail Christian liberty over secondary issues, one might regret the fact but one must also obey. Barnes also took a strikingly generous view of which questions the temporal power could legitimately order in this way, extending even to clerical celibacy.[45] The same kind of logic led Nicholas Shaxton, also in 1531, to put forward the perverse argument that it was permissible to disbelieve in purgatory, but not to deny it openly.[46]

If inconsistency of this kind did not seem an acceptable solution, deliberate ambiguity was another possibility. Thomas Becon trumpeted the necessity of confessing one's faith in apparently forthright terms:

> No manacynge wordes, no imprysonment, no chenes, no fetters, no sweard, no faggot, no fyre ought to plucke vs from this Confession. No tyranny ought so to be feared, that God & hys trueth shoulde not be confessed.

However, he did not define what constituted the faith which his readers must confess. All he said was that they must defend 'whatsoeuer the holy scriptures teach of God', while evading the critical question of who might authoritatively interpret them. It is perhaps not irrelevant that Becon was himself to recant abjectly scarcely a year after this was written.[47] Yet for Becon, obedience was a matter not only of expedience but also of conscience. And while his view of royal authority was certainly exalted, he was not alone in this approach. In 1546 Simon Heynes, the reformist dean of Exeter who was no faint-heart, advised Edward Crome to recant his attack on the Mass, chiefly on the grounds that the king had ordered Crome to do so.[48] John Hooper, hardly the most retiring or compromising of English reformers, was one of many who were troubled by the implications of the biblical story of Naaman. The prophet Elisha had apparently permitted Naaman to kneel beside his royal master in a pagan temple. Surely, Hooper suggested to Heinrich Bullinger, this and other texts implied that it was possible for evangelicals to obey royal authority and to conceal their faith without betraying their consciences?[49]

---

[45] William A. Clebsch, *England's Earliest Protestants 1520–1535* (New Haven and London, 1964), 63–4. This was an issue which was to return to haunt the reformers, as Gardiner argued against Martin Bucer that the king had an absolute right to outlaw clerical marriage. Cf. Turner, *Rescuynge of the romishe fox* sigs. L2^v–3^v.
[46] Wabuda, 'Equivocation and recantation', 229.
[47] Becon, *Potacion for lent*, sig. D6^v; Bonner Register fos. 44^r–5^r.
[48] PRO SP 1/218 fo. 44^v (*LP* XXI (i) 790.1).
[49] *ET*, 24–5 (*OL*, 38–9); II Kings 5:17–19. Cf. Peres Zagorin, *Ways of Lying: Dissimulation, Persecution and Conformity in Early Modern Europe* (Cambridge, MA, 1990), 69.

Indeed, quite apart from the issue of authority, even fervent reformers might admit that some points of doctrine or (especially) of order were simply not important enough to be worth a confrontation with the authorities. After all, while Christian tradition might celebrate true martyrs, it also condemned as suicides those who courted martyrdom. The most sure-footed conscience might stray from such a narrow line.[50] Hugh Latimer, on any showing one of the more robust voices of early English evangelicalism, is recorded as confronting just this difficulty in 1532, when he visited James Bainham in prison. Bainham was facing execution, and Latimer took him to task:

> I do not allow that any man should consent to his own death, unless he had a right cause to die in. Let not vain-glory overcome you in a matter that men deserve not to die for; for therein you shall neither please God, do good to yourself, nor your neighbour: and better it were for you to submit yourself to the ordinances of men, than so rashly to finish your life without good ground.

When he learned that the first article on which Bainham was condemned was that he had called Thomas Becket a damnable traitor, Latimer was confirmed in his original opinion: 'This is no cause at all worthy for a man to take his death upon; for it may be a lie, as well as a true tale, and in such a doubtful matter it were mere madness for a man to jeopard his life.' He changed his mind, however, on learning that the next article concerned the doctrines of purgatory and of the sacrifice of the Mass. These, he judged, were questions of sufficient importance that Bainham might die for them in good conscience. Even so, Latimer still urged caution. 'But yet beware of vain-glory; for the devil will be ready now to infect you therewith.'[51] Brad Gregory has movingly described the ideal martyr's preparation for death, building up faith and admitting a total reliance on God.[52] Yet not all of those who found the courage to go to the stake, much less those who were unable to escape, fulfilled this ideal. Latimer's stern words suggest what is already plausible: that amongst those who died were some who had courted martyrdom or who did not die in the sober, stable faith that the martyrologists liked to record. The maverick sacramentarian priest, Anthony Pearsone, who was burned in Windsor in 1543, is recorded as saying to the stake when he was bound to it, 'Nowe welcome myne owne sweete wife: for this day shalt thou and I be maried together in the loue and peace of God.' He followed this by putting a pile of straw on his head, saying, 'Thys is Gods hatte: now am I dressed

---

[50] Gregory is right to insist (*Salvation at Stake*, 104–5) that the enthusiasm of those who 'wished to die *as martyrs*' is not, by modern standards, suicidal or the manifestation of a 'death wish'. Yet by the harsher standards of the sixteenth century, those whose pursuit of a martyr's crown led them needlessly to put themselves in harm's way might well be described as suicides. True martyrs ought to be indifferent to their deaths, not complicit in them.

[51] Hugh Latimer, *Sermons and Remains of Hugh Latimer*, ed. George Elwes Corrie (Cambridge: Parker Society, 1845), 222–3.

[52] Gregory, *Salvation at Stake*, 129–33.

like a true souldiour of Christ.'[53] For all Foxe's tidying-up, the impression is of a man whose approach to his imminent painful death is some way from the accepted ideal.

The seemingly clear-cut ethics of recantation and martyrdom repeatedly dissolve into complexities. So do a cluster of other issues which gathered around that central problem. Were lies, for example, always sinful? A strong tradition of Christian thought held that they were. Augustine had argued that since God is truth, to lie is necessarily to sin. Latimer placed himself in that tradition, preaching that one lie will in due course require twenty more to defend it. Even Aquinas, however, had tempered this approach, arguing that officious and jocose lies were merely venial sins; and those who wished to find patristic precedents for muddying the water could cite Jerome and Chrysostom, who had both argued that, in some circumstances, dissimulation was permissible or even obligatory for the Christian. Nor was early Protestant opinion unanimous. Bullinger inclined towards the Augustinian view, as did Calvin, but even Calvin accepted that one might hide the truth as long as one did not actually state falsehoods.[54] Otto Brunfels' scepticism about the claims of temporal authority made him a fringe figure in early Protestantism, but his claim in his *Pandects* of 1527 that 'it is licit to feign and dissimulate in the presence of the impious to avoid or prevent danger' was backed up by an impressive range of biblical precedents, including the midwives who lied to Pharaoh to protect the Hebrew children; St Paul's proclaimed willingness to be all things to all people; and the old chestnut of Naaman and Elisha.[55] There is no direct evidence to connect Brunfels' view with anyone in England, although the *Pandects* were certainly known in scholarly circles.[56] However, even before Brunfels wrote, English reformers were beginning to make similar arguments. The comments which Thomas Bilney jotted in the margins of his Vulgate, apparently before 1527, include the remark that, in I Samuel 19, David's wife Michal practised deceit blamelessly. Bilney also described Jeremiah's rhetorical false prophecy in Jeremiah 28 as the prophet's 'pious lie'.[57] Tyndale's 1533 exposition of the Sermon on the Mount insisted that 'to lie . . . and dissemble is not alway sin', and

---

[53] *AM*, 1220.
[54] Johann P. Somerville, 'The "new art of lying": equivocation, mental reservation and casuistry', in *Conscience and Casuistry in Early Modern Europe*, ed. Edmund Leites (Cambridge, 1988), 161, 165, 183; Carlos M. Eire, 'Prelude to sedition? Calvin's attack on Nicodemism and religious compromise', *Archiv für Reformationsgeschichte* 76 (1985), 120–45.
[55] Zagorin, *Ways of Lying*, 68–9; Exodus 1:19; I Corinthians 9:22, which was also used by Martin Bucer to defend the Nicodemite position. Pettegree, *Marian Protestantism*, 93.
[56] Three copies appear amongst the probate inventories of Cambridge University in the period 1538–43. Leedham-Green, *Books in Cambridge Inventories*.
[57] J. Y. Batley, *On a Reformer's Latin Bible: Being an Essay on the Adversaria in the Vulgate of Thomas Bilney* (Cambridge, 1940), 47–8, cited in Wabuda, 'Equivocation and recantation', 229.

indeed that to lie to defend others can be 'the duty of every Christian man by the law of charity'. He cited another of the biblical precedents which Brunfels had used, namely the episode in which David feigned madness so as to escape from the king of Gath.[58] The attraction of this line of argument is plain. Augustine's approach had a certain bleak clarity, but his insistence that one must never lie, even when the alternative is to betray the innocent to their deaths, was hard to swallow even in the abstract, and far harder to cling to in the face of genuine persecution. If, however, the permissibility of such a lie was conceded, it became almost impossible to find a coherent and defensible position.

Other issues contributed to the confusion. For example, was exile a valid alternative to martyrdom for the persecuted Christian? Almost all reformers agreed that it was, although this was partly because those who did not rarely had a chance to argue their case. But if it was legitimate to flee from the power that had been appointed by God to wield the sword, might it not be permissible to employ other means of evasion and concealment? Such means might not involve direct, verbal untruths, but were nevertheless designed to deceive and thwart the temporal power. When the conservative pamphleteer 'Ponce Pantolabus' – actually John Huntingdon, soon himself to convert to reformist views – dismissed evangelicals as 'slepers / and corner crepers', John Bale retorted that this

maketh not agaynst them but rather with them, so longe as their cause is good and godlye. For soche a corner creper was Christ their master, whan Pantolabus spirituall generacion wolde ones haue stoned him to death. He hyd himselfe from their hastye furye, and so went preuylye out of the temple.[59]

Nor was this simply theoretical. After his arrest and recantation in 1543, Thomas Becon fled to the Midlands and ceased preaching and writing in support of the evangelical cause. He later defended both his flight and his silence as pragmatic necessities:

When neyther by speaking, nor by writing I coulde do good, I thoughte it best not rashly to throwe my self into the rauenynge pawes of these gready wolues, but for a certaine space to absent my selfe from theyr tyrannye accordynge to the doctrine of the Gospell.

By 'the doctrine of the Gospell', he meant a series of difficult and ambiguous texts that could be made to support such action. He cited the dictum of Ecclesiastes that there is a time to keep silent; the prophet Amos' saying that 'when the poore are oppressed and troden vnder the fote, then shal the wyse

---

[58] Zagorin, *Ways of Lying*, 234; I Samuel 21:13–15.
[59] John Bale, *A mysterye of inyquyte contayned within the heretycall Genealogye of Ponce Pantolabus* (RSTC 1303: Antwerp, 1545), fos. 71^r, 72^r.

man . . . holde hys peace, for the time is euyl'; and Christ's command not to cast pearls before swine.[60] This last passage was a favourite for reformers who wished to justify concealing their beliefs. Anne Askew, when pressed to give her understanding of the biblical passages she had quoted, told her interrogators that 'I wolde not throwe pearles amonge swyne, for acornes were good ynough.'[61]

A further problem was occasioned by evangelical suspicion of the use of oaths. Any process of recantation involved the swearing of an oath, so the question of how seriously these were to be taken was of direct importance. Swearing, however, was an issue which knotted a range of contentious problems together. Evangelicals enthusiastically condemned frivolous and profane oaths as an affront to public virtue, deploying the two New Testament texts which forbid the use of oaths.[62] However, reformers following this line of argument had to tread carefully, for fear of being associated with those Anabaptist radicals who used the same texts to oppose the use of vows and oaths under any circumstances. These arguments were made still more delicate by the reformers' other interest in the subject, through the topic of clerical celibacy; for many of the debates on clerical celibacy turned around the validity of the vow of celibacy, and whether it was binding. Four issues, then, were closely intertwined – recantation, profanity, the validity of oaths and clerical celibacy – and they reacted against each other in ways that were not always easy to control. This did not prevent evangelicals from devoting considerable attention to all of them.

The bane of profane swearing attracted a remarkable degree of attention from across the reformist spectrum.[63] Two of the most prolific evangelicals went so far as to write pamphlets devoted to the subject. It was a issue with which Thomas Becon was almost obsessively preoccupied. In addition to his *Inuectyue agenst the moste wicked & detestable vice of swearing*, five of the other eight books he published in this period touched on the problem.[64] Most of Becon's fire was directed against simple profanity, but he was obliged to present his views on the right use of oaths, and as such to give his opinion on the dangerous text from Matthew 5. He was careful to distance himself

---

[60] Becon, *Iewell of ioye*, sigs. B4^v–5^r; Ecclesiastes 3:7; Amos 5:11–13; Matthew 7:6.
[61] Askew, *The first examinacyon*, fo. 2^v.
[62] Matthew 5:33–7; James 5:12. The former of these was the text on which Tyndale had based his opinion, noted above, that it might be a Christian's duty to lie.
[63] For example, Crowley, *The opening of the woordes of the prophet Ioell*, sigs. C6^v–7^r; *A generall free Pardon or Charter of heuyn blys* (RSTC 19187: 1542), sig. B1^v; cf. Bonner Register fo. 40^r.
[64] Thomas Becon (ps. Theodore Basille), *A Christmas bankette garnyshed with many pleasaunt and deynty disshes* (RSTC 1715: 1542), sig. A3^v; Thomas Becon (ps. Theodore Basille), *Dauids Harpe ful of moost delectable armony, newely strynged and set in tune* (RSTC 1717: 1542), sigs. G3^v–5^r; Becon, *New yeares gyfte*, sigs. E7^v–8^r; Becon, *Newes out of heauen*, sigs. A4^v–5^r; Becon, *New pollecye of warre*, sig. H1^{r-v}.

from the Anabaptist position, emphasising that a magistrate might impose oaths without violating God's law. Nevertheless, he remained uneasy about this, admonishing magistrates that they should not require oaths lightly, but only for

> weighty & necessary matters concernyng eyther the glory of God or the profyt of the common weale. For menne ought not to be called forthe to swere for euery lyght trifle, nor yet to swere as many do, they can not tel what nor wherfore.[65]

Given Henry VIII's fondness for imposing oaths on his subjects, this was controversial enough. However, when he was not weighing his words so carefully, Becon could slip back into the language of Matthew 5 without qualification. The true Christian, he said, 'wyll sweare by nothynge that euer god made, nother by heauen nor by earth, nor ony other oth. His communicacion shall be, yea, yea, na, na.'[66] John Bale's approach in his *Christen exhortacion vnto customable swearers* was broadly similar. He, too, refused to go down the Anabaptist road, but he was sufficiently suspicious of oaths to compare swearing to homicide. Magistrates might lawfully require oaths, he argued, but only from the same God-given authority which permits magistrates lawfully to kill and to require others to do so. Swearing is no more permitted for the private citizen than murder.[67]

This thoroughly sceptical view of swearing led naturally, and very conveniently, to suspicion of the validity of vows of celibacy. George Joye, who bitterly resented clerical celibacy, began from the universally agreed point that such vows had to be taken advisedly in order to be valid. He argued, however, that the vow of celibacy was one that no one had the strength to keep, and which was in any case against Scripture. As such it was impossible to take it advisedly. The vow was therefore in no way binding and the Christian was free – indeed, almost obliged – to disregard it.[68] Heinrich Bullinger's tract on marriage argued a similar line (although the relevant section was included in only one of the English editions printed in the 1540s).[69] All these arguments led to the same point, widely agreed on by all these authors: that is, that an oath which was ill-advised, made under compulsion,

---

[65] Becon, *Inuectyue agenst swearing*, fos. 57ᵛ, 60ᵛ.   [66] Becon, *Dauids Harpe*, sig. G5ʳ.
[67] John Bale, *A Christen exhortacion vnto customable swearers. What a ryght & lawfull othe is: whan, and before whom, it owght to be* (RSTC 1280: Antwerp, 1543?), fo. 6ᵛ. This work is anonymous, and attributed by the *RSTC* to either Bale or Miles Coverdale. That Bale is the author seems clear both from his unmistakably pungent style and from his own later references to the book. Bale, *A dysclosynge or openynge of the Manne of synne*, fo. 90ᵛ; Leslie P. Fairfield, *John Bale, Mythmaker for the English Reformation* (West Lafayette, IN, 1976), 200, n. 6. However, the bland table graces and edifying poems at the end of the work do not appear to be from Bale's pen.
[68] Joye, *Defence of the mariage of preistes*, sig. B2ʳ⁻ᵛ.
[69] Heinrich Bullinger, *The christen state of Matrimonye*, tr. Miles Coverdale (RSTC 4045: Antwerp, 1541), fo. 29ʳ.

opposed to Scripture or in any other way suspect was not binding. An oath to do an evil deed is already damnable, Bale argued, but doubly so if it is carried out.[70] Becon deployed a range of patristic authorities to prove his assertion that breaking a foolish oath is not perjury. Rather, he argued, such oaths 'snarle the consciences of so many as kepe them'. The most compelling proofs of such an argument, however, were biblical. The oath taken by the conspirators who hoped to murder St Paul; the oath taken by Jephtha in the book of Judges which forced him to kill his own daughter; and, above all, Herod's rash oath to Herodias which led to the execution of John the Baptist, were repeatedly cited by a variety of authors as examples of oaths that should never have been made, but which having been made, should certainly never have been kept.[71]

These arguments made a firm line against recantation difficult to hold. The oath which was the centrepiece of a recantation was stripped of much of its power. These writers would certainly regard a promise to deny Christ and the Gospel as an oath which the Christian was obliged to break. The fact that such oaths were usually set about with the trappings of traditional religion undermined them still further. In 1546, one Essex heretic argued 'that yf he swere by the masse he swereth by none othe', since the Mass was itself false.[72] That an oath could be lightly broken need not, of course, imply that it could be lightly taken – quite the opposite; but this side of the argument, that to take an ill-advised oath was itself sinful, was rarely emphasised. This was perhaps natural, since most of these writers had in their younger days vowed both celibacy and loyalty to the papacy. Whether for this or other reasons, they tended to see vows and oaths as unfortunate facts to be dealt with, rather than as moral choices. Joye even spoke of the vow of celibacy as one which was extorted by compulsion. If the threat of not being ordained constituted compulsion, then so *a fortiori* did the threat of burning.[73] All of these arguments tended to steer those facing the dilemma of death or recantation towards conformity. All that that required was a hasty oath, with the knowledge that there would be leisure in which to repent of it.

These debates over the validity and right use of oaths also had a wider echo. Similar problems had been pondered in Lollard circles for over a century. At times the connection seems to be a close one. Lollards had also learned suspicion of oaths from the New Testament texts. Some denied the legitimacy of oaths altogether, but while their opponents certainly believed that

---

[70] Bale, *Christen exhortacion vnto customable swearers*, fo. 7^{r-v}.
[71] Becon, *Inuectyue agenst swearing*, fos. 45^v–9^r; Joye, *Defence of the mariage of preistes*, sigs. B2^v–3^r; Bale, *A dysclosynge or openynge of the Manne of synne*, fos. 73^v–4^r; Acts 23:12; Judges 11:30–40; Matthew 14:6–10.
[72] PRO SP 1/218 fo. *139^r (*LP* XXI (i) 836).
[73] Joye, *Defence of the mariage of preistes*, sig. B2^v.

this shocking view was the Lollard orthodoxy, the more common approach seems to have been to deny oaths sworn by created things, while allowing oaths sworn by God himself. This is the same fine distinction, based on the same close reading of the Matthew 5 text, that Bale was to make in his *Christen exhortacion vnto customable swearers*.[74] However, while in some ways Lollard views largely paralleled those of the evangelicals, in others they went a good deal further. Lollard texts cited Jephtha's and Herod's oaths as biblical types of evil oaths, as the evangelicals were to do. In Lollard hands, however, the connection between the debate over oaths and that over recantation became explicit. One Lollard went so far as to say that oaths were 'only ordained for preserving reputation in the presence of a judge'. Anne Hudson has this to say about Lollard views of abjuration:

> There is . . . a good deal of evidence to suggest that their rejection of oaths had considerable bearing upon the significance Lollards attached to those promises, and indeed to indicate that many did not hesitate to take the oath when forced but regarded it, because any oath was illicit, as of no account and certainly as having no bearing upon their future behaviour or beliefs.[75]

Whether or not this is the reason, it is undeniable that conformism, dissimulation and apparently cynical recantation were deeply embedded in Lollardy. Hudson's estimate is that 98 per cent or more of Lollards arrested for heresy recanted or abjured. There was some theoretical justification for such recantations, in addition to the devaluation of oaths. One early Lollard, Richard Wyche, was persuaded to recant in 1403 by an argument akin to the later theory of mental reservation.[76] The Lollard leader John Purvey apparently gave detailed instructions on how to evade interrogation, recommending that one should simply claim to understand the Eucharist as Christ and St Paul understood it. Purvey himself, however, was soon afterwards persuaded to recant unambiguously, and his example was repeatedly used against Lollards who might be considering standing firm. The prevalence of recantation amongst Lollards seems, in the end, to have had less to do with principle than with

---

[74] Henry G. Russell, 'Lollard opposition to oaths by creatures', *American Historical Review* 51 (1946), 669–76, 680. Lollards, however, were more exacting in their objection to the swearing of oaths on a book as a form of swearing by a creature. Hudson, *Premature Reformation*, 372.

[75] Hudson, *Premature Reformation*, 373–4.

[76] *Ibid*. 158–60. In the early Reformation, however, mental reservation seems to have been more closely associated with conservative opponents of the Henrician reforms. Friar Forrest, the one papal loyalist executed for heresy rather than treason, claimed that he had taken the supremacy oath 'with his outward man, but his inward man neuer consented thervnto'. One evangelical writing in the mid-1540s claimed that conservative clergy commonly argued that, while they were forced to conform outwardly, still 'they keepe their inward man free'. Hall, *The vnion of . . . Lancastre & Yorke*, fo. 232ᵛ; BL Royal MS 17.B.xxxv fo. 19ʳ; Peter Marshall, 'Papist as heretic: the burning of John Forest, 1538', *HJ* 41 (1998), 351–74.

self-preservation. Most tellingly, Lollard 'penitents' were commonly willing to betray their fellows to the authorities. They were most eager to denounce those who were long dead or already implicated, suggesting a level of passive resistance; but when, in 1521, Bishop Longland threatened those who had previously abjured with relapse (and therefore with death) if they would not incriminate others, the tactic proved highly effective.[77]

Lollard dissimulation extended not only to actual recantation, but to the kind of day-to-day conformity which kept dissent hidden from public view. According to John Thomson, fifteenth-century Lollardy was 'more concerned with self-preservation than with revolution, conforming to the normal practices of the Church to avoid detection'. Richard Rex describes late Lollardy as 'conformist to the point of quietism'.[78] The Mass may have been detestable idolatry to most Lollards, but they were rarely willing publicly to absent themselves from church. Some apparently believed that if they attended Mass with the right inward attitude and rejection of Catholic doctrine, they might derive the benefits of a 'true' communion service from it. One Lollard detected in 1521 rationalised his presence at Mass, saying, 'I will not denie, but it is a holy thing: but it is not the body of the Lord that suffered Passion for vs.' Others made their protest against the Mass in secret, for example by eating before communicating. Others still openly admitted that they attended church simply for their own safety, and apparently saw nothing wrong in this. Thomas Boughton of Salisbury, who abjured in 1499, said that 'I feyned with myn hondys to honour it [the Host] as cristen men vse to doo, but my mynd and entent was nothyng therto, but to God almyghty above in heven, thinkyng that he was not ther present in the blessyd sacrament.'[79] Over their century and a half of surviving as a persecuted minority, Lollards had developed a strong tradition of self-preservation, of which the keynotes were concealment and the avoidance of confrontation with the authorities.

Richard Rex has recently drawn on such evidence to stress the contrast between conformist, reclusive Lollardy and evangelicalism, a passionate and revolutionary movement which scorned such passivity and cowardice.[80] The point is well taken, but by the same logic, the persistence of habits of conformism and recantation within early English evangelicalism suggests that Lollard influence cannot be entirely discounted. By styling themselves as Lollardy's heirs and embracing Lollard texts, evangelicals laid claim not

---

[77] Hudson, *Premature Reformation*, 159–62; Andrew Hope, 'Lollardy: the stone the builders rejected?', in *Protestantism and the National Church in Sixteenth-Century England*, ed. Peter Lake and Maria Dowling (1987), 3–4.

[78] Thomson, *Later Lollards*, 19; Richard Rex, *The Lollards* (Basingstoke, 2002), 131.

[79] AM, 830; Hudson, *Premature Reformation*,149–51; James E. Oxley, *The Reformation in Essex to the Death of Mary* (Manchester, 1965), 9; Zagorin, *Ways of Lying*, 67.

[80] Rex, *Lollards*, 132.

only to the legitimacy which Lollardy's history could provide but also, willy-nilly, to a somewhat mixed bag of Lollard doctrines and practices.[81] Euan Cameron has shown how the Alpine Waldensians' tradition of dissimulation survived into the late sixteenth century, despite prolonged contact with Swiss Protestantism; it is very plausible that Lollardy informed early English Protestantism's similar tradition.[82]

Perhaps more importantly, even if English evangelicals were not the heirs to Lollardy's tradition of recantation, the religious conservatives of the early Reformation era were certainly heirs to those who had extracted recantations from Lollards for a century and a half. Recantation, like martyrdom, is a game for two players. It requires not only a heretic who is willing to recant, but a prosecutor willing to accept a recantation. Thomson sees the prevalence of recantations among the later Lollards as

> a measure of the comparative mildness of the bishops. Their main concern was to bring the offender back into the fold ... Even in the case of relapsed offenders ... the effort was made to secure their repentance before death so that they should die within the fold of the Church.[83]

This is a point of considerable importance. The rhetoric of the evangelical polemicists is full of denunciations of the conservative bishops as bloodthirsty persecutors, but in reality most conservatives saw burning a heretic as a defeat.[84] Like Gibbon's enlightened magistrates, their first priority was to secure a recantation rather than a condemnation. We should not forget that to burn a baptised Christian for obstinate heresy represented a catastrophic pastoral failure. Execution, like a just war, was a last resort. The logic cited to justify it was relentless, yet had it been fully put into practice the body count of heresy prosecution in the age of the Reformation would be terrifyingly high. Most of the time, a genuine reluctance to send heretics to the fire tempered the 'willingness to kill'.[85] When Bishop Gardiner admonishes John Marbeck to 'take heed least thou cast away thy selfe wilfully', we should hear the voice of the pastor as well as that of the politician.[86] Yet pragmatic considerations did reinforce this stance. The authorities had reason to be wary of the heightened tensions which public religious confrontations could cause. By contrast, those who recanted could be relied upon to provide the names of other heretics; it was her refusal to do this

---

[81] See below, pp. 232–8.
[82] Euan Cameron, *The Reformation of the Heretics: the Waldenses of the Alps, 1480–1580* (Oxford, 1984), 224.
[83] Thomson, *Later Lollards*, 235.   [84] Gregory, *Salvation at Stake*, 81.
[85] *Ibid.*, 82–90. Gregory's eloquent presentation of the logic driving heresy prosecutions does not fully acknowledge the extent to which authorities failed to implement it, whether from policy, partiality, mercy or simple squeamishness.
[86] *AM*,1214.

which made Anne Askew's burning such a disastrous failure for her conservative enemies. Moreover, executions and recantations were both public events with considerable value as propaganda for one side or the other. It was Richard Wyche's prosecutors who had suggested the device of mental reservation to him in 1403. Evidently the propaganda coup of a recantation was more important than the penitent's sincerity.[87]

In the 1540s, evangelicals and conservatives were both vividly aware of the power of recantations. Miles Coverdale deplored the fact that conservative preachers 'make such tryumphinge of reuocacions in your sermons', but the exploitation of recantations was not limited to preachers. When Alexander Seton and William Tolwin recanted in 1541, Bishop Bonner had their recantation sermons published in full, and the pamphlet quickly ran through two editions.[88] Those recantation sermons for which we have texts were carefully crafted to give the impression of sincerity. In 1541 Edward Crome was made to declare that he was 'resolued and fully perswadid in his harte and conscience' to stick to his new-found orthodoxy. Likewise, in 1543, the preacher Robert Wisdom's recantation began, 'Howe soever I haue counterfett before, thyncke not that I counterfett nowe.' For those who could not be present, he and his fellow-penitents were made to sign numerous copies of their recantation sermons.[89] Subsequently, overwhelmed by remorse, Wisdom lamented the 'moost grevouse slaunder that I gaue' to the Gospel by recanting. He did his best to undo the damage, claiming he had never seen the text of his recantation before the day he read it, and pleading that his own sin should not discredit his beliefs. As Coverdale put it, 'Loue not thou Christ the worse, though Iudas be a traytoure.'[90] However, the damage that such events could do was real and lasting. Nicholas Shaxton, the former bishop of Salisbury, made one of the most high-profile recantations of the reign in 1546. Two years later, in an open letter to Shaxton, Robert Crowley was still concerned by 'the great numbre of them that thorowe your recantation were established in your errroures'.[91]

Conservatives not only exploited triumphs of this kind, they were willing to go to some lengths to secure them. The most notorious example of this was the illegal racking of Anne Askew in 1546, but in 1543 also, according

---

[87] Hudson, *Premature Reformation*, 160.
[88] Coverdale, *Confutacion of . . . Iohn Standish*, sig. K2^r; Alexander Seton and William Tolwin, *The declaracion made at Poules Crosse in the Cytye of London, the fourth sonday of Aduent* (RSTC 22249.5: 1542). Only one edition of this pamphlet survives, but it claims on its title page to be 'newly corrected & amended'.
[89] Bonner Register fos. 26^r, 44^r.
[90] ECL MS 261 fos. 90^r, 130^r; Coverdale, *Confutacion of . . . Iohn Standish*, sig. N5^v.
[91] Wabuda, 'Equivocation and recantation', 226; Robert Crowley, *The confutation of .xiii. Articles, wherunto Nicolas Shaxton, late byshop of Salisburye subscribed and caused to be set forthe* (RSTC 6083: 1548), sig. A2^v.

to the evangelical courtier William Palmer, there was a deliberate policy of pursuing recantations. Although some of the reformers arrested that year were steadfast and would have gone to their deaths, Palmer alleged that the bishops preferred to

> ... wery them in preson
> wherby at lengith, we might them compell
> for there doctryne, to make recantation.
> We were not so dull, as to forget
> how the People wondryde at the constancye
> of doctor barnes, Iarame and garete
> that toke there dethe so pacientlye
> And that by their godly exhortation
> they made at there dethe, many dyde turne
> and that thes men of the same fasshion
> wold convart many, yf we dyd them burne.[92]

Palmer was certainly not above inventing such charges, but this account fits the facts as far as we know them. When Robert Wisdom was arrested in or before March 1543, he was initially defiant. He wrote a refutation of the charges against him while in prison, and at the time of writing he clearly expected to die. Rather than being burned, however, he was confined to the Lollards' Tower, and kept in the stocks for two months or more, until his nerve eventually broke.[93] As another evangelical writing in the 1540s put it, 'It is more for their purpose [the conservatives'] to suffer the true preachers to lyve in discredit, than to burne them for mainetenance of their doctrine.'[94]

It is understandable that evangelical writers should view this policy with dismay, but from the point of view of the heretic facing legal proceedings it had one great advantage. The authorities were frequently ready to be flexible in order to secure a recantation. Wisdom himself had been the beneficiary of such discretion when he was first arrested in 1541. When he was brought before Bonner, the bishop urged him to recant, using

> flaterye and faire promises with grett attestatyon by god and as he was trewe preste ... that I shulde finde him as gentill and as good vnto me, as he wolde be to his awn sowle. Yet when all this wolde not serue nether wolde I eyther submytt my selfe or wryte ony thinge at all to him, then began he to swere vnto me by god, and by his faithe and by his baptisme then if I wolde confesse my selfe fawltye, he wolde demysse me so free, that I shulde never more here of yt nor never more be trobled for yt.[95]

Wisdom accepted this offer with considerable reluctance, but it was hardly a rigorous application of the law. Despite his subsequent reputation, in Henry's

---

[92] TCC MS R3.33 fo. 138ᵛ. Peter Moone described a similar policy: Moone, *Short treatise*, sig. A3ʳ⁻ᵛ.
[93] ECL MS 261 fos. 115ʳ–16ʳ; BL Harleian MS 425 fo. 5ʳ; Bonner Register fo. 45ᵛ.
[94] BL Royal MS 17.B.xxxv fo. 8ᵛ.   [95] ECL MS 261 fo. 92ᵛ.

reign at least Bonner was not a blood-soaked persecutor. Indeed, it was Bonner who managed to negotiate a recantation of sorts from Anne Askew when she was first arrested. He interviewed her at some length, describing himself as a surgeon whose aim was to heal the wound of heresy in her; we should not allow her scorn to sweep away the likelihood that he meant this. She refused to state her beliefs, but instead of continuing with proceedings under the Six Articles, Bonner produced a general statement of orthodoxy which he asked her to sign. Askew still wished to add an escape clause to this statement, straining the bishop's frayed patience to the limit. He may nevertheless have accepted her suggested modification, although there is a discrepancy between the statement as recorded in Bonner's register (placed there after Askew's eventual death) and her own account. In any case, Bonner bent the rules considerably for her.[96] As Thomas More had commented when Cuthbert Tunstall had taken similar pains to avoid burning Thomas Bilney in 1527, the law was 'so far stretched forth that the leather could scant hold'.[97]

The danger of courting martyrdom; the imperative to obey the divinely ordained temporal powers; questions about the validity of lies or of other forms of dissimulation or silence which fell short of outright deception; an attitude to oaths which played down their importance; a Lollard heritage which saw recantation and conformism as perfectly normal; and a regime which was usually willing to make compromises in order to extract some kind of retraction – all of these things conspired to make it difficult to hold a firm line against creeping Nicodemism, equivocation and willingness to recant. These dilemmas were not peculiar to England. Indeed, in the 1540s the controversy about 'Nicodemism' amongst Continental Protestants was at its fiercest, and the debate was visibly beginning to move towards the absolutist position espoused by Calvin. However, there is little evidence of that debate being heard within English circles, other than amongst the small and unrepresentative group of exiles. A pamphlet published in 1544 contained English translations of two short anti-Nicodemite tracts by Bullinger and Calvin, but there is no evidence that any copies of this book even reached England during Henry's reign; certainly it appears on none of the surviving lists of prohibited books. The term 'Nicodemite' itself was not in general use. I have found only one use of the word by an English evangelical in this period, and

---

[96] Askew, *The first examinacyon*, fos. 23^v–39^r; Bonner Register fo. 109^r. Cf. Crome's recantation in 1541, which apparently deviated some way from what was expected of him. His only punishment was to have his preaching licence withdrawn. The account, however, comes from Crome's admirer Richard Hilles, and should not be swallowed whole. *ET*, 140–3 (*OL*, 211–15).

[97] Greg Walker, 'Saint or schemer? The 1527 heresy trial of Thomas Bilney', *JEH* 40 (1989), 223.

he, again, was a correspondent of Bullinger's.[98] The English debate was not unrelated to that on the Continent, but it was largely isolated from it; and England's peculiar political situation combined with the Lollard past to give a quite different flavour to the arguments.

When these theoretical concerns were combined with the eloquent persuasions of the fire and the rack, it is hardly surprising that for evangelicals during these years recantation and conformism were the rule rather than the exception. It is not merely that the recanters significantly outnumbered the martyrs. They were also a much more exalted company. None of those executed for heresy in this period were religious leaders of any great significance, except for Robert Barnes, Thomas Garrett and William Jerome in 1540. They had in any case recanted, with an ambiguity typical of this period, shortly before their deaths, and Susan Wabuda is surely right to suggest that they would most likely have survived had Cromwell not pulled them down with him when he fell.[99] The recanters, however, included Becon, the most popular evangelical author of the period; a series of influential evangelical preachers, including Crome, Wisdom, Seton, Tolwin and John Willock; and Shaxton, a former bishop. Had these people been unwilling to recant as they did, the death toll would have been significantly higher, and the religious atmosphere of the close of the reign markedly different.

In the event, however, when dealing with the actual danger of prosecution, many even of the most outspoken reformers allowed ambiguities to creep in. Latimer, who had taken such a principled approach to these issues on Bainham's behalf in 1531, was himself hauled before the Privy Council in 1546, accused of encouraging Edward Crome's defiance. Under questioning, he refused to confirm or to deny this. An oath was administered to him, and he was sent to answer a list of written questions. However, he was soon back to protest, claiming

the proceding therin to be more extreme then shuld be ministred vnto him if he lyved vnder the Turke as he lyveth vndre the kinges Maieste, for that he sayd it was sore taunswere for an other Manes facte; and besides he sayed he doubted whither it were his hieghnes pleasyr that he shuld be thus called and examyned, desiring therfore to speake with his Maieste himself before he made further aunswere.

---

[98] Heinrich Bullinger and Jean Calvin, *Two Epystles . . . whether it be lawfull for a Chrysten man to communycate or be pertaker of the Masse of the Papystes* (RSTC 4079.5: Antwerp, 1544). In a 1541 letter to Bullinger, Richard Hilles described how in the summer of 1540, Crome had been warned by 'homine quodam Nicodemico' that his arrest was imminent: *ET*, 138. In 1540 Richard Taverner used the term 'Nicodemes' to describe those who accept the facts of Christianity but have no actual faith, which would seem to confirm that the other definition was not yet in common use. Richard Taverner, *The epistles and gospelles with a brief postil . . . from after Easter tyll Aduent, . . . the Somer parte* (RSTC 2968: 1540), fo. 2^r.

[99] Wabuda, 'Equivocation and recantation', 233.

Finally, under pressure, he did give a set of answers, but these left the Council 'as wise almost as we were before'. The Council sent him for further interrogation, 'to fishe out the botom of his stomak', but we do not know who eventually won this battle of wills. Others interrogated the same day were equally evasive. The Council noted with exasperation that William Huick, a royal physician, provided 'long writinges and smal Matier, and he trusteth vs so well that he desireth in his writeng that twoo or three of the gentlemen of the pryvey chamber maye declare his writenges to the Kinges Maieste.' John Lassells, the boldest of this group, nevertheless 'wil not aunswere ... without he have the kinges Maiestes expresse commandement with his protection, for he sayd It is neither wisdom nor equitie that he shuld kyll himself'. And the Scottish preacher John Willock capitulated completely:

He is more mete for dunbar then for London ffor neither hath he any maner of wit or learneng mete for a precher but is a veray ignorant. . . . To be rydd he wil saye nowe what you wil byd him.[100]

Another prominent figure in the 1546 troubles was Rowland Taylor, a trusted agent of Archbishop Cranmer's who was to be one of the first victims of the Marian persecution. In 1546, however, Shaxton persuaded him to make an abject recantation. He was, the Privy Council noted, 'very penitent'. Moreover, in his defence he alleged that he 'did neuer directly but by conclusions affirme any thing against the most blessed Sacrament of thaultre'. In other words, he had dissembled before his arrest as well as after it.[101]

Again and again we meet a low-key, pragmatic attitude to the issues of recantation and dissembling. A group arrested in Oxford in 1539 for breaking the Lenten fast did not justify their actions, even in correspondence to Thomas Cromwell, but begged forgiveness on the grounds of their physical infirmity. They pleaded that their case should not be judged by those 'as will streyne a gnat and devo[ur] a Camele' – a biblical reference which strongly implies that they were downplaying their guilt, not denying it.[102] Robert Wisdom was eventually persuaded to make his first submission, in 1541, by family and friends arguing that 'yowe are of a weake complexion and lacke strengthe to abyde the punishment of enprisment'.[103] After Latimer was forced from the bishopric of Worcester in 1539, his conservative successor, John Bell, ordered four of Latimer's licensed preachers to preach several sermons around the diocese affirming conservative doctrinal views. All apparently complied. Indeed, one, John Joseph, impressed Bell sufficiently that the bishop renewed his preaching licence; but while Joseph may have been

---

[100] PRO SP 1/218 fos. 110^r–12^v (*LP* XXI (i) 823).
[101] PRO SP 1/224 fo. 99^v (*LP* XXI (ii) 58).
[102] PRO SP 1/141 fo. 232^r (*LP* XIII (ii) Addenda 19); cf. Matthew 23:23–4.
[103] ECL MS 261 fo. 93^r.

convincing he was not sincere, if his later distinguished career as a reformer in London and Canterbury under Cranmer's patronage is any guide.[104] To conservatives, this kind of discretion could seem sinister. Gardiner commented sourly in 1541 that 'it is lerned for a precept that the brethern shuld not be to rashe but walke soberly as they terme it soo as to the brethern ther meanyng maye appere and to other the same may be excused'.[105] There is some truth in this, but real conspirators are usually less willing to betray one another. Askew's memorable steadfastness is less typical than the attitude of the Gloucestershire heretic Thomas Mores, who in 1541 said that he would rather spend twenty shillings than testify against his brethren, but who nevertheless did so; or the approach of Thomas Thompkyns, a London weaver, who had boasted that he would be 'contentyd to shed his blode' to defend the doctrines contained in his heretical books but who readily denounced his friend William Mychell before the Court of Aldermen.[106]

Indeed, even those reformers who deplored the culture of recantation which suffused English evangelicalism in these years were often willing to make pragmatic compromises with it. John Bale, George Joye, William Turner and Henry Brinklow – four of the most uncompromising radicals writing in these years – all practised one kind of dissimulation by writing under pseudonyms. Bale described the prevalence of recantation as a sign of the Devil's power, but when dealing with actual cases, he tended to present recanters as the victims rather than the offenders. Indeed, his *A dyclosyng or openynge of the Manne of synne* is a quasi-martyrological account of William Tolwin's 1541 recantation, in which Tolwin is pitied as a 'poore manne ... enforced ... to proclame him selfe an heretyque'.[107] Bale was also willing to defend Askew's repeated evasion of the questions put to her.[108] Likewise, Henry Brinklow sought to prove the cruelty of the bishops not by citing those they had burned, but those they had compelled to recant. Perhaps most strikingly, in his play *King Iohan*, Bale presented his hero King John's submission to the pope as being at the same time abject, calculated and (under the circumstances) praiseworthy. To the Cardinal, John says, 'Ser, in euery poynt I shall fulfyll yowr pleasur,' and to the papal agent Archbishop

---

[104] WCRO MS BA 2764/802 pp. 153–9, cited in Susan Wabuda, 'The provision of preaching during the early English Reformation: with special reference to itineration, c. 1530 to 1547' (PhD thesis, Cambridge, 1991), 113–14; Fines, *Biographical Register*.
[105] PRO SP 1/164 fo. 108^v (*LP* XVI 391).
[106] WCRO MS BA 2764/802 p. 109; CLRO Repertory 11 fo. 158^{r-v}.
[107] John Bale, *The Image of bothe churches after the moste wonderfull and heauenly Reuelacion of Sainct Iohn the Euangelist* (RSTC 1297: Antwerp?, 1548?), sig. Hh3^r; Bale, *Mysterye of inyquyte*, fo. 75^r; Bale, *A dysclosynge or openynge of the Manne of synne*, fo. 3^r; Bale, *Epistle exhortatorye*, fo. 15^r. Cf. Alec Ryrie, 'The unsteady beginnings of English Protestant martyrology', in *John Foxe: An Historical Perspective*, ed. David Loades (Aldershot, Hants., 1999).
[108] Askew, *The first examinacyon*, fos. 2^v–3^r, 12^v, 29^r, 32^r; *The lattre examinacyon*, fo. 17^r.

Langton, he adds, 'I am ryght sory that euer I yow offended.' He then explains this surrender to the audience in an aside:

> More of compassyon for shedyng of Christen blood
> Than anye thyng els, my crowne I gave vp lately
> To the pope of Rome, whych hath no tyttle good
> Of ivrysdycion, but vsurpacyon onlye.[109]

Whatever the principles might have been, when dealing with real cases pragmatic considerations could not be ignored. The culture of recantation was sufficiently strong that it was hard to maintain an unforgiving attitude to it, even long after the event. In 1554, Turner was still writing of Crome and Shaxton's recantations as if they were victims. And in the first edition of the *Actes and Monuments* in 1563, John Foxe felt compelled to take an indulgent view of those who recanted in Henry's reign. There were simply too many of them, and only the most spectacular recantations were airbrushed out of his account.

Yea in all kinges Henris times, how fewe were they that burned, which did not reuoke before? So did Bilney, Garret, Barnes, Ierom, Ather with diuers mo. Bishop Latimer who suffered in Quene Maris time, though he bare no faggot, yet he subscribed to theire articles . . . The like is to be said of M. Wisdome, D. Crome, Alexander Seton; Tolwing, Singleton with the rest which all recanted in kinge Henries time, and yet good soldiers after in the church of Christ.[110]

For Foxe, as also for Bale and the other exiled writers in Henry's reign, the culture of recantation was an embarrassment; but it was too dominant to be simply ignored.

This is not what it meant to those within it. Nor was it simple cowardice, although, as Andrew Pettegree has remarked, those who lacked the combination of unshakeable commitment and superhuman courage which made for a martyr do not deserve the moral condescension with which library-bound historians have often treated them.[111] Recantation in this period was not merely a process by which reformers submitted to the regime. As Bilney, Crome, Wisdom, Latimer and many others discovered, it involved an element of negotiation. The ambiguity of the regime's religious policies, and the doctrinal compromises it repeatedly made during this period, helped to foster a climate in which recantation was possible. The regime's compromises, reinforced by the evangelical ethic of obedience, called forth compromises from the reformers. Those compromises were in turn met by a regime which was often willing to accept submissions which were legally shaky or patently

---

[109] Bale, *King Iohan*, lines 1763, 1803, A87–90.
[110] Turner, *Huntyng of the romyshe vuolfe*, sig. E5ᵛ; *AM* (1563), 674.
[111] Pettegree, *Marian Protestantism*, 116–17.

false. In other words, the culture of recantation in 1540s English evangelicalism created a circle – vicious or virtuous, according to taste – which achieved that rare thing in the European Reformation: a lowering of the ideological temperature. It fostered, and was in turn fostered by, a climate in which compromise was possible. In the event, of course, this climate would be short-lived. In the reigns of Henry VIII's children, religious confrontation would become more feverish than ever, and the ambiguities which had made recantation possible would be stripped away. However, the brevity of this interlude does not mean that it is unimportant; merely that as well as exploring its causes and its dynamics, we must also consider how it came to an end.

PART II

The faces of reform

3

The exiles

How shall we synge the Lordes songe in a straunge lande? Psalm 137:4

Between 1539 and 1547, a handful of English evangelicals went into exile. These men and women formed part of what was already becoming an honourable tradition of exile within European Protestantism. For those reformers faced with the unenviable choice between recantation and death, exile was an acceptable third alternative. The study of exile movements has long held an equally honourable place in Reformation historiography. The importance of exile movements in supporting Protestant churches 'under the cross' in France and the Netherlands has become a historical commonplace. Moreover, this is one part of the drama of the European Reformation in which England is generally acknowledged to have played a leading role. England provided a home for Protestant refugees, from the days when Scottish reformers such as Alexander Alesius and George Wishart took refuge south of the border, through the shelter which Edward VI's regimes gave to Protestant grandees such as Martin Bucer and Bernardo Ochino, to the formal 'stranger churches' which became permanently established in London and elsewhere. Equally, English reformers were themselves forced into exile in large numbers under Queen Mary. The Marian exiles both formed the backbone of Protestant resistance to the Marian regime and had a lasting impact on English Protestantism. After their return, another exile movement played an equally important part in maintaining, and influencing the direction of, English Catholicism.[1] In the light of this historiographical tradition, it is perhaps unsurprising that the evangelical exiles of the last years of Henry VIII's reign have been portrayed as the keepers of the

---

[1] On the importance of exile generally, see Christina Hallowell Garrett, *The Marian Exiles: A Study in the Origins of Elizabethan Puritanism* (Cambridge, 1938); R. M. Kingdon, *Geneva and the Coming of the Wars of Religion in France, 1555–1563* (Geneva, 1956); Pettegree, *Foreign Protestant Communities*; Pettegree, *Marian Protestantism*; Ole Peter Grell, *Calvinist Exiles in Elizabethan and Stuart England* (Aldershot, Hants., 1996).

English Protestant flame. M. M. Knappen's still-powerful study of Tudor puritanism entitles its chapter on the early 1540s 'The second Henrician exile', as if nothing that happened within England itself in this period had any importance for the later development of the movement. Much more recently, Nicholas Tyacke has suggested that the 'underlying trajectory of evangelical activity' which he discerns in these years was maintained predominantly through the publication of reformist books on the Continent.[2] However, a closer examination of the late Henrician exiles and their work suggests that to concentrate so much attention on this group may be an error.

I have been able to trace thirty-three men and four women (all of whom were married to evangelical clergy) who spent some time abroad between 1539 and 1547 at least partly because of their faith. This includes four Scottish reformers who had earlier settled in England. Most of the exiles settled in Germany, Switzerland or the Netherlands, although the universities of Italy attracted some and George Marshall went as far afield as Danzig.[3] Counting religious exiles is not, of course, an exact science. Some who now appear as exiles may have gone abroad for more secular reasons. Christopher Hales, the nephew of the attorney-general, was certainly sympathetic to his Protestant hosts during his studies at Strassburg, but he may not have been an exile in the strict sense. John Philpot was in the unusual position of having his studies while in exile funded by the king himself.[4] And William Thomas seems to have fled more because he had stolen from his master than because of his religious views. Conversely, there were certainly many genuine exiles of whom we know nothing. In August 1546 John Dymocke, the English agent in Bremen (and himself a committed reformer), reported the arrival there of some sixty Englishmen, including Robert Wisdom; they had fled 'the grat persecucion which ys done by the byschopes'.[5] If it were not for Dymocke, we would know nothing about this group. It is reasonable to suppose that there were others we do not know about at all. Nevertheless, this episode also serves to remind us that some 'exiles' spent a comparatively short time abroad. William Peterson moved to Zurich in 1536, but had returned home by 1541 after his business enterprises failed. An evangelical servant of Richard Hilles also returned from Strassburg in 1541, finding poverty, homesickness and the rigours of Reformed worship too much for him.[6]

Alongside the exiles, there were substantial English expatriate communities across northern Europe, and these communities, uniquely exposed to

---

[2] 'Introduction', in *Long Reformation*, ed. Tyacke, 6, 8.
[3] See Appendix I.   [4] Bodleian Library, MS Jones 3 fo. 6^v.
[5] PRO SP 1/223 fo. 152^r (*LP* XXI (i) 1491).   [6] See Appendix I.

Continental Protestantism, no doubt harboured merchants who had reason to be grateful that their profession made exile an unnecessary choice. It would, however, be wrong to see these groups, vulnerable as they were to the unpredictable winds of diplomacy, as nests of radicalism. The only definite connection that can be established between the expatriate communities as such and evangelical activity hardly indicates a firm commitment. In 1540, in the wake of Robert Barnes' execution, copies of his protestation from the stake found their way to Germany. George Everat, an English agent in Danzig, heard a rumour that several of the English community in Hamburg were planning to have a Latin version of this document printed. On investigating, he learned that the project had collapsed because some of the Englishmen involved 'wolde not ha[ve] ther namys in & so the reste lefte of like wisse'. The book was eventually printed at Lübeck. Some of the expatriates were clearly sympathetic to the Lutherans amongst whom they lived, but not to the point of risking the wrath of the English authorities.[7] Indeed, some evangelical exiles saw English expatriates as a source of danger rather than of support. George Joye believed that one governor of the merchant-venturers in Antwerp was an informant for Bishop Gardiner, and John Bale alleged that the bishops regularly used English merchants as sources of information about the exiles. Such merchants certainly seem to have had a ready supply of doctrinally conservative English books for sale.[8]

The group of English evangelicals which we can meaningfully refer to as the exiles, therefore, was numerically very small. It is in keeping with the low level of persecution in late Henrician England that there were as few reformist exiles as reformist martyrs. The Protestant exiles of Mary Tudor's reign were not only far more numerous, but far more organised. There is no hint that the formal exile congregations of the 1550s had any parallel a decade earlier. Apart from a loose group in Strassburg, few of the 1540s exiles seem to have been in regular contact with one another.

Spending time abroad had its compensations. William Turner's travels around the universities of Italy, Switzerland and Germany were apparently thoroughly stimulating, although his wife may not have agreed.[9] However, for most, exile was far from romantic. It meant poverty, insecurity and isolation. In 1542, John Bale, admittedly the most lugubrious of the exiles, wrote that

---

[7] PRO SP 1/163 fo. 52^r (*LP* XVI 105); Ryrie, 'Unsteady beginnings', 59–60.
[8] George Joye, *George Ioye confuteth, Winchesters false Articles* (RSTC 14826: Antwerp, 1543), fo. 22^{r-v}; Askew, *The first examinacyon*, fo. 43^r.
[9] Whitney R. D. Jones, *William Turner: Tudor Naturalist, Physician and Divine* (1988), 13–17; Turner, *Rescuynge of the romishe fox*, sig. K5^v.

I haue exyled my selfe for euer from myne own natiue contrye, kyndred, fryndes, acquayntaunce (which are the great delyghtes of this lyfe) and am well contented for Iesus Christes sake & for the comforte of my brethren there, to suffre pouerte, penurye, abieccion, reprofe, and all that shall come besydes.[10]

Likewise, George Joye lamented that he was forced 'to wander and trauell in a strange contrye, the more is my heuines and sorowe and payne especially in my syknes & olde age'. He was particularly aggrieved that in fleeing Cambridge he had been forced to abandon his fellowship at Peterhouse.[11] These humdrum miseries accounted for most of the exiles' sufferings, but they were not free from actual danger. One exile, the Yorkshire friar Dennis Tod, was executed: arrested by the French at Neuchâtel, he was handed over to the English at Calais and burned.[12] Thomas Rose also spent a month in a French prison, at Dieppe, although he was released along with a number of other English prisoners of war.[13] Nor were English exiles in the Netherlands safe. No one suffered Tyndale's fate in this period, but there were intermittent attempts by the English regime to restrain the exiles' activities. The Anglo-Imperial treaty of 1543 laid down that the emperor should prohibit any printing in English within his realms. In the spring of 1546, Joye was vexed by 'trouble and vnquietnes . . . sustained in flying & fliting from place to place' after such a clampdown on printing. Joye attributed this, like most of the ills of the world, to Stephen Gardiner, who had indeed lamented that 'a knave lurkyng in a corner, as Joye doth at Antwerpe, shalbe nurrished to trouble the realme'.[14]

These, then, were the exiles: few in number, poor, isolated and in danger. A mere head count is admittedly misleading, for amongst the exiles were individuals whose presence on the religious battlefield was worth thousands: Miles Coverdale, John Bale, William Turner, George Joye, John Hooper, John Philpot. However, this roll-call is less impressive than it appears. The fame which these men subsequently acquired was built on very particular foundations. Coverdale and Joye's renown springs largely from the supporting (or, in Joye's case, opposing) roles they played to Tyndale in the production of the English Bible. The others are joined by Coverdale in being famous for their exploits under Edward VI and subsequently. In the new reign many of the Henrician exiles found themselves at the heart of the establishment. Coverdale and Hooper were given English bishoprics, Bale an Irish one;

---

[10] Bale, *Image of bothe churches*, sig. B2^v.
[11] Joye, *Refutation of the byshop of Winchesters derke declaration*, fo. 31^v; Joye, *Present consolation*, sigs. A6^v–7^r.
[12] PRO SP 1/171 fos. 53^r–5^r (*LP* XVII 427); Fines, *Biographical Register*.
[13] *AM*, 2083.
[14] PRO SP 1/176 fo. 17^{r-v} (*LP* XVIII (i) 144.5); Joye, *Refutation of the byshop of Winchesters derke declaration*, sig. A2^v; Gardiner, *Letters*, 159–60.

Turner became dean of Wells and Philpot archdeacon of Winchester. Edmund Allen became a chaplain to Princess Elizabeth, who was later to appoint him bishop of Rochester. Christopher Hales helped to negotiate the flight of leading Continental Protestants to England after the Schmalkaldic War. Perhaps more importantly, these men were to become the heroes of Foxe's *Actes and Monuments*, the lens through which most subsequent ages have viewed the English Reformation. Rose, Philpot, Hooper and John Rogers were all high-profile victims of the Marian persecution, and all featured prominently in Foxe's work; and Bale was Foxe's mentor and one of his most important sources. These men were the winners, and they quite literally wrote the history books.

Even Foxe, however, had little to say about the late Henrician exile as such. The exiles' fame as exiles is based largely on their publications, which are the focus of studies such as Knappen's. Their numerous printed treatises and polemics produced in the last years of Henry's reign have a striking stylistic and doctrinal unity. Their tone is as ferocious and intemperate as we expect from religious controversialists in the Reformation period, characterised by (in C. S. Lewis' phrase) 'indisciplined armies of adjectives'. They rarely stop at calling their opponents knaves when they can describe them as 'lecherous locustes leapinge out of the smoke of the pytt bottomlesse'.[15] As we have seen, these writers were readier than almost any of their contemporaries to be sceptical about Henry VIII's reformism, to defy his authority and to scorn compromise and dissimulation. Doctrinally, almost all of them inclined towards the 'Reformed' brand of Protestantism which was coalescing in Switzerland and south-western Germany. Except for a few around Heinrich Bullinger, few of them saw the division between Lutheran and Reformed as unbridgeable. Bale, for example, translated Justus Jonas' account of Luther's death for publication in 1546, and Joye described Luther, Zwingli and the Reformed theologian Œcolampadius together as the chief enemies of Antichrist.[16] Nevertheless, their loyalties are clear. Bale emphasised that he respected Philip Melanchthon, but that Œcolampadius and Zwingli 'were auncyent men whan Melanchton was but a chylde, & were promoters of the Lordes veryte whan he knewe nothynge of yt'. With an irony rare among these writers, Turner described himself as 'a zuinglian heretik'. In 1543 Joye translated Zwingli's 1530 statement of faith, describing his subject as 'the good heerdman, that lett his lyfe for his sheep'.[17] Respect for

---

[15] C. S. Lewis, *English Literature in the Sixteenth Century Excluding Drama* (Oxford, 1954), 196; Bale, *Image of bothe churches*, sig. B2r.
[16] Joye, *Daniel*, fo. 229r.
[17] Bale, *Mysterye of inyquyte*, fo. 24v; Turner, *Huntyng and fyndyng out of the Romishe fox*, sig. C1v; Huldrych Zwingli, *The Rekening and declaracion of the faith and beleif of Huldrik Zwingly, bisshoppe of Zijryk*, tr. John Bale (RSTC 26138: Antwerp, 1543), sig. A1v.

the Reformed theologians' ablest English interpreter, John Frith, was also widespread.[18] The exiles' embryonic Reformed identity, however, was rooted less in allegiances to particular theologians than in their doctrinal priorities: the eradication of all vestiges of Roman ceremonial, ferocious attacks on idolatry and, above all, the rejection of the Mass and of any Eucharistic doctrine which involved Christ's objective presence in the elements. 'If anye thynge vndre the heauens hath nede of reformacyon', Bale wrote, it was the Mass.[19] This was, of course, much the same spirit in which the Edwardian Reformation would be conducted, and in which many wished to pursue further reform under Elizabeth. These books, then, are not merely numerous and eye-catching. They lend their authors an air of being the forefathers of mature English Protestantism.

The exiles' publications are an invaluable source for any history of evangelicalism in this period. Printed books are amongst the primary sources which are the most conspicuous and also, thanks to the spread of microfilm, the most accessible to historians. Nevertheless, we should be aware of the distorting effect which the survival of printed books over time can give. In the 1540s, they stood alongside manuscript books, sermons, the liturgy, private letters and, most importantly of all, private conversations as influences on religious thought and behaviour. However, time does not muffle these different forms of communication even-handedly. Precious scraps of conversation have been preserved, in accounts of varying degrees of unreliability. Written versions of a few sermons survive, as do a scattering of letters. The survival rate of printed books, by contrast, is very high indeed. Probably a majority of all such imprints survive, with the sample usefully weighted towards those which were more substantial, more popular and more widely circulated. This skewed pattern of sources can skew our view of events. We can only use the sources we have, but it is easy to give printed books a disproportionate importance. This matters for any consideration of the exiles, for just as we have far better access to early printed books than to any other form of communication used in the sixteenth century, so did they. Their physical absence meant that it was only through the printed word, and occasional personal letters, that they were able to communicate with their co-religionists in England. In the sixteenth century, exile did not simply mean physical relocation; it meant isolation and exclusion, separation from those primitive networks of communication that existed. Evangelical books printed within England are the tip of a huge iceberg of ephemeral religious communication which is lost to us. Beneath the evangelical books

---

[18] Bale, *Mysterye of inyquyte*, fo. 31^v; Turner, *Huntyng and fyndyng out of the Romishe fox*, sigs. C1^{r-v}.
[19] Bale, *Epistle exhortatorye*, fo. 20^v.

printed abroad, however, there is almost nothing. Print was the exiles' only significant means of interacting with events at home.

While we have the exiles' own writings, we have very little to indicate how they kept themselves informed of events in England. What hints we do have suggest that this was a serious problem for them. Gardiner seems to have believed that the exiles had networks of informants. In an attack on Joye, he wrote that 'for the mutual intelligence, in the fraternite, ye can not in your absence, but knowe, how publique thynges go'.[20] In reality, however, while the exiles were familiar enough with 'publique thynges', especially politics and diplomacy, they were often strikingly ill-informed about the broader picture in England. A notorious example of this is John Hooper's account of the recent news from England in his letter to Bullinger of January 1546, written from Strassburg. Much of this is a fair account of the state of diplomacy between England, France and the empire; much of the rest is so plainly hyperbole that it would be perverse to criticise its inaccuracy. He also, however, gives a well-known list of six royal counsellors who 'truly favoured the Gospel' and who had died over the previous two years. It is an impressive list, headed by two privy councillors: Lord Chancellor Audley and Charles Brandon, the duke of Suffolk. Yet there is rather less to it than meets the eye. Audley did incline somewhat towards reform, but after Cromwell's fall his efforts on behalf of the evangelical cause were slender in the extreme. Brandon, too, may have acquired a degree of sympathy with reformist views under the influence of his fourth wife, Katherine Willoughby; but his biographer is inclined to think that Hooper was simply wrong.[21] Next on Hooper's list is Sir Edward Bainton, vice-chamberlain to the queen and a former client of Anne Boleyn's. Bainton had a reputation as a reformer, but his favouring of the Gospel in the 1540s is restricted to breaking Lent in 1543, for which he may in any case have had a licence.[22] Hooper also named Sir Thomas Poynings, the king's deputy in Boulogne; but Hooper's word is our only evidence for Poynings' supposed reformism, and if Hooper was right, it would have made Poynings' membership of a commission against heretics in Calais in 1543 somewhat ticklish.[23] Only the last two on Hooper's list, Thomas Wyatt and William Butts, were active supporters of reformism in the 1540s, and although Hooper claimed all these had died in the past two years, Wyatt had been dead for more than three by the time he wrote.[24] This was not a list which someone familiar with the English situation would have

---

[20] Gardiner, *A declaration of such true articles as George Ioye hath gone about to confute*, fo. 96ᵛ.
[21] Steven Gunn, *Charles Brandon, Duke of Suffolk c. 1484–1545* (Oxford, 1988), 199. On Audley, see above, pp. 30–40, and below, p. 160.
[22] HPT; *APC*, 114–15.   [23] PRO SP 1/177 fo. 64ʳ (*LP* XVIII (i) 420).
[24] *ET*, 23; cf. *OL*, 36–7, where the six are wrongly described as privy councillors.

composed. This is not only because of the dubious qualifications of most of those on it; nor because some prominent and committed evangelicals who had died recently, such as Sir George Carew, were omitted.[25] The oddity is that he should draw up such a list at all. At the same time as Hooper claimed that 'those in England who most favour the Gospel are dying by the hour', the careers of Edward Seymour, John Dudley, William Parr, William Paget and other reformist sympathisers were in the ascendant. Parliament had just thrown out a bill against heretical books; Archbishop Cranmer was optimistic that a further tranche of traditional ceremonies might be abolished; the queen was allowing her household to become a centre for reformers. Yet Hooper showed no awareness of any of this. Instead, he reeled off a list of names familiar from the 1530s, the last time he had spent any time in England. He may have had access to some of the basic facts, but his hyperbole cannot conceal the fact that his whole view of the English situation was badly out of date.

Hooper, of course, was a young man with limited contacts. However, all the exiles had trouble keeping properly informed about events at home. Occasionally, there are signs that they had functioning lines of communication with England. Richard Hilles was a friend of Walter Bucler, the English ambassador to the Schmalkaldic League in 1545. When Bucler visited Strassburg, he stayed with Hilles and surely brought him up to date with events in England.[26] Likewise, when Bale's wife Dorothy visited England briefly in 1545, she was presumably able to bring some news back to her husband. Most remarkably, Bale somehow managed to come by Anne Askew's accounts of her interrogations. How Askew managed to write these and smuggle them out is a mystery. Bale simply says that 'out of the prison she wrote vnto a secrete frynde of hers'.[27] Nor do we know how they came to make their way to Bale. All we can say with certainty is that Bale did not fabricate them, since Askew's terse style is so strikingly different from (indeed, superior to) Bale's vitriolic expostulations. In the first volume of the *Examinacyons*, Bale claimed to be working from Askew's holograph originals. In the second, he claimed to have received the text 'in coppye, by certen duche merchauntes commynge from thens'. John King has suggested that the manuscript was sent to Bale by Mary, duchess of Richmond, who was later a patron of Bale's. This is perhaps less implausible than any of the other

---

[25] As Captain of the Rysbank in Calais, Carew was singled out as one who favoured 'all such as love the word of God'. In 1540, he was arrested for protecting heretics and for breaking Lent. His military prowess restored him to favour, but also won him the command of the *Mary Rose*. He went down with the ship on 19 July 1545. Byrne, *Lisle Letters*, vol. V, 352, 489, vol. VI, 105; *LP* XIV (ii) 397; HPT.

[26] Patricia Cole Swensen, 'Noble hunters of the Romish fox: religious reform at the Tudor court, 1543–1564' (PhD thesis, University of California at Berkeley, 1981), 202–7.

[27] Askew, *The lattre examinacyon*, fo. 11^r.

possibilities.²⁸ This impressive *coup* apart, however, Bale struggled to piece together a picture of events in England, based apparently on evidence much more skewed and fragmentary than that which has survived for modern historians to use. High political events were common knowledge, and Bale could sometimes find some mileage in these. His gibe that the English bishops' role in the French war was one of 'bakynge, bruynge, broylynge, gryndynge, seasonynge, saltynge, sowsynge and sethyng' is a clear reference to Gardiner's work in military logistics.²⁹ Bale's only explicit acknowledgement of his sources, however, came in his 1543 tract *A dysclosynge or openynge of the Manne of synne*. He claimed that German merchants brought him a supply of printed books produced by English conservatives – books which they gave him 'with no small laughter'. This conduit seems to have been effective, since Bale knew of a wide range of conservative imprints, including some which no longer survive. John Huntingdon's *Genealogy of heresy*, although it went through two editions, is known to us only through Bale. Bale is also the only source which tells us that Bishop Bonner's advertisements urging restraint in the use of the English Bible were printed.³⁰ In addition, he received William Peryn's sermons on the Mass, John Standish's refutation of Barnes' *Protestacion*, at least some of the ballads exchanged in 1540 between William Gray and Thomas Smith, and Alexander Seton and William Tolwin's recantation.³¹

Although there were other conservative publications which Bale's merchants do not seem to have brought for him,³² he managed a good haul. However, these polemics formed the better part of all of Bale's information about events at home. They determined the structure of his output over this period; for he wrote refutations of most of the conservative pieces he received.³³ Moreover, he laid far more significance on these conservative

---

²⁸ Askew, *The first examinacyon*, fo. 5ʳ; *The lattre examinacyon*, fo. 11ʳ; John N. King, *English Reformation Literature: The Tudor Origins of the Protestant Tradition* (Princeton, 1982), 71–3; Brigden, 'Henry Howard', 522. Leslie Fairfield has suggested that Bale did make some amendments to Askew's text: Fairfield, 'John Bale and Protestant hagiography in England', *JEH* 24 (1973), 158–9.
²⁹ Bale, *Epistle exhortatorye*, fo. 25ᵛ.
³⁰ Bale, *A dysclosynge or openynge of the Manne of synne*, fo. 97ᵛ. 'The .ii. draffyshe Declaracyons of my lorde Boner' are apparently the notices recorded in the Bonner Register fos. 26ᵛ–7ʳ; see also below, pp. 220–21.
³¹ Bale, *A dysclosynge or openynge of the Manne of synne*, fo. 87ᵛ; Askew, *The lattre examinacyon*, fo. 60ᵛ; John Bale, *Scriptorum illustrium maioris Brytanniae, quam nunc Angliam & Scotiam uocant: Catalogus*, 2 vols. (Basle, 1557, 1559), vol. I, 704. On Gray and Smith, see below, pp. 113–14.
³² For example, William Chedsay and C. Scott, *Two notable sermones lately preached at Pauls crosse. Anno 1544* (RSTC 5106.5: 1545); Richard Smith, *A defence of the blessed masse, and the sacrifice therof* (RSTC 22820: 1546); Richard Smith, *Assertion and defence*.
³³ Bale, *A dysclosynge or openynge of the Manne of synne*; Bale, *Mysterye of inyquyte*; and see Appendix II. His reply to Peryn was presumably never finished: Askew, *The lattre examinacyon*, fo. 60ᵛ.

tracts than they could bear. John Huntingdon and John Standish, the authors of two of these pieces, were fairly lowly foot-soldiers in the conservative army. Other than writing the *Genealogy* – whose quality is questionable even by the standards of early modern polemical balladry – Huntingdon's main contribution to the conservative cause was to be one of the witnesses against Alexander Seton in 1541. He held no exalted office, he does not seem to have had a patron, and there is no evidence for his being given a benefice at all in the years after Cromwell's fall. After his conversion to reforming ideas in 1543–5, he became respected in evangelical circles, but the height of his career was appointment as a canon of Exeter in Elizabeth's reign.[34] Standish was more prominent: an Oxford theologian and a prebendary of Whittington College in London, who was given a London living by Bonner in 1543. In 1545, he stood for the vice-chancellorship in Cambridge, although he perhaps regretted it after securing only eight votes against Matthew Parker's seventy-nine.[35] Neither man, however, deserves to be named, as Bale repeatedly did, as being amongst the chief lieutenants of the conservative bishops.[36] It is hard to see how Bale could have come by this impression unless printed material were almost his only source of fresh information.

The others whom Bale labelled as major persecutors are equally ill-suited to the role. William Wattes was an aggressively conservative former friar who, in the autumn of 1539, had engaged in a high-profile pulpit war with Barnes which ended in his arrest. In other words, Wattes was prominent around the time Bale went into exile. After 1540 there is no trace of any further activity from him, but in 1544 Bale was still denouncing him as one of England's leading conservatives.[37] Like Hooper, he was forced by his isolation repeatedly to recycle personal knowledge which was becoming steadily more out of date. We know nothing at all about five of those whom he named as leading opponents of evangelicals, except what Bale himself tells us: that they were 'blind Popish poetes and dirty metristes', in other words, that Bale's view of them was derived only from printed ephemera.[38] Other

---

[34] Bale, *Mysterye of inyquyte*; AM, 1205; Askew, *The first examinacyon*, fo. 12ᵛ; Gina Alexander, 'The life and career of Edmund Bonner, bishop of London, until his deprivation in 1549' (PhD thesis, London, 1960); PRO E 334/2, 3; Fines, *Biographical Register*.
[35] Standish, *Lytle treatise against the protestacion of Robert Barnes*, sig. A1ʳ; Alexander, 'Life and career of Edmund Bonner', 357, 359, 370; Matthew Parker, *Correspondence of Matthew Parker, D.D., Archbishop of Canterbury*, ed. John Bruce (Cambridge: Parker Society, 1853), 18; Brinklow, *Lamentacion of a Christian*, sig. C5ᵛ.
[36] Bale, *A dysclosynge or openynge of the Manne of synne*, fo. 12ᵛ; Bale, *Mysterye of inyquyte*, fo. 9ʳ.
[37] PRO SP 1/155 fos. 189ʳ⁻ᵛ, 196ʳ (*LP* XIV (ii) 750); BL Cotton MS Titus B.i fo. 477ʳ (*LP* XV 438); Bale, *Mysterye of inyquyte*, fos. 9ʳ, 16ᵛ; Bale, *Epistle exhortatorye*, fo. 14ʳ; Elton, *Policy and Police*, 102.
[38] The five were Richard Dallison, William Stawne, Steven Prowet, Friar Adrian and Quarrye the pardoner. Quarrye earned three mentions from Bale. *Image of bothe churches*, sig. h1ᵛ; *Mysterye of inyquyte*, fos. 9ʳ, 16ᵛ.

prominent conservatives such as Henry Cole, John London and Richard Smith were passed over entirely. Bale did succeed in naming one cleric who could with justice be labelled a leading hardliner, Nicholas Wilson, although he is only mentioned once. His list of persecuting bishops bears a closer resemblance to reality, although in 1544 he seemed unaware that Richard Sampson had been translated from Chichester to Coventry and Lichfield more than a year previously.[39]

Bale's case is worth dwelling on, since his output was much greater than that of any other exiled author and since his works contain more explicit references to events and people in England. None of the other exiles seem to have been significantly better informed. Coverdale's works were mostly translations of Continental Protestant texts, apart from a refutation of Standish's attack on Barnes. Joye, too, produced several translations. After long years in exile, both men found that their intellectual centre of gravity was on the Continent. Likewise, William Turner, a less prolific but perhaps more influential writer, was hardly up to date on his English news. He apparently did not hear about the 1543 Act for the Advancement of True Religion until nearly four months after the end of the parliamentary session in which it had been passed.[40] All of these books may be scoured in vain for any reliable information about events in England other than those incidents which are well known from, and better documented in, other sources. The isolation of which the exiles spoke was not metaphorical.

More important than the question of how much they knew about events in England, however, is that of how far they were able to influence those events through their books. Their output is impressive: we know of some fifty-eight editions of English-language evangelical works printed abroad between 1540 and the king's death, including four reprints of works which first appeared before 1540.[41] For all their isolation, the printing press gave the exiles a voice. However, while printing was one of the most effective means of communication in this period, it was also the least precise. It was not only a monologue, but a monologue broadcast by a speaker with only the vaguest idea of who his audience might be and how it might react. The

---

[39] Bale, *Epistle exhortatorye*, fo. 14^r, where he lists the bishop of Chichester but not that of Coventry and Lichfield. It is possible that he meant to refer to the new bishop of Chichester, George Day; in that case, however, his omission of Sampson, widely viewed as a conservative leader, is even more remarkable. Sampson was translated to Coventry and Lichfield in March 1543; Bale's book is dated August 1544.
[40] The Act was debated in the House of Lords on 8 and 10 May; Parliament was prorogued on 12 May. After he had finished his *Huntyng and fyndyng out of the Romishe fox*, Turner heard about the Act and added a brief postscript attacking it. The book was printed on 14 September. *LJ*, 230, 232; Turner, *Huntyng and fyndyng out of the Romishe fox*, sig. F4^v.
[41] RSTC, and see Appendix II. This total also includes two lost pieces by Coverdale: a translation of the Danish Church's baptismal and Eucharistic liturgies, and his *Fruitfull lessons, vpon the passion*, known from a later edition to have been printed in 1540.

number of imprints which the exiles flung at England is less important than the question of whether this material was actually being read.

Evidence on this point is hard to come by, but there are enough fragments to allow a partial picture to be built up. The most important document is a long list of prohibited books which were burned at Paul's Cross in London in July 1546.[42] Of thirty-nine evangelical titles which were apparently printed abroad between 1540 and 1545, and which might therefore be expected to have found their way into England, only seventeen appear on this list. Bale does better than most. All his surviving works are represented except for the *Christen exhortacion to customable swearers*, although there is also no mention of his three lost works.[43] Indeed, two of his works – the *Epistle exhortatorye of an Englyshe Christiane* and *A dysclosynge or openynge of the Manne of synne* – are two of only four books to be mentioned twice on this list, although this should not be taken to mean that they were the only ones of which more than one copy was captured. Coverdale's canon is slightly less well represented, with only six of the nine pieces he had published by 1545 being on this list. Joye's showing was miserly, with only three works of his nine. William Turner wrote only two polemics during his exile; his *Huntyng and fyndyng out of the Romishe fox* was burned, but his sequel, *The rescuynge of the romishe fox*, does not appear. To put this patchy showing in perspective, Thomas Becon, the most prolific of the evangelical authors who remained in England, produced twelve works in this period, including two which are now lost and one which he retitled when it was reprinted. Despite the fact that all imprints of these works were more than three years old, all twelve appear on this list, including both editions of the one whose title he had changed. Domestically produced books which could be printed, distributed and sold legally would be available in greater numbers, with greater ease and at significantly lower prices than those smuggled in from abroad. When competing for a share of the English market, the exiled authors had the odds stacked against them.

No other surviving list approaches this one for comprehensiveness. In 1542, however, Edmund Bonner, the bishop of London, circulated a list of prohibited books to his clergy. This is shorter than the 1546 list – thirty-eight books as against eighty-nine – but for our purposes it is almost as striking. Not a single one of the exiles' books printed between 1539 and 1541 can be found in Bonner's 1542 list, even though at least five exile works printed during that period were to be present on the 1546 list. Most of the books on the 1542 list dated from the 'first exile', in the late 1520s and early 1530s.

---

[42] Bonner Register fo. 92^{r-v}. This list was edited and reorganised by Foxe, and placed in the first edition of the *Actes and Monuments* as a list of books prohibited at various times in Henry's reign. *AM* (1563), 573–4.

[43] See Appendix II.

Perhaps Bonner had used an older list, but if so he had updated it: at the least, the last named item on it, 'A lytell Treatyse in frenche of the supper of the Lorde made by Calvyne', was certainly more recent. And it would have been thoroughly peculiar for Bonner to have added Calvin while ignoring an influx of new English-language imprints.[44] The most plausible explanation is simply that, up to 1542, exile literature had not been arriving in London in large enough quantities to catch the bishop's attention. Around 1541 Bale wrote of one of his books, 'I knowe there wyll be great thonderinges, lyghtnynges, and earth quakes at the coming forth therof'. The reality, however, was that his labours were having no discernible effect on the climate at all.[45]

Several other fragments of evidence point us in the same direction. In 1541 an evangelical conventicle in Salisbury was broken up and its library seized. No list survives, but it is clear that this group had access to a wide range of books. The evidence which Bishop Salcot uncovered included the disturbing report that this group supported a travelling dealer in evangelical books, a man who was based in London but travelled widely across the country. Yet the book of theirs which Salcot singled out as particularly offensive was Richard Taverner's carefully edited translation of the Augsburg Confession. This was a text which had been commissioned by Cromwell and published with the approval of the regime. The political landscape had since changed, of course, but compared to most of the exile publications this was tame. Bale, indeed, lambasted this edition as a shameful departure from the sense of the original.[46] If this was the most damaging book which Salcot could come up with, it seems unlikely that the Salisbury heretics owned any of the exiles' works. Likewise, when William Tolwin was made to recant in December 1541, the heretical volumes in his extensive and esoteric library were listed in the printed recantation. The seventeen printed books ranged from Frith and Luther to Lollard authors and the Anabaptist Balthasar Hubmeir. Some were recent: Lancelot Ridley's commentary on Ephesians, Richard Taverner's postils on the liturgical epistles and gospels, and John Gough's edition of the prologue to the Wycliffite Bible were all published in 1540. But again, none of the recent exile publications were found.[47]

Coverdale's translation of Bullinger's treatise on matrimony, *Der Christlich Eestand*, printed in 1541, must have been noticed in England,

---

[44] Bonner Register fo. 40^v.
[45] Bale, *Image of bothe churches*, sig. B1^v; Katharine R. Firth, *The Apocalyptic Tradition in Reformation Britain 1530–1645* (Oxford, 1979), 39.
[46] PRO STAC 2/34/38 fo. 8^r; Richard Taverner (tr.), *The confessyon of the fayth of the Germaynes. To which is added the apologie of Melancthon* (RSTC 908: 1536), fo. 2^r; Bale, *A dysclosynge or openynge of the Manne of synne*, fo. 7^r.
[47] Seton and Tolwin, *Declaracion made at Poules Crosse*, sig. B3^v; Bale, *A dysclosynge or openynge of the Manne of synne*, fos. 47^r–55^v.

for Thomas Becon plagiarised it the following year. Another translation produced by exiles, of Charles V's reply to Paul III's convocation of a general council, was likewise republished in England, although shorn of its polemical introduction.[48] These republications are the earliest evidence of any of the exiles' works being read in England, and until we reach 1544 they are the only such evidence.[49] Before 1544, any attempt by exiled writers to provoke a response to their books failed. Even when they were joining in an ongoing controversy they seem to have been ignored. By that year, however, the domestic evangelical press in England had been silenced, allowing the exiles to be heard more easily. The book which finally succeeded in attracting some attention was Turner's 1543 *The huntyng and fyndyng out of the Romishe fox*. This donnish, somewhat pedantic and atrociously printed volume was an unlikely bestseller, but Turner had hit on a powerful formula for tackling the perennial problem of how to deal with the king. Henry VIII had, he argued, done 'as myche as one man is able to do' to drive the pope from England. However, the agents whom he had trusted to do this – the bishops – had traitorously concealed and defended the Romish fox instead. Turner was thus able simultaneously to defend the king's authority and attack the bishops who exercised it.[50] While hardly plausible, this was at least coherent. Bale adopted the approach wholesale. When he published his *A dysclosynge or openynge of the Manne of synne* a few months later, he surtitled it *Yet a course at the romyshe foxe*, in a deliberate bow to Turner, and in his *Epistle exhortatorye* of 1544, he both praised Turner's book directly and modelled his title page on Turner's.[51] Far more importantly, however, Turner's book managed to rouse Gardiner himself to pen a reply, *The examination of the hunter*, printed in the summer of 1544.[52]

From then on signs begin to gather that the exiles' books were being read. William Palmer later wrote that it was in 1544–5 that significant numbers of exile publications began to reach England.[53] In 1545 Gardiner involved himself in the debate again, replying to an attack by Joye called (with characteristic subtlety) *George Joye confuteth Winchesters false articles*. In

---

[48] Charles V, *The answere of Carolus the fyfte . . . vnto the letters conuocatorye of Paule the thyrd Bysshope of Rome concerninge A Generall Concell to be celebrated at Trident* (RSTC 5014: Antwerp, 1543), esp. sig. A2^{r-v}; Charles V, *The answer of Charles the fyft . . . vnto the letters conuocatorye of Paule the thyrde bishop of Rome, concernyng a generall councell to be held at Trident* (RSTC 5015: 1543).

[49] However, William Palmer's narrative of Henry's reign mentioned Coverdale's 1541 defence of Robert Barnes: he may have known of it nearer the time of publication. TCC MS R3.33 fo. 126^v.

[50] Turner, *Huntyng and fyndyng out of the Romishe fox*, sigs. A2^r–6^v.

[51] Bale, *Epistle exhortatorye*, fos. 1^r, 7^r.

[52] Datable from Bale, *Epistle exhortatorye*, fo. 29^r.   [53] TCC MS R3.33 fo. 147^r.

January 1545, an artisan conventicle in London was broken up. Its members owned a book of Frith's, but also Joye's 1544 *A present consolacion for the sufferers of persecucion* and 'lorde cobhams boke' – most likely Bale's 1544 hagiography of the Lollard rebel Sir John Oldcastle.[54] Bale even acquired some notoriety. His massive commentary on the book of Revelation, *The image of bothe churches*, was clearly circulating in London evangelical circles by 1546, when the conservative William Peryn deplored the fondness of 'busy readers' for it.[55] In the same year, Gardiner described Bale, Joye and Turner as a new trinity of sacramentaries who had sprung up to replace Frith, Œcolampadius and Zwingli.[56] On 7 May 1546, the Privy Council instructed the mayor of London to examine two men 'touching certaine heretike bokes of Bales making lately broughte in a hoye of Flaunders'. Two or three months later, John Geffyre, a Welshman and a former servant to the old earl of Arundel, was accused of owning, and prophesying from, one of Bale's books – probably, again, *The image of bothe churches*. The evidence which the Privy Council examined during the heresy scare of the spring of 1546 convinced them that 'a greate number' of imported heretical books were circulating.[57]

The exiles responded to this increase in interest by redoubling their efforts. After 1543–4 their output of polemic increased significantly. Fourteen exile imprints can be dated with some confidence to the period 1539–42, as against thirty-two for 1543–7. Moreover, after 1544, occasional exile works began to be reprinted. The second edition of Turner's *The huntyng and fyndyng out of the Romishe fox* is probably datable to that year, and Bale's *Epistle exhortatorye*, printed in August 1544, even ran to a third edition. An unfinished version of *The image of bothe churches* was printed in 1545, apparently to be followed by the complete text the following year.[58] By contrast, there are some indications that in the early 1540s the exiles had difficulties having their work published at all. Bale's first book to have any success, *A dysclosynge or openynge of the Manne of synne*, was written in 1542 but not printed until December 1543. His *A mysterye of inyquyte*, also written in 1542, was only published in 1545, by which time Bale had to deal

[54] CLRO Repertory 11 fo. 158ʳ; Brigden, *London*, 358.
[55] William Peryn, *Thre godlye and notable sermons, of the sacrament of the aulter* (RSTC 19786: 1546), sig. *4ʳ.
[56] Stephen Gardiner, *A detection of the Deuils Sophistrie, wherwith he robbeth the vnlearned people, of the true byleef, in the most blessed Sacrament of the aulter* (RSTC 11591: 1546), fo. 71ᵛ.
[57] APC, 409, 509; PRO SP 1/218 fo. 92ʳ (*LP* XXI (i) 812).
[58] The earliest surviving complete text of the *Image*, RSTC 1297, dates from 1548?, but since the list of books burned in 1546 specifies all three parts of the *Image*, there must be a lost impression dating from 1545 or 1546.

with the embarrassing fact that Huntingdon, whom the book attacked so viciously, had since become a reformer.[59]

It appears, therefore, that in the last two or three years of Henry's reign the impact of the exiles' writings in England was steadily increasing. However, it would be wrong to overemphasise this change, much less to see it as an inexorable gathering of the momentum that would drive the Edwardian Reformation. The problems of exile publication remained daunting. Although many of the printers used by the exiles were technically excellent, they were not always able to use English-speaking compositors, which could lead to garbled texts; a frustrated Bale wrote that the 'heady hast, negligence, and couetousnesse' of printers 'comonly corrupteth al bokes'.[60] Print runs were short, and the need for secrecy complicated the logistics of distribution. Joye claimed that 'one secret .C.[hundred]' copies of his attack on Gardiner were printed, while a thousand copies of Gardiner's reply were openly distributed. This was hyperbole, but the problem was a real one.[61] When illegal books could be obtained, their prices were considerably inflated.[62] Moreover, such dangerous works were likely to circulate only within tightly confined circles of committed evangelicals. For such material to reach the general reading public, reformers had to adopt desperately inefficient tactics such as giving away these expensive texts freely, or – worse – simply dropping them or other, shorter texts in places where they might be found. These practices thoroughly alarmed conservatives, but can hardly have made many converts.[63]

The exiles did not feel themselves to be on the verge of a triumph by the mid-1540s. Turner believed that England was drifting towards a re-establishment of the papacy.[64] If the exiles were optimistic about the future, it was not because they felt that events were moving in their favour but because they were living through 'this laste time'. Indeed, it was the outward

---

[59] Bale, *A dysclosynge or openynge of the Manne of synne*, fo. 99^r; Bale, *Mysterye of inyquyte*, sigs. A1^r, 2^{r-v}, fo. 88^v.

[60] Bale, *Image of bothe churches*, sig. a3^v. The first, Bonn edition of Turner's *Huntyng and fyndyng out of the Romishe fox* was a crude imprint laden with errors; the second edition, produced by the more professional printers of Antwerp, was a great improvement.

[61] Joye, *The refutation of the byshop of Winchesters derke declaration*, fo. 171^r; Charles C. Butterworth and Allan G. Chester, *George Joye 1495?–1553: A Chapter in the History of the English Bible and the English Reformation* (Philadelphia, 1962), 230.

[62] See, for example, PRO SP 1/244 fo. 9^r (*LP* Addenda 1548).

[63] Gardiner, *Declaration of such true articles as George Ioye hath gone about to confute*, fo. 83^r. For radical 'bills' being dropped in public places during this period, see Nichols (ed.), *Chronicle of the Grey Friars*, 48; Gardiner, *Letters*, 160; PRO SP 1/119 fo. 196^v, 1/210 fos. 72^v–3^r, 1/218 fo. 86^r (*LP* XII (i) 1147, XX (ii) 769, XXI (i) 810); Wriothesley, 159; *Statutes of the realm*, 997 (37° Henry VIII c. 10); and see R. W. Hoyle, 'Petitioning as popular politics in early sixteenth-century England', *Historical Research* 75 (2002), 388.

[64] Turner, *Rescuynge of the romishe fox*, sig. I3^{r-v}.

desperation of their situation that assured them that it must be so. Joye's commentary on the book of Daniel contained an extended application of that book's apocalyptic prophecies to the current international situation, with the burgeoning religious wars in Germany and the ever-present Turkish threat becoming the final conflict which will usher in the day of judgement. Bale took the same view, adding a parallel interpretation of events within England. He likened the pope to the beast in the book of Revelation who is healed from a mortal wound; the pope, wounded by Henry VIII's schism, had been healed by England's return to *de facto* popery. This apparent triumph of evil was, of course, grounds for confidence. If the beast was healed, 'destroyed yet vtterly shall that execrable monstre be within short space'. The forces ranged against the Gospel were so vast that they could be defeated only by God's hand. Joye explained that persecution was coming to a peak because the devil 'seith his kyngedom almost at an ende and his heuey iugement at hand, manis wikednes beinge al moste at the rypiste and higheste'. In other words, their view was that, in worldly terms, matters were bad and getting worse. Bale believed that those who trusted in princes for a true reformation would be disappointed, and feared that young Prince Edward was being poisoned by the 'contagious drinkes' of the papists; but he had no practical alternatives to propose. Indeed, the only outward sign of hope which he and others admitted was that popery no longer bothered to disguise its corruption and tyranny, and that 'theyr lowsye legerdemaine is almost perseyued of all menne'. Likewise, the true Gospel had at last been revealed, so that the gulf between Christ and Antichrist was becoming unmistakable. Even so, the exiles believed that the Gospel's followers would be no more than a remnant – the 'smal flocke of fayth' preserved against 'the infinite table of infideles'.[65] As such, all that they themselves could do was to act as faithful witnesses. Even this role was being curtailed. Bale was undaunted by the clampdown on heretical books in 1546, but he admitted that the new circumstances would force the exiles to change their tactics: 'It wyll from hens forth occasyon vs, to set fourth in Latyne also, that afore we wrote onlye in the Englysh, and so make their spirytuall wyckednesse and treason knowne moche farther of.' He returned repeatedly to this threat to publish the iniquities of the English bishops in Latin, 'that all christendome ouer, it shall be knowne what ye are'. Turner made a similar threat.[66] These

---

[65] Joye, *Vnite and Scisme*, fo. 9^r; Joye, *Daniel*, fos. 230^r–2^v; Bale, *Image of bothe churches*, passim, esp. sigs. B3^r–4^r, O7^r, i7^v, Ii3^v; Bale, *Mysterye of inyquyte*, fo. 88^v; Joye, *Present consolation*, sig. C6^v; Bale, *Epistle exhortatorye*, fos. 5^r, 23^v–4^r; Bale, *A dysclosynge or openynge of the Manne of synne*, fo. 7^v, 98^r; cf. Revelation 13:3.

[66] Askew, *The first examinacyon*, introduction fo. 5^v, fo. 1^v; Askew, *The lattre examinacyon*, fo. 51^v; Turner, *Huntyng and fyndyng out of the Romishe fox*, sig. F3^v.

were brave words, but hardly the terrors of the earth; they were in effect an admission that the attempt to further the Reformation through sending polemic into England was failing. Bale's view in 1542, quoted above, was that he had exiled himself 'for euer', and in 1546 there was little reason to change that assessment. The exiles did not believe themselves to be the standard-bearers of a rising evangelical movement, but the outcast prophets of a cause which would be rescued by God against all worldly expectation.

Before we leave the exiles, one revealing curiosity deserves to be noted. Those who wished to publish inflammatory religious material in this period were forced to use the overseas presses to do so. However, publishing abroad did not necessarily entail exile. Richard Tracy was able to have his *Supplycacion to kynge Henry the eyght* published in Antwerp while he sat on the commission of the peace in Worcestershire. The most extreme of all the authors whose work was published abroad in this period, Henry Brinklow, remained in England, although his mercantile business presumably took him abroad every so often. This approach was not without risk, and also required a degree of dissimulation,[67] but it greatly enhanced these authors' ability to aid the reformist cause. This was partly because their physical presence gave them opportunities to do so unconnected to their writing. Brinklow stood surety for Robert Wisdom during his imprisonment in 1543, so that, as Wisdom gratefully noted, he did not have to wear chains.[68] Perhaps more importantly, however, these authors' work had an immediacy which that of the exiles lacked. Brinklow and Tracy both blended their doctrinal views with political and social polemic which could be precise and biting. Only their status as eye-witnesses made this possible.[69] Living at home and publishing abroad did not solve the logistical problems associated with exile publication. Brinklow's *Lamentacion of a Christian*, for example, was first printed in 1542, but did not come to the attention even of the keen-eyed bishop of Winchester until a second edition appeared in 1545.[70] Nevertheless, the polemicist who was able to remain in England was unquestionably in a stronger position.

This serves to remind us that, for all that Bale emphasised the spiritual sacrifice of the exiles and depicted himself as a latter-day St John producing a new Revelation from his personal Patmos in Antwerp, exile was a

---

[67] Brinklow claimed quite falsely that he was 'a man banished my natyue contry'. Brinklow, *Complaynt of Roderyck Mors*, sig. A4^r.
[68] Bonner Register fo. 45^{r-v}; ECL MS 261 fos. 115^v–16^r.
[69] For example, Brinklow's denunciation of clerical pride draws much of its power from his eye-witness account of the opening of Parliament in January 1542 – an account whose political precision has only recently been demonstrated. Brinklow, *Complaynt of Roderyck Mors*, sigs. H2^r–4^r; MacCulloch, *Cranmer*, 294.
[70] Gardiner, *Letters*, 159–60.

brutally practical affair.[71] For those who merely wished to escape a local reputation for heresy, internal exile was a perfectly acceptable alternative, and some reformers did take this route. Thomas Becon, from Norfolk, took refuge in Kent after one recantation and in the Midlands after a second one. During the heresy-hunts of 1546, two London sacramentaries fled to York. Robert Ferrar, the future bishop of St David's, also went to ground in Yorkshire during the mid-1540s, perhaps sheltering with family. The radical Anthony Gilby seems to have sat out the last years of Henry's reign in rural obscurity – this, at least, seems to be the meaning of his comment that 'I haue dwelled fully seuen yeres in a place where I neuer hearde sermon'.[72] The lack of preaching may have been frustrating, but compared to exile overseas such arrangements were very agreeable indeed. Many of those who fled abroad, however, did so because they were guilty of more than holding heterodox opinions: they were clerics who had married or who wished to marry.[73] Opinions could be concealed, but wives usually could not, unless their husbands had the resources (and the finely balanced conscience) of the archbishop of Canterbury. Clerical marriage was one of the most unambiguous and irrevocable public statements of reformist allegiance which it was possible for a magisterial Protestant to make, somewhat akin to rebaptism for Anabaptists. In Helen Parish's phrase, it 'amounted to a highly visible act of doctrinal iconoclasm'.[74] It was also an issue which, however much the Henrician regime and the evangelicals who lived under it might incline towards compromise, was almost impossible to finesse. The Six Articles imposed the death penalty on clerics who married. After the Act, the only alternatives to flight were concealment, which was both difficult and extremely dangerous, or abject submission. As laymen, Brinklow and Tracy were of course spared this dilemma. Exile was neither a vocation nor the natural consequence of doctrinal radicalism. It was, in large part, a function of Henry VIII's loathing for clerical marriage.

For all their subsequent fame, the Henrician exiles were simply that: exiles. They were shut out of the mainstream of religious life in England, and struggled to keep up with the progress of events at home. They were stood on the sidelines, trying to make themselves heard through their books. While

---

[71] Bale, *Image of bothe churches*, sig. A5^{r-v}.
[72] Bonner Register fo. 44^r, Becon, *Iewell of ioye*, sig. B6^v–7^v; PRO SP 1/227 fo. 170^r (*LP* XXI (ii) 596); Andrew J. Brown, *Robert Ferrar: Yorkshire Monk, Reformation Bishop and Martyr in Wales (c. 1500–1555)* (1997), 81; Anthony Gilby, *An answer to the deuillish detection of S. Gardiner* (RSTC 11884: London?, 1548), fo. 141^v. I owe this reference to Catharine Davies.
[73] This, William Palmer claimed in 1547, was the key issue which had driven the exiles overseas. TCC MS R3.33 fo. 52^v.
[74] Parish, *Clerical Marriage*, 1.

they became significantly more successful from about 1544 onwards, they were still a very long way from taking centre stage. In Mary's reign, arguably, the exiles were the keepers of the reformist flame. In Henry's last years, they were a sideshow. Moreover, their success or failure did not lie in their own hands; their resurgence after 1543 owes little to them and much to events in England. Perhaps unsurprisingly, if we are looking for the real centres of English evangelicalism, we need to look within England.

4

Pulpit and printshop

And Elia came vnto all the people, and sayde: how long halte ye betwene two opynions?
I Kings 18:21

A LOYAL OPPOSITION

After the *coup* against Thomas Cromwell in 1540 failed to become a full-scale purge, most of the leaders of English evangelicalism did not take the paths of exile or of outright rejection of the regime. Instead, they waited for the world to turn and the fortunes of officially sponsored reform to rise again. In the meantime, they continued working to spread the evangelical message, to build up the evangelical community and to call the nation as a whole to repentance. It was a mission which they shared with their exiled brethren, but which they pursued in a very different way. The ambiguities of late Henrician religious politics and the moderation of their own beliefs led these evangelical preachers and authors to engage constructively with their opponents in a way that more radical reformers could not or would not. The result was the emergence of a new and highly distinctive strain of evangelicalism.

Over the winter of 1540–1, the new limits within which evangelicals were going to have to operate became plain. Edward Crome's confrontation with Nicholas Wilson over Masses for the dead was the most public drama of these months, but two other incidents which excited less public comment were of more long-term importance. In the wake of Cromwell's fall, an anonymous ballad appeared, reviling him as traitor and heretic. William Gray, a former client of Cromwell's, found the attack on his old master too much to stomach, and replied with another ballad. The clerk of the queen's council, Thomas Smith, then took up the cudgels on the anonymous author's behalf. Centring around Smith and Gray, the controversy seems to have echoed more or less tunefully through London's streets for much of the autumn. We know of nine ballads and two longer contributions.[1] Finally, in January 1541, both men appeared before the Privy Council, and both were imprisoned, with two of their printers. The Council's treatment of them was not even-handed. Smith, the conservative, was apparently summoned only as an afterthought, and the imprisoned printers, Richard Grafton and John Gough, were both evangelicals. Nevertheless, as in the Crome case, the Council's main concern seems to have been the threat to public order.[2] A more serious case came to light at the end of December 1540, when the Council heard that manuscripts of an English translation of Philip Melanchthon's tract against the Six Articles were circulating in Norfolk. This was, of course, a direct attack on the regime and could not be tolerated. For ten days, the matter dominated the Council's business. The translation was eventually traced, despite several false leads, from a Norfolk bookseller, through a chaplain to Bishop Goodricke of Ely, through the wife of the well-connected London evangelical John Blage, to the printer Richard Grafton – the same man who had printed some of William Gray's invectives.[3] The message was uncomfortably clear. If evangelical publicists stirred up public dissent, or openly challenged the political and religious status quo, they could expect to be silenced.

In the spring of 1541, however, the political winds began to change in the reformers' favour and the printers Grafton and Gough were released. They had learned their lesson. Both men now began to produce a different variety

---

[1] Brigden, *London*, 322–3; William Gray, *A balade agaynst malycyous Sclaunderers* (RSTC 1323.5: 1540); Thomas Smith, *A lytell treatyse agaynst sedicyous persons* (RSTC 22880.4: 1540); *A brefe apologye or answere to a certen craftye cloynar, or popyshe parasye, called Thomas Smythe* (RSTC 22880.7: Antwerp, 1540); Thomas Smith, *A treatyse declarynge the despyte of a secrete sedycyous person, that dareth not shewe hym selfe* (RSTC 22880.6: 1540); William Gray, *An answere to maister Smyth* (RSTC 12206a.3: 1540); Thomas Smith, *An Enuoye from Thomas Smith vpon thaunswer of one WG* (540, RSTC 22880.2: 1540); William Gray, *The returne of M. Smythes enuoy* (RSTC 12206a.7: 1540); R. Smyth P. (a pseudonym), *An artificiall apologie, articulerlye answerynge to the obstreperous Obgannynges of one WG* (RSTC 22877.6: 1540); *A paumflet compyled by G. C. / To master Smyth and Wyllyam G.* (RSTC 4628.5: 1540); Ernest W. Dormer, *Gray of Reading: Sixteenth-century Controversialist and Ballad-Writer* (Reading, 1923); Bale, *Catalogus*, vol. I, 704. Smith seems not to have been the author of the first ballad.

[2] *P&O* 103, 105, 107, 110. Initially, on 30 December 1540, the only persons summoned by the Council were Gray, Grafton and another of Gray's suspected printers, Richard Bankes.

[3] *P&O* 94–107. Despite Grafton's involvement, it appears that the treatise was never printed. There were relatively few copies involved, and it appears on neither of the lists of prohibited books issued in the 1540s. (Bonner Register fos. 40^v, 92^{r-v}). The involvement of Thomas Goodricke, the evangelical bishop of Ely, in this case seems to be a red herring. Since one of his chaplains and one of his servants were involved, the Council naturally suspected his complicity, but the investigators were instructed to search his study only if it 'appered certainly' that he was involved. There is no reason to believe that they did so, and it is in any case unlikely that so cautious a reformer would involve himself with so dangerous a document. *P&O* 98.

of evangelical propaganda. They were two of the principal figures behind a remarkable, if short-lived, strain of moderate reformist printing which cautiously pressed for continued reform while remaining within the law. During 1542 and 1543 these works dominated the output of vernacular works of religious controversy, and they continued to be produced in smaller numbers for the remainder of the reign.[4] Easily the most eye-catching of these works are those written by Thomas Becon, under the pseudonym Theodore Basille, and published by Gough with his associate John Mayler. Becon was a reformist Norfolk priest who had been brought to recant, probably in 1540, for his heretical preaching. After this, he moved to Kent, began to write and became the evangelical publishing phenomenon of the decade. In something like eighteen months, he wrote nine full-length books; a long preface to a translation of Heinrich Bullinger's *Der Christlich Eestand*; and two lost works, a metrical catechism and a collection of Christmas carols. The books are direct and accessible, and they were bestsellers. At least twenty-two editions were in print by 1543, and more reprints would probably have followed if Theodore Basille had not been forced into premature retirement that year.[5] One of his works was even translated into Dutch and printed in Antwerp in 1543.[6] It is no surprise that when Gough and Mayler printed the Bullinger piece, they chose to set it forth under Becon's pseudonym 'for the more redy sale . . . to make it the more plausible to the Readers'.[7]

While no other writer approached Becon's success, several other broadly similar reformist works appeared during the same period. All were produced in England, within the law, and pursued a studiedly moderate reformist line. A treatise by Richard Tracy on justification was published by Richard Grafton's business partner Edward Whitchurch in 1543. Gough printed a moderate (indeed, anodyne) Lollard text, *A generall free Pardon or Charter of heuyn blys*, in 1542. A work printed by William Middleton which only survives in a small fragment and appears to have been called *A meane to dye well* probably also belongs to this group,[8] as does a piece published by Richard Lant entitled *A compendyous treatyse of sclaundre*. Reformist

---

[4] See Appendix II.
[5] Derrick Sherwin Bailey, *Thomas Becon and the Reformation of the Church in England* (Edinburgh, 1952), 16; RSTC; Bonner Register fos. 45^r, 92^{r-v}.
[6] Willem Heijting, 'Early Reformation literature from the printing shop of Mattheus Crom and Steven Mierdmans', *Nederlands archief voor kerkgeschiedenis* 74 (1994), 155. The bulk of Dutch evangelical printing in this period was also moderate in flavour: *ibid.*, 157–9.
[7] Thomas Becon, *The worckes of Thomas Becon*, 3 vols. (RSTC 1710: 1560–4), vol. I, sig. C 5^v.
[8] This fragment is dated by RSTC to c.1545, but a dating of 1543 or earlier would explain the Privy Council's otherwise peculiar decision to arrest Middleton for printing reformist books in 1543: Middleton's only other known religious publication from this period is a conservative devotional work. *APC*, 107.

printers also produced several editions of sympathetic patristic or humanist works in this period, some of which were given a reformist twist by their editors. The master of this practice was Richard Taverner, in whose hands Erasmus became a full-blown evangelical. Taverner's reworking of his material could be blatant, as when Erasmus' proverb 'Non omnes qui habent citharum, sunt citharaedi'[9] was rendered as 'All that have the gospel hangynge at theyr gyrdels be no gospellers. Nor agayn all that disprayse the leude facions of the Papistes be not forthwith Heretiques.'[10] Even Polydore Vergil could be repackaged as unmasking 'these manyfolde swarmes of popish religions' and demonstrating 'what hath crepte in to the congregacion to the peruertyng of our faithe and seducyng simple people with supersticion'.[11] However, venturing into scholarly territory carried its own dangers. Gough and Mayler produced a translation of a sermon of John Chrysostom's in 1542 apparently unaware of the existence of a markedly better translation by Thomas Lupset. The king's printer, Thomas Berthelet, rushed the Lupset translation into print.[12]

One important subgroup of these domestically produced evangelical texts consists of collections of homilies or 'postils'. These were preachers' handbooks which provided outlines for sermons on the set readings for each Sunday in the liturgical year. The most important such collection was Richard Taverner's semi-official set, which, although collected from a variety of sources, bears a strong editorial voice.[13] Parts of this set predate Cromwell's fall. However, the second volume was printed during the dangerous summer of 1540 itself – prompting Taverner to add, needlessly as it turned out, a panicky preface which assured the reader (and the censor) that he had no intention of teaching disobedience or heresy. The final volume, which contained the postils for holy days, dates from 1542. Moreover, the set continued to be reprinted throughout this period, with twelve known editions before Henry VIII's death. Taverner's was much the most widely circulated set of

---

[9] 'Not all those who have lutes are lute-players.'
[10] John K. Yost, 'German Protestant humanism and the early English Reformation: Richard Taverner and official translation', *Bibliothèque d'Humanisme et Renaissance* 32 (1970), 618.
[11] Polydore Vergil, *An abridgement of the notable woorke of Polidore Vergile conteignyng the deuisers and firste finders out aswell of Artes, Ministeries, Feactes and ciuill ordinaunces, as of Rites, and Ceremonies*, ed. T. Langley (RSTC 24656: 1546), sig. A7^r. This was the book which the shepherd Robert Wyllyams bought when he was unable to buy an English Bible (see above, p. 49). In fact, however, a great many references to traditional religious practices were permitted to remain in this edition – see, for example, fos. 62^v, 85^r, 102^v, 110^v–12^v, 125^v. Indeed, Langley carefully distanced himself from Vergil's dangerous advocacy of clerical marriage (fo. 106^r).
[12] Both editions are dated 1542. However, Gough and Mayler's translator believed that the sermon was 'hyd from such as vnderstand not the Laten tonge', presumably indicating that their edition (RSTC 14640) predates Berthelet's (RSTC 14639).
[13] Yost, 'German Protestant humanism', 622.

postils, but, perhaps inspired by his commercial success, other sets followed. Richard Grafton printed a single-volume set of postils, which shows the signs of having been composed in some haste.[14] Stephen Cobbe, a scholar in John Gough's household, prepared a translation of another set, presumably for publication, although these are now lost. The preparation of a full set of postils was a major undertaking, easier to start than to finish. One unknown author, whose work is certainly late Henrician, set out to produce such a set but, having written nine folios of close script for the first homily, was apparently too daunted to write any more. One John Pokysfene, the author of another late Henrician set which again survives only in manuscript, tackled the problem in another way. The postils in his (complete) collection are highly condensed and tediously bland, often doing little more than paraphrasing the biblical text.[15] All of these texts have an evangelical slant to them (although in the case of Pokysfene's set it is faint). The author of Grafton's collection went so far as to take his biblical texts, not from the authorised Great Bible, but from Tyndale's illegal 1534 New Testament.

This flourishing trade in moderate evangelical books was, for a time, permitted to continue unchecked. Gough, Grafton and their associates printed their works openly in London and cited their royal privilege as printers. When Bishop Bonner issued a list of prohibited books in 1542, none of these publications were included.[16] This toleration came to an abrupt end in the spring of 1543, when, as we have seen, the regime took steps to close down domestic evangelical printing and to silence several leading evangelical preachers. Grafton, Whitchurch, Mayler and others were imprisoned; Gough was interrogated; Becon compelled to make a humiliating recantation. After this, the legal trade in evangelical books was reduced to a shadow.[17] The few evangelical imprints which appeared after 1543 only underline the point. Most reformist printers were driven to such bland projects as Grafton's 1544 *Praiers of holi fathers*, an unadorned collection of biblical prayers. William Middleton printed another book of prayers, perhaps in 1546, which is a little more plain-spoken. Its long discussion of penitence makes no mention of auricular confession, instead insisting that true repentance is performed through private prayer and that it arises from divine grace rather than from the sinner.[18] The most outspoken of these imprints to survive is a small

---

[14] *The ende of this brefe Postyl, vpon the Epystles and Gospelles of all the Sondayes in the yeare* (RSTC 2972.7: 1543). The postils decrease dramatically in length through the work, and towards the end of the collection, the author begins simply to give outline sermons in note form, or even to omit some postils entirely, referring the reader to relevant texts earlier in the book. See, for example, fos. 159^v, 229^v, 299^r.

[15] APC, 115; BL Harleian MS 1197 fos. 144–203; BL Royal MS 7.C.xvi fos. 182–91.

[16] Bonner Register fo. 40^v.   [17] See above, pp. 46–7; Appendix II.

[18] *A boke of prayers called ye ordynary fasshyon of a good lyuynge* (RSTC 3326.5: 1546?), sigs. B1^r–5^r.

pamphlet, *Twoo fruitfull and godly praiers*, printed in 1545. Towards the end it comes close to affirming a Protestant view of justification:

> No merites nor good workes, now of myself I haue
> Before ye to knowledge, wherfore my flesh doth quake
> But only it lieth in the good lorde, my soule to saue
> Not able I am to ye, for my synnes amendes to make
> Through thy mercy by faith, yet in thy blod I take
> A perfect hope & trust, thou wilt not impute my syne
> But accept into thy grace, through ye heuen to winne.[19]

This stanza was the height of the evangelical printers' daring in the last years of Henry's reign.

A few other post-1543 domestic imprints were more clearly evangelical, but were produced in safer circumstances. Even so, they were painfully moderate. William Hughe's 1546 work *The troubled mans medicine* was more Erasmian than evangelical, but it did take a reformist line on justification. Philip Gerrard's preface to his 1545 translation of Erasmus' *Epicurus* went so far as to attack as papists those 'whiche bee not wyllyng that gods woorde shoulde bee knowen'. The most apparently innocuous of all was Arthur Kelton's long poem, *A commendacion of welshmen*, printed in 1546. This included, some two-thirds of the way through, a substantial section in which the king was praised in exalted terms for the English Bible, as well as for destroying images and shrines and for expelling the pope (who seduced the people to have 'more trust / in thynges vniust / Then in Cristes passion'). Kelton also prayed that Prince Edward would finish what his father had begun. These three books, however, only underline the weakness of the evangelicals' position after 1543. Kelton's praise of the king for the English Bible, and Gerrard's similar celebration of the fact that 'the swete sound of gods worde is gone thorough out all this realme', required heroic evasion of reality after 1543. More importantly, these books could only be printed because of their authors' connections. Hughe, as chaplain to Lady Denny, belonged to one of the most influential evangelical households in the realm; Gerrard was a groom of Prince Edward's privy chamber; and Kelton was a client of William, Lord Herbert, the king's brother-in-law.[20] It is perhaps more striking that, even with such powerful patrons, these authors had to be so

---

[19] *Praiers of holi fathers, Patryarches, Prophetes, Iudges, Kynges, and renowmed men and women of eyther testamente* (RSTC 20200: 1544); *Here after foloweth twoo fruitfull and godly praiers, the one in laude and praise of the trinitie, and the other desiryng grace to with stande the feare of death* (RSTC 20197.3: 1545).

[20] William Hughe, *The troubled mans medicine*, 2 vols. (RSTC 13910: 1546), vol. II, sigs. A1^v, E5^r–8^r; Desiderius Erasmus, tr. Philip Gerrard, *A very pleasaunt and fruitful Diologe called the Epicure* (RSTC 10460: 1545), sigs. A8^r, B1^v–2^r, B3^r; Kelton, *A commendacion of welshmen*, sigs. F6^v–G5^v, G8^v–H1^r; Williams, *Wales and the Reformation*, 149. See below, p. 199.

circumspect. The point is reinforced by the caution of the most vulnerable of all these moderate reformers, Queen Katherine Parr. Her book of evangelical devotions, the *Lamentacion of a Sinner*, which undoubtedly belongs to this group, remained unpublished until after the king's death. The final domestically printed evangelical work from after 1543 is a complete reprint of Taverner's postils on the epistles and gospels, probably dating from 1545–6. This is an oddity. The work had been commissioned by Cromwell and so had semi-official status, but while this might explain the fact that it was never banned it remains peculiar that it continued to be reissued. It is probably significant that Richard Bankes, Taverner's printer, was one of only three major printers operating in London in 1543 who was not arrested in April of that year. If so, this only serves to underline the impact of those arrests.[21]

This whole body of work, both before and after 1543, is highly diverse in form. Nevertheless, it is strikingly congruent in its doctrinal content and, equally importantly, in how it deals with the problems of being an evangelical in a society which was at the same time predominantly conservative and bitterly divided. Nor was this approach restricted to the printed and written word, although that is both where it is most visible to us and also one of the arenas where, by its nature, it flourished most readily. Preachers such as Crome and Robert Wisdom took a similar line, and echoes of their views and methods can be found in most of the sources where religious views are recorded in this period. This group was not a party or faction. No clear boundaries can be drawn, and they lacked even the self-conscious coherence of many of the exiles. They were, however, quite as united in their approach as the exiles were in their rejectionist, quasi-Reformed position, and they were far more numerous. Despite the disparate nature of this group, two distinctive doctrinal priorities stand out and can serve to define them. First of all, they stressed the importance of a Protestant understanding of justification by faith alone. Secondly, and critically, they were not sacramentaries; they wished to maintain a belief in Christ's objective presence in the Eucharist.

These doctrinal touchstones were matched with political priorities which, at least initially, complemented them. The high doctrine of obedience and

---

[21] Bankes was also one of the two printers involved in the *Twoo fruitfull and godly praiers*. It is less clear, however, quite how Bankes escaped arrest in April 1543. Part of the answer may lie in the investigation into the 1540 pamphlet war between Gray and Smith. Bankes was arrested for printing four of Gray's pamphlets, which indeed bear his colophon, but he apparently persuaded the Council that Grafton was responsible for these, and was released. Whether or not Bankes was innocent in 1540 – and it seems unlikely – some aspect of the Council's experience with him then may have convinced them that it was unnecessary to rearrest him in 1543. *P&O* 103, 105–6; E. Gordon Duff, *A Century of the English Book Trade* (1905); RSTC.

associated culture of recantation prevalent amongst English evangelicals, and the regime's genuine openness to some parts of the evangelical agenda, limited the extent to which this group of reformers was willing to oppose or denounce the regime. Given the pervasiveness of dissimulation, it should be no surprise that, in some cases, this moderation was a matter of policy rather than of principle. Becon's publishers, John Gough and John Mayler, both favoured ideas far more radical than those they were prepared publicly to support. In 1540 Mayler was arrested for unmistakably sacramentarian beliefs – he had called the Mass 'the baken god' – and in the early 1530s John Gough appears to have been involved with a conventicle importing Anabaptist books.[22] They presumably found the milk-and-water reformism that they were being forced to publish in the 1540s somewhat distasteful. However, there is no reason to suspect that, as a whole, this phenomenon of conformist evangelicalism was a conspiracy to conceal more radical views. The opinions of these reformers seem to have been much the same in public and in private. If they were ambiguous, their ambiguity was, as Annabel Patterson has written of their Elizabethan successors, 'creative and necessary'. The reformers and the regime shared an interest in avoiding confrontations.[23] For authors writing for the domestic printing press, such considerations affected tone more than content. In 1544, Richard Tracy followed his piece on justification with a polemic calling for social reform. Since this second piece was printed abroad, Tracy had an entirely free hand, but while his beliefs were expressed more forcefully they were not markedly different. These writers and preachers unanimously protested their loyalty to Henry VIII and exalted his authority. They certainly had their criticisms of his Church, but they remained essentially loyal to it and saw themselves as part of it. They understood it to be a true Church, flawed but capable of reformation. When Tracy denounced those who trusted in the power of works to save, he denounced *us* rather than *you*, seeing himself as a part of an erring Church rather than an external critic of an apostate one. Becon praised 'the commendable order of thys Realme nowe a dayes vsed amonge vs'. To be sure, further reformation was needed, but the principal obstacle to it was the irreligion of the common people, not the papistry of the hierarchy.[24] While this faith in the regime was neither bottomless nor sustained by goodwill

---

[22] PRO SP 1/237 fo. 290^v (*LP* Addenda 809); PRO SP 1/243 fo. 79^r (*LP* Addenda 1463). However, if Gough had ever had Anabaptist sympathies, he had abandoned them by 1539, when he went out of his way to insert an attack on Anabaptism in a text he had prepared for publication. Jennifer Britnell, 'John Gough and the "Traite de la difference des schismes et des conciles" of Jean Lemaire de Belges', *JEH* 46 (1995), 72.

[23] Annabel Patterson, *Censorship and Interpretation: The Conditions of Writing and Reading in Early Modern England* (Madison, WI, 1984), 11; see above, pp. 88–9.

[24] Richard Tracy, *The profe and declaration of thys proposition: Fayth only iustifieth* (RSTC 24164: 1543), sigs. B4^r–5^r; Becon, *Pathway vnto praier*, sigs. L1^r–2^r, R4^v.

alone, it remained the starting point for a short-lived but strikingly eirenic form of evangelicalism.

POLEMICISTS AND THEIR AUDIENCES

One of the most important characteristics of these conformist writers is somewhat less tangible than their political loyalties. Their work is suffused with a certain mood of calm, favouring persuasion and even dialogue over polemical denunciations. This was, of course, a significant departure from the vitriolic conventions of sixteenth-century religious debate. No modern reader can spend long in the company of Reformation-era polemic without beginning to wonder whether this was a literature which was in any way effective, and, indeed, quite what it might have been trying to achieve. Much the same could be said of many of the recorded sermons of the period. Indeed, on closer examination, some fundamental questions become increasingly vexed – such as, who religious polemicists believed their publics to be, what they were trying to communicate to them, and what the purposes of polemical literature and preaching actually were.

Proselytisation was perhaps the obvious task for evangelical publicists in this period, but it was neither the only objective nor always the most important. The exiles' polemic was so violent that it is difficult to imagine many conservatives being converted by it, even granting that rhetorical norms were a good deal more robust in the sixteenth century than in our own. It batters the reader, inviting retaliation rather than agreement. Indeed, the exiles rarely addressed themselves to doubters or the uncommitted, as we might expect apologists to have done. Bale's *Epistle exhortatorye*, the most popular (or at least the most reprinted) of the exiles' works, was not even addressed to reformers but to the conservative clergy. Likewise, William Turner's *The huntyng and fyndyng out of the Romishe fox* was addressed to the king, and Henry Brinklow's blistering tracts were addressed respectively to the House of Commons, the City of London, the clergy and – if the last tract is his – the king.[25] On one level, of course, this was merely a rhetorical device. Most of those who actually read these works were presumably committed evangelicals. However, while propagandists certainly used such devices, it is worth emphasising that these authors had other objectives than propaganda. The conservative polemicist Richard Smith claimed that his first reason for writing in defence of the Mass was to avoid burying his talent. The truth had been impugned, and he was duty-bound to defend it. This was principally an act of piety rather than of apologetics, since the effectiveness of such a

[25] Bale, *Catalogus*, vol. II, 105.

defence was in the hands of God.²⁶ Reformers as well as conservatives were drawn to such acts of piety. Robert Crowley argued that those whom God had called to preach had no option but to obey, whether single or married, lay or ordained, and if they might not preach with their mouths then they must needs do so with their pens.²⁷ John Hooper compared himself to Caleb and Joshua, fulfilling their duty to describe the promised land truthfully even though no one was willing to hear them; and Anthony Gilby claimed that he would have replied to Gardiner's writings even if he had only been able simply to assert that they were false.²⁸ The best modern analogues to Bale, Joye, Turner, Hooper and others who rushed to rebut conservatives would not be the leaders of a carefully crafted publicity campaign; but rather, the outraged letters-page correspondents who cannot allow the smallest murmur of dissent to pass without smothering it in refutation.

Nevertheless, some of even the most venomous and personal of the attacks penned by the exiles and those who thought like them were put in print, meaning that reaching a wider audience was at least one of their subsidiary aims. It was, however, an audience which they judged would be edified by such violent polemic: those who had already accepted the reformers' Gospel. When such people read a tract of Bale's or Brinklow's, they were in a sense spectators. Most such tracts were formally addressed to conservatives, whom they lambasted. The response they clearly expected from their evangelical readers was a hearty cheer and a renewed commitment to the battle themselves. If such people were to remain committed, they had to remain convinced that their estrangement from traditional religion was a reflection of the cosmic gulf between Christ and Antichrist. Bale thus justified his bitter attacks on Bishop Bonner, saying, 'Moche better ys yt to the Christen beleuer that Sathan apere Sathan, and the deuill be knowne for the deuil, than still to lurke vnder a faire similitude of the angell of lyght.'²⁹ Joye, too, half-apologised for writing a 'sharpe tothed' book, asking his readers to 'consider in howe sharpe a tyme it was writen'. Making a similar apology, Anthony Gilby declared that in such a time 'there is no meane for styll and ware politicke persons'. If one was not with Christ, one was against him.³⁰

Manifestly, the audiences which these books would find would principally be committed gospellers, and most of their authors were content with this.

[26] Richard Smith, *Assertion and defence*, fos. 2ᵛ, 4ʳ.
[27] Crowley, *The opening of the woordes of the prophet Joell*, sigs. F8ᵛ–G1ʳ.
[28] John Hooper, *An answer vnto my lord of wynchesters booke* (RSTC 13741: Zurich, 1547), sig. A3ᵛ (cf. Numbers 14:6–10); Gilby, *An answer to the deuillish detection*, fos. 2ᵛ–3ʳ.
[29] Bale, *A dysclosynge or openynge of the Manne of synne*, fo. 96ʳ. Cf. Alec Ryrie, 'The problem of legitimacy and precedent in English Protestantism, 1539–47', in *Protestant History and Identity in Sixteenth-Century Europe*, ed. Bruce Gordon (Aldershot, Hants., 1996), vol. I, 87–8.
[30] Joye, *The refutation of the byshop of Winchesters derke declaration*, sig. A2ᵛ; Gilby, *An answer to the deuillish detection*, fos. 5ʳ⁻ᵛ, 10ᵛ.

Coverdale's reply to John Standish's attack on Robert Barnes was dedicated 'to all them that either reade or heare gods holy worde, and geue ouer them selues to lyue vnfaynedly acording to the same'.[31] George Joye's *A present consolacion for the sufferers of persecucion* proclaims its limited audience in its title (although he also professed the hope that he might reach more faint-hearted reformers). Bale made it clear that he had ceased believing that conservatives might convert at all. In 1546 he declared that while he expected to be labelled a heretic by his enemies, 'neyther loke I for reasonable answere of them, nor yet for amendement of theyr knaueryes'. When one conservative, John Huntingdon, did convert, Bale was of course delighted, but he described the event in such a way as to maximise God's action in saving Huntingdon and to portray Huntingdon's own role in his conversion as entirely passive.[32] This was simply the practical application of the doctrine of election which was very widely held amongst English evangelicals in this period, but the fatalism it engendered was hardly conducive to proselytisation.

The priorities of, and the approach taken by those evangelicals who preached and published within England during these years could hardly be more different. Thomas Becon's works were written in a far less aggressive style. He could certainly show his teeth when dealing with those he judged to be heretics, but most of the time he genuinely seems to have been trying to make himself heard by the uncommitted and the sceptical. Aware that his books might be 'a songe sunge to them that are deafe', he went to some trouble to ensure that they did not grate too offensively on conservative ears.[33] He also repeatedly emphasised the importance of reaching the unconverted. Several of his tracts from this period are couched in the accessible form of a dialogue between a godly host, Philemon, and three guests who are eager to learn the Gospel. At the end of the first of these tracts, Philemon urges the guests to good works, 'that by your vertuous conuersacion ye myghte not plucke men from, but vnto the Gospell . . . not hynder but prouoke the Euangelical trueth'. To emphasise proselytisation at all was unusual for the exiles, let alone to suggest that it should be done through so non-confrontational a method as providing an example of virtuous living. The theme is picked up at the beginning of the next of Becon's dialogues, when Philemon rejoices at the change in the guests' lives. 'By theyr meanes', he soliloquises, 'there are, I thancke my LORDE God, many of oure neighbours whiche nowe begyn to folowe that trade and to practyse like godlynes.'

---

[31] Coverdale, *Confutacion of . . . Iohn Standish*, sig. A2^r.
[32] Joye, *Present consolation*, sigs. B5^v–6^r; John Bale, *The actes of Englysh votaryes, comprehendynge their vnchast practyses and examples by all ages* (RSTC 1270: Antwerp, 1546), fo. 6^v; Bale, *Mysterye of inyquyte*, sig. A3^v.
[33] Becon, *Inuectyue agenst swearing*, fo. 11^r. For Becon's more forthright side, see his *Potacion for lent*, sigs. C4^r–D1^r.

Elsewhere, Philemon declares, 'I desyre & wysh with all my herte, that all menne lyuinge were in the bowelles of Christ.'[34] Becon was as passionate on this subject when he was speaking with his own voice. One of the main motivations for the Christian to do good works, he believed, was 'that we may wynne our neyghbour also vnto Christ', and indeed one of the most important good works was to strive 'to brynge all men to the true knowledge of God & euen to engraffe them in the bodye of Christ'. Becon felt his evangelistic responsibilities heavily. 'Certes', he wrote, 'he is no true Christen manne, that prouideth for hys owne saluacion, and carethe not for the helthe of other.' This was one of the driving forces behind his publishing campaign. He compared himself to the watchman in the book of Ezekiel who, if he does not warn the people of impending doom, will not be free of guilt for their destruction.[35]

Most of the other domestic authors and preachers were less explicit about this priority than Becon, but it is ever-present in their work. Richard Tracy ended his tract *The profe and declaration of thys proposition: Fayth only iustifieth* with a prayer for those who refused to believe his doctrine: for God 'to open theyr eyes, and to mollifye theyr hartes, that they may be conuerted, and that he maye make them hole'. His next tract opened with a biblical text which Becon also quoted: the harvest is great but the labourers are few.[36] Richard Lant's imprint, *A compendyous treatyse of sclaundre*, betrays similar preoccupations. It is addressed to convinced evangelicals, but its purpose is to urge them to renounce conduct which, while not inherently sinful, 'scarreth men from the gospell'. Readers are urged to practise 'sobrenesse and dyscrecyon, for euen amonge enemyes ther be some that rather shuld be reconsyled than styred & prouoked'. Their concern instead should be to 'beutyfye the gospell' with the excellence of their conduct.[37]

The very form which some of these works took was informed by this concern with reaching the unconverted. The various sets of postils, intended as they were to reach into the pulpits of ordinary parish churches, are unmistakably a tool of proselytisation. It is no surprise that the postils' contents repeatedly reflect this priority. The author of the set published by Grafton urged Christians to good works, 'that the Heathen thoroughe theyr good conuersation maye be lyke wyse conuerted to the Lorde'. The reason one

---

[34] Becon, *Christmas bankette*, sig. G4^v; Becon, *Potacion for lent*, sigs. A7^v–8^r; Becon, *Pleasaunt newe Nosegay*, sigs. B6^r–7^r.

[35] Becon, *New yeares gyfte*, sig. O3^{r-v}; Becon, *Dauids Harpe*, sig. C1^r; Becon, *Inuectyue agenst swearing*, fos. 10^r–11^v; cf. Ezekiel 3:16–21, 33:1–9. In 1543 Becon was made to recant the presumption of claiming Ezekiel's mantle for himself: Bonner Register fo. 45^r.

[36] Tracy, *Profe and declaration*, sig. D8^v; Tracy, *Supplycacion to . . . Kynge Henry the eyght*, sig. A1^r. Cf. Becon, *Dauids Harpe*, sig. B3^r.

[37] *A compendyous treatyse of sclaundre, declarynge what sclaundre is* (RSTC 24216a: 1545?), sigs. A3^r, B1^r, B4^r.

should love one's enemy, we read, is to 'helpe to conuerte him to Christ'. One model suggested for Christians to imitate is that of the friends of the deaf and dumb man in Mark's gospel, who brought him to Christ: 'Thus also we praye for all them that haue no fayth. Noman yet can be saued by another mans fayth, yet it maye be by another mans fayth, that he maye get fayth of his owne.'[38] The priority thus proclaimed was put into practice by the author of another homily, who compared his audience to Saul on the Damascus road. He suggested that the objections which they made to the Gospel might just as plausibly have come from the apostle's lips, and urged that they follow Saul's example in resisting such temptations:

He made no such carnall reasons vnto Christe, sayenge: Shall I forsake thys fashion of seruynge God, and thys maner of lyuynge, that I haue led hetherto? Shall I now begynne to lyue otherwayes, than my fathers haue done before me? Doth not all the whole multitude of the prestes, scribes, and pharises cleue to the tradicions of the fathers? Ame I wyser than so many learned men?[39]

The evangelistic purpose is unmistakable. So too is the sense that conservatives had arguments which needed to be engaged with, and which were worth countering. The author of this sermon, and the authors of the other sets of homilies, were not intending to preach to the converted.

Indeed, proselytisation had an apocalyptic significance in these authors' minds. Like their co-religionists in exile, these authors feared divine judgement on the nation if it did not repent, but they differed from the exiles both in their assessment of the prospects for national repentance, and in their understanding of what such repentance entailed. The exiles were resigned to being Jeremiahs, prophetic voices which were doomed not to be heard. But those writing and preaching within England understood themselves to be Ezekiels, or even Jonahs, whose words genuinely might bring the nation to repentance and true faith. As such, they were less exacting than the exiles about quite what that true faith might mean, concentrating on a simple willingness to hear the Gospel and on moral renewal. Becon quoted a series of biblical stories to demonstrate that if a nation was granted preachers to call them to repentance, but ignored them, then judgement would follow.[40] The beginning of such judgement would be that England would be given up to its sins:

Excepte we shortely repent, & receyue this glorious lyght of christes most blessed gospel which nowe is come amonge vs ..., God wyll surely take it away againe from vs, & throw vs into more blynd darkenes than euer we were inuolued & wrapped in before.[41]

---

[38] *Brefe Postyl, vpon the Epystles and Gospelles*, fos. 173^{r-v}, 201^v, 245^v; cf. Mark 7:32.
[39] BL Royal MS 17.C.xvi fo. 186^r.   [40] Becon, *Pathway vnto praier*, sigs. R7^v–S4^v.
[41] Becon, *Newes out of heauen*, sig. A7^v; cf. Constantine, 'Memorial', 59.

The set of postils published by Grafton made a similar point, warning that 'thys tyme of helpe & felycite' would not last for ever. It urged repentance 'whyle we haue lyghte, for the nyghte commeth in the whyche no man can worke'. John Pokysfene's postils, too, stressed the urgency of repentance.[42] The fate not only of individual souls but of the nation, indeed of Christendom was in the balance. The reformers needed to make their message heard – even if a few corners had to be cut in the process.

This set of priorities engendered an approach to religious controversy that was wholly different from the confrontational methods of the exiled polemicists and their allies. The exiles sought to accentuate the divisions between reformer and conservative, so as to convince reformers that any compromise was a doomed attempt to straddle a chasm. Bale celebrated the stark division of humanity into the righteous and the reprobate, and rejoiced that God's Word was 'the marke of contradiccion and rocke of reproch'.[43] Those who remained in England and preached and published within the law were more concerned to make straight the way of the Lord. They sought to minimise and indeed to disguise any doctrinal divisions. Their hope was that if they could bridge the chasm, they might tempt conservatives to cross. Most of the printed works produced by these reformers do not draw attention to the fact that they are works of religious controversy. The sets of homilies are, at first glance, simply resource-books for preachers; Becon's works, merely pious treatises. Indeed, two of Becon's books go further. His *New pollecye of warre*, hurriedly produced when war broke out in late 1542, concealed the evangelical pill in a spoonful of patriotic saccharine. And his version of Bullinger's book on matrimony, *The golden boke of christen matrimony*, presents itself as a general advice-book on marriage. It is possible that this book's considerable commercial success in this period arose from its being given as a wedding present.[44]

This trend of surreptitious reformism reaches its logical conclusion in a set of imprints which quietly advance the evangelical cause despite not being works on religious topics at all. In 1542 Grafton printed an anonymous book called *A glasse for housholders*, one of the dreary tracts on ordering one's life prudently and piously that were a staple of sixteenth-century publishing. However, unwary traditionalists who bought this volume at the St Paul's book market would find themselves being instructed in the basics of justification by faith. Readers are also admonished to give to the poor on the grounds that they are the true images of God, and that 'other deed Images hath nothing commune with these Images but onely the shadowe, wherfore

---

[42] *Brefe Postyl, vpon the Epystles and Gospelles*, fo. 130[r–v]; BL Harleian MS 1197 fo. 144[r].
[43] Bale, *Image of bothe churches*, sigs. E5[v], Ff6[r].
[44] I am grateful to Carrie Euler for discussions on this point.

they might be called better tokens or signes of remembraunce': a familiar argument in both the Zwinglian and the Lollard traditions.[45] A number of other purportedly 'secular' imprints from this period are also spiced with evangelicalism. Early in 1543 Grafton printed an edition of John Hardyng's violently anti-Scottish *Chronicle*, to celebrate the victory of Solway Moss, and he incorporated other histories to bring the chronicle down to 1540. In the process, he added a few comments of his own. For example, Hardyng's account of King John's reign contrasts 'kyng Iohn his great misgouernance' with the pope's 'full greate pitee', but Grafton's marginal note describes how John 'by the Roomyshe byshop and his adherentes was most shamfully & vylanously abused'. Similarly, Grafton's brief account of the 1530s consists mostly of praise for the king for the expulsion of the pope and the suppression of idolatry.[46] Grafton was not the only evangelical printer to use such opportunities. In 1542–3 John Gough printed a translation of a news pamphlet describing recent developments in the Franco-Imperial wars. The translation, prepared by Gough's partner John Mayler, left the anti-French polemic of the original untouched, but presented Francis I's alliance with the papacy as conclusive proof of the French king's perfidy: 'hys deades declare hym to be the mooste vn-Christen Kynge, lyke as the Bysshoppe of Romes workes declare hym to be very Antechriste'. Likewise, *The order of the greate Turckes courte*, also translated from French, was given a new preface before Grafton printed it. The preface's description of Ottoman tyranny, and of God's coming judgement on Islam, is essentially the standard evangelical diatribe against the papacy, with only the minimum of changes to names. A third translation, the *Lytle treatyse of the instruction of chyldren* printed by Jean le Roux in 1543, has a more explicit evangelical subtext. While its ostensible purpose is to teach French, the texts which it uses to do so are unmistakably Lutheran.[47] Yet another work which might be considered as part of this group is *The Plowman's Tale*, a Lollard pseudo-Chaucerian text

---

[45] *A glasse for housholders, wherin thei maye se, bothe howe to rule them selfes & ordre their housholde* (RSTC 11917: 1542), sigs. A2^r–3^r, 7^v. For Lollard uses of this argument, see John Gough (ed.), *The dore of holy scripture* (RSTC 22587.5: 1540), sig. L5^{r-v}; Geoffrey Chaucer, *The workes of Geffray Chaucer newly printed with dyuers workes whiche were neuer in print before* (RSTC 5070: 1542), fo. 124^r (the *Plowman's Tale*). Cf. John Phillips, *The Reformation of the Images: Destruction of Art in England 1535–1660* (Berkeley and Los Angeles, 1973), 33–4. Thomas Bilney had taken a similar line: Batley, *On a Reformer's Latin Bible*, 48.

[46] John Hardyng and Richard Grafton, *The chronicle of Jhon Hardyng in metre, from the first begynnyng of Englande*, 2 vols. (RSTC 12766.7: 1543), vol. I, fos. 149^v–50^v, vol. II, fo. 160^r.

[47] Alfonso d'Avalos, *A ioyfull new tidynges of the goodly victory that was sent to the Emperour*, tr. John Mayler (RSTC 977.5: 1543?), sig. E3^r; Antoine Geoffroy(?), *The order of the great Turckes courte* (RSTC 24334: 1542), sigs. *2^v–4^r; [Ends:] *Here ends thys lytle treatyse of the instruction of chyldren* (RSTC 14106.2: 1543), esp. sigs. A7^v–B1^v.

which was included in a printed edition of Chaucer's works for the first time in 1542, although its printing probably owed more to Chaucer's fame than to reformist zeal.[48]

Dressing evangelical works in innocuous covers was a strategy which may have annoyed the book-buying public, but other evangelicals could hardly object.[49] The same cannot be said of the other main way in which these moderate reformers tried to appeal to conservatives: that is, by adjusting the content of their message, playing down controversial doctrines and presenting reformist ideas in traditional terms. This was hardly a new idea. Indeed, it was an obvious way of making 'new' doctrines palatable to a people profoundly suspicious of novelty. In 1536 Thomas Talley, a protégé of Bishop Barlow of St David's, was accused of preaching that

> if the Sowles that be departed haue any nede of our prayers (if it myght doo them any goode) ye shall praye that Christe the soner at the Contemplacion of our prayers may take them to the fruition of his glory.[50]

In other words, rather than condemning prayer for the dead outright, Talley tried to strip away its troublesome doctrinal implications while allowing the practice itself to remain. Likewise, it was said in London in 1537 that some reformers 'praying for theym that be departid, craftely ment of theym that be separated from God by synne, and not of the deade'.[51] In the early 1540s, however, this rhetorical trick began to appear more frequently. The area which was most commonly subject to this kind of blurring was the veneration of the saints and the piety which went with it. While all evangelicals were uncomfortable with prayer to saints, these authors and preachers were often willing to overlook it or to treat it as a second-order issue. Becon attacked the cult of Thomas Becket, which had been suppressed on the king's orders in 1538, but left it to his readers to draw the implications for the cult of saints more generally.[52] Robert Wisdom's careful consideration of the subject concluded that actually to invoke saints was to supplant God and

---

[48] That fame meant that it was exempted from the controls on books in the 1543 Act for the Advancement of True Religion. For a more conspiratorial assessment of the *Tale*'s importance, see Andrew Wawn, 'Chaucer, *The Plowman's Tale* and Reformation propaganda', *Bulletin of the John Rylands Library* 56 (1973).

[49] Indeed, more radical texts were occasionally repackaged in this way. The conservative Richard Whitford wrote with some annoyance in c. 1541 that he had seen one of his own books being sold bound together with an anonymous text which he identified as a work of Luther's. Even John Bale's plays of the 1530s have been seen as an attempt to provide an evangelical alternative to traditional play-cycles. Richard Whitford, *Here foloweth dyuers holy instrucyons and teachynges very necessarye for the helth of mannes soule* (RSTC 25420: c. 1541), sigs. A1^v–2^r; Ruth H. Blackburn, *Biblical Drama under the Tudors* (The Hague, 1971), 48–9.

[50] BL Cotton MS Cleopatra E.v fo. 415^r.

[51] Cranmer, *Letters*, 340; cf. the case of Thomas Wylley, above, pp. 1–4.

[52] Becon, *New yeares gyfte*, sigs. H1^r–2^r.

was unacceptable, but 'to desire them to praye with vs and for vs I thinke it after a maner tollerable'.[53]

This comparative openness to the cult of saints was matched by a willingness to appropriate the piety which went with it. For example, when Becon emphasised that Christ will pray for the believer, he used language strikingly reminiscent of traditional piety: 'His watching, fastynge, prayenge, almes dedes, & al that euer he dothe, shall be done for you.'[54] Writing in 1546, William Hughe laboured heroically to come up with a doctrinally acceptable substitute for the comfort provided by prayer for the dead. Addressing the bereaved, he emphasised that they are only parted from the deceased for a little while before being forever reunited, and added: 'You may at al times ... in the meane space, in youre myndes, and memoryes, se hym, talke with him, and embrace him.'[55] Similarly, a 1545 imprint gave a clearly evangelical view of Christ's sacrifice but described the Passion in terms borrowed from the old piety of devotion to the Name of Jesus.[56] Most intriguingly of all, Katherine Parr's *The lamentacion of a sinner* emphasised that the Christian should learn from 'the booke of the crucifixe'. In a delicately balanced passage, she implied that the piety associated with the use of images such as crucifixes was of real value, without either condoning or condemning – indeed, without explicitly mentioning – images as such. And all this in the context of a thoroughly evangelical exposition of justification.[57]

Not all controversial ideas could be given traditional veneers in this way. Nevertheless, the need to avoid unnecessary provocation was a constant theme amongst these reformers. They were painfully aware that their opponents needed no excuses to tar them with the more extreme heresies of the quasi-Reformed group represented by the exiles. As one moderate reformer wrote in the mid-1540s:

Whoso preacheth faith shalbe accused of sedition and disorder for denying good woorkes: if he set foorth Christ, he shalbe noysed to contemne sainctes, if he say Iesus is our onely mediator and peasemaker he is persecuted as an anabaptist.[58]

Many of these evangelical authors therefore went out of their way to embrace as much traditional religious practice as their consciences could bear.[59] The

---

[53] BL Harleian MS 425 fo. 5ʳ.
[54] Becon, *Newes out of heauen*, sig. F6ʳ. Cf. *Brefe Postyl, vpon the Epystles and Gospelles*, fo. 34ʳ.
[55] Hughe, *Troubled mans medicine*, vol. II, sig. F7ʳ.
[56] *Here after foloweth twoo fruitfull and godly praiers*.
[57] Katherine Parr, *The lamentacion of a sinner, bewayling the ignorance of her blind life* (RSTC 4827: 1547), sigs. B8ᵛ–D2ᵛ; cf. Ann Eljenholm Nichols, 'Books-for-laymen: the demise of a commonplace', *Church History* 56 (1987), 457–73.
[58] BL Royal MS 17.B.xxxv fo. 8ᵛ.
[59] While such attitudes sat uncomfortably with the stern rejectionism which Protestantism cultivated, it is becoming clear that pastoral and evangelistic imperatives led later generations

most comprehensive attempt to do this is in Becon's *Potacion for lent*, where he showed himself willing to accept almost the full panoply of traditional Lenten ceremonial as long as its meaning was explained in evangelical terms. This line of argument had several advantages. Creative reinterpretation of the ceremonies could yield distinctly evangelical messages. Mischievously, Becon had one of the 'guests' in his dialogue suggest that one reason for the covering of images in Lent is 'to put vs in remembraunce that although we haue in ony parte of the yeare paste commytted Idolatry with them, yet at this tyme we shoulde vtterly gyue ouer this abhominacion, & only cleue to God.'[60] Moreover, this approach gave the evangelicals a polemical edge over their opponents, because explaining the spiritual significance of laudable ceremonies to the people was certainly royal policy, and policy which some conservatives resisted.[61] As we have seen, several reformers applied the same kind of constructive criticism to auricular confession.[62]

If compromise on an issue was impossible, the usual response from these reformers was obfuscation. For example, several of them were outspoken in their denunciations of their religious opponents while maintaining a studied vagueness as to who those opponents actually were. Philip Gerrard attacked the 'blind stiffe hearted, and obstinate' who were opposed to God's Word. In a detailed and unpleasant passage, Becon argued at length that the Jews who had persecuted Christ had modern equivalents, but never stated who they might be. Elsewhere, when he lamented that Christians' enemies 'cruelly assayle vs', he appeared to mean spiritual rather than corporal enemies.[63] Others simply ignored difficult issues. For example, the author of Grafton's set of postils – the most radical of those sets to survive – simply ducked the problem presented by the Epistle for Passion Sunday, from Hebrews 9. This text, which vigorously asserts the uniqueness of Christ's sacrifice, was a key proof-text for the Protestant attack on the sacrifice of the Mass. As such, in 1546 this passage was to be at the centre of a major religious confrontation. However, it drew from Grafton's author a wholly anodyne homily that is one of the shortest in the set.[64] Some of the other texts produced by these reformers are extraordinarily bland. Gough's *A generall free Pardon or Charter of*

---

of Protestants to accommodate themselves to their audiences' cultures in similar ways. See, for example, Walsham, *Providence in Early Modern England*; Bruce Gordon, 'Malevolent ghosts and ministering angels: apparitions and pastoral care in the Swiss Reformation', in *The Place of the Dead*, ed. Bruce Gordon and Peter Marshall (Cambridge, 2000).

[60] Becon, *Potacion for lent*, sigs. H4^v–5^r.
[61] See, for example, CCCC MS 128 pp. 11–12, 15–16, 59 (*LP* XVIII (ii) 546 pp. 293, 295–6, 309).
[62] See above, p. 32.
[63] Erasmus, *A Diologe called the Epicure*, sig. A7^v; Becon, *New pollecye of warre*, sig. D4^v; Becon, *Pathway vnto praier*, sig. A4^v.
[64] *Brefe Postyl, vpon the Epystles and Gospelles*, fo. 153^{r-v}; cf. Hebrews 9:11–15. See below, p. 142.

heuyn blys is manifestly Lollard in origin, but is simply an exhortation to devotion to Christ and to good works.

At times, we find evangelicals raising their heads a little above the parapet, and implying provocative ideas without openly committing themselves to them. For example, in his preface to *The golden boke of christen matrimony* Becon praised matrimony and deplored celibacy in immoderate terms, but he did so while maintaining the pretence that he was speaking only of the laity, and did not mention the clergy at all.[65] The author of Grafton's *A glasse for housholders* also had serious reservations about clerical celibacy, urging parents to discourage their sons from ordination so that they should not be forced to promise the celibacy which only God can give, and arguing that Christian marriage was chaste. Again, however, this author did not explicitly discuss the legitimacy of the practice.[66] Elsewhere Becon spoke of the need to worship God as he had commanded, rather than according to human whims, but made no attempt to move from this to criticise established practices and ceremonies.[67] Perhaps the most delicately balanced example of this approach is in Becon's *A Christmas bankette*. This dialogue begins by describing the godly host's idealised evangelical home. His living space has been sacralised without embracing idolatry or superstition, by the means of inscribing a series of apposite Bible verses at various points around the house. One such verse – 'He that eteth my flessh, & drinketh my bloud, he dwelleth in me, and I in him' – is inscribed on the crockery. In answer to his guests' questions, the host explains:

This putteth vs in remembraunce when we eate oure meate of the breakynge of Christes moost blessed body and the shedding of his moost precious bloud & by the remembraunce of it, & the beleuyng of the same, our soules at that very present, are no lesse fed and susteyned, than oure bodyes are wyth the meate that is brought vnto vs in these dysshes.[68]

Becon was thus able to bring in the evangelical emphasis on remembrance of Christ's Passion in the Eucharist without actually mentioning the Mass at all.

Intriguingly, this technique of playing down differences, conceding what could safely be conceded and appropriating the opposition's language, was also used by some moderate conservatives in this period.[69] Two sermons published under Bishop Bonner's supervision in 1544 are outspoken in their

---

[65] Heinrich Bullinger, *The golden boke of christen matrimonye, moost necessary and profitable for all them, that entend to liue quietly and godlye in the Christen state of holy wedlock*, ed. and ascribed to Thomas Becon (ps. Theodore Basille), (RSTC 4047: 1543), sigs. A3ʳ–4ʳ.
[66] *A glasse for housholders*, sigs. F4ᵛ–5ᵛ.   [67] Becon, *Newes out of heauen*, sigs. E4ᵛ–5ʳ.
[68] Becon, *Christmas bankette*, sig. B2ʳ.
[69] These themes have been explored, principally for a later period, in Wooding, *Rethinking Catholicism*; although Wooding downplays the extent to which any polemical purpose shaped such apparent moderation.

denunciations of the papacy, speak positively of the doctrine of the priesthood of all believers, and condemn clerical greed and corruption – all themes to which evangelicals would have warmed.[70] Bonner's own injunctions to his clergy in 1542 ordered them to engage in a rigorous programme of study of the Bible and the *Bishops' Book*; to expound the meanings of ceremonies; and to avoid preaching from fables or legends in the manner which the reformers so despised.[71] The Bristol preacher Roger Edgeworth had a knack for using the evangelicals' arguments against them. A favourite early evangelical line of argument pointed out that Christ had promised that the Gospel would bring division and persecution, and argued that the absence of such troubles before Luther indicated that the true Gospel had been lost. Edgeworth took up this claim and accepted that the Church had been deeply corrupted; but he then suggested that it was only because of this corruption that Luther's heresies had been so widely received. Or again, Edgeworth agreed that salvation came only through Christ's merits, but countered the evangelical argument that faith gave rise to good works with the suggestion – couched in strikingly similar language – that good works arise from the fear of God.[72] The Oxford theologian Richard Smith went one better. He turned the Protestant emphasis on assurance of salvation on its head by arguing that no one can be sure of the steadfastness of their own faith, but everyone can be certain of the efficacy of the Mass.[73] Even in Edward VI's reign, one somewhat idiosyncratic conservative could write that 'gospeller' was an honourable name, but that those who claimed it for themselves were not applying Scripture to their lives; rather, they had abandoned the false gods of popery but put nothing in their place.[74] For the evangelicals, as also for the conservatives, such approaches may have lacked candour, but they were a sensible way of trying to deal with the situation of religious confusion which partisans of both sides faced. If they could reduce the polemical volume, they might succeed in making themselves heard.

Unsurprisingly, those evangelicals who adopted this style met with the scorn and contempt of more uncompromising reformers. Bale, in particular, reviled the 'worldlye wyse brethren . . . which are neither hote nor colde'.

Some there be abrode in the worlde, walkynge vndre the pretence of the gospell, whych do all they can to hyde the fylthye partes of that monstrouse madama, that rose couloured whore of Babylon. . . . The bokes whych hath bene putt forth

---

[70] Chedsay and Scott, *Two notable sermones*, sigs. G3^v–6^v, H1^v–2^r.
[71] Bonner Register fos. 39^v–40^v. On Bonner's own religion, see below, pp. 216–18 and 220–21.
[72] Roger Edgeworth, *Sermons very fruitfull, godly and learned: preaching in the Reformation c. 1535– c. 1553*, ed. Janet Wilson (Cambridge, 1993), 160, 168–9.
[73] Richard Smith, *Assertion and defence*, fo. 63^r.
[74] John Proctor, *The fal of the late Arrian* (RSTC 20406: 1549), sigs. A8^v, B4^r.

by menne of lernynge to discouer her myscheues, do they now gelde, myngle, hacke, cutte, take fro and putt to. . . . Easye it is to perseyue, what hath brought these menne to the gospell . . . ther owne fylthie lucre and dampnable deuylyshe pleasure.

He did not spell out precisely which books he meant, but an obvious candidate would be Coverdale's translation of Bullinger's *Der Christlich Eestand*. Becon expunged the most controversial chapters and added a new preface to his version of this. Likewise, Bale's attack on those who print English Bibles 'whych now hath neyther annotacyons nor table' can only be directed at Grafton, the publisher of the officially authorised Great Bible. He also made clear his disgust with Richard Taverner's editions of the Augsburg Confession and of Sarcerius Erasmus' *Commonplaces*.[75]

George Joye had equally little time for those who were willing to make compromises: 'These vnright rightwysemakers wold serue two contrary masters at once, the Pope and God to, the gospel and the popis lawis but whyls thei thus halt on both sydis with Baals preistes thei serue trwlye the deuill.'[76] Anne Askew flung the same text at Lord Chancellor Wriothesley shortly before her condemnation, asking how long he would 'halte on both sydes'. In his 'elucydacyon' of her words Bale took up the theme, seeing this as a description of the whole English Church, and added references to two more texts which were favourites amongst anti-Nicodemites:

For all our newe Gospell, yet wyll we styll beare the straungers yoke with the unbeleuers, and so become neyther whote nor colde, that God may spewe vs out of hys mouth.[77]

Nor was this a problem confined to the printed page. John Foxe related how William Smith, a radical preacher in Calais in the late 1530s, was approached by some reformist members of the Calais council. They suggested 'that he should not be so earnest against them that yet could not away with [God's word], willing him to beare with suche, for by bearing with them they might hap to be wonne'. Smith, however, felt that this was mere dissimulation, and gave his reply from the pulpit: 'Let all such take heede, for before God, I feare that God for their contemning of his word, will not long beare with them, but make them in suche case as some of them shall not haue a head left them vpon their shoulders to beare vp their cap withal.'[78]

The most obvious accusation which could be made from the moral high ground of exile was that of cowardice – although Bale's criticism of those

---

[75] Bale, *Image of bothe churches*, sig. B1^v; Bale, *A dysclosynge or openynge of the Manne of synne*, fos. 6^v–7^r.
[76] Joye, *George Ioye confuteth, Winchesters false Articles*, fo. 4^r. Cf. I Kings 18:21.
[77] Askew, *The lattre examinacyon*, fo. 19^{r-v}. Cf. II Corinthians 6:14; Revelation 3:16.
[78] *AM*, 1224.

reformers who did nothing to help their imprisoned or exiled brethren was at least tinged with personal bitterness.[79] It is true that persecution did not appeal to those evangelicals who were trying to operate within the law, and it is also true that their commitment to proselytisation could lead them into the familiar grey areas of dissimulation. This, however, was only part of the truth. The mildness which these reformers showed to their opponents was a symptom as well as a cause of their distinctive doctrinal position. The exiles were as divided from these writers and preachers in doctrine as they were in style. Moreover, the doctrines of the more moderate writers were more palatable to the unconverted. The radicals' fear of their conformist brethren was, in other words, entirely justified.

JUSTIFICATION AND THE MASS

If a single theme ran through the work of these moderate evangelical writers and preachers, it was the Protestant doctrine of justification by faith alone. It would be difficult to exaggerate the extent to which this topic dominates the printed output of this group. Becon's first book, *Newes out of heauen*, is essentially an extended exposition of the doctrine, although, in keeping with his general approach, he uses the associated theological jargon sparingly. Most of his subsequent books return to this subject, tackling it from several different angles. It is of course also the subject of Tracy's book, *The profe and declaration of thys proposition: Fayth only iustifieth*. Taverner's postils repeatedly emphasise the importance of faith; those in Grafton's set repeat the doctrine *ad nauseam*. It also seems to be the theme of the fragmentary pamphlet printed by William Middleton, whose only surviving leaf expounds the link between faith and assurance.[80] The *Lytle treatyse of the instruction of chyldren*, published by Jean le Roux, includes a brief but comprehensive exposition of justification by faith. It is the only controversial issue to which John Pokysfene's anodyne postils allude. For example, he notes, in his account of the parable of the Pharisee and the publican, that the publican called on God's mercy alone: 'he doth not allege for to haue his workes, his merytes his good dedes, to be exalted'. The doctrine of justification is the subtext of much of Grafton's *A glasse for housholders*. For example, it retells the gospel story of the rich man and Lazarus in such a way that the rich man is damned for placing his trust in his wealth, and for rejecting God when he came to him in Lazarus: in other words, he is damned for lack of faith rather than evil deeds. William Hughe's *The troubled mans medicine* not only teaches the doctrine, but uses the technical Protestant terminology

---

[79] Bale, *Image of bothe churches*, sigs. S2ᵛ–3ʳ.
[80] *A meane to die well* [= headline, sig. B1ʳ] (RSTC 17760.5: c. 1545).

of imputation to do so.⁸¹ Several anonymous manuscript treatises on the subject which are datable to this period survive; one has been attributed to Cromwell's publicist Richard Morison.⁸²

This preoccupation also dominated evangelical pulpits during Henry's last years. The Scottish reformer Alexander Seton felt strongly enough about the doctrine that in 1541, goaded by a conservative's preaching of free will at Paul's Cross, he assembled a gathered congregation at St Antholin's church in London to denounce the preacher and to expound predestination and the inability of good works to aid one's salvation.⁸³ Robert Wisdom, too, was troubled for a sermon in which he preached 'howe vnperfecte all our rightwisnes is, and . . . moved all men to sett hand vpon the rightwisnes of faith'.⁸⁴ The dossier of heresy charges against Kentish reformers drawn up in 1543 reveals that the doctrine was widely preached in that county. An agent of Archbishop Cranmer's called Humphrey Churden took it to one of its more contentious logical extremes when he preached in February 1543 that 'if Iudas had gone to god, & confessed his fawte, saying Peccaui ['I have sinned'], as he went vnto the priests, he had not been damned'.⁸⁵ Indeed, Cranmer himself, the most highly placed proponent of this conformist evangelicalism, was passionately convinced of the Protestant doctrine of justification. He risked the king's anger by opposing to the last the treatment of the doctrine in the *King's Book*; and he remained quietly but unshakeably convinced that salvation was through faith alone and by grace alone.⁸⁶

Justification by faith was, of course, common ground to all Protestants, and it may seem unnecessary to labour these reformers' commitment to the doctrine. Nevertheless, three aspects of that commitment are worth emphasising. First, for all the apparent moderation they showed in dealing with their opponents, there was nothing moderate in the commitment these reformers showed to this doctrine. It was not the most politically convenient of sticking-points, given the king's well-known antipathy to it; but while these authors certainly shaped their expositions of justification in response to that antipathy, their commitment to the doctrine did not waver. Secondly, while all evangelicals affirmed justification by faith, there were significant differences of emphasis. The exiled writers rarely treated it as a doctrine important in itself. In the whole body of works Bale published in this period, he only once discussed the subject at any length.⁸⁷ The only substantial exile treatments of justification are George Joye's pamphlets written

---

[81] BL Harleian MS 1197 fo. 190ᵛ; *A glasse for housholders*, sigs. A3ᵛ–4ʳ; Hughe, *Troubled mans medicine*, vol. II, sig. E5ᵛ. Cf. Luke 16:19–31, 18:9–14.
[82] BL Harleian MS 423 fos. 12–33; PRO SP 6/11 no. 7, pp. 315–21 (*LP* XVIII (i) 611.3).
[83] Seton and Tolwin, *Declaracion made at Poules Crosse*, sigs. A2ʳ–3ᵛ.
[84] BL Harleian MS 425 fo. 4ʳ.   [85] CCCC MS 128 p. 29 (*LP* XVIII (i) 546 p. 299).
[86] MacCulloch, *Cranmer*, 338–47.   [87] Bale, *Epistle exhortatorye*, fos. 17ʳ–18ʳ.

against Stephen Gardiner, in which he took his lead from the bishop's rejection of the evangelical interpretation. When the exiles did mention justification and related doctrines, they usually did so in order to make more provocative points. Joye, for example, argued from St Paul that faith justified the believer, but only if that faith was openly confessed: 'For fayth in oure herte iustifyeth and the confession with oure mouthe bringeth saluacion.'[88] More commonly, the exiles pointed out that justification by faith was incompatible with the sacrifice of the Mass; for as we have already seen, the Mass was the issue which dominated their outlook. While they affirmed justification by faith, it was something of a side issue.[89] A central emphasis on justification by faith, which does not attempt to use the doctrine as a bridge to more radical beliefs and behaviour, is one of the most distinctive characteristics of those writers and preachers who remained in England in these years.

Finally, while the emphasis on justification was certainly an end in itself, most of these works do give that doctrine a particular slant. It was one of the central concerns of these reformers to rebut the charge, so frequently made, that the evangelical doctrine of justification was antinomian. The claim was that if good works played no part in the salvation of the Christian – as all evangelicals did indeed preach – Christians were thus licensed to sin without thought of the consequences. This was an unjust parody of the evangelical doctrine, but it was a parody which that doctrine invited. This accusation was made across Europe, but Henry VIII's strong views on the subject made it essential for English evangelicals to engage with the problem. Archbishop Cranmer's response to his failure to convince the king of his view of justification in 1543 was to gather authorities to support his position, and a central purpose of this collection was to refute the charge of antinomianism. The political problem was reinforced by these reformers' general concern to reach the unconverted. The result was a remarkable concentration of polemical resources on this subject. Becon rarely mentioned justification without also emphasising the Christian's absolute obligation to perform good works. In print and in the pulpit, others went out of their way to make the same point.[90] Tracy's piece on justification is largely focused on this question; so too is the manuscript treatise ascribed to Richard Morison. Robert Crowley described evangelicals as taking a virtuous middle way between Pelagianism and libertinism.[91]

It was a subject to which these writers devoted not only time, but passion. Becon's usual moderation of tone deserted him when he launched withering

---

[88] Joye, *Daniel*, fo. 34^r; Romans 10:9.   [89] Davies, *Religion of the Word*, 18.
[90] MacCulloch, *Cranmer*, 345–7. See also, for example, BL Harleian MS 425 fo. 4^r; PRO SP 1/119 fos. 185^v–7^r (*LP* XII (i) 1147).
[91] Crowley, *The opening of the woordes of the prophet Joell*, sigs. A5^r–7^r.

attacks on those whom he called 'the grosse Gospellers, the rayling readers of the scripture . . . and brayneles bablers of the gospell, whych bable muche of gods trueth, and yet lyue no part therof'.[92] Tracy, likewise, reviled the 'wanton christians' who 'euer haue in their mouthes, thys proposition: fayth onely iustifyeth, whyche neuer tasted in theyr harte, any parte of that lyuyng fayth'.[93] Such libertines probably were a genuine problem rather than a polemical straw man.[94] In any case, they were a staple of conservative polemic, and so dangerous whether they existed or not. 'Such grosse gospellers', Becon wrote, 'haue much hyndered the prosperous progresse of Goddes worde.' Katherine Parr agreed that 'suche gospellers are an offence, and a sklaunder to the worde of God'. Richard Lant's piece on slander was almost entirely concerned with this last issue. Likewise, the author of Grafton's postils urged his audience not to 'hurte . . . the conscience of the hearer, beynge an offence vnto hym'.[95]

It is entirely typical of these moderate reformers, however, that some of them were not content with railing against antinomianism, and tried to find more creative solutions to the problem. Protestant theology may have denied works any role in salvation, but salvation need not be the only issue. Within the kingdom of heaven, a strong scriptural tradition suggested, some of the saved would have exalted positions, others lowly ones. Perhaps these gradations, if not salvation itself, were influenced by one's deeds. Philip Melanchthon argued that 'there will be different rewards for different labours' and 'distinctions in the glory of the saints'. Luther was content to see these rewards as, in Emma Disley's phrase, an 'unmerited recompense' for good works; an integral part of the process of sanctification which his theological system had separated so assiduously from justification.[96] Such ideas appear to lie behind Richard Tracy's insistence that 'to beleue that good workes shall not be rewarded of god, is deuelyshe and dampnable'.[97] One anonymous writer embraced this argument explicitly, arguing that 'no man maye merite of his owne power, but it is true that our lorde will rewarde everye man after his owne deedes'. The elect, he continued, are rewarded for their works with a higher place in heaven; whereas if one of their number sins and repents 'notwithstandinge that repetaunce he shall have for that evill deade the lower place in heavyn'. This was a complex and highly problematic argument. For 1540s evangelicals, however, its usefulness for

---

[92] Becon, *Christmas bankette*, sig. O4ᵛ. [93] Tracy, *Profe and declaration*, sigs. D3ʳ–4ʳ.
[94] Ryrie, 'Counting sheep', 98–105.
[95] Becon, *Potacion for lent*, sig. F4ᵛ; Parr, *Lamentacion of a sinner*, sig. F1ᵛ; *Compendyous treatyse of sclaundre*; *Brefe Postyl, vpon the Epystles and Gospelles*, fo. 140ᵛ.
[96] Emma Disley, 'Degrees of glory: Protestant doctrine and the concept of rewards hereafter', *Journal of Theological Studies* ns 42 (1991), 99–101.
[97] Tracy, *Profe and declaration*, sig. D4ʳ⁻ᵛ.

emphasising the importance of works outweighed the dangers of its potentially treacherous theology.[98]

On the question of justification, the differences between the exiles and their brethren in England were more of style than substance. The same cannot be said of the other hallmark of this moderate evangelicalism, the Eucharist. The Eucharistic presence was the most explosive doctrinal issue in 1540s England. Both to Henry VIII, and to the exiles and other evangelicals who held to a quasi-Reformed position, it was the most fundamental litmus test of religious allegiance. Perhaps unsurprisingly, these more cautious reformers preferred to engage with the question indirectly, or to avoid it altogether. However, enough of them were unable or unwilling to evade the issue in this way for a clear consensus to appear. Part of this consensus was a distaste for the Mass, and in particular for the doctrine of the sacrifice of the Mass, although it is uncertain quite how widely this distaste was shared. The other, far more solid part of the consensus was a firm unwillingness on the part of any of these moderates to be associated with rejection of the Real Presence. If there was a single fault line dividing English evangelicalism, this was it.

Within a decade of Henry VIII's death, the Mass had become the critical issue delineating Protestant from Catholic in England. Few then tried to straddle the line; and few of those who had once done so cared to remember the fact. Becon, for example, moved towards a Reformed view of the sacraments at some stage after 1543, and when the folio edition of his works was printed in Elizabeth I's reign he removed embarrassingly Catholic phrases such as 'the sacrament of the altar' from his earlier books. This folio edition formed the basis for the Parker Society's editions of Becon's works, through which most modern readers have come to know him.[99] The success of Becon's retrospective doctrinal clean-up is symbolic of the extent to which modern scholarship has viewed Henrician evangelicals through an Edwardian and Elizabethan prism; a prism whose blind spot largely conceals the moderate reformism with which this chapter is concerned.[100] It has always been apparent that there was a division amongst Henrician evangelicals between those who took a Reformed view of the Eucharist and those whose opinion was more akin to that of the Lutherans: the latter view being that Christ's body and blood were objective, corporally present in the consecrated elements, but that the substance of bread and wine still remained, rather than being

---

[98] PRO SP 6/3 no. 20, pp. 164–5 (*LP* XIV (i) 376).

[99] John Ayre, editor of the Parker Society volumes, was aware of these changes but simply commented that Becon's views 'did not and could not at once arrive at all the clearness and decision by which they were afterwards distinguished'. Thomas Becon, *The Early Works of Thomas Becon*, ed. John Ayre (Cambridge: Parker Society, 1843), xviii.

[100] Witness, for example, Foxe's unenthusiastic comment that, in the 1540s, Cranmer was 'yet but a Lutheran'. *AM*, 1224.

miraculously transformed ('transubstantiated') into the substance of Christ. The quasi-Lutheran views of some leading reformers, notably Archbishop Cranmer and Robert Barnes, are well known. One Elizabethan writer even added that 'the most part of the other byshoppes and learned men' also held such views.[101] Yet the powerful evidence for a more widespread evangelical suspicion of the Reformed position has rarely been acknowledged.[102] Rory McEntegart, in one of the most careful assessments of late Henrician religious politics in recent years, has acknowledged that by 1539 English evangelicalism has to be divided into two camps, which he characterises respectively as sacramentaries and (more cautiously) as Lutherans. He places Thomas Cromwell into this second group, and emphasises, quite correctly, that 'during the 1530s there was in fact no contradiction at all in being an evangelical and opposing denial of the real presence'.[103] Becon (later in life), Foxe and later Protestant generations were consistently concerned to downplay the prevalence of such opinions in the 1530s, but contemporary evidence suggests otherwise.

William Gray, the balladeer who defended Cromwell's reputation after his execution, conceded that his former master had been a traitor and had suffered justly. He was not, however, willing to admit that Cromwell had been a heretic. He was proud to proclaim that

> The sacrament of the aulter, that is most hyest
> Crumwell beleued it to be the very body of Chriest.[104]

It is hard to doubt that this claim is true, especially since less than a year before the veteran evangelical George Constantine had been writing to Cromwell with a mixture of indignation and alarm to counter accusations that he was a sacramentary – a crime, Constantine protested, as heinous as treason.[105] Another of Cromwell's correspondents, Henry Goderick, the parson of Hothfield in Kent, was as hot-headed a reformer as one might hope to find. He had preached in Folkestone that Christians should trust in Christ's passion rather than in the elevated Host – which was certainly an attack on the Mass, although not on the Real Presence. He was also accused, probably falsely, of preaching that Christ took no flesh from the Virgin. In 1539 he

---

[101] This was Cranmer's anonymous biographer, whom Diarmaid MacCulloch has tentatively identified as Stephen Nevinson. Nichols (ed.), *Narratives*, 224; MacCulloch, *Cranmer*, 633–6.
[102] For example, Basil Hall argues that 'from the beginning of the reformation in England ... almost all' English reformers were 'uneasy and even hostile' toward Lutheran sacramental ideas. Basil Hall, 'The early rise and gradual decline of English Lutheranism (1520–1660)', *Reform and Reformation: England and the Continent c. 1500–1750*, ed. Derek Baker, *Studies in Church History: Subsidia* 2 (1979), 109.
[103] McEntegart, *Henry VIII*, 135–7.
[104] Gray, *Balade agaynst malycyous Sclaunderers*. [105] Constantine, 'Memorial', 77.

wrote to Cromwell in a fury to denounce idolatry in the neighbouring parish of Ashford. There was a rood in the north aisle of the parish church, he alleged, to which illegal offerings were made and at which

> dayly the people blaspheme god . . . for they make reuerence & Inclination vnto it as many as goith by it, it is in there way as they goo to see the sacrament of the body & blode of Crist mynystered at the high aulter.[106]

For all his loathing of idolatry, Goderick was prepared to use archetypally conservative language to describe the Mass, and to allow reverence to the sacrament to pass without comment. Like Gray and Constantine, his unmistakable evangelicalism apparently did not extend to sacramentarianism.

For Cromwell's clients, there were obvious advantages in being seen to be on the safe side of such a dangerous doctrine, but evangelicals who remain convinced of Christ's presence in the Eucharist can be found outside Cromwell's circle; nor did they disappear after the minister's death. These include many of the authors and preachers with whom we are already familiar. Becon happily referred to the sacrament simply as 'Christes body'. He wrote that when Christians receive it, they receive 'the very body of our lord Iesus Christ, of al treasures moost precious' and 'taste of the true Paschall Lambe, which was offered & slayne for our sake'. He implicitly supported the traditional practice of fasting before receiving the sacrament; and he urged his readers 'to be present at the ministracion of the moost blessed Sacrament of the altare Christes very body and bloud'. By contrast, he was bitter in his attacks on 'the Anabaptistes, Sacramentaries & other Phanaticall & frentyke Spirites which haue vayne visions inuented of theyr owne braynes'. Even Becon's enemies tacitly conceded that his views on the sacrament were not actively heretical. In the recantation sermon prepared for him in 1543, he was made to admit to having preached on the cult of saints, prayer for the dead and clerical celibacy 'vntruylie', but the worst fault that could be found with his preaching on the sacrament was that 'men were offended with me'.[107] Other evangelicals can also be found using resolutely realist language about the Eucharist. A book of prayers published by William Middleton even provided a set of Mass devotions, emphasising that Christ 'hath lefte his body here amonge vs in fourme of breade & wyne'.[108] One anonymous writer, laying out principles for scriptural interpretation which were otherwise highly damaging to traditional religion, insisted that the Real Presence should be maintained because the plain words of Scripture,

---

[106] PRO SP 1/152 fo. 1^v (*LP* XIV (i) 1053); BL Cotton MS Cleopatra E.v fo. 397^r (*LP* IX 230). For the dating of this document, see Elton, *Policy and Police*, 163.
[107] Becon, *Potacion for lent*, sigs. K4^v–L4^v; Becon, *Pathway vnto praier*, sigs. L1^r–2^r; Becon, *Dauids Harpe*, sig. K4^v; Bonner Register fo. 44^v.
[108] *A boke of prayers called ye ordynary fasshyon of a good lyuynge*, sig. B6^r.

'Hoc est corpus meum', admitted no other interpretation.[109] Robert Wisdom was equally explicit: 'We confesse and knowledge ... that the Lorde Iesus giveth at all tables of his holie sowper to all that receiue yt his very bodie and bloude.' And he refused to defend the condemned sacramentaries John Frith and John Lambert.

This was not capitulation to the conservatives. No sooner had Wisdom affirmed the Real Presence than he moved to the attack, using (typically enough) his opponents' terminology against them. He claimed that while traditionalists gloried in their commitment to transubstantiation (a term which Wisdom carefully neither criticised nor endorsed), 'their was never heritique did so grett dishonoure to the blissed Sacrament of Christes souper' as they did. In the Mass, Christ's institution had been replaced with 'an Ordinaunce of their awne Imagination'. As such, he claimed, it was the conservatives who were the true sacramentaries: a term which Wisdom clearly still regarded as a wounding insult.[110] Richard Tracy made a similar point once Henry VIII was safely dead. He affirmed that those who receive the sacrament 'eate Chrystes flesshe, and drynk hys bloude', but added: 'Note well Chrysten Reader, whether our clargy be not most detestable sacramentaryes, which take awaye christes woordes of Instytucyon, of the sacramente of hys body and bloude.'[111] Wisdom and Tracy's dislike of the Mass was by no means incompatible with their commitment to the Real Presence. There were plenty of other aspects of the Mass to which reformers objected. For example, much traditional piety ascribed considerable spiritual value simply to witnessing Mass, and especially to seeing the elevation of the consecrated host. The cleric John Cardmaker mocked this piety: 'it is as profitable to a man to heare Masse, and see the Sacrament, as to kysse Iudas mouth, whyche kyssed Christ our Sauiour'. But while this was clearly inflammatory and anticlerical, it does not appear to have been sacramentarian. The implication is that those who hope for contact with Christ mediated through the priest (Judas) are deluded, but that if they receive the sacrament themselves they will indeed be receiving Christ.[112]

Likewise, reformers of all stripes rejected the Catholic understanding of the Mass as a sacrifice as inimical to the Protestant doctrine of justification.

---

[109] PRO SP 6/3 no. 20, p. 158 (*LP* XIV (i) 376). Cf. *Brefe Postyl, vpon the Epystles and Gospelles*, fos. 160^r–1^r, where the sacrament is referred to as 'the true Easter lambe whyche is oure Lorde Iesus Christe ... our Easter feaste, in the whyche oure sauyoure Christ was offered to the heauenly father'. Taverner, *Catechisme*, sigs. K4^v–6^r, insists that 'we must fastly beleue that chryst with all his rychesse is here gyuen and presented vnto vs, no lesse then yf he stode euen personally present'.

[110] ECL MS 261 fos. 116^{r-v}, 121^{r-v}.

[111] Richard Tracy, *A bryef & short declaracyon made, wherby eue[ry] chrysten man maye knowe, what is a sacrament* (RSTC 24162: 1548), sigs. A3^r, B6^v.

[112] *AM*, 1205; PRO SP 1/243 fo. 64^r. Cardmaker was also known as Taylor.

Many English reformers can be found who either directly or indirectly made this distinction. Even Becon went out of his way to stress that Christ's sacrifice was unique and unrepeatable, although with his characteristic caution he did not explicitly connect this to the Mass.[113] Thomas Hancock, the curate of Amport in Hampshire, was suspended from his cure in 1546 for denying that the Mass was a sacrifice. On the same day, preaching from the same text, Edward Crome sparked the last major religious crisis of Henry's reign by preaching that 'the Bisshopp of Rome hath wrongly applyed the sacrafice of the Masse making yt a satysfaccyon for synnes of the quyck and the deade. . . . A sacryfice it is of thankes geving.' With his usual precision, Crome did not extend his attack to the Real Presence.[114]

The Eucharistic presence was a dangerous issue, and the wiser and more prominent of these moderate reformers either left it alone or affirmed the Real Presence only in vague terms. However, several less cautious reformers can be found attempting to formulate more complex viewpoints, denying transubstantiation but insisting on some other form of real, objective presence. The author of one treatise on this subject affirmed a corporal presence as the necessary meaning of the words of institution, but denied transubstantiation, arguing that there was no scriptural evidence or logical reason that the substance of bread and wine should be absent after the consecration. He even turned a favourite conservative argument to his own use, suggesting that to affirm transubstantiation is to deny that Christ had the power to maintain two substances together, and thus to blaspheme.[115] Another anonymous treatise takes the form of a dialogue. In the portion that survives, a master instructs 'D.' (presumably a disciple) as to the meaning of Christ's presence in the Eucharist. Christ's body is indeed present corporally and naturally, the master argues, but it is not corporal and natural in the same sense as our own bodies. This much is orthodox, but he then goes on to suggest that the words 'corporal' and 'natural' are approximations chosen simply for convenience. The disciple wonders if other terms might be preferable, and the master briefly considers 'supernatural' and 'supercorporal' before deciding that they would mislead and create doubt among the unlearned. The traditional terms should be retained, but their purpose, he insists, is

not to schewe or signifi the state or maner of the thyng but most serteynly to confyrme & ratyfy the veryte therof. For the veryte of cryst body in the sacrament is the thyng that we ar most bound to beleve & not after what maner & sorte it is there, whiche passit the reche of al mens wyttes.

---

[113] Becon, *Newes out of heauen*, sigs. F8^v–G1^r.
[114] Nichols (ed.), *Narratives*, 71; BL Harleian MS 425 fo. 66^r.
[115] BL Cotton MS Cleopatra E.v fos. 179^r–83^v (*LP* XIV (i) 1067).

'Natural' and 'corporal', therefore, become code-words for a 'true' presence, and the question of quite *how* Christ is truly present becomes unimportant. The terms should be retained, both to protect the faith of the simple and to refute the Manichean heresy that Christ was not incarnate; but the learned will know what actually lies behind them.[116] Although we have only a fragment of this dialogue, it is unmistakably an exercise in doctrinal double-speak. The author is attempting to smuggle evangelical views in under the cover of orthodox terminology. The fact that this fragment is found amongst the State Papers suggests that the attempt failed.

However, while some arguments may be flavoured with political expediency, there is no reason to doubt that such attempts to find a compromise were sincere. The regime certainly had little interest in differentiating among those who, by rejecting transubstantiation, had already broken the bounds of acceptability. People who held ambiguous views such as these were already anathematised by the Act of Six Articles. One Coventry heretic who clearly accepted the Real Presence within the context of a celebration of Mass was troubled by the reservation of the sacrament: he had said that

The bodie of our lorde Ihesu Christ is not now in the Canapee or pixe ouer the high aulter, ther. It is not ther at euery tyme but at the tyme of consecracion therof by a priest beying at masse.[117]

Thomas Trentham, a London pinner, was likewise arrested for claiming that the sacrament 'was a very good thing but it was not as men toke yt, very god'.[118] We know from the zealous young Zwinglian Richard Hilles that Richard Mekins, burned in 1541, 'did not entirely deny the corporal presence, but claimed (as our Wyclif did) that the accident of bread did not remain there without the substance'. This did not save him, and the conservative chronicler Charles Wriothesley simply noted that he died for heresy against the sacrament.[119]

In the early 1540s, these two doctrinal boundary-markers – justification by faith and the objective presence of Christ in the Eucharist – enclosed a very substantial body of reformers. It is, however, perhaps from outside that the potential strength of their position is most visible. English conservatives apparently felt the preaching of justification by faith to be a serious threat. The conservative John Standish had to admit that the preaching of justification by faith alone was popular: 'It is commonly sayde no venym or poyson is wurse or more pestylent then that whiche to the tast semyth swete and

---

[116] PRO SP 1/152 fos. 23^r–4^v (*LP* XIV (i) 1066).
[117] PRO KB 9/129 fo. 5^r (*LP* XVII 537).
[118] PRO SP 1/243 fo. 73^r (*LP* Addenda 1463).
[119] Wriothesley, 126; *ET*, 147 (*OL*, 221).

dilycious.'[120] Gardiner agreed with him, claiming that those who preached grace were popular because they irresponsibly refused to confront their audiences with the reality of sin: 'In a miserable state of iniquitie and synne, some wolde haue nothynge preached, but mercye, with onely Christe, and howe he beareth al synne, payeth all, purgeth all, and clenseth all.'[121] Across the confessional divide, Robert Crowley shared the worry that congregations did not wish to be reprimanded for their sins, but merely to be told that 'Christes bloude doth suffice'.[122] This part at least of the evangelical message was apparently winning a sympathetic hearing.

Perhaps the clearest demonstration of the strength of the conformist evangelicals' doctrinal position is the concern which some conservatives showed to break it up. For example, in a printed poem from around 1540 which only survives in a fragment, the author tried to refute justification by faith by associating it with sacramentarianism:

> They saye that confessyon, is ryght nought ...
> They saye it is ynough, god knoweth our thought
> We shall be safe, Christ hath so dere vs bought.
> But who so dothe, confessyon dispyse
> The sacrament of the aultre, setteth as lytell pryse.[123]

This author was clearly hostile to any doctrinal innovation. However, he recognised that the evangelical attack on confession might well appeal to his readers. It is an attack which he summarised fairly deftly, and whose connection with evangelical views on justification he recognised. Yet he also assumed that the same readers would find attacks on the Mass repugnant. Therefore he attempted to discredit the one by association with the other. Discrediting moderate beliefs through association with radical ones is an old trick; but as here, it will only prove effective when it is false, that is, when the moderates are not in fact willing to embrace more radical views. Likewise, Gardiner argued in 1547 that belief in the Real Presence was incompatible with justification by faith, citing Zwingli to prove 'that these things are so joined and interdependent that whoever has admitted the doctrine of "only faith" in justification is compelled to reject the Sacrament of the Eucharist in the way we profess it.'[124] The unlikely alliance between Gardiner and Zwingli is a reminder that conservatives and radical reformers shared an interest in partitioning the doctrinal territory which these moderate evangelicals occupied. In the early 1540s, however, their eventual success in doing so was still only on the horizon.

---

[120] Standish, *Lytle treatise against the protestacion of Robert Barnes*, sig. C2^r.
[121] Gardiner, *Detection of the Deuils Sophistrie*, fo. 114^v.
[122] Robert Crowley [fragment on the prophet Joel] (RSTC 6088.9: 1547?), sig. D6^r.
[123] *Here beginneth a good lesson for yonge men* (RSTC 15525: 1540), sig. A2^v.
[124] Gardiner, *Letters*, 335.

This is the distinctive, conformist, moderate yet unmistakable evangelicalism of the world of England's pulpits and printshops in the years after Cromwell's fall. This was the acceptable face of reformism: the loyal opposition, working within the system rather than against it, persuading rather than denouncing. If we wish to, we can invent party labels for these reformers. 'Eirenic evangelicals', perhaps, although their eirenicism did not extend to compromise on their core beliefs, in either direction. 'Anglo-Lutherans', perhaps – their doctrinal emphases were distinctly those of Lutheranism; but their political quiescence and moderated style were very un-Lutheran, and they did not acknowledge any direct connection with Luther and his circle. Yet such labels are not especially helpful. They suggest a self-conscious unity which these reformers do not appear to have had. They also suggest that this set of identities – doctrinal and political moderation – formed the essence of one breed of English reformism. This is not the case, for two reasons. First, this was not so much a subset of English evangelicalism as its public face, the face it wore for preaching and publishing. As we shall see, in other, less visible settings, different patterns of reformist behaviour were being set, and different battles were being fought. Secondly, this variant of evangelicalism was not so much a party as a process. It was intimately tied to a particular set of political circumstances. In the early 1540s sacramentarian views were utterly rejected by the regime, but many of the other doctrines preached by evangelicals were accepted or afforded a degree of toleration. Heresy prosecutions were usually half-hearted and frequently negotiated with their targets. In such circumstances we might expect a moderate, non-confrontational evangelicalism to flourish. Rather than postulating a short-lived Anglo-Lutheran movement, we might instead think of an Anglo-Lutheran *moment*. This was a strain of evangelicalism whose time had come; and its time was to pass, almost as quickly. As political events moved on so these reformers would be carried with them. Moreover, even in the early 1540s, there were internal tensions within this kind of reformism which were signs of less compromising times to come.

THE COMMONWEALTH

These conformist evangelicals were moderate in their doctrinal and political ambitions, but they pursued them with genuine commitment. These were not merely fair-weather reformers. At times, on some subjects, they were willing to abandon their characteristic caution, or felt obliged to do so. One such subject was the free availability of the English Bible.[125] Another was the broader issue of the welfare of the commonwealth. This was the set of problems that was once called the Condition of England Question, and

---

[125] See below, pp. 250–4.

which would nowadays be called social policy. A number of these reformers held and expressed forthright views on social questions, and were not afraid to criticise the status quo in doing so. This thread of social radicalism in their thought linked them to the exiles and some of their doctrinally radical allies. Evangelicals of all stripes were broadly agreed in their view of the commonwealth, and this agreement is the earliest sign of the mainstream of English evangelicalism expressing public discontent with the rule of Henry VIII. It was a symptom of the instability of evangelical moderation, and a catalyst for more confrontational attitudes to come.

The 'commonwealth men' are a now somewhat discredited staple of mid-Tudor history. In the reign of Edward VI, so the argument went, a coherent body of authors and preachers set forward a robust criticism of existing social and economic structures, which arose from a consistent and consistently radical programme for the renewal of society along Gospel lines. This thesis was subjected to a typically meticulous mauling by Geoffrey Elton in 1979 and has never fully recovered. Recent attempts to rescue something from the wreckage have been a good deal more cautious. It is clear that a great many writers did address such themes, especially in the early years of Edward's reign, and indeed that Protector Somerset dallied with the language and ideas of the 'commonwealth' to a dangerous extent. It is equally clear that such social criticism was uncoordinated, naive and idealistic, as considerations of genre should lead us to expect. Preachers such as Hugh Latimer preached sermons; they did not present balanced policy papers. There was, indeed, no 'commonwealth party'. However, the hope for reform of the commonwealth interacted with the hope for reform of religion in a way that many contemporaries found compelling.[126]

It has also long been recognised that this evangelical interest in the state of the commonwealth stretches back into the last years of Henry VIII's reign. One of the set texts of the 'commonwealth men' was written in 1542, and republished in 1548: Henry Brinklow's *The complaynt of Roderyck Mors*. But the breadth of interest in 'commonwealth' questions in Henry's last years has not been fully appreciated. Moreover, such blunt social views were being expressed not only by religious radicals such as Brinklow, but by individuals who were much more softly spoken on doctrinal and political matters. Brinklow's two surviving polemics dealt principally with social matters; a third, lost text probably did the same. He may also have been the author

---

[126] The best recent treatment of this question is in Davies, *Religion of the Word*, 140–76. See also G. R. Elton, 'Reform and the "commonwealth-men" of Edward VI's reign', in *The English Commonwealth*, ed. P. Clark, A. Smith and N. Tyacke (Leicester, 1979), 23–38; Ethan Shagan, 'Protector Somerset and the 1549 rebellions: new sources and new perspectives', *English Historical Review* 114 (1999), 34–63; Diarmaid MacCulloch, *Tudor Church Militant* (1999), 122–6.

of another social polemic, *A supplication of the poor commons*, which was printed anonymously in 1546, the year after his death. But more conformist evangelicals wrote on such topics as well. Richard Tracy followed his careful defence of justification by faith with *A supplycacion to our moste soueraigne lorde kynge Henry the eyght* in 1544. A number of Becon's works touched on social issues, in particular his *New pollecye of warre* and *Inuectyue agenst the moost wicked vyce of swearing*. Richard Grafton's household manual *A glasse for housholders* also included a good deal of forthright social commentary. Numerous other authors and preachers, including such prominent figures as Robert Barnes and Robert Wisdom, emphasised 'commonwealth' ideas. Robert Crowley's verse commentary on the book of Joel was not published until 1547 (or perhaps not even 1567), but was written during the last year of Henry VIII's life and pays close attention to social questions.[127] In particular, one unpublished text is worth mentioning: an untitled supplication addressed to the king and written during the period 1543–6, which lays out comprehensive and ambitious plans for the reform of the commonwealth and does so from a distinctly yet cautiously evangelical perspective. It was written by an anonymous Londoner whom I have come to think of as the London Commonwealthman.[128]

Much of the social agenda which these authors and preachers were pressing was uncontroversial in its ambitions, although hardly realistic. The Christian obligation to care for the poor was a constant theme.[129] Becon's description of the ideal evangelical home had the text 'Break thy bread to the poor' inscribed above the dining table. He returned repeatedly to his insistence that 'the poore peple ought to be better prouyded for'.[130] *A glasse for housholders* also urged almsgiving on its readers as a form of true worship of God.[131] This much is mere platitude, but most 1540s evangelicals were also willing to point the finger of blame for failure on this score. Brinklow's attacks on the rich were uncompromising: 'their heades are so geuen to seke their awne particular welthes', he wrote, that they ignored their duties to the poor. And he warned the rich that their goods would be witnesses against them on the day of judgement.[132] Yet *A glasse for housholders* was if anything blunter, stating that 'greate riches can neyther be eyther gotten or els kepte without synne'. Crowley argued that during times of dearth the wealthy must use their goods for the welfare of the poor, even to the extent

---

[127] Crowley, *The opening of the woordes of the prophet Joell*. The earliest surviving (near) complete text is the 1567 edition, but several uncut sheets apparently printed in 1547 survive. The text itself refers to Henry VIII as the reigning king (sig. E2ʳ).
[128] BL Royal MS 17.B.xxxv. [129] Davies, *Religion of the Word*, 162–7.
[130] Becon, *Christmas bankette*, sigs. A7ᵛ–8ʳ (cf. Isaiah 58:7); Becon, *Newes out of heauen*, sig. B3ᵛ; Becon, *Potacion for lent*, sig. G4ʳ.
[131] *Glasse for housholders*, sigs. A7ᵛ–8ʳ.
[132] Brinklow, *Lamentacion of a Christian*, A2ᵛ, B3ʳ.

of impoverishing themselves.[133] And even Becon was ready to threaten the rich with the fires of hell if they failed to use their wealth for others, spelling out their duties at some length and quoting the fearsome story of the rich man and Lazarus. All too many of the gentry, in his view, were hoarders of grain and avaricious collectors of lands and titles.[134] Robert Wisdom was scathing towards those who

> pilleth the pore and scrapeth them even to the bones; their pride and ambytion; their excesse and vayne apparell; their banketting and dronkenshippe till every place be full of vomyt; their vayne buildinges as though thei wolde liue here ever; their layinge howse to house and cowpling feld to fealde till pore men be eaten owt of the contraye; their engrossinge of fermes some man xx^{ti} in to his handes; their raysing of rents vnto the vtter empoverishinge of the pore.[135]

This was more than platitude.

A similarly robust attitude towards the wealthy runs through evangelical commentary on broader social morals. Fashionable and expensive clothing was a favourite target. Becon compared tailors inventing new fashions to Satan inventing new ways to tempt the faithful. Tracy's complaint was that expensive clothes were beggaring people – especially, this married layman emphasised, women's clothes. Robert Wisdom was particularly offended by the purchase of luxurious clothes for images, while the poor were naked – a theme on which Becon also touched. The London Commonwealthman renewed the old call for sumptuary laws to be enforced. He, too, was particularly concerned about women's fashions.[136] Other favourite themes were the scourge of profanity[137] and the perceived irresponsibility of wealthy parents towards their children. Miles Coverdale's popular translation of Heinrich Bullinger's work on matrimony included stern denunciations of parents who were unwilling to educate their children, and especially of the practice of wet-nursing. *A glasse for housholders* includes a long section on childrearing, and devotes even more attention to the evils of wet-nursing.[138] A further moral failure which excited evangelical comment was the treatment of prisoners. In 1542 Wisdom urged his congregation to visit and care for those in prison. While evangelicals who might themselves face arrest clearly had a

---

[133] Crowley, *The opening of the woordes of the prophet Joell*, sigs. A8^v–B1^v.
[134] *Glasse for housholders*, sig. A4^v; Becon, *Pleasaunt newe Nosegay*, sigs. M2^v–3^r (cf. Luke 16:19–31); Becon, *Pathway vnto praier*, sig. N 2^v; Becon, *New pollecye of warre*, sigs. H2^v–4^r.
[135] ECL MS 261 fo. 118^v.
[136] Becon, *Pleasaunt newe Nosegay*, sigs. E2^v–3^r; Tracy, *Supplycacion to Henry the eyght*, sigs. D1^v–2^r; ECL MS 261 fo. 110^r; Becon, *Pathway vnto praier*, sig. R2^r; BL Royal MS 17.B.xxxv fo. 20^{r-v}.
[137] See above, pp. 76–7.
[138] Bullinger, *Christen state of Matrimonye*, fos. 68^v–71^v; *Glasse for housholders*, sigs. D5^r–F8^v.

vested interest in this traditional work of mercy, deeper principles were also at work. Wisdom himself, when a curate in Oxford in the mid-1530s, had won widespread admiration by ministering to the sick during an epidemic, apparently with little regard for his own safety.[139] In 1546, Richard Cox, an academic who was normally careful about expressing his evangelical views, urged Sir William Paget with quite uncharacteristic passion to see to the provision of good counsel and pastoral care for prisoners, and denounced the 'wolves of the world' who preferred enriching themselves to following Christ's commands in this way.[140] Even otherwise moderate reformers understood these questions to have an apocalyptic significance. Richard Grafton saw the Turks' military victories as a judgement on 'our synfull lyuynge'. When Becon spoke of England's need for repentance, it was these social ills that he had at the forefront of his mind. The use of profane oaths, he wrote, was so widespread that it alone was 'ynough to bryng final destruccion to thys Realme'. Indeed, he claimed that England's immorality 'is an euident token that the great & terrible daye of iudgement is at hande'.[141] Crowley agreed that the oppression of the poor was one of the signs of the last days, and lamented that even in those last days worldliness would continue:

> Some shall plante vines,
> And some presse wines,
> And some shall marry wiues:
> And some shall bie,
> To gaine therby,
> But few shall mende their liues.[142]

So far, these denunciations are preachers' generalisations, forthright and dramatic while avoiding any criticisms or proposals that were too specific. Yet evangelicals with an interest in these matters also made specific proposals for changes to established laws and practices. Brinklow denounced the increase of rents and the spread of enclosure.[143] The London Commonwealthman laid out a detailed programme of economic reform. He called for all enclosures made during the previous twenty years to be revoked and for a triennial national survey of rents to prevent increases. Land which was left untended was to be confiscated and the wealthy were to be barred from any farming activity other than the breeding of horses. Both the export

---

[139] ECL MS 261 fo. 115^{r-v}; PRO SP 1/123 fo. 145^r (*LP* XII (ii) 374).
[140] PRO SP 1/225 fo. 202^r (*LP* XXI (ii) 282).
[141] Geoffroy, *Order of the great Turckes courte*, sig. *3^r; Becon, *Pathway vnto praier*, sig. A7^{r-v}; Becon, *Inuectyue agenst swearing*, fo. 6^r; Bullinger, ed. Becon, *Golden boke of christen matrimonye*, sig. A6^r.
[142] Crowley, *The opening of the woordes of the prophet Joell*, sigs. A2^v–3^v, F2^v; cf. Luke 17:26–9.
[143] Brinklow, *Complaynt of Roderyck Mors*, sigs. A6^v–B3^r, B5^r–6^v.

of unworked goods, and the import of any goods to which there was a domestically produced alternative, were to be banned.[144] The legal system was always a favourite target. An evangelical treatise on the reform of the common law from this period, probably written by Richard Morison, both deprecates the greed and ignorance of lawyers and sets about suggesting remedies.[145] For Becon, lawyers were 'gaping wolfes' more interested in prolonging cases and lining their pockets than in justice. John Bale had earlier described lawyers as profiting from the corruption of the Church.[146] The anonymous set of postils published by Richard Grafton took a different tack, picking up the Pauline warning against Christians taking one another to law.[147] The most thorough attack on the legal system, however, came from Brinklow. He demanded a comprehensive overhaul of English law, of which the most radical elements were his call for a stipendiary Bar and judiciary, and his argument that the two houses of parliament should be merged. He also directly attacked some of the Henrician legal innovations, notably the seizure of first-fruits from the clergy and the 'cruelnesse and suttyltes' of the Court of Augmentations.[148] Most dangerously, he challenged the new doctrine that statute law was absolute – a challenge in which he was joined by Robert Crowley and the courtier-poet William Palmer.[149]

However, the social problem which most alarmed evangelicals was sexual immorality. This subject had a polemical edge to it, since reformers were keen to depict clerical celibacy as a cloak for sexual misconduct of all kinds, and some of them – notably John Bale – made little effort to conceal their prurience. However, they were aware that the sexual conduct of the laity was hardly exemplary either. Becon denounced with some vigour the popular view that faithfulness to one's wife was unmanly, and lamented that 'honeste wyues syt at home and allmoost perish for honger but harlottes are sumptuously fed wyth al kynde of deyntyes'. Worse still, not all wives were such paragons; and loose-living men were also willing to wink at their wives' indiscretions.[150] An early pamphlet by George Joye gave a confessional twist to these claims. He suggested (most implausibly) that the Six Articles' bar on clerical marriage was the result of a plot by married nobles, who wished to separate priests' wives from their husbands in order to lure them into harlotry.[151] Again, almost all the reformers who wrote on

---

[144] BL Royal MS 17.B.xxxv fos. 17^v, 19^v–20^r.
[145] BL Cotton MS Faustina C.ii fos. 5–22. I owe this reference to John Jackson.
[146] Becon, *New pollecye of warre*, sigs. H1^v–2^r; Bale, *King Iohan*, lines 1263–4.
[147] *Brefe Postyl, vpon the Epystles and Gospelles*, fo. 105^v; I Corinthians 6:1–8.
[148] Brinklow, *Complaynt of Roderyck Mors*, esp. sigs. A6^v, C3^v–4^v, E1^r–2^r.
[149] Ibid., sig. D5^v; Crowley, *The opening of the woordes of the prophet Joell*, sig. G4^{r-v}; TCC MS R3.33 fo. 109^r.
[150] Bullinger, ed. Becon, *Golden boke of christen matrimonye*, sigs. A4^v–7^v.
[151] Joye, *Defence of the mariage of preistes*, sig. A4^{r-v}.

sexual morals had concrete remedies to suggest. Aside from the legalisation of clerical marriage – which no one could safely advocate within England after 1539 – two main proposals were put forward. First, the death penalty should be imposed for adultery, although some evangelicals conceded that this should only be for the second offence.[152] Secondly, prostitution should be both outlawed and vigorously prosecuted. Evangelicals were aware of the traditional view that prostitution should be permitted as a social safety-valve, but treated it with contempt.[153] The former demand was a gruesome pipe dream, but the Southwark stews were indeed closed by royal order in the spring of 1546. This may have had as much to do with levels of syphilis as with any moral concern, and one sour evangelical grumbled later that it had merely scattered prostitution across the country. However, the proclamation was couched in strongly moralistic terms, lamenting that prostitution kindled God's wrath and corrupted the commonwealth.[154] Evangelicals could be forgiven for believing that they had won the argument.

Few of these issues were directly connected to doctrinal questions, and they may seem relatively uncontroversial. Certainly, a number of religious conservatives agreed with their evangelical opponents on many of these points. In the same year as Becon denounced those who preferred drinking to attending church, Edmund Bonner, the bishop of London, was taking practical steps to control this problem, by ensuring that alehouses closed for the duration of divine service.[155] In 1544 the conservative preacher William Chedsay doubted the legality of prostitution and attacked the miserliness of the rich. In a passage glistening with irony, he praised the charity of landowners, whose love was so great that they wished to bring as many lands as they could into their embrace. Another conservative preacher, John Feckenham, denounced the payment of first-fruits and called for tithes to be reformed. A more prominent traditionalist, Richard Smith, went so far as to argue that tithes were only due to clergy who were resident and ministered to their flocks.[156]

---

[152] Bullinger, *Christen state of Matrimonye*, fo. 35^v; Bullinger, ed. Becon, *Golden boke of christen matrimonye*, sig. B7^{r-v}; BL Royal MS 17.B.xxxv fo. 20^v; Davies, *Religion of the Word*, 153.

[153] Bale, *Christen exhortacion vnto customable swearers*, fo. 3^r; Bullinger, *Christen state of Matrimonye*, fos. 33^v–4^r; Turner, *Huntyng and fyndyng out of the Romishe fox*, sigs. F1^r–2^v.

[154] TRP, 365–6; Whitney R. D. Jones, *William Turner*, 155; Elis Gruffyd, ed. and tr. M. Bryn Davies, 'Boulogne and Calais from 1545 to 1550', *Bulletin of the Faculty of Arts, Fouad I University, Cairo* 12 (1950), 13–14.

[155] Bonner Register fo. 40^r.

[156] Chedsay and Scott, *Two notable sermones*, sigs. D8^v–E2^r, E5^{r-v}; PRO SP 1/228 fos. 55^v–6^r (*LP* XXI (ii) 710); Richard Smith, *A godly and fayhfull Retraction made and published at Paules crosse in London* (RSTC 22822: 1547), sig. B2^r.

Such cross-party agreement does not, however, mean that these sentiments were uncontroversial. The regime's own view was very different. Official publications during this period gave little space to the plight of the poor. Where it was mentioned, the flavour of the discussion was far less charitable. Poverty was blamed not on the greed of the rich but on 'sturdy beggars', the able-bodied who chose to beg because they were too lazy to work.[157] Or holy days were blamed, for limiting the amount of work which the poor were permitted to engage in.[158] Henry VIII himself was very keen that poverty should be blamed principally on the poor. His manuscript amendments to the *Bishops' Book* emphasised the need to compel sturdy beggars to work, and he replaced a passage emphasising that our daily bread is a gift from God with an address to 'the tru labouryng man', who will attain prosperity and salvation through hard work. Indeed, some of his amendments might, to the unkind eye, suggest a tender conscience. The king who had dissolved the monasteries, imposed questionable taxes and forced a number of leading clergy into damaging exchanges of property qualified the commandment not to covet one's neighbour's goods. His rewritten version stipulated that one should not do so 'wrongfully or vniustely'. Faced with a later passage which claimed that attempting to obtain another's property was a violation of the commandment, Henry added that this was only the case if it was done 'withowght due recompence'.[159] It was in keeping with this spirit that, when John Pylbarough paraphrased the *Magnificat* in his panegyric to the king, he entirely omitted the central verses which preach justice for the poor and vengeance on the mighty.[160] Those who took a different view of these matters had to watch their step. Richard Smith was made to recant his views on tithes shortly after Henry's death. It was said that he had denied that tithes might legitimately be impropriate to lay persons, and that this was 'seditious and sclaunderous to the kynges maiesties procedinges'.[161] Evangelicals were in a somewhat more exposed position. Brinklow and Tracy published their social polemics abroad, either pseudonymously or anonymously. The London Commonwealthman rather naively submitted his to the king instead; and so, although it was clearly written with publication in mind, the manuscript simply disappeared into the royal library. The much more cautious Becon was permitted to publish, for a while at least, but even he insisted on going out of his way to deny that he was advocating the communion of goods.[162]

---

[157] *King's Book*, fos. 65^{r-v}.   [158] PRO SP 1/143 fo. 202^v (*LP* XIV (i) 402).
[159] Bodleian Library, 4° Rawlinson 245, fos. 54^v, 77^r, 85^{r}–7^{r}. These attempts to rewrite Scripture drew a tart rebuke from Cranmer, who insisted that even if compensation was made the commandment had still been broken. Cranmer, *Letters*, 100, 106.
[160] Pylbarough, *Commemoration*, sig. C3^v; cf. Luke 1:51–3.
[161] Richard Smith, *Godly and faythfull Retraction*, sig. B2^r.
[162] Becon, *Potacion for lent*, sig. G4^r.

Even on the comparatively safe subjects of charity, social morals and the legal system, then, evangelicals with an interest in the commonwealth found themselves pulling away from the regime. In addition, however, the 'commonwealth' agenda led these authors into positions critical of the English Church itself. The Church's structure, its wealth and the ways in which it used them offended even otherwise moderate reformers. Moreover, such matters led directly to conflict with a regime which had its own reasons for taking a close interest in Church property. Henry VIII's known willingness to seize ecclesiastical wealth for his own ends gave this issue its sharp edge, because while evangelicals were usually content to see the Church stripped of its property, their ideas about what should be done with it differed dramatically from the king's.

Simple denunciations of ecclesiastical wealth were controversial but straightforward enough. Bale declared that the clergy had no interest in using their riches for the benefit of the commonwealth, but rather in toadying to 'great lordes and ladyes . . . & soche as hath fat benefices'.[163] Brinklow used the language of sturdy beggars – 'lusty Lubbers' in his version – but applied it to chantry priests, who should labour for their livings while their stipends should go to the poor. The author of *A supplication of the poor commons* – perhaps, again, Brinklow – inveighed against the financial burden the clergy laid on the poor with real bitterness. 'They commaunde vs to buylde them goodly churches with hyghe steaples, & greate belles to ryng oure pence into theyr purses when our frendes be dead.'[164] George Joye used the gospel story of the rich young ruler who was reluctant to give his wealth to the poor to mock his particular hate-figure, Stephen Gardiner: 'I dare say he wold skratche his head twyse (as did this riche man) ere he sold his bisshopryke & had geuen it to the pore.' Joye and Becon both cited the Pauline injunction – 'whoso labore not, let him not eat' – to argue that non-preaching clergy should be deprived of their incomes.[165]

However, the Supreme Head of the Church of England could not easily be excluded from these criticisms. Richard Tracy's attack on clerical pluralism drove him to confront the state of affairs which the king had authorised. His first swipe was at court chaplains, who supported themselves from benefices they never visited. 'Haue not Kynges and other rulers sufficyent to endowe their chapelaynes?', he wondered. He moved on to attack the statute of 1529 which permitted such men to be non-resident. Eventually, as well as calling on the king to reform such matters, he insisted that in the meantime he strip

---

[163] Bale, *Epistle exhortatorye*, fos. 21^v–2^r.
[164] Brinklow, *Lamentacion of a Christian*, sig. B1^v; Brinklow?, *Supplication of the poore Commons*, sig. B3^r.
[165] Joye, *George Ioye confuteth Winchesters false Articles*, fo. 12^r; Joye, *Daniel*, fo. 67^r; Becon, *New pollecye of warre*, sig. H 7^v; Luke 18:18–23; II Thessalonians 3:10.

such idle and useless clergy of their lands.¹⁶⁶ *A supplication of the poor Commons* made a similar point in more intemperate language, and directly blamed the king. Crowley again singled out royal chaplains, but widened his attack to include the nobility and the magistrates who permitted such abuses.¹⁶⁷ The payment of tithes to a non-preaching ministry was another particularly sore point, although not all reformers agreed on how tithes ought to be reformed.¹⁶⁸ Yet the regime was quite uncompromising. In 1539, even a modest attempt to ameliorate the effects of lay impropriations of tithes on clerical incomes was blocked in parliament.¹⁶⁹ Evangelical attitudes hardened in return. Richard Cox's correspondence with William Paget in 1546 included a remarkably unguarded attack on impropriations, which he argued were irreversibly destroying any chance of a godly preaching and pastoral ministry across large parts of England. 'Wo be to the beginner, wo bee to the Continuers, wo be to the Aiders, and Abetters', Cox wrote, knowing that this attack must embrace the king as well as his councillors.¹⁷⁰ It was a truism amongst evangelicals of every stripe that ecclesiastical wealth could have only one justification: the support of a preaching ministry. However, as George Constantine complained in 1539, 'in all our visitations we have had no thin[g]e reformed but our purses'.¹⁷¹ Wealth that should have been supporting preachers or being taken from the Church for other godly ends was instead being spent on war and on supporting the kind of clergyman whom Archbishop Cranmer called a 'good viander'.¹⁷² The result was a dangerous erosion of evangelical goodwill towards the regime.

Some reformers moved from these general expressions of alarm to policy suggestions that were more detailed and, consequently, more politically delicate. The London Commonwealthman's proposed solution to the ills of the commonwealth was a campaign of mass deprivation of the clergy, with the wilfully ignorant to be pensioned on a pittance and the well-meaning to be restored once they had acquired sufficient education. The large number of vacant benefices that would result were to be leased to laymen who would be required to use the revenues to maintain the chancel, provide hospitality and to host visiting preachers. And as the keystone of this programme, the bishoprics were to be dissolved and the cathedrals refounded as preaching centres. This was sugared with a bribe to the king. The dissolution of the twenty-seven bishoprics and their cathedrals should, he claimed with back-of-envelope insouciance, raise £27,000 for the Crown. The mass deprivations

---

¹⁶⁶ Tracy, *Supplycacion to Henry the eyght*, sigs. A8ʳ–B1ʳ, C3ʳ⁻ᵛ.
¹⁶⁷ Brinklow?, *Supplication of the poore Commons*, sig. B5ʳ; Crowley, *The opening of the woordes of the prophet Joell*, sigs. B5ʳ–C3ᵛ.
¹⁶⁸ ECL MS 261 fo. 111ʳ; Tracy, *Supplycacion to Henry the eyght*, sigs. E6ᵛ–7ʳ; Gough (ed.), *Dore of holy scripture*, sigs. C4ʳ, 7ᵛ; Brinklow?, *Supplication of the poore Commons*, sigs. A 8ʳ–B 2ᵛ.
¹⁶⁹ Lehmberg, *Later Parliaments*, 63.   ¹⁷⁰ PRO SP 1/225 fo. 202ᵛ (*LP* XXI (ii) 282).
¹⁷¹ Constantine, 'Memorial', 59.   ¹⁷² MacCulloch, *Cranmer*, 264.

would, he guessed, yield a further £100,000 in the revenue from vacant benefices and in first-fruits. But this cannot conceal the fact that this writer was proposing the abolition of sacramental ministry across most of England. He believed it would be 'much more commodioose necessarie and profitable for the realme to haue no preestes at all, than ignoraunt and vnlearned, vicioose and of evyll conuersation'. In other words, he did not really envisage a priestly ministry at all, but was calling for a revolution in the English Church, and implicitly challenging a king who had knowingly allowed such a state of affairs to continue.[173]

Henry Brinklow's theology was more radical than this author's, but his plans for ecclesiastical wealth differ only in mood and detail. Those few differences can be accounted for by the difference between a consciously illegal polemic and a document actually presented to the king in the apparently sincere hope of redress. He was more concerned to channel the proceeds of a mass seizure of Church lands towards care for the poor and for education, and the bone he threw to the king was rather meaner than that which the London Commonwealthman offered. Brinklow suggested that the incomes of non-preaching clergy should be forfeit directly to the king, but – echoing Tyndale's ideas – proposed that the Crown should receive only half of the value of England's church plate, and a tenth or less of church lands seized. Brinklow, however, allowed his bitterness to show more plainly. He approved of the dissolution of the monasteries, but also pointed out that they had provided some alms for the poor, a degree of hospitality and some patronage of godly clergy. As a result, the dissolution had stripped many of the poorest places of England of even the little they had.[174] Few others dared express such suicidal views at the time, but this was to become the evangelical orthodoxy. In 1554, William Turner laid out an even more thoroughgoing plan for restructuring the Church, which envisaged the creation of more than 150 elected 'bishops', the suppression of cathedrals and the ending of all impropriations. In the process, he roundly criticised 'King Henry the eight, with his couetous counsell', who, through seizing monastic property rather than using it for godly ends, 'spoiled the churche and hole realme miserably after suche a fashion, that all the hole realme smarteth for it vnto this day'. He proceeded to compare Henry to Ananias, struck dead for attempting to defraud the Holy Spirit.[175] Hindsight soured even the dissolution of the monasteries.

---

[173] BL Royal MS 17.B.xxxv fos. 2^v–4^r, 11^v–12^r, 17^v.
[174] Brinklow, *Complaynt of Roderyck Mors*, sigs. D4^r–5^r, E2^r, F3^{r-v}; Brinklow, *Lamentacion of a Christian*, sig. D7^{r-v}.
[175] Turner, *Huntyng of the romyshe vuolfe*, sigs. D6^{r-v}, E6^v–F3^r; Acts 5:1–6. Cf. Anthony Gilby's similarly jaundiced view of Henry's proceedings in 1558: Anthony Gilby, 'An admonition to England and Scotland, to call them to repentance', in *The Works of John Knox*, ed. David Laing, vol. IV (Edinburgh, 1895), 563–4.

An emphasis on the need for self-sacrificial action to secure the prosperity of the commonwealth was shared across the evangelical spectrum. It may have been an emphasis which contributed to the appeal of reformist preaching, as it was elsewhere in Europe.[176] It is certain, however, that this emphasis divided evangelicals from Henry VIII. While the leaders of evangelical opinion within England in the early 1540s were predominantly moderate in both doctrine and politics, their views on the commonwealth both united them with their more radical brethren in exile and set them at odds with the king. For most of Henry VIII's reign, this division remained largely potential – although, as we shall see in the next chapter, in one arena the regime's high promises and miserly actions collided dangerously with values which were particularly dear to evangelicals. Yet even a potential division reminds us that the moderation of evangelicalism as preached and printed in England in the 1540s was more than mere quietism or conformity. Where conviction led these reformers into a degree of confrontation with their king, they were willing to follow. This underlines the fact that their moderation, too, was as much a matter of conviction as of convenience; and suggests that their wider loyalty to the religious settlement also had its limits.

[176] Larissa Taylor, *Soldiers of Christ: Preaching in Late Medieval and Reformation France* (Oxford, 1992), 219–20.

5

The universities

For the Jewes requyre a sygne, and the Grekes seke after wysdome. But we preache Christ crucifyed, vnto the Jewes an occasyon of fallynge, and vnto the Grekes foolysshnes.   I Corinthians 1:22–3

GODLINESS AND GOOD LEARNING

The Reformation was perceived by those who made it, and by those who were made by it, as an intellectual event. Nowadays we are interested in 'popular religion' and the religious culture of the unlearned, but this preoccupation would have bemused most of the religious reformers of the sixteenth century – including many outside the elites. It is worth emphasising the extent to which, in the early sixteenth century, learning was next to godliness. A Lutheran catechetical dialogue which was translated into English in 1545 provides a typical example. One of the characters, the 'unlearned man', begins with a soliloquy in praise of the learning he lacks:

Whan I do considre with my selfe (ryght gentle neyghbours) how many greate, learned, wyse, and connynge men there be in the worlde, vnto whome the knowledge of the truthe is so plentuously opened, so that they knowe at large what is neadfull & necessary to theyr saluacyon: I can not otherwyse thynke but that all suche learned men muste neades haue here vpon earth an heauenly treasure, & an ouerflowinge fownteyne, out of the whiche they may at all tymes featche all suche thinges as theyr hartes can desyre, beynge neadefull and necessary to theyr soules healthe.[1]

This parallel between godliness and good learning was particularly close in evangelical eyes. 'The Lorde oure God', wrote Anthony Gilby, 'is the God of knowledge'; and those who would follow him needed above all to learn.[2] Especially in this first generation of the Reformation, the process of spreading the new doctrines was seen as one of education. Conversions

---

[1] Robert Legate (tr.), *A Breife Catechisme and Dialogue betwene the Husbande and his Wyfe. . . . Item dyuerse other Dialogues betwene the Truthe and the Vnlearned man* (RSTC 4979.3: Antwerp, 1545), sig. B7ᵛ.
[2] Gilby, *Answer to the deuillish detection*, fo. 2ʳ.

to reforming ideas were frequently described in intellectual terms. In the few early conversion narratives that survive, the occasion for conversion is commonly the reading of a book, above all of the New Testament.[3] The Holy Spirit's contribution to this process was usually understood in terms of opening the convert's eyes and leading him or her out of ignorance. John Foxe's famous description of the town of Hadleigh in Suffolk, one of the first centres of popular reformism, did not use the terms which modern writers would usually choose when speaking of an explosion of piety in a small area. There is no mention of the emotional intensity, or the radical changes in behaviour, which we expect from a religious revival. Instead, Foxe drew on academic and intellectual terms:

A great number of that parishe became exceeding wel learned in the holye scriptures, as well women as men: so that a man might haue found among them many that had often read the whole Bible through, and that coulde haue sayd a great part of S. Paules epistles by hart, and very wel & readily haue geuen a godly learned sentence in any matter of controuersie. . . . The whole towne seemed rather an Uniuersitie of the learned, then a town of Cloth-making or labouring people.[4]

Similarly, the London Commonwealthman hoped that England might in due course 'more resemble an vniuersite of lerned men, than of a vile and laboroose multitude'. He meant, of course, that the multitude should learn the simple truths of the Gospel, not the subtle problems of theology. However, he emphasised that while godly wisdom was grounded in the workings of the Holy Spirit, even the wisest need actual education to become truly wise, just as even the most skilled of carpenters needs tools.[5]

This emphasis on learning was not, of course, solely the province of the reformers. The heirs of Colet, Fisher and More, as much as any evangelical, believed education to be vital to the welfare of a Christian commonwealth. William Chedsay, the vice-president of the eminently humanist foundation of Corpus Christi College, Oxford, was a moderate conservative who was later to play a minor part in Cranmer's trial. Preaching in 1544, he cited the dreadful precedent of Emperor Julian the Apostate, who had tried to close down Christian schools,

---

[3] Thomas Bilney, for example, was famously converted by reading I Timothy; Nicholas Shaxton confessed in 1546 that heretical books had been the occasion of his conversion. Wriothesley, 170. See also Peter Marshall, 'Evangelical conversion in the reign of Henry VIII', in *The Beginnings of English Protestantism*, ed. Peter Marshall and Alec Ryrie (Cambridge, 2002), 16–17, 24–8.

[4] *AM*, 1518. The extent to which this obviously stylised description is removed from reality has only recently become clear. John Craig, *Reformation, Politics and Polemics: The Growth of Protestantism in East Anglian Market Towns, 1500–1610* (Aldershot, Hants., 2001), 152–75.

[5] BL Royal MS 17.B.xxxv fos. 4^r, 18^r; Davies, *Religion of the Word*, 45.

well knowynge that whan all learnyng were gone, the fayth wolde soone decaye after. Wherfore we maye gether of the contrary that the chiefest meanes to mayntayne the fayth is to sette vp learnyng, to mayntayne scoles to put youre chyldren to knowe, what the wyll of god is, and so to be able afterwarde to teache other the same. It was neuer more nede to speke and crye vpon it. The vniuersitees decaye: Grammer scoles be desolated. . . . It is to be feared that the fayth wyl away.[6]

Such views – to say nothing of the apocalyptic language in which they are couched – were the common currency of the Renaissance, truisms in an age of extraordinary intellectual self-confidence. Christianity's long tradition of wariness towards learning and towards the elevation of the intellect was as marginal in the early sixteenth century as perhaps it has ever been. However, such a recurrent theme could not be suppressed altogether, and as we shall see, in this period it was chiefly in conservative circles that it was remembered. It is amongst evangelicals that an untempered zeal for education and learning stands out most clearly. The London Commonwealthman argued not only that ignorance was the root of all other evils, but also that 'the true remedie of all evills consisteth in theducation of yewth'. Few conservatives would have been willing to go quite that far.[7]

It should therefore be no surprise that perhaps the most insistently repeated item on the 'commonwealth' agenda was education, and in particular university education. This was an emphasis with a long history. The Lollard Disendowment Bill, probably presented to Parliament around 1410, had urged that revenues be confiscated from the clergy to be used, amongst other things, for the foundation of either five or fifteen new universities. Wyclif's disciple John Purvey had argued for the foundation of fifteen universities a decade before. This plan, wildly unrealistic in any case, vanished entirely along with Lollardy's social respectability in the early fifteenth century, but Anne Hudson has argued convincingly that it was symptomatic of a Lollard emphasis on education which survived long after the heretics had been drummed out of the universities.[8] In the wake of the break with Rome, this emphasis was taken up by the new reformers. Thomas Becon deplored poverty largely because it meant that

no man is able to set forth hys chylde vnto learnyng, wherby it is come to passe, that such blynde ignorancy, and rude Chaos of barbarous and rusticall manners reygne nowe in the world vniuersally.

His hope for the future was that

the ciuile magistrates and head rulars . . . prouyde that there be learned curates, which maye teache the people the true worde of God, that they maye knowe howe to worshyp hym accordyng to the holy scriptures.

---

[6] Chedsay and Scott, *Two notable sermones*, sigs. F2^v–3^r.
[7] BL Royal MS 17.B.xxxv fo. 17^v. [8] Hudson, *Premature Reformation*, 114, 174–227.

Such an ideal commonwealth would also have many schoolmasters, that children

> maye learne euen from theyr cradles, as they saye, to knowe God, to vnderstond his worde. . . . By this means shall all Idolatry and false worshyppyng of God shortely decay & vanysh away, and the true seruyce of God remayne among vs.[9]

In the same year, Henry Brinklow called for ecclesiastical wealth to be used to establish schools in scores of towns, with public lectures on Latin, Greek and Hebrew.[10] This emphasis explicitly embraced the universities; Bale's sour observation that they had been popish foundations appears to be an isolated comment.[11] Others were enthusiastic about their role. The London Commonwealthman's schemes for the renewal of the Church included the sending of vast numbers of unlearned clergy to university for three years; the restriction of ordination to graduates, or to those who could expound Scripture and knew Latin; the requirement that each cleric with an annual income of more than twenty pounds should support a poor scholar at one of the universities; and the foundation of schools for the poor in every major town, from which the sons of the nobility and gentry should be barred.[12] George Joye demanded that 'the chirche muste nedis haue scolis', and made the remarkable claim that 'there were flourishing scoles or vniuersites as thei now call them, in the tyme of the apostles'.[13] Even if the evidence was vanishingly thin, evangelicals were concerned to find a scriptural basis for something so dear to their hearts.

A few evangelicals even found themselves in a position in which they could begin to put this agenda into practice. Lord Chancellor Thomas Audley was hardly a model reformer, a fair-weather friend whose administration of Chancery earned him the reputation of being 'a good seller of justice whenever he can find a buyer'.[14] He nevertheless made a few significant contributions to the reformist cause, not least of which was the securing of substantial monastic wealth in order to refound his alma mater of Buckingham College, Cambridge, as Magdalene College in 1542 – the only foundation at either university between Cardinal College in 1528 and the creation of Trinity and Christ Church in 1546. Simon Heynes, the evangelical dean of Exeter, proposed an ambitious set of reforms to his cathedral in the late 1530s. Had they been implemented, they would have seen schools for a hundred children

---

[9] Becon, *New pollecye of warre*, sigs. H3^r, K6^{r-v}.
[10] Brinklow, *Complaynt of Roderyck Mors*, sig. F4^v.
[11] Bale, *Image of bothe churches*, sigs. L1^v–2^r.
[12] BL Royal MS 17.B.xxxv fos. 13^v–14^v, 18^r.
[13] George Joye, *Our sauiour Iesus Christ hath not ouercharged his chirche with many ceremonies* (RSTC 14556: Antwerp, 1543), sig. C3^r. Joye's source for this claim is the reference to there being teachers in the church at Antioch: Acts 13:1.
[14] Kaulek (ed.), *Correspondance Politique de Marillac*, 195 (*LP* XV 804).

established, twenty-four students supported at the universities and a salaried lectureship in theology endowed.[15] Several bishops, including evangelical fellow-travellers of varying degrees of enthusiasm such as Robert Holgate of York and Nicholas Heath of Rochester, also took some pains to promote education within their dioceses.[16] One of William Barlow's few solid achievements as bishop of St David's (other than alienating virtually the entire clerical elite of the diocese) was the establishment in 1541 of a grammar school at Brecon. His hope for this, he wrote with characteristic tenderness towards his cure, was that 'gods honour princypally preferred, the welsh rudenes decreasynge, Christian cyvilitye maye be introduced'. The foundation also provided for public lectures on Scripture twice a week; Barlow had originally hoped that these would be daily.[17]

Like many others, Barlow's project was funded by a grant of ecclesiastical lands which had been seized by the Crown. This was the example which reformers of every shade hoped to see repeated across the country. Their principal hope for the wealth of the suppressed monasteries was that it might be used for a massive investment in education. Even some of monasticism's defenders were willing to concede that this would be a worthy use of its riches. Lady Margaret Beaufort and Cardinal Wolsey provided impeccably orthodox precedents for such action, and the regime used these precedents to justify its actions.[18] In 1536, Thomas Starkey wrote to Cromwell, describing the indignation roused on the Continent by the dissolution of the smaller monasteries, but he added:

I thynke the troth ys thys, that yf the world myght see thes grete monastarys wych yet stond, conuertyd & turnyd in to lytyl vnyuersytes, and made therby, as hyt were commyn scoles of lernyng & vertue to the ryght educatyon of youthe, al thes droonys wych consume the hunnye dryuen out of the hyuys as vnprofytable to god & to the world, then schold not the suppressyon of thes lytyl abbays gyue so much occasyon, among blynd pepul ful of foly, of any sklaunderouse infamy.[19]

For this very reason, the regime was eager to portray itself as intending to use the proceeds of the dissolution for education and other public goods. The 1540 statute permitting the erection of new bishoprics had a preamble which may have been written by the king himself. This provided the only statutory statement of a positive purpose behind the dissolution: that

---

[15] George Oliver, *Lives of the Bishops of Exeter and a History of the Cathedral* (Exeter, 1861), 480–1.

[16] A. G. Dickens, *Robert Holgate, Archbishop of York and President of the King's Council in the North* (1955), 22; Walter Frere and William Kennedy, *Visitation Articles and Injunctions of the Period of the Reformation*, 3 vols., Alcuin Club Collections 14–16 (1910), vol. II, 93. On Heath, see below, pp. 214–15, 218–19.

[17] BL Cotton MS Cleopatra E.iv fo. 142^r (*LP* XIII (i) 634); Glanmor Williams, *The Welsh and their Religion* (Cardiff, 1991), 130.

[18] Wooding, *Rethinking Catholicism*, 38.   [19] PRO SP 1/105 fo. 48^v (*LP* XI 73).

Gods worde myght the better be setforth, Childern brought upp in lerning, Clerkes norished in the Universyties, olde servantes decayed to have lyvynges, Almeshouses for poore folke to be susteyned in, Reders of Grece, Ebrewe, and Latten to have good stipend, daylie Almes to be ministred, mendinge of highe weyes, exhibicion for mynisters of the Churche.[20]

This promised all that the reformers could hope for.

The promise may not have been made entirely cynically. However, in the event, very little monastic wealth ever trickled down into such worthy projects. Despite occasional grants such as those secured by Audley and Barlow, the more common experience was that of Barlow's protégé and successor at St David's, Robert Ferrar, whose appeal for his priory of St Oswald's Nostell to be preserved as 'a colledge for the norishement of yowth in vertue and learnynge' went unheeded.[21] Whether there was a deliberate deception in royal policy from the beginning cannot be known, but there is good evidence that by April 1543 at least the king had consciously, if privately, abandoned his stated good intentions. In that month he wrote to Ralph Sadler, the English ambassador in Scotland. Sadler was advising the earl of Arran on how to consolidate his precarious position as regent by pursuing a Reformation on Henry's pattern. The dissolution of monasteries, the king wished Sadler to tell Arran, 'requireth politique handelyng'. In particular, the bishops should be bribed with lands – some for their own estates, but also to provide for scholars to be sent to the universities, 'wherby the state of the clargie, shalbe better preserved and in a more decent ordre'. Only then might Arran safely divert the lion's share of the proceeds to the Crown.[22]

The emptiness of the promise of rich new endowments for education quickly became apparent. The immediate impact of the dissolution of the monasteries was close to catastrophic. Several colleges in the two universities had been monastic foundations, and they promptly disappeared. In addition, the religious orders had provided a steady stream of students at the other colleges, which now dried up. There was a sharp numerical decline at both universities, such that between 1542 and 1548, only 173 students were admitted BA in Oxford, and only 191 in Cambridge. Numerical decline inevitably also had financial implications. The embryonic university library at Cambridge was forced to sell books to remain solvent during the 1540s, and on one occasion Cambridge's common chest dipped below twenty pounds.[23] Conservative and reformer alike lamented that 'the poore studentes ... were

---

[20] *Statutes of the realm*, 728 (31° Henry VIII c. 9); Lehmberg, *Later Parliaments*, 66–7.
[21] Dickens, *Lollards and Protestants*, 149.
[22] BL Additional MS 32650 fo. 125^{r-v} (*LP* XVIII (i) 364).
[23] James Bass Mullinger, *The University of Cambridge from the Royal Injunctions of 1535 to the Accession of Charles the First* (Cambridge, 1884), 27–8, 49–51.

neuer fewer in number, and yet they that be lefte, be ready to runne abrode into the world and to leaue their study for very nede'.[24] Far from bringing in the promised new endowments, the dissolution had significantly impoverished the universities. Some of the more optimistic evangelicals tried to continue holding their hopes for education together with loyalty to the Crown. In 1544 Richard Tracy stated his confidence

> that your magestye will prouide and make ordinaunce, that all suche landes and possessyons whereupon so many ydle hypochrytes and deceyuers be greate burden & charge to your realme . . . maye from henceforthe be . . . conuerted to the supportation and mayntenaunce of common scoles, wherby errours crept vp through ingnorance [sic] maye be through knowlege repressed.

He must, however, have been aware that the king was no more likely to grant this than any of the other requests in his *Supplication*.[25] Likewise, the London Commonwealthman's attempt to show how his plans could be funded by seizures of episcopal and cathedral property was a tacit admission that the wealth of the monasteries had already been squandered.

By this time, many reformers were openly disillusioned. Even in 1536, John Skip had feared that the universities would be impoverished by the dissolution.[26] By July 1540, Robert Barnes' petition to the king from the stake to use the wealth of the monasteries for the poor was openly provocative.[27] In 1542 Brinklow roundly condemned the use of monastic wealth:

> I wold to GOD the distribucyon of the same landes and goodes had bene as godly distributed, as the act of roatyng vp was, which distribucyon, I darre saye, all Christen hertes lament. For the fatte Swyne onely were greased, but the poare Shepe to whom that thing belonged had least, or nothyng at all.[28]

Brinklow avoided a direct attack on the king only through the flimsy device of blaming Parliament. Equally implausibly, John Bale chose to lay the blame at the bishops' feet when he made a similar attack two years later.[29] The most thorough condemnation of the waste of monastic wealth, however, came in 1545 from George Joye, in his commentary on the book of Daniel. Bringing fresh and bitter experience to a theme which his one-time friend William Tyndale had raised in the 1520s, he asked rhetorically 'whether the seculare kynges and princes, maye take awaye the chirche goodes?' Indeed they might, he answered:

---

[24] Edgeworth, *Sermons*, 155.   [25] Tracy, *Supplycacion to Henry the eyght*, sig. C3^v.
[26] Eric W. Ives, 'Anne Boleyn and the early Reformation in England: the contemporary evidence', *HJ* 37 (1994), 397–8.
[27] Standish, *Lytle treatise against the protestacion of Robert Barnes*, sig. F3^{r-v}.
[28] Brinklow, *Lamentacion of a Christian*, sig. D8^r.
[29] Bale, *Epistle exhortatorye*, fos. 21^v–2^r.

The chirche goodis belong to the pore. . . . The goods and iewels of oure temples, abbeys and bisshoprykis are not consecrated to siche vses by gods worde, but by their owne inuented couetuose charmings, wherfore emprowrs, kynges and princes maye take them awaye and putt them to beter vses, as to the maintenance of scoles, vniuersities, to sustain trewe techers and godly prechers.

However, he argued that since ecclesiastical goods were originally gifts from the people (albeit gifts given in superstition and ignorance) princes had a duty to use them for the people's benefit:

As they be praised which, the ydle bely burdens remoued, substitute apt and lerned labourers, euen so synne they which translate the chirche goodis into prophane vses (which thing is now to comon) suffering the pore chirches congregacions, and scoles to be cold and hongrye. . . . Nether haue the princes power to translate to themselues thecclesiasti[c] goodis, with the defrauding of the pore chirches and scoles.[30]

Although the exiles were more willing than their brethren in England to confront this problem squarely, evangelical unity on this issue is more apparent than opposition. Most reformers considered the regime's failure to use monastic wealth for educational and other social ends to be at best a waste and at worst a betrayal.

This process of disillusionment came to a point of crisis at the close of the reign, when it became clear that, so far from giving the universities generous new endowments, the king could not be trusted to safeguard even what they had. The crisis began in the parliament of 1545, with the so-called Chantries Act. The bill was introduced into the Lords as 'Billa pro Dissolutione Cantariarum, Hospitalum, et Liberorum Sacellorum' but the eventual statute was titled, 'An Acte for dissolucion of Colledges'; and as this indicates, the chantries were not its only, or even its main target.[31] It is striking that a House of Commons with as large an evangelical contingent as that of 1545 should have put up a much fiercer fight against this bill than the parliaments of 1536 and 1539 did against the legislation which destroyed the monasteries. The bill 'was driven euen to the last houre, and yet then passed onely by division of this Hous'.[32] An attack on the chantries, almost the last visible representatives of the old purgatorial system, was of course an evangelical priority – as was to become clear early in Edward VI's reign. However, the 1545 Act was not a measure of godly reformation. During the destruction of the monasteries, the regime had at least felt the need to maintain the pretence that the funds would be used for education and for the poor. In the 1545 Act only a shadow of this pretence remained. Its preamble mentioned only 'thexcedinge greate & inestimable charges costes and expences which your

---

[30] Joye, *Daniel*, fos. 66ᵛ–8ʳ.
[31] *LJ*, 275; *Statutes of the realm*, 988–92 (37° Henry VIII. c. 4.).
[32] PRO SP 1/212 fo. 112ᵛ (*LP* XX (ii) 1030); MacCulloch, *Cranmer*, 347.

Majestie hathe had and susteyned and dayly doeth susteyne' in war, and in the maintenance of his estates. For this reason, the king was now empowered to seize the endowments of foundations which had been plundered by their own administrators. The Act's most draconian clause, however, was buried in its centre, and here some lip-service was paid to the social role fulfilled by chantries, colleges, hospitals and other foundations. Many of them, the Act states, had endowments 'to thentent that almes to the poore people and other good vertuouse and charitable deedes mought be made done & executed'. It adds, however, that 'it is right well knowen' that this duty is usually not fulfilled, 'to the great displeasure of Almightie God and to the discontentacion of the Kinge'. The response to this deplorable state of affairs was simply to give the king the power to seize at will any foundation at all, whether it was failing to fulfil a social role or not. The scope of this power clearly alarmed Parliament, for in the speech which closed the session, Henry personally thanked those present for trusting in his good intentions, and promised to

use all things to the best ... minding in the use of this liberty to declare openly unto them, how much he feared God, and tendred the maintenaunce of his Service, and the relief of Povertye.

However, the currency of royal promises was already debased, as the Act's own text indicates. The king's new powers of dissolution at will extended to 'Colleges Freechappells Chaunties Hospitalles Fraternities Brotherheddes Guyldes' and perpetual endowments for stipendiary priests. Amongst the most prominent and tempting of these foundations were the already struggling colleges of Oxford and Cambridge. If anything, the universities were more directly in the regime's sights than were the chantries. The Act stated that colleges which did not pay first-fruits nevertheless fell under its jurisdiction: a clause which, as Alan Kreider has noted, can only have been inserted specifically to bring the universities within the Act's scope.[33]

During the following month England's universities faced what Elisabeth Leedham-Green has called the gravest threat in their history.[34] For a short time it seemed that the king might exercise his new powers to plunder the universities' endowments, such that if they survived at all it would be as husks. On 16 January 1546, barely three weeks after the passage of the Act, commissions were issued for surveys of the universities' lands. (The commissions for surveying chantry lands, by contrast, were not to be issued for another month.) The commissions' ostensible purpose was 'thencrease of good learninge and the Comen wealthe of thys our Realme', but few can have

---

[33] PRO SP 1/212 fo. 111ᵛ (*LP* XX (ii) 1030); Alan Kreider, *English Chantries: The Road to Dissolution* (Cambridge, MA, and London, 1979), 179–80.

[34] Elisabeth Leedham-Green, *A Concise History of the University of Cambridge* (Cambridge, 1996), 49–50.

been reassured.[35] However, remarkably enough, this is more or less what happened. The threat was diverted, and the king was instead persuaded to endow the enormous foundations that became Trinity College, Cambridge and Christ Church in Oxford. The significance of these events for our purpose is the manner in which the universities were defended, the threat dissipated and the new foundations secured, for the key players were all friends of the reformers.

In retrospect, the decisive element in thwarting the attack on the universities was probably the decision, at the very beginning of the process, to allow the universities to conduct surveys of their own lands.[36] The three surveyors appointed for Cambridge were Matthew Parker, William May and John Redman. Parker, the future archbishop, was then vice-chancellor of the university and master of Corpus Christi College. He was a moderate but committed reformer, and an able politician; he was also a loyal tenant of Queen Katherine Parr, a relationship which is a silent but important ingredient in this story. May was the president of Queens' College, a good friend of Parker's and a long-standing client both of Cranmer and of Thomas Goodricke, the reformist bishop of Ely. At the same time as he was carrying out his commission in Cambridge, the Privy Council was forcing through his election as dean of St Paul's Cathedral. Redman was the Lady Margaret Professor of Divinity, the master of King's Hall, and a royal chaplain. By Cambridge standards he was something of a conservative, having been involved in drafting the section on justification in the *King's Book*, but he had taken the reformers' side in the dispute over Greek pronunciation in the early 1540s and was on excellent terms with the leading evangelicals.[37] It is not known how these three men came to be chosen, but from their appointment on 16 January 1546 the evangelical mobilisation can be traced. Two aspects in particular stand out. John Cheke and Thomas Smith, the young royal lecturers[38] in Greek and civil law at Cambridge, were both former pupils of Redman's, and were also firmly aligned with reformist ways of thinking. In 1546, their status as royal tutors put them in a pivotal position. Smith in particular took his petition to an increasingly important friend of the

---

[35] CCCC MS 108 p. 448; Kreider, *English Chantries*, 179–80.
[36] Alan Kreider plausibly suggests that Thomas Smith persuaded the king to use university men rather than, in Parker's words, 'any of his costly officers'; which would make the decision one of Henry VIII's more spectacular false economies. Kreider, *English Chantries*, 180.
[37] DNB; Parker, *Correspondence*, 31–3; LP XIX (ii) 613; Haigh, *Reformation and Resistance*, 164; Redworth, *In Defence of the Church Catholic*, 168; MacCulloch, *Suffolk and the Tudors*, 162; APC, 322. For the dispute over Greek pronunciation, see below, pp. 183–7.
[38] Often, and anachronistically, called 'regius professors'. F. Donald Logan, 'The origins of the so-called Regius Professorships: an aspect of the renaissance in Oxford and Cambridge', *Renaissance and Renewal in Christian History*, ed. Derek Baker, Studies in Church History 14 (Oxford, 1977), 271–8.

evangelicals, Queen Katherine. We cannot know how much influence the queen had on her husband's decisions, but it is clear from the letter that she wrote to the university on 26 February that they had approached her for help through Smith and that she was able to report that all was well:

> I (according to your desires) have attempted my lord the King's Majesty, for the stablishment of your livelihood and possessions; in which, notwithstanding his Majesty's property and interest, through the consent of the high court of parliament, his highness being such a patron of good learning, doth tender you so much, that he will rather advance learning and erect new occasion thereof, than to confound those your ancient and godly institutions.[39]

For once, this promise of largesse was to be fulfilled.

Alongside the queen's intervention, another evangelical manoeuvre seems to have been critical. Richard Taverner, the prolific but moderate evangelical author and translator, was also a clerk of the signet. Three days after the issue of the commission to Parker, May and Redman, Taverner was approached by the sinister figure of Richard Rich, the chancellor of the Court of Augmentations. Rich, one of the century's most reliable villains, is as plausible a candidate as any for that role in this drama. Any spoil from the universities would have passed through his hands. Rich's message was that the king wished the commissioners to report in person forthwith. Taverner wrote to Parker with this information, addressing Parker as 'right worshipfull and his singular freend'. He was aware that the interview with the king which was being arranged would be critical, and wrote, with more confidence than he perhaps felt, that 'we doubt not but ye woll so handle your self herin as ye shal answer to vs your friendes expectacions'. Despite the gravity of the situation, Taverner clearly felt that there was no particular hurry. He did not write to Parker until two days after his conversation with Rich, doubtless being aware that the survey would take some time to complete.[40] Parker, however, appears to have had other ideas. As Jane Dawson has established, his interview with the king must have taken place on or before 28 January – that is, within a week of Taverner's letter, and a month before the survey was complete.[41] Parker and his colleagues presented to the king findings which can have been no more than a provisional summary. Provisional figures are, of course, peculiarly susceptible to massage, and these appear to have done the trick. The king's response, as Parker described it shortly afterwards, would warm the heart of any higher education institution fighting to preserve its funding. He 'diligently perused' the summary, 'and in a certain

---

[39] Parker, *Correspondence*, 34–7.   [40] BL Additional MS 19400 fo. 23^{r-v} (*LP* XXI (i) 101).
[41] Jane Dawson, 'The foundation of Christ Church, Oxford and Trinity College, Cambridge in 1546', *Bulletin of the Institute of Historical Research* 57 (1984), 209. The answers even to their preliminary enquiries were only being written on 1 February. BL Additional MS 19400 fo. 24^{r-v} (*LP* XXI (i) 152).

admiration said to certain of his lords which stood by, that he thought he had not in his realm so many persons so honestly maintained in living, by so little land and rent'. As the lords saw their hopes of rich pickings from university lands fade, the king apparently turned to them and said 'that pity it were these lands should be altered to make them worse'. He concluded with a promise to the commissioners that the university should not be forced to part with any lands unwillingly.[42]

This was not quite the end of the threat. In February, Parker was writing to the king and to Sir William Paget, praising the king's love of learning but also asking Paget to ensure that the universities continue to be protected. A few days later, however, the heads of house at Oxford wrote to the king formally thanking him for his assurances received through Richard Cox, the dean of the former Osney Cathedral who was now apparently masterminding Oxford's petitions to the king.[43] Little else is known of the campaign Oxford mounted. What is known is that on or shortly after 26 January – in other words, at almost exactly the same time as the interview with the Cambridge commissioners – the king halted the process of granting the St Frideswide's site in Oxford to be a new cathedral.[44] This former abbey had been the site of Wolsey's grand foundation of Cardinal College; after Wolsey's fall, the college was drastically slimmed down and renamed King Henry VIII College. In May 1545, the king apparently determined to transfer the cathedral of the new diocese of Oxford from Osney Abbey, outside the city, to this site.[45] He also appears to have been envisaging a substantial new educational foundation on the site. If that plan had been threatened by financial pressures and the tempting opportunities created by the new legislation, it was now restored and enlarged. The result was Christ Church, a college larger than any in Oxford and which incorporated a cathedral. Cambridge, too, received a huge new foundation, Trinity College. Quite how a programme of asset-stripping came to be replaced by a plan for huge new colleges in each university is unknown, but the turning-point can be dated with some certainty to those few days in late January 1546.[46]

As the new projects gathered momentum, it was the men who had defended their universities from the threat of dissolution who profited most. Richard Cox became the first dean of Christ Church. In Cambridge, John Redman

---

[42] Parker, *Correspondence*, 34–6.
[43] PRO SP 1/214 fos. 53^r, 54^r, 110^{r-v} (*LP* XXI (i) 203, 204, 244).
[44] Dawson, 'Foundation of Christ Church', 209.   [45] *LP* XX (i) 775, 776.
[46] As Christopher Haigh has argued, the preparations in Oxford in 1545 demonstrate clearly that 'Christ Church was intended: it was not an accident or an afterthought'. The king was, however, quite capable of changing his mind on such subjects. Given the timing of the decisions, it still seems likely that Christ Church owes its survival, if not its existence, to 'the political skills of a Cambridge vice-chancellor'. Christopher Haigh, *1546, Before and After: The Making of Christ Church* (Oxford, 1996), 3–6.

became the first master of Trinity College when his own college, King's Hall, was absorbed into the new foundation.[47] In the universities' hour of need, it was the evangelicals and their fellow-travellers who had defended them: led, of course, by the reformers within the universities, but with invaluable help from outsiders. The queen's intervention may be hard to assess but was surely important. Richard Taverner's involvement is suggestive, for he was a man of many parts. He had studied at both universities before entering Cromwell's service in the 1530s. As well as having a position at court and contacts in the book trade, he was known as a lay preacher in London's conventicles.[48] In this context it is tempting to wonder if his reference to 'vs your friendes' is more than a conventional civility. Be that as it may, the reformist mobilisation of which he was a minor part proved more successful than anyone might sensibly have hoped. Thanks almost entirely to the efforts of the evangelicals, it proved possible not only to save the universities from plunder, but to strengthen them with the addition of two spectacular new colleges, each with a friend of the reformers at its head.

In January 1546, the evangelicals' commitment to the reform of the commonwealth forced them into a confrontation of sorts with the regime: and they won. The episode certainly seems to have stiffened the backs of some of those immediately involved. In October of the same year, Cox, now dean of Christ Church, apparently felt that the danger might be returning. His approach was less than diplomatic. His letters to Paget urged that the seizure of university and cathedral lands should be halted, and that impropriations should be reversed. If these pleas were ignored, Cox warned, the realm would sink into 'foul Ignorance, and Barbarousness'. He concluded with an unmistakable threat: 'As touching those things, whereof I wrote to you seriously . . . I trust ye will not forgett them, ffor then God will forget you.'[49] This new confidence, and new willingness to be confrontational, underlines the importance which the reform of the commonwealth held for evangelicals. Their hopes for social reform, and especially their aspirations for education, tied otherwise diverse reformers together; at the same time, those hopes were in constant tension with the king's own actions. This placed evangelical loyalty to and confidence in the regime under considerable pressure. It was a sign that the patience of even apparently conformist evangelicals had its limits. It also fed into the more discreet but bitterer battles which were already being fought within the universities themselves.

---

[47] The king had even grander schemes for the reshaping of the universities. In October 1546 Cox wrote that 'the kynges maiesti as of hym self hath determyned, that the ciuilians [lawyers] in Oxforde shall be to gether in one College, The phisitions & Cyrurgions in a nother'. Oxford reacted to this plan to create something akin to modern faculties with predictable horror, although Cox himself was more sanguine. PRO SP 1/226 fo. 16^r (*LP* XXI (ii) 321).
[48] *AM*, 1204.   [49] PRO SP 1/225 fos. 185^{r-v}, 202^r (*LP* XXI (ii) 260, 282).

'THE CORRUPTION OF THE REALME'

The evangelicals' principled defence of learning was heavily reinforced by more practical considerations. In the simplest sense, of course, when Henry VIII threatened the universities in 1546, men such as Parker, May and Redman were trying to protect their own livelihoods and a way of life which they personally cherished. Not all assaults on learning met with the same level of outrage from evangelicals. The loss of the monastic libraries was a grievous blow to English scholarship, but Parker was almost alone in his strenuous efforts to rescue some portion of them. The evangelical defence of the universities, however, was also driven by self-interest of a more enlightened variety. The spread of evangelicalism in England, like that of Wycliffism a century and a half before, was rooted in the universities. Most of the leaders of Henrician evangelicalism had studied at Oxford or Cambridge; many of them had been converted there. The story of the early growth of reformist ideas in the universities has often been told.[50] Cambridge was the setting for the first set-piece confrontation of the English Reformation, Robert Barnes' Christmas sermon of 1525 and the events which followed. Oxford was the setting for England's first quasi-martyrdoms, when three of the evangelicals arrested at Cardinal College in 1528 died after being imprisoned in the dean's salt fish cellar.[51] By the 1540s those heady days already seem to have acquired a slightly mythic feel. In 1543 William Turner, himself a Cambridge man, located his stylised account of the beginning of the Reformation in the universities. 'Certayn scolares of Cambrygd [sic] and of Oxford,' he wrote, 'euen streyght way after he [the Romish fox] had kylled certayn of theyr felowes, folowed hym to haue catched hym.' However, he ran to hide in a church, 'and when the scolares wold haue folowed hym in to the chirche the bisshoppes and prestes bet them out agayn with blody pates'.[52] The universities were, and were seen to be, one of the key arenas in which evangelicalism had to fight its battles.

By the 1540s there was also a clear sense of the difference between the religious atmospheres of the two universities. Evangelical ideas clearly had a foothold in both in the 1520s, and, as Richard Rex has pointed out, the crisis at Cardinal College in 1528 provides rather firmer evidence of heresy at Oxford than the stubborn legend of the White Horse Inn does for Cambridge. However, Rex's statement that 'there is no particular reason for the

---

[50] Most recently and perhaps most convincingly in Richard Rex, 'The early impact of Reformation theology at Cambridge University, 1521–1547', *Reformation and Renaissance Review* 2 (1999), 38–71.

[51] James P. Lusardi, 'The career of Robert Barnes' in *The Complete Works of St Thomas More*, vol. VIII part iii (Yale, 1973); *AM*, 1032; Lambeth Palace Library, MS 113 fo. 79^r; cf. Brown, *Robert Ferrar*, 293, n. 82.

[52] Turner, *Huntyng and fyndyng out of the Romishe fox*, sig. A3^{r-v}.

traditional priority given to Cambridge over Oxford in the history of English Protestantism' cannot be sustained much beyond the late 1520s, if at all.[53] The Cambridge foundation myth, if myth it was, had taken root by the end of Henry VIII's reign, in part because the leadership of the evangelical movement was dominated so heavily by Cambridge men. Of all the discernibly evangelical bishops appointed under Henry, only one, John Hilsey, was an Oxford graduate; he was converted after he had left.[54] Thomas Cranmer, Hugh Latimer, Nicholas Shaxton, Edward Foxe, Thomas Goodricke, John Bird, Robert Holgate and Henry Holbeach were all Cambridge men. The proportion of Oxford to Cambridge graduates among the leading reformist preachers and authors of the 1540s was just as low. After the deaths of Thomas Garrett and William Jerome in 1540, the most prominent reformers with an Oxford connection were Richard Taverner (who had spent more time at Cambridge than at Oxford) and the preacher Robert Wisdom (who had held a benefice in Oxford, but was not a graduate). These were certainly important figures, but hardly pivotal.

The domination of English evangelicalism by Cambridge men in the last years of Henry's reign was matched by the enormous disparity in the levels of support for reform within the two universities. That Cambridge had a reputation as the more evangelically inclined institution has never been in doubt. Perhaps the most striking example of this comes from Canterbury, where a corps of cathedral preachers was created when the cathedral was refounded in 1541. The six posts were split between three reformers and three conservatives, quite deliberately and with the approval (at least) of the king. It was one of the few occasions in Henry's reign when the doctrinal fault line running through the higher clergy was formally recognised, and as such one of the few occasions when it was felt necessary to coin passably objective terms to describe the two parties. In 1543, William Cockes, a petty canon of Canterbury, claimed that Cranmer had described the arrangement by saying 'that there were vj prechers appoynted iij of oxforde and iij of Cambridge, to thentente that thei myght betwene theym trie oute the trueth of doctrine'.[55] In Canterbury at least, the two universities were being used as convenient shorthand terms for conservative and reformer.

It has only recently become possible to chart the true extent of the religious disparity between the two institutions with any accuracy. Elisabeth Leedham-Green and R. J. Fehrenbach have catalogued the books listed in probate

---

[53] Rex, *Henry VIII*, 140.
[54] William Barlow may also have studied at Oxford, although as A. B. Emden has argued, the evidence for this is at best slender.
[55] CCCC MS 128 p. 133 (*LP* XVIIII (ii) 546 p. 323). This was more than simply a description of the Six Preachers' backgrounds: one of the 'iij of Cambridge', Michael Drum, had spent most of his academic career in Oxford.

Table 5.1 *Works by Protestant authors owned by Cambridge testators 1535–47*

	No. of vols.		No. of vols.
Martin Luther	29*	Johannes Bugenhagen	7
Philip Melanchthon	14	Huldrych Zwingli	6
Martin Bucer	14	Jean Calvin	5
Heinrich Bullinger	9	Conrad Pellican	4
Johannes Œcolampadius	8	Otto Brunfels	3

* Fifteen of these twenty-nine volumes were owned by one testator, Oliver Ainsworth, d. 1546.

inventories surviving from the period in both universities. These allow us to see the personal libraries of deceased scholars, from which we may cautiously attempt some comparison of what was being read in each university. There are thirty-two such book-lists from Cambridge probate inventories which survive for the period from 1535 (the date of the earliest list) to January 1547, and they are thick with the works of evangelical authors.[56] Table 5.1 summarises by author the number of volumes of controversial or theological material preserved in the book-lists. In addition to those works listed in the table, the book-lists also include seven copies of the highly influential *Unio dissidentium*;[57] two copies of the Augsburg Confession; and individual works by a number of other reformers, including Wolfgang Capito, Andreas Osiander and Johannes Sleidanus. Miles Eglesfylde of Christ's College also apparently owned a work by Jan Hus. English-language works, however, are much more slenderly represented: there are single works by John Frith, William Tyndale, Hugh Latimer and Thomas Becon,[58] and a copy of *The summe of the holye scripture*, probably translated by Simon Fish. These reformist books were widely distributed, being drawn from the libraries of eighteen of the thirty-two testators. Three more men owned English translations of at least part of the Bible.

These figures can be given a little perspective through a comparison with some of the other authors represented. The opponents of evangelical reform are present, but in substantially smaller numbers. Johannes Cochlæus leads the field, with seven volumes listed. There are four by Thomas More, and two each by John Fisher and John Rastell. Johannes Eck's *Enchiridion*

---

[56] Leedham-Green, *Books in Cambridge Inventories*.
[57] On this, see Robert Peters, 'Who compiled the sixteenth-century patristic handbook Unio Dissidentium?', ed. G. J. Cuming, *Studies in Church History* 2 (1965).
[58] Roger Soresby, d. 1546, owned 'The polises of Warre', listed by Leedham-Green as ?Erasmus, but presumably Becon's *New pollecye of warre*.

locorum communium aduersus Lutteranos was, John Bale alleged in 1542, on virtually every clerical bookshelf in London:

> Euerye ser Iohan must haue yt that can rede . . . verye fewe popyshe prestes with in my lordes dyocese [of London] are at thys same houre with out yt. . . . No lesse myght Harrye Pepwell in Paules churche yearde haue out of Michael Hillenius howse in Antwerpe at one tyme than an whole complete prynte, at the holye request of Stokyslaye. In a short space were they dyspached and a newe prynte in hande.[59]

In Cambridge in these years, however, there are only four copies of it to be found, and only two of Eck's other works. There is no question that scholars who wished to find such books could have done so: they had been sold openly in Cambridge since the 1520s.[60] In addition, the official Henrician line is poorly represented. There is a copy of that embarrassing volume, the king's *Assertio Septem Sacramentorum*, but there were a mere three copies of the *Bishops' Book* and only one of the *King's Book*.[61] All of these works and authors are outnumbered by the thoroughly unfashionable Duns Scotus: ten volumes of his works are listed.

It would be unwise to try to deduce too much detail about individual testators or texts from the book-list data. Academics are very likely to have books in their libraries with which they disagree. In several of the lists authors who would have objected violently to one another can be found jostling for shelf-space. In addition, controversial works such as these form only a small proportion of even the most theological of collections, and all of these authors are dwarfed in the lists by Erasmus and the major classical and patristic writers. Nevertheless, some useful conclusions can be drawn. The presence of such large numbers of books by Continental Protestant authors makes it clear that theirs was a respectable position in the academic life of the university. Even the more radical, Reformed authors made a strong showing. The presence of conservative works makes it clear that evangelical ideas were not uncontroversial, but the numerical weakness of those works suggests that the reformers would be, at least, on an equal footing. The paucity of official Henrician publications suggests that the regime's attempts at enforcing unity had not penetrated Cambridge life particularly deeply. To put the case at its weakest, it seems unlikely that any student or fellow could

---

[59] Bale, *A dysclosynge or openynge of the Manne of synne*, fos. 54ᵛ–5ʳ.
[60] Rex, 'Early impact', 60.
[61] This may, of course, be because such books were bought by college libraries. Nevertheless, it is suggestive that there were also two copies of a more reformist-leaning official publication, Cranmer's English processional, despite its being published in the summer of 1544, late in the period and more than a year after the *King's Book*. John Perman, d. 1545, owned 'The letany', identified by Leedham-Green as the 1531 *Golden Litany*, but probably the Cranmer text; and William Porter, d. 1546, owned 'An ynglysshe processyonall', unidentified by Leedham-Green, but also presumably this text.

avoid coming into contact with reforming ideas in 1540s Cambridge; nor that any discreet scholar who wished to pursue an interest in them would find it unduly difficult to do so. If such ideas were not yet the new orthodoxy, they were thoroughly intellectually fashionable. Stephen Gardiner, the chancellor of Cambridge, was alarmed by this state of affairs. As he put it in May 1545: 'Each youth [in Cambridge] . . . follows his own inclinations, rendering obedience only in so far as it suits his fancy; indeed, most of them refuse to submit to restraint or authority, and, in the words of a famous writer, "the larger part dominates the better part".'[62] This is hyperbole, but it is plausible that in 1540s Cambridge Catholic orthodoxy had become a minority stance.

The book-list data from Oxford are not precisely parallel to those from Cambridge, and any attempt to make detailed comparisons would be fraught with problems. There are many fewer probate inventories which include itemised book-lists: seven for the period 1534–47, as against Cambridge's thirty-two. The Cambridge lists also appear to have been considerably more detailed. Nevertheless, once all this has been taken into account, it remains striking that not a single work of theology or religious controversy from a reformer's pen is recorded in any of the Henrician book-lists from Oxford. The closest approach is in one list from 1543, which includes two textbooks by Philip Melanchthon – a rhetorical text and a commentary on Aristotle's *Politics* – and a work on topography by the Swiss reformer Joachim Vadianus. There is not even an English Bible in the Oxford lists until 1551. The first genuinely evangelical work to appear is a copy of Calvin's *Institutes*, in 1552. Moreover, none of the controversial works by the opponents of reform are present either. Still generously represented, however, is Duns Scotus, with either four or five volumes.

Such a comprehensively blank slate does, of course, raise suspicions. The Oxford lists are indeed less full than their Cambridge counterparts, and it may be that the compilers of probate inventories chose to omit volumes which savoured of the frying-pan (although such a policy would in itself be revealing). Texts opposing the reformers, at least, are known to have been circulating in Oxford. Robert Croft of New College was in 1538 accused of owning Eck's *Enchiridion*.[63] However, there is no obvious reason why the inventory-makers should have been unwilling to list works by Cochlæus or Eck, especially when they were willing, in 1539, not only to include a work of John Fisher's but actually to list it under that dangerous name. It would be almost as peculiar to be willing to list Melanchthon's philosophical works and balk at his biblical commentaries.[64] The simplest explanation is that the

---

[62] Gardiner, *Letters*, 136.   [63] *LP* VIII 799.
[64] R. J. Fehrenbach and Elisabeth Leedham-Green, *Private Libraries in Renaissance England: A Collection and Catalogue of Tudor and Early Stuart Book-Lists*, vol. II (Binghamton, NY, 1993). The Fisher text was a Latin version of his penitential psalms.

Reformation controversy was cooking over a much lower heat in Oxford than in Cambridge. Stephen Gardiner's opinion, while seen through increasingly jaundiced eyes, nevertheless underlines this impression. In Cambridge, he wrote in 1545, 'there is hardly a college in which one may not find party antagonisms. . . . At Oxford there is none of this.'[65] Neither the advocacy of evangelical reform, nor opposition to it, seem to have been amongst the major preoccupations of John Wyclif's university in the 1540s.

This impression from the book-lists is confirmed and fleshed out by evidence of a more anecdotal nature from Oxford. In November 1539, Owen Oglethorpe of Magdalen College recommended to Cromwell that Dr George Cotes should be the next head of Balliol College,

for his iudgement in scripture is very well amended & is not addicte to manis doctrine nor scholemennis phantasies but onely to goddes worde, And besides that taketh much paynes here in reding and preaching. Yf your Lordeshippe somwhat tender his cawse & gratifie him in this behalf, I dowght not but yow shall confirme him & make him a hartie favourer of goddes trowthe, and by him many mo, seinge he is here a commune reader.[66]

However, although Cotes may have looked decidedly reformist to the Oxford establishment, this was the man who in the 1530s had crossed swords with Hugh Latimer (Latimer dismissed him as 'Dunsly learned'), and who was to go on to be the bishop responsible for the only Marian heresy execution in the north of England.[67] The religious centre of gravity was far closer to traditional beliefs in Oxford than in Cambridge. This is not to say that there were no reformers in 1540s Oxford. For all the importance of the 'Cambridge connection', a great many Henrician reformers were Oxford graduates, and amongst the students and fellows at Oxford in the last years of Henry's reign were a number of the future leaders of English Protestantism. John Parkhurst, later bishop of Norwich, was at Merton College in the 1540s; his pupil John Jewel was at Corpus Christi. Gilbert Berkeley, Elizabeth's first bishop of Bath and Wells, took his BTh at Oxford in 1540. Nicholas Bullyngham, a fellow of All Souls from 1536 to 1546, was to become a chaplain to Cranmer in 1547 and bishop of Lincoln in 1559. Magdalen College had a particularly strong contingent of future Protestant luminaries. Thomas Bickley, who became a fellow of Magdalen in 1541, violently attacked the Mass in 1548 and became bishop of Chichester in the 1580s. John Mullins, Elizabethan archdeacon of London, was also at the college. Nicholas Cartwright had been a fellow there since 1507 but was no conservative, siding with Peter Martyr in the debates over the Eucharist in 1549. John Harley, briefly bishop of Hereford in 1553

---

[65] Gardiner, *Letters*, 139–40.   [66] PRO SP 1/154 fo. 154ʳ (*LP* XIV (ii) 498).
[67] R. V. H. Burne, 'The Founding of Chester Cathedral', *Journal of the Chester and North Wales Archaeological and Historic Society* ns 37 (1948), 51–2.

and an outspoken reformer from the very beginning of Edward's reign, was a student at Magdalen until 1542 and thereafter an usher at Magdalen School. At the time, however, the most prominent of these future leaders was Richard Cox. Cox had been involved in the Cardinal College troubles in 1528, but had taken his BTh and DTh from Cambridge in the 1530s and entered Thomas Goodricke's service at Ely before returning to Oxford as dean of Osney in 1544. He remained as dean when that cathedral was refounded at Christ Church and merged with what remained of his old college. However, like many of these men, Cox's open commitment to reform in this period was generally of the restrained, Oxford variety.[68]

Alongside such illustrious figures were others who made their evangelical commitment at the time somewhat plainer. William Hughe, who took his MA from Corpus Christi in 1543, was thereafter a chaplain to Lady Denny and the author of a moderate reformist tract, *The troubled mans medicine*, in 1546. The tract was apparently written at the instigation of his friend John Faukener, another Oxford graduate who left the university in the mid-1540s to become a tutor in the household of the redoubtable Warwickshire reformer and JP, William Lucy. Several Oxford reformers won patronage from reformist bishops while the old king still lived. Thomas Young, Elizabeth's first archbishop of York, won his first preferment in his home diocese of St David's from William Barlow after leaving Broadgates Hall, Oxford. Michael Drum had been involved in the troubles at Cardinal College in 1528, and from 1531 was a fellow of Magdalen. Despite having made a credible run for the presidency of the college in 1536, he left in 1541 for the (apparent) safety of Canterbury Cathedral, to be one of the new Six Preachers. Cranmer's patronage extended to other Oxford men, such as John Joseph, a former client of Hugh Latimer's who took his DTh in 1542. In 1545 Joseph became a chaplain to Cranmer, and he was appointed to the Canterbury peculiar of St Mary le Bow, London, in October 1546. Other Oxford men were more direct about their reformism. When William Ford left New College in 1543, and returned to Winchester College as an usher, he was apparently responsible for a bizarre act of surreptitious iconoclasm, and was severely beaten by the masters and scholars as a result.[69]

The striking feature of this creditable list of Oxford reformers is that none of them made their evangelical commitment clear while at the university. There were some, at some stages, who did feel able to do so. Most notably, in October 1538, a group of reformist scholars at Corpus Christi College accused a number of their colleagues of potentially treasonous religious

[68] See below, p. 249, but also above, pp. 149 and 154.
[69] Fines, *Biographical Register*; Emden; *DNB*; Hughe, *Troubled mans medicine*, vol. I, sig. A2^{r-v}; Glanmor Williams, *Welsh Reformation Essays* (Cardiff, 1967), 121, 125; Nichols (ed.), *Narratives*, 29–30.

conservatism. In the same year, Matthew Goodrich, a chaplain at New College, joined a scholar there called John Emerson in accusing a third member of the college of treason. The troubles at Cardinal College in 1528 also seem to have left a legacy in its successor institution, King Henry VIII College, where in 1538 a reformist chaplain called John Hatley, and John Best, a renowned preacher later to be bishop of Carlisle, had a public falling-out with a conservative chaplain, Henry Spicer.[70] It is no coincidence that all of these events took place in 1538, near the high-water mark of Cromwell's Reformation, for to provoke such confrontations in Oxford was a dangerous business. Even in 1538, in the same month as the ructions at Corpus Christi, there was a burning in Oxford.[71] The New College reformers were particularly foolhardy, since John London, warden of the college and later the first dean of Osney Cathedral, was one of the most notorious heresy-hunters of his time.[72] In 1538 London did his best to turn Goodrich and Emerson's accusation against them, forwarding the case to Cromwell and to the mayor of Oxford despite the inconclusive evidence they had given.

A more substantial case followed in April 1539, when the mayor and aldermen of Oxford discovered a ring of Lent-breakers meeting in the house of a bookseller called Horman Men. The list of guests which Men gave to the authorities included John Best and three others of King Henry VIII College, three of the reformist ringleaders at Corpus Christi, several scholars of New College whom he refused to name, and others from All Souls, Canterbury and Oriel Colleges.[73] Such circles were common to both universities,[74] but the response in Oxford was far more vigorous. Oxford's traditionalists had the support not only of heads of house such as John London, but also, at least until 1542, of a thoroughly sympathetic diocesan bishop, John Longland. In August 1539, four and a half months after the arrests in the Horman Men case, Longland was pressing Cromwell to ensure that firm action was taken against the offenders.[75] William Huyck, who at Robert Ferrar's instigation had spent a portion of the previous year as a travelling preacher in Yorkshire, seems to have lost his fellowship at Oriel as a result of this affair.[76] Through the 1540s, Oxford reformers continued to be vulnerable. John Man, who had

---

[70] Elton, *Policy and Police*, 93–8.
[71] William Cowbridge was burnt for heresy on 10 October. However, while Cowbridge may have come from a Lollard background, his views were repugnant to reformer and conservative alike: he claimed, amongst other things, that Christ was a deceiver and that there was no Hell. Bowker, *Henrician Reformation*, 179–80; Fines, *Biographical Register*.
[72] Elton, *Policy and Police*, 352–3; MacCulloch, *Cranmer*, 300, 314, 321.
[73] PRO SP 1/146 fo. 252^{r-v} (*LP* XIV (i) 684).
[74] Gardiner ordered a crackdown on Lent-breakers in Cambridge in 1543. It is striking, however, that the Cambridge Lent-breakers offended in a far more obviously dangerous year, and that they were drawn from more prestigious circles, apparently including regents of the university. Gardiner, *Letters*, 121–2.
[75] *LP* XIV (ii) 71.   [76] Brown, *Robert Ferrar*, 55–7.

been proctor of the university in 1540, was soon afterwards expelled from New College for heresy.[77] In 1545, John Foxe, the future martyrologist, was forced to leave Magdalen for his conscientious refusal to comply with college regulations.[78] It was perfectly possible for an evangelical sympathiser to survive and even prosper in 1540s Oxford – but only as long as he remembered that he belonged to a marginalised minority, and kept his head down.

The contrast with Cambridge is stark. As the book-list evidence suggests, Cambridge evangelicals were able to follow their consciences with a remarkable degree of impunity. There was, of course, always an understanding that scholars were permitted a greater degree of latitude in religious matters than ordinary folk. The anti-heresy proclamation of November 1538 had forbidden discussion of the Eucharist on pain of death, 'except and reserved to learned men in Holy Scripture, instructed and taught in the universities, their liberty and privilege in their schools and places accustomed'.[79] This liberty, however, was apparently substantially greater in Cambridge than in Oxford. As early as 1534, a convicted heretic was appointed as one of Cambridge's official stationers.[80] From the same year, the bishop of Ely (and thus the Visitor of the university) was the cautious evangelical Thomas Goodricke, although his relations with the leading reformers in Cambridge were not always smooth.[81] A *laissez-faire* local bishop, combined with the sheer numbers of evangelicals in positions of influence, gave reformers a degree of security within the university. The broader movement certainly seems to have thought of Cambridge not only as the cradle of reformism but as a safe haven. When William Tolwin was forced to recant in 1541, John Bale contrasted Tolwin's troubles in London to his former security in Cambridge:

Neuer coude Tolwyn throughlye knowe what these rhetoryckes ment, as are denuncyacyon, deteccyon, and presentacyon, so longe as he was in Cambryge . . . tyll he came to my lorde of Londons howse.[82]

The influence that evangelicals could wield at the highest level of university administration is illustrated by the voting in the election of the vice-chancellor in January 1545. Of the ninety-eight votes cast – an unusually high number – the unmistakably evangelical Matthew Parker won seventy-nine. His closest challenger, the conservative John Standish, managed only eight. A further five votes went to another reformer, Nicholas Ridley.[83]

---

[77] Nichols (ed.), *Narratives*, 33.   [78] Fines, *Biographical Register*.   [79] *TRP*, 273.
[80] Mary Bateson (ed.), *Grace Book B: Containing the Proctors' Accounts and Other Records of the University of Cambridge for the Years 1488–1544*, 2 vols. (Cambridge, 1903, 1905), vol. II, xvi, 163.
[81] From 1540 to 1545 he was involved in a running dispute with John Taylor, the master of St John's: Mullinger, *University of Cambridge*, 39.
[82] Bale, *A dysclosynge or openynge of the Manne of synne*, fo. 26^r.
[83] Mullinger, *University of Cambridge*, 72.

The near-unanimous support that Parker was able to command was to prove important for evangelical scholars, because not all of the university's authorities displayed Goodricke's tolerant attitude towards them. Stephen Gardiner became chancellor of the university after Thomas Cromwell's death, and he took his responsibilities seriously. Gardiner was a Cambridge man, and still master of his old college of Trinity Hall, but he had been gone too long and his views were too far from the emerging new consensus to retain much of a power base in the university. Trinity Hall itself seems to have been a nest of reformers, and its fellows spurned Gardiner in their wills.[84] It is symptomatic of Cambridge's cool relations with its chancellor that none of the Cambridge book-lists from this period include copies of any of Gardiner's works, not even the influential *De vera obedientia*.[85] It is perhaps not surprising that in his correspondence he so frequently insisted on the dignity of the office of chancellor and the respect due to him as such, for he clearly had little authority in the university other than that bestowed on him by his office.[86] His control over the situation in Cambridge was also seriously undermined by his inability to give the university more than intermittent attention. Gardiner was a busy man throughout these years. He was abroad on diplomatic missions in 1540–1 and 1545–6, and had enormous logistical responsibilities during the height of the French war in 1544–5. All of this contributed to a weakness which meant that in two critical and high-profile confrontations with his religious opponents in Cambridge, he was able to claim no more than Pyrrhic victories.

The less important of these two confrontations took place in the spring of 1545. At some point between mid-January and mid-March, 'the yought in Christes College . . . playde a tragedie called Pammachius'.[87] Although a Latin play written by a German Lutheran, Thomas Kirchmeyer, *Pammachius* had strong English connections. Kirchmeyer had dedicated it to Cranmer. John Bale had prepared an English translation, most likely when he was in Cromwell's service in the late 1530s. The play tells of Pammachius, a fictional fourth-century pope, who transfers his allegiance from Christ to Satan and forces the Roman Empire to submit to him until Christ sends a messenger to Wittenberg to reawaken the Church.[88] The semi-official status suggested by its dedication and translation, as well as its anti-papal theme, may have encouraged the students of Christ's to believe that it fell within the bounds of acceptability. Such an innocent explanation seems unlikely, however, since

---

[84] Rex, 'Early impact', 53–4; MacCulloch, *Cranmer*, 300.
[85] Leedham-Green, *Books in Cambridge Inventories*.
[86] Gardiner, *Letters*, 122, 130, 134, 140.   [87] Ibid., 130; Parker, *Correspondence*, 26.
[88] Blackburn, *Biblical Drama*, 40; James Arthur Muller, *Stephen Gardiner and the Tudor Reaction* (1926), 123; Charles H. Herford, *Studies in the Literary Relations of England and Germany in the Sixteenth Century* (Cambridge, 1886), 125–9; *LP* XIV (i) 631.

the players went to the trouble of preparing a bowdlerised version of the text for the performance. What remained was provocative enough. 'They reproved Lent fastinges, al ceremonies, and albeit the wordes of Sacrament and Masse wer not named, yet the rest of the matier wryten in that tragedie in the reprofe of them was expressed.'[89] Perhaps more important than any specific doctrinal controversies was the new historical paradigm which the play assumed, and which Bale was even then developing further in his *Image of bothe churches*. The perception of history as a struggle between a true, persecuted Christian Church and an oppressive, Roman Antichrist went beyond any Henrician orthodoxy, but the audience of such a play would find themselves being drawn into this world-view.[90] The mere fact of the performance is a wayside marker in the establishment of an evangelical mindset as Cambridge's orthodoxy.

That mindset was not universally accepted in Cambridge, however. If it had been, the whole event might have vanished from the historical record; but Cuthbert Scott, a young fellow of Christ's who was to be bishop of Chester under Mary, was sufficiently outraged by the performance that he reported it to the chancellor, describing the play as poisonous.[91] On 27 March 1545 Gardiner wrote to Vice-Chancellor Parker that he had heard of the performance, and that parts of the play were 'soo pestiferous as wer intollerable'. He assured Parker silkily that he did not believe such rumours but would be grateful if Parker could look into the matter. Parker replied a week later, confirming that the performance had indeed taken place. However, he assured Gardiner that this was not, as he had thought, an action taken 'contrary to the mynde of the Master and President', but had rather been authorised and indeed funded, to the tune of some six pounds or more, by the college. He also confirmed that the offensive sections of the play had been excised, and added that although he was not at the performance himself, 'hitherto I have not seen any man that was present at it to shew himself grieved'.[92]

If Parker had hoped that this would reassure Gardiner he was mistaken. Gardiner instead raised the stakes when he wrote again on 23 April, having received fuller information on the performance from other sources. It was, he said, to be expected that students, 'eyther of fraylte, lightnes, or malyce, wold abuse ther giftes'. However, if members of the college or university hierarchy were involved, that was far more serious. He ordered Parker to assemble the heads of house and the doctors of the university 'to require them to assiste youe in the tryal of the truth concernyng the said tragedye', through examining those who were present at the performance. The bowdlerisation

---

[89] Gardiner, *Letters*, 131. [90] Ryrie, 'Problem of legitimacy', 81, 85.
[91] *APC*, 162; Parker, *Correspondence*, 25; Mullinger, *University of Cambridge*, 75.
[92] Gardiner, *Letters*, 130; Parker, *Correspondence*, 21–2.

of the text was, Gardiner felt, particularly sinister. 'If, as youe wrote to me, they left out sumwhat unspoken, it shuld appere that the rest, being spoken, was, upon a jugement by consideration and deliberation, allowed.' And finally, without breaking the fiction that chancellor and vice-chancellor were as one concerning this matter, he added a threat:

Many hath of late repyned at the Kinges Majesties munificence in our privileges and otherwise, and let not us geve cause that they shuld justely soo doo. Our obedience shuld be an example to al other in publique directions without occasion of al slaunder. If lernyng shuld nowe be an instrument to sterre up dissension and trouble the commen quietnesse, ther opinion shuld be confermed which not many yeres past have laboured to prove, in bokes prynted in Englyshe, that the universities be the corruption of the realme. Oxford lyveth quietly with fewer privileges thenne we have; ther be that wold we had as fewe as theye.[93]

Parker's response, two weeks later, showed that he had complied with Gardiner's instructions in as minimal a fashion as possible. He assembled the heads of house, and had them return to their colleges to examine those who had been present at the performance. Once again, 'none of all their companies declared unto them that they were offended with any thing'. Gardiner wanted solid information as to whether the play was heretical; Parker was instead giving him an opinion poll on the subject. Only two people could be found to have objected to it, he wrote, one being Scott, who had made himself thoroughly unpopular in the college by his objections. Parker did, however, feel it was necessary to send Gardiner a copy of the excised text that had been used for the performance.[94]

Gardiner now moved to bring the affair to a conclusion. He replied almost by return of post. His patience with Parker's stonewalling was evidently wearing thin, and by sending the script Parker had given him all the ammunition he needed. 'Perusyng the booke of the tragedie which ye sent me, I finde moch matier not stryken out, al which by the parties own confession was uttred, very nought, and on the other parte sumthing not wel omitted.' The openness of the offence, he wrote, required that it should be dealt with sternly. 'Touching those that wer chief players in the tragedie, I here very evel matier, and I pray youe cal them unto youe and knowe whither they wyl acknowledge and confess ther faulte or noo.' Six days later, on 18 May, he sent a formal letter to the regents and non-regents at Cambridge on the general need to maintain good order and religious unity, citing the performance of *Pammachius* as the most visible symptom of a deeper problem. He also brought in more weighty authority to reinforce his orders. On 16 May,

---

[93] Gardiner, *Letters*, 131–2.   [94] Parker, *Correspondence*, 24–6.

Gardiner was one of the signatories of a letter from the Privy Council to Parker which required that he act to discipline the players.[95]

Nothing further is heard from Cambridge on the matter, and the chancellor seems to have had the last word. However, the limitations of Gardiner's apparent victory are worth emphasising. A remarkable feature of the affair is the apparent confidence of the organisers at Christ's that such a play could be staged, before an intercollegiate audience of reasonable size, without creating repercussions. Gardiner wrote that 'you can scarcely have expected that what is done publicly among you, and in such a way as to receive publicity, would remain confined within your own walls and not get abroad' – yet this seems to be precisely what they had expected, and had it not been for Scott's outrage they would have been correct. Possibly they relied on the play's central anti-papal theme to silence opposition, a theme which even Gardiner was compelled to praise. It is, of course, impossible to know whether there were other, similar events which were concealed more successfully. However, it seems unlikely that the *Pammachius* affair would have been entirely effective in deterring the staging of similar events in the future. The only substantial demand which Gardiner made was that the university leadership 'do, for the reformation of those that have misused themselves in playing of the said tragedy, as to your wisdoms shall be thought requisite'. Parker was asked to inform Gardiner if the players 'wyl acknowledge and confess ther faulte or noo', although there is no record of whether or not he did so (or indeed of any of the results of the process which presumably followed Gardiner's instructions). This is noteworthy not only because the examination and punishment of the offenders was left in Parker's decidedly sympathetic hands, but also because Gardiner chose, in the end, to make nothing of the admitted fact that the play had been procured with the consent and at the cost of the master and company of Christ's College. Only the most obvious and vulnerable offenders were tackled. Gardiner's ability to control events was hamstrung by his physical absence, but also, as he was well aware, by the real independence which the vice-chancellor could exercise. As he wrote in frustration in his formal letter: 'At Oxford there is none of this, and it has been suggested to me that the administration of your affairs would be more satisfactory if the chancellor's deputy were appointed, in accordance with the Oxford practice, by the chancellor alone.'[96] However, while Gardiner could wish that his old university would embrace both Oxford's practices and its doctrines, there was little that he could do to bring it about. Within Oxford, evangelicalism was present, but able to do

---

[95] Gardiner, *Letters*, 133–40; Parker, *Correspondence*, 29–30; *APC*, 162. It is intriguing that John Dudley and William Parr, who were both becoming aligned with the reformist faction at court, were present at the Privy Council on 16 May yet did not sign the letter.

[96] Gardiner, *Letters*, 135, 140; Parker, *Correspondence*, 21–2, 29.

PRONUNCIATION AND AUTHORITY

The *Pammachius* affair was a flash in the pan. By 1545, a more serious conflict had been rumbling on for three years: a dispute over Greek pronunciation. This was an abstruse academic issue which all participants agreed was of trifling importance, but which nevertheless laid bare profound intellectual differences. It served as an arena in which some of the central issues of the Reformation could be confronted by proxy. The debate itself stemmed from the difference between the pronunciations of ancient Greek and of contemporary Greek. The contemporary usage was followed for the pronunciation of classical texts in Western Europe. The first systematic attempt at deducing what the ancient pronunciation might have been was made by Erasmus in 1528, but he continued to follow the established pronunciation for everyday academic use. However, Erasmus' ideas were picked up in about 1535 by the young Cambridge scholars Thomas Smith and John Cheke. Both men began to use a reconstructed ancient pronunciation in teaching and to suggest that it should become the norm. Despite the controversial nature of this project, and the almost uniformly hostile response it met with on the Continent, Smith and Cheke were appointed to two of the new royal lectureships created in 1540: Smith to that of civil law and Cheke to that of Greek. Both continued to spread the word of the reconstructed pronunciation. However, early in 1542 Gardiner, as chancellor, wrote to Cheke to ask him not to introduce such speculations into the university's teaching. On 15 May 1542 Gardiner issued an edict upholding the established usage and providing various penalties for scholars who insisted on the novel forms.[97] Smith protested, but without success.

This apparently irrelevant academic spat is in fact of considerable importance to the religious conflicts of the age, in several ways. First of all, it is a further demonstration of the chancellor's inability to enforce his authority. Exactly a year after the initial edict, Gardiner, writing to Vice-Chancellor John Edmunds, felt it necessary to reiterate the ban on the reconstructed pronunciation.

---

[97] Muller, *Stephen Gardiner*, 121–2. A fuller account of the origins of this controversy may be found in Mullinger, *University of Cambridge*, 54–63. See also John Strype, *The Life of the Learned Sir Thomas Smith* (Oxford, 1820), 10–25; Winthrop S. Hudson, *The Cambridge Connection and the Elizabethan Settlement of 1559* (Durham, NC, 1980), 43–6.

I pray youe be persuaded that I wyl not be deluded and contempned. I did it seriously and wyl maynteyne it. If youe see the transgressours punished I have cause to be contented, but otherwise I entende, in your and the proctours persons, to use myn auctorite geven me by the Universite; whereunto I trust ye wyl not enforce me.

His letter to the regents and non-regents on the *Pammachius* affair also returned to this question, saying that the youth of the university

> in dealing with the very letters of the Greek alphabet . . . are learning to contemn and make light of my office as well as your authority. . . . While they are flaunting as the truth something extremely frivolous, the truth actually is that they reject your authority, scorn my office, and disagree with everyone else.[98]

The attempt to suppress the reconstructed pronunciation had evidently had very limited success.

This is, of course, the kind of issue which is capable of generating a great deal of heat within a university. However, both sides in the debate were aware that the issue itself was a minor one. Despite his fierce edict and his repeated insistence that it be obeyed, Gardiner freely conceded that the question was 'of exceedingly slight importance'.[99] Nevertheless, the principles which lay behind it gave it a stubborn significance which meant that neither side was willing to yield. For Gardiner, of course, one of those principles quickly became that of defending his own authority.[100] (And likewise, the spectacle of Gardiner as one 'so wonderfully learned that ye will teach the scolares of cambridge to pronunce Greke' was too choice a target for evangelical polemicists to resist.[101]) But the pronunciation issue raised questions which went to the heart of the Reformation debates. Gardiner's reason for enforcing his edict was the religious implications raised by this issue. 'It is a trifling matter, I admit', he wrote in his letter to the regents and non-regents of 1545, 'if one considers this point [pronunciation] only, but it paves the way for more serious things . . . In fact, I perceive that the attitude of which I complain has already made such headway that it affects even religious practices.' The *Pammachius* affair was portrayed in this letter as a direct consequence of the disputes over pronunciation. Two years before, in his instruction to Vice-Chancellor Edmunds to enforce the edict, Gardiner had seen the issues of pronunciation and religious division as intimately connected. Using the potent rhetoric of unity, he concluded his reaffirmation of the edict with the words,

---

[98] Gardiner, *Letters*, 122, 136–7.   [99] *Ibid.*, 137.

[100] Rex Pogson, 'God's law and man's: Stephen Gardiner and the problem of loyalty', in *Law and Government under the Tudors*, ed. Claire Cross, David Loades and J. J. Scarisbrick (Cambridge, 1988), 86.

[101] Turner, *Rescuynge of the romishe fox*, sig. H7ᵛ.

The Kinges Majestie hath, by the inspiration of the Holy Ghost, componed al matiers of religion; which uniformite I praye God it maye in that [i.e. the issue of pronunciation] and al other thinges extende unto us; and forgetting al that is past goo forth in agrement as though ther had been no such matier.[102]

Disunity over pronunciation would lead, Gardiner feared, to the spread of heterodox doctrines.

Modern spectators will find themselves almost instinctively siding with Smith and Cheke in this debate. If ancient Greek is being spoken, surely ancient Greek pronunciation is appropriate. If the established pronunciation can be shown to be, as Smith and Cheke contended, 'corrupt, barbarous, misguided', it should be altered or abandoned. Smith's argument might have been calculated to appeal to modern historians: 'It is a fine thing to rebuild what has collapsed, to set up what has been torn down, to put together again what has been pulled apart, to restore to things their own proper splendour.' Nor, he added, does the impossibility of completing such a task render it any less worthwhile.[103] Smith and Cheke's opponents, by extension, can all too easily seem to be mere obscurantists. Foxe mocked Gardiner for defending the old usage regardless of its merits, even though (indeed, because) it was 'rotten with age'.[104] It is therefore important to understand exactly why Gardiner objected to this project, for he was no mean scholar, and his argument is both subtle and powerful. In his reply to Smith's treatise in September 1542, Gardiner was happy to agree that the established pronunciation differed, sometimes dramatically, from the ancient usage. However, he continued, 'you maintain that this is done incorrectly. It is precisely there that the point at issue lies. My contention, indeed, is not that it is done because it is correct but that because it is done it is the correct thing to do.' Both the pronunciation and the meaning of words are, he argued from Aristotle, merely conventional and so subject to change over time:

You will say that the change occurs by means of 'misuse'. I grant you that; but it is a 'misuse' which authority supports and upholds in the face of the older usage. The passage of time possesses this characteristic property: working slowly and tranquilly, with the co-operation of usage, it alters, to a considerable extent, the character of things; it changes rude to refined and refined to rude, and makes clear what is obscure and discordant what is harmonious.

The religious implications of the battle-lines thus sketched are clear enough. The reformers viewed the Church of the apostolic age as normative, an absolute standard against which all else was to be judged, and

---

[102] Gardiner, *Letters*, 122, 137.
[103] However, the project appears in a slightly different light when compared to Smith's other great linguistic scheme, to produce a rationalised English alphabet, containing twenty-nine letters and no Q. Strype, *Smith*, 20–1.
[104] AM, 1786.

besides which the accretions of subsequent ages were at best indifferent and at worst blasphemous. Conservatives understood the Church to be a single body developing over time, whose development and reinterpretation of the authorities it received was itself authoritative. This was the debate of Scripture against unwritten verities; of the Church as the recipient of revelation against the Church as participant in revelation; of the conviction of the individual conscience before God against the authoritative settlement of the Church. These were the central questions of authority which underlay the entire Reformation crisis. In the debate on pronunciation, the same questions were being fought out at one remove. Gardiner defended the established usage in terms calculated to turn a reformer's stomach:

> You and your friends consistently maintain that there is error in the present pronunciation – ours, I mean, not yours. I do not deny that the change from the old pronunciation is obvious. Indeed, error there truly is, since you will have it so. But it is a collective error, an established error, an error accepted and approved of everywhere, by every single living human being except by the two of you, an error held in honour among scholars.

He had, he claimed, 'learned to regard a collective error as justice and on occasion to deal with the truth as a matter of secondary consideration'.

An analogy took Gardiner to the heart of the question. A court of law always aims at justice, but cannot always achieve it. Nevertheless, jurists agree that the judgements of a court should be called justice, even if on a particular occasion they are unjust,

> so that it is actually given the name of justice when it is unfair and of truth when it is false. If this were not so, we should never have anything sure, anything fixed on which to rely. But, you say, whatever name is given to it, in actual fact it remains unfair or false, and the name does not change its nature. On the contrary, by reason of the formal conditions which attach to a matter when it has been adjudicated, it is now called justice and is justice, and similarly it ought to be received as truth and regarded as such.

These are perennial Reformation themes: the Catholic insistence that religious truth can be firmly established only by a process of divinely authorised interpretation, as against the Protestant assertion that biblical truths are self-evident. Gardiner's use of the legal analogy to describe this is a genuinely powerful argument – not least because it is reminiscent of the language of forensic justification.

Gardiner proceeded to draw a moral for the question of pronunciation, a conclusion which represents an entire pattern of thought repugnant to this generation of reformers. Scholarship, he stated, must take second place to authority: and this was an argument which applied as forcefully to the theologian as to the classicist. 'Let us ignore the question of true and false, for that, disposed of by a sort of previous verdict, may well lie quiescent, and let us all embrace and follow that which is in force by general agreement.' Finally, he turned to Smith's argument that the restoration of a lost pronunciation is a worthwhile endeavour. While not denouncing it as an academic exercise, he was profoundly opposed to any attempt to introduce a restored pronunciation for everyday use, simply because any such restoration was bound to be imperfect and incomplete. At this point the religious subtext of the debate became explicit. Gardiner related how Philip Melanchthon ('a young man addicted to introducing innovations') had suggested that Duns Scotus should be removed from the list of approved writers, and how Erasmus had replied that 'when he had determined upon a better theology to substitute for it, and not till then, would he consult about altering the scholastic theology'. Gardiner concluded by refuting the suggestion that 'it is something . . . to make any advance at all, even though we are not permitted to go on further', comparing this to re-tuning an orchestra and stopping halfway through. It is an image which vividly portrays the traditionalist understanding of the Church, and which must count as one of the more telling hits against the reformers.[105]

The attack on the reconstructed Greek pronunciation, therefore, was an indirect attack on evangelical patterns of thinking at Cambridge. The failure of that attack was one of the more important conservative failures of the period. This was partly because it underlined Cambridge's status as an evangelical stronghold, but also because the same approach that underpinned Gardiner's attack on reconstructed Greek pronunciation can be seen in much of the broader attack on evangelical thought. Gardiner himself, and other conservative preachers and polemicists, came increasingly to attack reformist thought through an emphasis on authority and faith, and through scorn for the intellectual pride and reliance on naked reason which, in their view, characterised the reformers. As so often in the English Reformation, academic skirmishes presaged broader battles.[106] In 1546, conservatives finally engaged their evangelical opponents in print.[107] In particular, Gardiner wrote a major piece of English polemic, a book for conservatives to rally to. *A detection of the deuils sophistrie* is a lively, lengthy and scholarly defence of the Mass. It includes the obligatory clause-by-clause justification of traditional belief, but Gardiner pointedly refused to go too far down that particular road. Instead, he took a step back from the conventional exaltation of learning, and attacked the gospellers for their reliance on 'carnall reason'. Such reason cannot, he admitted, prove the doctrines of the Mass, but nor can it prove doctrines such as the Trinity or the Incarnation. In these matters, 'carnall reason is excluded, by certentie of faithe: so shulde it be in all other

---

[105] Gardiner, *Letters*, 101–18. Muller's translation of Gardiner's Latin is used throughout.
[106] Wooding, *Rethinking Catholicism*, 192.   [107] See Appendix II.

mysteries, which all together, be the body of our religion'. Good Christians may be unable to understand a particular doctrine, but their doubts should not lead them to question the universally accepted teaching of the Church,

> agaynst which teaching, good men kicke not, with howes, & whattes, for that is a token of incredulite. . . . If thou wilt not byleue more then thyne owne capacite can comprehende, then haste thou no byleef at al of god, which can not be of man comprehended, & haste onely a vayne deceytfull ymaginacion of thyne owne . . . and so is there fynally by thy conclusyon, no stedfaste fayth in our religion, but waueryng opinion.

The reformers, of course, would deny this characterisation of themselves, and argue that they placed their 'stedfaste fayth' in the fixed revelation of Scripture. Gardiner, however, argued that Scripture is composed of words, and that words (as he had argued against Smith four years before) are mutable. It is the Church which has their authoritative interpretation. He compared the reformers who defied that interpretation to the wilfully ignorant who use ambiguous abbreviations and spellings to misread a written text. As such, it is impossible to allege any biblical passages against the traditional teachings of the Church in good conscience:

> How so euer thapparaunce of wordes be in scriptures, we beleue the truth taught vs by the churche. . . . Hath not the churche had, and vnderstanded these wordes of scripture, that ye so vehemently alledge? Hathe not the churche delyuered those worde vnto vs? And hathe not the same church notwithstanding, taught this truth, how the bread by the consecracion, is conuerted into the precyouse bodye of Christe?

Gardiner's appeal to the reformers was for them to renounce the pride through which they question established belief, and rejoin the united mind of the Church. 'Beleue, without howes, as is preached vnto thee by the church of christ.'[108]

This appeal, however, emotive as it doubtless was to conservatives, by its nature came too late for the reformers. It could have no purchase on those who had already crossed the intellectual Rubicon of deciding that authority lay in bare Scripture, and that the Church's interpretation of it was prone to error. As at Cambridge in 1542, Gardiner was trying to apply the rules of one intellectual world to those who had crossed over into another. They could be brought to outward compliance through threats, but arguments such as these could not reach them. Other conservatives openly admitted that reproaches which had once brought people to repentance now only provoked derision.[109] In the decades that followed, of course, as a Protestant orthodoxy became defined and established, Protestants were driven to make very similar arguments in order to justify their particular interpretation of Scripture as authoritative, despite having jettisoned many of the intellectual

---

[108] Gardiner, *Detection of the Deuils Sophistrie*, fos. 6^r–7^v, 15^v, 17^{r-v}, 101^v–3^r, 106^r.
[109] *An inuectiue ageinst glotony*, sig. B7^r.

tools which gave such arguments their power. In 1540s England, however, the reformers had the twin luxuries of opposition, and of having no clear confession of faith. As such, the double-edged principle of *sola scriptura* could, for the time being, still be wielded.

Gardiner, as a lawyer, was perhaps peculiarly attracted to arguments which centred around the need to defer to intellectual authority. However, the themes he raised recur almost wherever conservative arguments are to be found in this period. William Chedsay was as shocked as Gardiner by the disunity in the Church provoked by the evangelicals, and he employed a similarly musical metaphor. 'Then,' he said, meaning the golden days of twenty years before, 'was preachyng swete melodye, whan the pypes were in tune: Nowe it is an vnswete noyse: for the pipes yarryth.'[110] However, these themes are most prevalent in discussions of the Mass. The *King's Book*'s comment on transubstantiation was that 'in this moste high misterie, no man ought to reason, ouer farre, nor go about to compasse, the wyll and worke of god, by his weake sense and ymagination'.[111] William Peryn's 1546 tract, *Thre godlye and notable sermons, of the sacrament of the aulter*, is a turgid piece which was largely plagiarised from the work of John Fisher, but which proved reasonably popular: it went through two editions within a year, and John Bale took it sufficiently seriously to plan a refutation of it.[112] Peryn positively celebrated the difficulty of bending natural reason to believe in the Mass. He appealed to the reader to make a leap of faith, despising 'suche grosse and stubburne blyndnesse, that wolde not haue reason subiugate and obedient, vnto goddes myghtie worde & power, but wolde that the omnipotent worde and power of God, shulde take suche auctoritie & place, as theyr blynd carnall wytte wyll geue leue'. He deliberately presented the miracles of the Mass so as to arouse incredulity, and admonished his readers and hearers 'not to be so curious & inquisitue, howe, or what wayes, God maye do thys or that'. When the patriarchs and prophets encountered miracles, they 'consellyd not wyth nature, neyther serched neyther skanned them, wyth blynd reason. But with mooste humble & obedient fayth they receyued them.' This is not merely a way of justifying a troublesome set of doctrines, but a principle of the Christian life:

We ought not to seke, to proue wyth reason, the matters of our faith. For yf we shulde be so grosse and carnall, that we wolde beleue no more, then we can proue by naturall reason, we shulde sone dyscharge our selfes, of all the articles, of oure fayth.... It is agaynst the nature of faythe (which is of thynges that appeare not vnto reason or sense) to be proued by reason.[113]

---

[110] Chedsay and Scott, *Two notable sermones*, sigs. C3ᵛ–4ʳ. [111] *King's Book*, fo. 26ᵛ.
[112] Richard Rex, *The Theology of John Fisher* (Cambridge, 1991), 90; Askew, *The lattre examinacyon*, fo. 60ᵛ.
[113] Peryn, *Thre godlye and notable sermons*, sigs. A4ᵛ, A8ʳ–B1ᵛ, C1ᵛ–2ʳ, L3ʳ⁻ᵛ.

Reason, if not properly directed, was corrosive. As one conservative worried early in Edward VI's reign, once the Mass was discredited, the Trinity and the Incarnation would be next.[114]

The submission of reason to the will of God was, of course, a truism, and reformers were ready to join conservatives in affirming it.[115] The issue remained whether reason should submit to God's will as revealed through the Church, or only to Scripture. Scripture's ambiguity, and the latitude thus possible in interpreting it, left the reformers open to the conservative accusation that they bent Scripture to their prejudices. Many evangelicals were aware that this position left them somewhat exposed. Some felt that attack was the best form of defence, and denounced conservatives for 'wrestyng and writhyng' Scripture:

> Do ye take the holy scripture to be lyke a shypmans hose?
> Nay nay, although a shypmans hose, wyll serue all sortes of legges
> yet Christes holy scrypture, wyll serue no rotten dregges.[116]

Others tried to develop more objective formulae governing the interpretation of Scripture. Simon Heynes, the dean of Exeter and former master of Queens' College, Cambridge, insisted that doctrines should 'be manifestly grownded vpon holy scripture writen, or at the lest wise manifestly & plainly deduced owte of holy scripture'.[117] Some of the more moderate reformers found this dilemma particularly uncomfortable. One late Henrician evangelical writing on the Eucharist played down the role of natural reason in the Christian life. 'It wer oon of the gretteste dyscomfortes that myght come to a crysten man yf it could be provyd that ther fayth myght be comprehendyd by reason: for then it were neyther of there godenes, worthynes nor perfeccion that it is of in dede.' A few paragraphs later, however, when disputing the 'oppinion' of transubstantiation, the same author stumbled over his own raw incredulity in the familiar manner which Gardiner and Peryn deplored. 'As me semyth it soundeth very nygh to a impossybilytye to sey that the colour: savour: taste: fasshon: moystenes ponderousenes: & measure of the wyne remayn, & that the substaunce ys gone.'[118] The core beliefs and doctrines of authority shared by all evangelicals continued to draw them towards assertions of this kind – however non-confrontational they might be.

It was this self-reliance, this willingness to pit one's own individual reasoning and interpretation of Scripture against the collective judgement of the Church, which drew forth one of the commonest accusations against the reformers, that of pride. The specific claim of assurance of salvation, which

---

[114] Proctor, *The fal of the late Arrian*, esp. sigs. A6^v–A8^r, D8^v.
[115] For example, Taverner, *Catechisme*, fo. 3^r.   [116] Gray, *Answere to maister Smyth*.
[117] BL Cotton MS Cleopatra E.v fo. 60^v (*LP* XIV (i) 1035).
[118] *Ibid.*, fos. 179^v, 180^r, 182^r (*LP* XIV (i) 1067).

arose out of the Protestant theology of justification, was especially offensive to conservatives. When Robert Barnes stated at the stake that 'yf Sayntes do praye for you, then I truste within this halfe houre to praye . . . for euery christen man', conservative commentators were outraged by

> the pryde, and grea[t] presumpcyon
> Of the false heretyke, that wolde become
> A saynt in the deuyls name.[119]

But this was only the most visible point of a more general spiritual pride that seemed, to conservatives, to suffuse the evangelical outlook. In 1544, Cuthbert Scott – the man who was to bring the *Pammachius* affair to light the following year – preached at Paul's Cross in London. He deplored the laity's reluctance to submit to clerical authority in matters of doctrine: 'If they haue redde ouer once the newe testament in englyshe, they wyll not stricke to enterprete the moost darkest places in scripture, contrary both to the auncient and moost holye doctors, and also the decrees of the churche.' He added that such a person, if asked to justify this behaviour, will say,

I am one whose eyes it hath pleased god to haue opened that I shold se his truthe: the churche hath erred, the doctors haue ben disceaued, as I knowe I my self can not be, for I am suere that I am one of the predestinate and electe. & therof they wyl largely and lyberally dispute and reason, not knowynge what the scripture doth meane by predestination and election.[120]

The Bristol preacher Roger Edgeworth likewise derided those 'greene Diuines' who, having gained a passing familiarity with Scripture, 'presumeth vppon this facultye, and teareth it, and teacheth it afore they learn it'.[121] Such pride, in other words, arose directly from the evangelical view of authority. Conservatives perceived this self-confidence as arrogance, and drew attention to it whenever possible, exploiting opportunities such as recantations to the full. When Thomas Becon recanted in 1543, for example, he was made to focus not on the heretical doctrines he had taught – these were spread fairly thinly through his works in any case – but on his supposedly overweening spiritual pride. The author of his recantation noted that this extended even to his pseudonym, Theodore Basille – 'whiche ys asmoch to say, as a kynge gyven of godd, ys yt not a prowde name to be of myne owne chosynge?'[122]

---

[119] Standish, *Lytle treatise against the protestacion of Robert Barnes*, sig. D6r; *This lytle treatyse declareth the study and frutes of Barnes borned in west smyth felde* (RSTC 1473.5: 1540). I am grateful to James Lawson of Shrewsbury School for making this unique tract available to me.
[120] Chedsay and Scott, *Two notable sermones*, sig. H7r–v.   [121] Edgeworth, *Sermons*, 140.
[122] Bonner Register fos. 44r–5r. Becon himself clearly remained enamoured of the name, as he named four of his sons Theodore and Basil – two each. Bailey, *Thomas Becon*, 125–6.

Reformers, too, were ready to accuse their opponents of pride. After all, if conversion means coming to understand the truth of God, and if that truth is perceived primarily on an intellectual level, then those who do not perceive it are necessarily either ignorant or wilful. Reformers faced with opponents who had had the opportunity to conform to their own views, but who had remained opposed, could draw only one conclusion: that they were deliberately rejecting what they knew to be the truth, either for some material gain or out of a damnable pride through which they allowed the devil to deceive them. Becon himself, in his panegyric to humility, stated that pride was the reason why 'the proude papisticall Romanistes can not perceyue the verite of Gods worde, & here in Englond & suche other lyke places euen the verye poore & base sort of people are godly learned & espy the truethe of Gods wyl'.[123] The courtier William Palmer took this even further, claiming that Gardiner was fully aware that the reformers' doctrines were true but that he continued to serve the Pope out of greed and vanity.[124] This is an important reason for the violence of so much Reformation polemic. Such proud and obstinate opponents were past persuasion and could only be denounced. They had deliberately closed their minds to the truth – and it was a truth which was to be apprehended almost exclusively through the mind. John Bale justified his violent style by the fact that his opponents were monsters, indeed devils, and so beyond reason:

> Gentyll and soft wyttes are oft tymes offended, that we are now a dayes so vehement in rebukes. But thys wolde I fayne knowe of them, what modestye they wolde vse (as they call it) if they were compelled to fyght with dragons, hyders, and other odyble monsters.... Surelye I knowe no kynde of Christen charyte to be shewed to the deuyll.... Salomon sayth, there is ... a tyme as wele to hate, as a tyme to loue.[125]

As we have seen, however, these attacks had a different flavour when made by traditionalist writers. Conservative polemicists were almost the sole representatives in the early sixteenth century of the Christian tradition of distrust of untrammelled natural reason. The polemics of Gardiner, Peryn and others were marked by suspicion of carnal reason and an appeal for assent to the mind of the Church, and underpinned by contempt for the reformers' intellectual pride. Such an approach was to an extent forced on them by their material. If they had engaged with the reformers on other terms, the underlying issue of authority would have been implicitly conceded even if particular traditional doctrines had successfully been defended. This was not anti-intellectualism. It was an attempt to ensure that the intellect did not break its banks, and in doing so sweep away all faith, all humility and, in the

---

[123] Becon, *Pleasaunt newe Nosegay*, sigs. D3^v–4^r.
[124] TCC MS R3.33. Cf. Riordan and Ryrie, 'Stephen Gardiner'.
[125] Askew, *The first examinacyon*, fos. 44^v–5^v. See above, p. 122.

end, all reason. Nevertheless, because they ran against the prevailing intellectualism of the time, such arguments were necessarily made from a position of weakness – whatever their intrinsic merits. In a society which valued learning so highly, there were limits to how effectively a movement which was aggressively and self-consciously cerebral could be opposed through questioning the role of reason. If the possibility that the Church could be wrong was once conceded – and the rejection of the papal supremacy was easily interpreted as just such a concession – these conservative arguments began to look dangerously flimsy.

These themes, of course, affected debates between reformer and conservative across the country and in print, not merely in the universities. The universities were, however, the cockpit of the intellectual nation, and the arena in which one of the more prominent and clear-cut rounds of this battle was fought. Gardiner was clear that the outcome of his trials of strength with Cambridge had implications which carried well beyond the walls of the colleges. 'If the Kinges Majesties directions be not obeyed there, and by us dissembled', he asked Parker rhetorically, 'howe shal we charge the rudenesse abrode that maye allege ther example for pretense of ther fault?'[126] The religious spectrum was united in seeing the universities as critical for the welfare of the Church: not merely through providing the next generation of leaders, but through their example to, and intellectual leadership of, the Church of the moment. In this sense, Cambridge's stubborn reformism during these years was of enormous importance to the evangelical movement's survival and development. On one level, Cambridge provided a safe haven for embattled reformers, a nationwide network of evangelical contacts and a reasonably steady supply of sympathetic graduates. On another, the experience of defending the universities led many moderate reformers to doubt the value of their alliance with the regime. This was the more so as within the safety of the colleges the regime could be defied on a scale which was not possible in the public arena. More importantly, however, the intellectual battles being fought there during these years were critical to the broader movement. The view of authority which emerged from the pronunciation debates was one which left little intellectual space for pragmatic compromises and politic silences. The elevation of Scripture which these debates implied overshadowed the spiritual authority of kings as well as that of bishops. Gardiner's failure in the pronunciation dispute to contain the contagion which rejected properly constituted intellectual authority was an ominous sign of conservatism's inability to control the same disease in society at large.

---

[126] Gardiner, *Letters*, 132.

6

The court

What shall be done vnto the man whom the kynge wolde fayne brynge vnto worshippe?
                                                                    Esther 6:6

IN THE SHADOW OF THE KING

During the 1540s most English evangelicals were safely hidden from view. One of their strongholds, however, was the most terrifyingly public place in England: Henry VIII's court and the upper echelons of his government. Since Anne Boleyn's rise to influence, evangelicals had received irregular but significant patronage from the regime. One of the key facts of the last years of Henry's reign is that this patronage continued. There was no mass cull of reformers after Cromwell's fall, although there were occasions on which such a purge threatened. A significant body of evangelicals and their sympathisers survived, and indeed won new recruits: in personal service to the king, amongst the nobility and gentry who dominated the court and who administered both peace and war, and amongst the senior clergy. Their proximity to the crown made their experience of the 1540s markedly different from that of their co-religionists in more humble positions. It was of course more dangerous. As the king's vindictiveness and paranoia accelerated during the last years of his life, royal service became increasingly perilous. Yet the reformers at court could also draw on royal protection. The king would not readily dispose of trusted or favoured servants simply on the say-so of their enemies, especially when he was at least as suspicious of the enemies themselves. As we have seen, in 1543 and again in 1546 he intervened to protect evangelical courtiers who were threatened with heresy charges, sometimes showing real anger on their behalf.[1] Most strikingly, he protected both Katherine Parr and Thomas Cranmer from their accusers. In Cranmer's case, in 1543 Henry was persuaded that the archbishop was 'the gretest heretique in Kente' – but he nevertheless chose to forgive him, directing his anger

---

[1] See above, pp. 48, 55–6.

instead at the 'confederacie' which had gathered the evidence.² Although the court reformers' security was precarious, they did remain tolerably secure for most of this period. And by way of compensation, they could wield some real power. They could influence national politics, and those who had the king's trust did at times succeed in doing so. And they could further the reformist cause in more local and low-key ways, not least by offering patronage to other evangelicals. Of course, balancing the use of such power for reformist ends against their own interests was a game of very high stakes. Nor did all those courtiers who could be linked to the reformist cause wish to use their influence in the same way. Most had other political interests and obligations to balance against their religious interests; all of them had the distinctive perspective on national affairs that the hothouse of Henry VIII's court afforded. Yet even their muted impact makes these men and women a disproportionately important part of contemporary evangelicalism, as well as a disproportionate influence on its future.³

The court of an opinionated and instinctively conservative king is perhaps not the most obviously hospitable environment for evangelicals. They were not there on account of their religion – at least, not in a straightforward way. Broadly speaking, evangelicals seem to have found their way to Henry's court by one or more of three means. The first and most obvious is through winning the lotteries of birth or of connections. Many of the most prominent and powerful evangelicals at court owed their position to matters wholly unconnected to their religious views. Edward Seymour did not climb steadily in the king's esteem because he had allies among the court evangelicals. He did so because he had the good fortune to be Prince Edward's uncle, and also because he had a modicum of military skill, the talent Henry valued above all else. Henry did not marry Katherine Parr because she was a reformist sympathiser – although he may have found her piety appealing, especially in contrast to her predecessor.⁴ Katherine Willoughby, the duchess of Suffolk, was perhaps the most aggressive of the reformers in the higher reaches of the court; but she was not there because of her beliefs, but because the king's childhood friend Henry Brandon had married her when she was a wealthy fourteen-year-old ward in his care. William Butts, the physician who is credited with quietly pressing a reformist view on his royal master on several occasions, rose in Henry's service from the 1520s principally

---

² Nichols (ed.), *Narratives*, 252–3.
³ On court reformers and their influence, see Maria Dowling, 'The Gospel and the court: Reformation under Henry VIII', in *Protestantism and the National Church in Sixteenth-Century England*, ed. Peter Lake and Maria Dowling (1987); Swensen, 'Noble hunters of the Romish fox'; Michael Riordan, 'Gospellers at court during the conservative reaction, 1539–47' (MA dissertation, St Andrews, 1998).
⁴ James, *Kateryn Parr*, 194–5.

because the king trusted his doctoring. The nobility and gentry included a number of men and women who found some evangelical ideas persuasive. Naturally, the younger generation were more inclined to such novelties, and those of a more scholarly bent were also more likely to be drawn to heresies which made so much of their intellectual pretensions. The court was stiff with such people. It is no surprise that the reformers found friends amongst them.

The second group of court evangelicals found themselves in the centre of power for reasons more closely connected to their beliefs. These were the scholars, a group welcome in a self-consciously Renaissance court. The world of fashionable humanist scholarship still included plenty of energetic opponents of evangelical doctrines,[5] but it was also a world in which reformist sympathisers were commonplace. A project like the translation of Erasmus' *Paraphrases*, to which Katherine Parr lent her patronage, was impeccably orthodox. Princess Mary, an undoubted conservative who had had an excellent humanist education, was one of the contributors. The royal doctor George Owen, who had evangelical friends but does not seem to have shared their views, was also involved. Yet the other leading participants were not quite so sound. Nicholas Udall was a humanist reformer and friend of Richard Cox. In the 1530s he had become headmaster of Eton College, but was thrown out of his post after Cromwell's fall. He was recruited, apparently by Parr herself, to translate the paraphrase of Luke's gospel. His preface to the translation is a remarkably unguarded celebration of Cromwell's Reformation and a call for further change, in particular for the abolition of Masses for the dead. Other contributors were more circumspect. Thomas Key, who translated the paraphrase of Mark, was an Oxford humanist who may have already had the reformist sympathies he displayed later in life. Francis Malet, who took over the work on John's gospel when Princess Mary withdrew due to illness, was a former vice-chancellor of Cambridge and a chaplain to both Cranmer and Cromwell, although he was also close to the princess.[6] Nor did this project exhaust the queen's willingness to secure royal patronage for evangelical scholarship. John Marbeck, the Windsor organist, narrowly escaped execution for heresy in 1543, but the English concordance to the Bible which he had been laboriously compiling was confiscated and

---

[5] Richard Rex, 'The role of English humanists in the Reformation up to 1559', in *The Education of a Christian Society: Humanism and the Reformation in Britain and the Netherlands*, ed. N. Scott Amos, Andrew Pettegree and Henk van Nierop (Aldershot, Hants., 1999).

[6] Desiderius Erasmus, *The first tome or volume of the Paraphrase of Erasmus vpon the newe testamente* (RSTC 2854: 1548): Mark, fos. i^r–ii^r, Luke fos. i^r–vi^v; Blackburn, *Biblical Drama*, 65–7; Swensen, 'Noble hunters of the Romish fox', 181, 184–5, 195; *LP* XVI 27; Riordan, 'Gospellers', 55.

destroyed. Undeterred, Marbeck began again, and when he had completed it set about securing royal patronage for its publication. A friend promised his assistance, but felt that the best course was to give it to Queen Katherine, who 'would so prefer it to the Kyng, that his Maiestie would commaunde it to be published'. In the event, the king's death scuppered this plan, but it is clear that by the end of the reign, reformist scholars both looked to the queen as a reliable advocate, and trusted that her husband would look kindly on her petitions on their behalf.[7]

The most prominent evangelical scholars at court, however, were not the queen's clients but those employed as tutors for Prince Edward. The leading tutors, John Cheke, Richard Cox and Roger Ascham, were three of the finest young scholars in the land. All also had clear connections to modish religious ideas. We have already met Cheke as a prominent university reformer. Cox had taken a cautiously evangelical line during the process of revising the *Bishops' Book*, and his evangelical connections were clear. Both Cranmer and Bishop Goodricke of Ely acted as his patrons, and he in turn supported rising reformist scholars such as Nicholas Ridley.[8] Ascham was a more ambiguous figure whose allegiance to his own career overrode his religious instincts. In the early 1530s, he had ruffled some feathers in Cambridge by speaking against the pope before it was quite politic to do so, and he learned his lesson. He supported Cheke and Smith over the pronunciation dispute, but until 1545 his principal patron was Edward Lee, the conservative archbishop of York, and he had to watch his step. In 1543, Ascham somewhat carelessly produced a translation (of a commentary by the tenth-century Greek theologian Œcumenius) which seemed to cast doubt on clerical celibacy. Lee was displeased, and Ascham back-pedalled furiously, assuring Lee that he knew nothing of heretical ideas. His correspondence with Cranmer has a quite different flavour. In 1545, he asked the archbishop to dispense him from the Lenten fast, and took the opportunity to display a healthily blasé attitude towards such traditions. This malleability, together with his undoubted brilliance, won him patrons of all persuasions, from Stephen Gardiner and the duke of Norfolk, through William Paget, to Ridley and Anthony Denny. Yet he was clearly a product of the Cambridge which had been so thoroughly infiltrated by evangelical patterns of thought.[9]

---

[7] John Marbeck, *A concordance, that is to saie, a worke wherein ye maie finde any worde conteigned in the whole Bible* (RSTC 17300: 1550), sig. A3^v.

[8] Rex, *Henry VIII*, 170; Felicity Heal, 'The parish clergy and the Reformation in the diocese of Ely', *Proceedings of the Cambridge Antiquarian Society* 66 (1977), 151; BL Cotton MS Cleopatra E.v fos. 41–3 (*LP* XV 826); MacCulloch, *Cranmer*, 326; *LP* XIX (ii) 726.

[9] Roger Ascham, *The Whole Works of Roger Ascham . . . with a life of the author*, ed. J. A. Giles, 3 vols. (1864–65), vol. I, 26, 31–5, 63–6; McConica, *English Humanists*, 210–12; Laurence V. Ryan, *Roger Ascham* (Stanford, 1963), 23–4.

The presence of this evangelical clique in the young prince's schoolroom has excited a good deal of scholarly attention.[10] Edward's precocious reformism was probably shaped by this environment, and also by the influence of the other adults who kept a close eye on his progress – most notably his stepmother, Katherine Parr, and his godfather, Archbishop Cranmer. This influence may or may not have extended actually to teaching the young prince doctrines to which his father would have objected. It would have been intensely dangerous to do so, but one can imagine that – for example – Cranmer might have been unwilling or unable to dissemble his views on justification to his future sovereign. The real mystery is the king's own purpose. It is obvious that he did not appoint his son's tutors intending to expose the next Supreme Head of the Church to heresy. But neither did he make undue efforts to keep gospellers away from the boy. Edward's tutors were certainly scholars of the first rank, and they were reformers of the most cautious shade; but men of comparable gifts and more conservative inclinations could have been found had they been wanted. Moreover, the tutors were not as careful to conceal their advanced views as was once thought. In 1545 or 1546, Cheke presented the king with a New Year's gift of a Latin treatise which was moderately but plainly evangelical in its leanings.[11] Cheke clearly did not expect that he would run into any difficulties for associating himself with these views, and he was right. Where his son was concerned, Henry was if anything more alarmed by crypto-papalists than by closet evangelicals.[12] Although this did not give the reformers licence to shape his heir in their image, it did give them a systematic advantage.

The combination of royal patronage of fashionable scholarship, and the more simply partisan support of evangelically inclined nobles, ensured that Edward's household was a reliable refuge for evangelicals. Richard Grafton, for example, held the title of the prince's printer. The prince did not, of course, require much printing to be done on his behalf, but this left Grafton well-placed to gather up the crumbs from under the presses of the king's printer, Thomas Berthelet. Most significantly, Grafton and his regular associate Whitchurch were commissioned to print the 1545 King's Primer – which may imply, as Pamela Neville-Singleton has suggested, that that evangelically flavoured document was connected to the prince's education.[13] And indeed,

---

[10] Lacey Baldwin Smith, 'Henry VIII and the Protestant triumph', *American Historical Review* 71 (1966); McConica, *English Humanists*, 214–15; Scarisbrick, *Henry VIII*, 474; Hudson, *Cambridge Connection*, 68–75.

[11] John F. McDiarmid, 'John Cheke's preface to "De Superstitione"', *JEH* 48 (1997).

[12] Eric W. Ives, 'Henry VIII's will: a forensic conundrum', *HJ* 35 (1992), 797–8; Ives, 'Henry VIII's will: the protectorate provisions of 1546–47', *HJ* 37 (1994), 913.

[13] *TRP*, 353; Pamela Neville-Singleton, 'Press, politics and religion', in *The Cambridge History of the Book in Britain, Vol. III: 1400–1557*, ed. Lotte Hellinga and J. B. Trapp (Cambridge, 1999), 595.

on the old king's death, Grafton became king's printer in Berthelet's place. Other reformers attached to the prince's establishment included John Tonge, a chaplain who was to become a prominent evangelical preacher as soon as his master became king, and who may have sheltered a fugitive heretic as early as 1539.[14] Philip Gerrard, a groom of Edward's privy chamber, even produced an openly evangelical book in 1545: a translation of Erasmus' *Epicure* prefaced by a vehemently scripturalist dedication to the prince. The book was, of course, published by Grafton.[15]

The third group of court evangelicals were those who sheltered in the long shadows of Anne Boleyn and, especially, Thomas Cromwell. The queen and the minister had been powerful, partisan and passably generous patrons. Although they were gone, many of their protégés survived and, in some cases, flourished – much as Wolsey's influence had outlived him, through such former clients as Cromwell and Stephen Gardiner. Boleyn's and Cromwell's clienteles, however, had a distinct ideological flavour. By the mid-1540s, the Boleyn allegiance was failing. Latimer and Shaxton had resigned from their bishoprics, Edward Foxe was dead and Edward Crome's political capital had been spent several times over. Matthew Parker, whose career was in the long run perhaps the most significant one which Boleyn boosted, was becoming a man to be reckoned with in Cambridge, but carried no great weight at court. Some of her clerical clients retained or acquired bishoprics in the 1540s, but of these William Barlow was the only clear evangelical. Her vice-chamberlain, Edward Bainton, retained that post under each of Boleyn's four successors as queen, but died in November 1544. Bainton was in any case no great warrior in the evangelical cause, although in the early 1530s he had worked to promote and protect Latimer at court. The most important of her evangelical clients who remained at court in the 1540s was also the one with whom she had had the murkiest relationship: Sir Thomas Wyatt, who despite his death in 1542 is at the heart of one of the most intriguing evangelical groupings of the period, and to whom we shall return.

Cromwell's patronage was more far-reaching, although less partisan than Boleyn's. His numerous clients included some, like Thomas Wriothesley and John London, who seem never to have favoured evangelical reform, and some whose views genuinely changed after his fall. Yet a great many of Cromwell's people retained a clear if cautious sympathy for the reforming cause during the 1540s, and these included some who held the highest office. Thomas Audley, lord chancellor from 1533 until his death in 1544, was certainly no zealot, but he did give evangelicals some protection and lent his support to

---

[14] Brigden, *London*, 426; MacCulloch, *Cranmer*, 370; Byrne, *Lisle Letters*, vol. V, 611.
[15] Erasmus, *A Diologe called the Epicure*, sigs. A4^v–B1^r, F6^r; see above, p. 118.

some minor reforms.[16] Ralph Sadler was secretary to the Privy Council from 1540 to 1543, and as the regime's most experienced Scottish hand, remained an important figure as policy towards Scotland sank into a morass after 1543. His continued evangelicalism is undoubted, although he was no great patron of reformers; but then, given that he had nearly lost his head on a charge dredged up by Gardiner and the duke of Norfolk in 1541, some caution is perhaps understandable.[17] A little further down the hierarchy, we find more active reformers. William Gray had publicly defended Cromwell after his fall, but continued in worthy if unspectacular royal service, becoming a chamberlain of the court of general surveyors. He also remained a supporter of reformers, in 1546 urging Edward Crome not to recant for 'a playnes at Pol's Crosse'.[18] Likewise, Richard Taverner had been taken up by Cromwell as a translator and propagandist, and given the office of clerk of the signet. He retained this post for the remainder of the reign (despite a brief spell in the Tower as a rumour-monger), and as such was well placed to assist reformers during the crisis at the universities of 1546.[19] The Kentish magnate Sir George Broke, Lord Cobham, had been propelled into national politics and an alliance with Archbishop Cranmer through Cromwell's patronage. He stayed there in the 1540s, remaining on excellent terms with Cranmer and becoming lord deputy of Calais in 1544. He continued to support reformers, acting as one of Thomas Becon's patrons in the early 1540s; and he had one of his sons educated in the evangelical London household of Stephen Vaughan.[20] And Thomas Legh, one of Cromwell's enforcers from the days of the suppression of the monasteries, survived as a master of Chancery and was able to put his old ruthlessness to partisan use on Cranmer's behalf during the plots of 1543.[21]

One of the highest concentrations of Cromwellian evangelicals in court circles was in diplomatic service. Sustained posting abroad was agreeable to those who were already evangelical, and was liable to expose the unconverted to new ideas. Cromwell's propagandist Richard Morison dusted off his diplomatic credentials in 1546–7, as an appropriately evangelical ambassador to Denmark. John Dymocke had been in royal service before Cromwell's time, but Cromwell had nurtured him and given him some (fairly

---

[16] See above, pp. 40, 160; Wilkins, *Concilia*, vol. III, 862.
[17] Arthur Joseph Slavin, *Politics and Profit: A Study of Sir Ralph Sadler 1507–47* (Cambridge, 1966), 37–8, 56, 137; David M. Head, *The Ebbs and Flows of Fortune: The Life of Thomas Howard, Third Duke of Norfolk* (Athens, GA, 1995), 182–3; *LP* XXI (i) 718.19, 963.67.
[18] HPT; *APC*, 227, 466–7.   [19] *P&O*, 279; see above, pp. 167, 169.
[20] Becon, *Dauids Harpe*, sigs. A2^r, B2^v–3^v; *APC*, 114; Cranmer, *Letters*, 411; Arthur John Edwards, 'The sede vacante administration of Archbishop Thomas Cranmer, 1533–53' (MPhil thesis, London, 1968), 138–9; BL Harleian MS 283 fo. 240^r (*LP* XXI (i) 1494); *LP* XIX (i) 812.59.
[21] MacCulloch, *Cranmer*, 318; *LP* XX (i) 775–6.

limited) advancement. He was an English agent in Germany and the Netherlands throughout this period, and during the wars of the mid-1540s had particular responsibility for arranging German mercenary reinforcement for English armies. Because he was both abroad, and indispensable, he did not need to try to conceal his vehement reformist views from his masters – although those views cost him a spell in a Dutch prison in 1546.[22] The most prominent evangelical diplomat was Stephen Vaughan, who had been in Cromwell's circle since the mid-1520s, and who, in the early 1530s, had acted as the go-between for Cromwell and William Tyndale. His service was uninterrupted by Cromwell's fall. He served as a royal agent in the Netherlands until 1546, and in 1544 he was appointed one of the under-treasurers of the mint. But he also remained up to his neck in the evangelical underworld. In 1543, Stephen Cobbe, an evangelical scholar, was imprisoned by the Privy Council for preparing a 'seditious ande erroneows' biblical commentary for publication by John Gough. Not long after this, Vaughan found Cobbe work as a tutor in his London household, and he used his contacts to defend Cobbe when Bishop Bonner wanted to question him. The children whom Cobbe tutored were to become a formidable Protestant dynasty. Vaughan's protection of evangelicals even extended to marriage. In April 1546, he married Margery Brinklow, widow of Henry, the radical polemicist.[23]

The real centre of evangelical strength which Cromwell left behind him, however, was the king's privy chamber. This body, consisting of the king's personal servants, was not staffed by politicians of the first rank or by senior nobles. However, a modestly titled servant such as Sir Anthony Denny, groom of the stool and (for the last few months of the reign) first chief gentleman of the privy chamber, might wield influence comparable to that of a privy councillor: the raw political power that close and continuous physical contact with a personal monarch brings. Especially as the king's health deteriorated and his moods blackened, the men of the privy chamber were the only group who could not be barred from his presence. Evangelicals came to rely on their co-religionists in the privy chambers as a secure route to the king, allowing them to bypass conservative councillors.[24] Moreover, as we have seen, the king was often reluctant to let the inconveniences of religious politics rob him of personal servants he had come to trust. To the outside world, George Blage (for example) was an unrepentant sacramentary in a dangerously influential position, who ought to be brought to justice. To the king, he was 'my pig',

---

[22] Swensen, 'Noble hunters of the Romish fox', 150–5.
[23] *APC*, 115; PRO SP 1/208 fos. 39^v–40^r, 71^v (*LP* XX (ii) 416, 444); *LP* XIV (i) 6, XIX (i) 1035.91; *HPT*; *DNB*; Patrick Collinson, *Godly People: essays on English Protestantism and Puritanism* (1983), 276–7.
[24] PRO SP 1/218 fos. 111^v–12^r (*LP* XXI (i) 823).

a reliable fellow whose readiness to be a butt of the unwieldy royal humour overrode other considerations.[25]

In 1539, Cromwell oversaw a restructuring of the chamber, and filled the expanded body with his own clients, many of them evangelicals.[26] These joined men such as Denny and William Butts who were already well established. This new intake included most of those who in 1543 were to be charged with supporting Anthony Pearsone.[27] Philip Hoby, once a diplomatic protégé of Cromwell's, became a gentleman usher of the chamber. Thomas Cawarden, another of Pearsone's supporters in the chamber, was quite undamaged by the affair: he was knighted and made keeper of the royal palace at Nonsuch the following year, and was left a generous personal bequest in the king's will. Edmund Harman had also supported Pearsone, and also received a similar bequest: he was one of the king's barbers. Sir Thomas Sternhold, a groom of the robes, was one of the most clearly committed evangelicals of the group: the Privy Council noted that in his case, the connection with Pearsone had actually been proved. He was to remain on close terms with a wide range of evangelicals and, famously, to give his name to the collection of metrical psalms which became a cornerstone of Protestant England. Yet he too benefited from the king's will; and in 1544 he was granted the leases on several estates which had belonged to the executed Germain Gardiner.[28]

Nor was privy chamber evangelicalism limited to this group. As we have seen, in September 1540 several of the chamber's reformers conferred on the prospects for the Gospel in the king's Great Chamber, and apparently felt at ease doing so there, where they might expect to have been overheard.[29] One of this group, John Lassells, was later to have a dramatic political impact: in 1541 he provided the evidence which destroyed Queen Katherine Howard, and in 1546 his defiant sacramentarianism ensured that he accompanied his friend and (perhaps) pupil Anne Askew to the stake. Another privy chamber evangelical, William Worley, was also arrested in 1546, for 'unsemely reasoning . . . apon Scripture matters, and for his sinistre opinions upon certain poinctes'.[30] Chamber office was also held by a few more prominent figures, such as Sadler and Sir George Carew.[31] William Knyvet, one of the gentlemen of the chamber, was also a diplomat and an evangelical partisan.

---

[25] *AM*, 1246. On the privy chamber generally, see David Starkey, 'Intimacy and innovation: the rise of the Privy Chamber, 1485–1547', in *The English Court: From the Wars of the Roses to the Civil War*, ed. David Starkey (1987), esp. 109–17.
[26] G. R. Elton, *The Tudor Revolution in Government* (Cambridge, 1953), 385–97.
[27] See above, p. 48.
[28] HPT; Brigden, *London*, 420; *APC*, 97; *P&O*, 48; *LP* XVIII (ii) 241.6, XIX (i) 610.91, XX (ii) Appendix 2, XXI (ii) 634.
[29] See above, p. 22. [30] *APC*, 402, 418–19.
[31] Slavin, *Politics and Profit*, 30; on Carew, see above, p. 100, n. 25.

As part of the English embassy to the Regensburg colloquy in 1541, he enthusiastically gathered evidence of potentially treasonous contacts between Stephen Gardiner and Cardinal Pole. A few years later, he helped the reformist exile Edmund Allen secure permission from Corpus Christi College, Cambridge, to remain overseas while continuing to draw his stipend.[32] With luck, indeed, privy chamber office could be the starting point for an illustrious career. William Herbert became a member of the chamber in 1540, and soon thereafter married Anne Parr, Katherine's sister. In 1543, therefore, Herbert rather unexpectedly found that he was the king's brother-in-law, and he made the most of it. A knighthood and, in due course, noble title followed. He acquired very substantial lands, and eventually became one of the more prominent councillors of Edward VI's reign. Yet he also used his position to give a degree of patronage to reformers. The 'hot-gospeller' Edward Underhill was said to have been in his service. More significantly, he supported several scholars with an interest in taking reformist ideas to his native Wales. Arthur Kelton's nationalistic and quietly evangelical text *A commendacion of welshmen* was published in 1546 under Herbert's oversight. He was also the patron behind *Yny lhyvyr hwnn y traethir*, a Welsh-language primer produced in 1546 by Sir John Price, which was the first book ever printed in Welsh. From a starting point in the privy chamber, Herbert was well on the way to becoming a patron of the first rank himself.[33]

In doing so, he became one of a handful of court evangelicals willing and able to extend significant patronage to other reformers. The patronage of individuals like Katherine Parr, Denny and the duchess of Suffolk is well established, to say nothing of the vigorously partisan establishment created by Cranmer.[34] Other figures are a little murkier. Edward Seymour, the earl of Hertford and future Lord Protector, showed few signs in Henry VIII's last years that he would shortly become a vigorous promoter of the Reformation. He maintained passably warm contacts with court evangelicals such as Peter Carew, Thomas Wyatt the elder and the duchess of Suffolk, and even with such partisan figures as Hugh Latimer and Edward Crome. Crome, indeed, baptised his son. But Seymour gave very little actual patronage to reformers during this period.[35] A more reliable friend of the reformers, although no less political than Seymour, was Sir William Paget, the king's principal secretary from 1543. Paget forged a close alliance with Archbishop Cranmer, working

---

[32] TCC MS R3.33 fos. 127^r–9^r; Robert Masters, *The History of the College of Corpus Christi . . . in the University of Cambridge* (Cambridge, 1753), 213.
[33] Williams, *Wales and the Reformation*, 149; HPT; *DNB*.
[34] James, *Kateryn Parr*, 145–63; Dowling, 'Gospel and the court', 64–6; Swensen, 'Noble hunters of the Romish fox', 141–5; MacCulloch, *Cranmer*.
[35] Brigden, 'Henry Howard', 516, 523; Riordan, *Gospellers*, 60. In 1545 he secured a parliamentary seat for William Sharington, whose affection for reform was more financial than doctrinal. Lehmberg, *Later Parliaments*, 211; Brigden, *London*, 361.

with him on the English litany and on plans to reform ceremonial. He took the reformers' message seriously enough that during the desperate diplomatic situation of August 1546, he thought it worth pursuing the possibility that Charles V might be persuaded to break with the papacy 'by reformacion of his conscience, to be moved therto by goddes worde'. He also nurtured contacts amongst the evangelical diplomats who had once been Cromwell's clients. John Dymocke wrote in 1546 that Paget was now the only person in England whom he could trust. Paget was also apparently a congenial point of contact for the unapologetically reformist diplomats Christopher Mont and Walter Bucler. Stephen Vaughan appealed to him to help his tutor Stephen Cobbe. Similarly, Richard Cox saw Paget as a close friend and a kindred spirit. William Broke, son of the evangelical Lord Cobham, was given the office of a 'spear' in Calais in 1546 through Paget's preferment.[36]

Royal service at all levels, in other words, was shot through with evangelical sympathisers. Amongst them, some individuals might be and were threatened, but the body of reformers, their friends and their fellow-travellers was too great to be stamped out without the kind of mass purge which Henry VIII was unwilling to permit. This perhaps is the most significant fact about court reformism: its stubborn durability. Although the direction of religious policy might shift, the persistence of evangelicalism in high places ensured that reformers in need of powerful friends could often find them. While enduring the lean years of the 1540s, evangelicals were able to derive some benefit from the political capital stored up during the previous decade. Indeed, they were at times able to use that capital to strengthen, rather than merely protect their positions. Henry VIII's regime spoke with many voices. It is a significant political fact that some of those voices were persistently evangelical.

The character of court evangelicalism is a different matter. These reformers rarely made their doctrinal allegiances explicit, but it appears that they ran the gamut of evangelical opinion from Erasmianism flavoured with solifidianism through to sympathy with the doctrines of the Swiss reformers. Many of them would have been entirely at home with the moderate evangelicalism which we have seen dominating the domestic presses before 1543. George Broke, Lord Cobham, even patronised the most prominent of those moderate authors, Thomas Becon. Katherine Parr herself wrote a book which sits comfortably alongside theirs. The scholars also tended to be comparatively cautious in their reformism. But there are some traces of more radical ideas. Anne Askew and John Lassells, of course, held openly sacramentarian convictions; so, apparently, did George Blage. William Gray and William

[36] MacCulloch, *Cranmer*, 329–30, 351; Northampton Record Office MS Fitzwilliam (Milton) Correspondence 21 fo. 21^r; PRO SP 1/208 fos. 39^v–40^r, 1/223 fo. 152^r, 1/225 fo. 185^r (*LP* XX (ii) 416, XXI (i) 1491, XXI (ii) 260); Swensen, 'Noble hunters of the Romish fox', 202–3; *LP* XIV (i) 157, XXI (ii) 475.5; Riordan, *Gospellers*, 39.

Worley's support for Edward Crome's defiance in 1546 need not have implied that they subscribed to especially radical doctrines, but it spoke of an uncompromising mood and set them at odds with more circumspect court reformers such as Cox. The evangelical diplomats can also be associated with radical ideas. When Katherine Parr's secretary Walter Bucler was in Strassburg in 1545, he stayed with Richard Hilles, an English exile who was a doctrinaire Zwinglian.

Yet there is very little to suggest that this doctrinal variation caused any tensions amongst court evangelicals. If a crisis point such as Askew's interrogation came, they might split, with moderates urging her to defuse the crisis by recanting. But most of the time most reformers were united in working to avoid such crises. The intimacy of personal friendships, contacts and enmities apparently counted for more than doctrinal disagreements, as is fitting in the court of an intensely personal monarch. Moreover, while doctrinal purity might appear to be the supreme concern when viewed from the harsh clarity of exile, the heady atmosphere of Henry VIII's court gave matters a rather different colour. To survive as reformers at court, all of these people had had to learn that valour was all but swallowed up in discretion. They could use their position to serve the Gospel only if they were also willing to conceal or even dissemble their beliefs. Even some of the exiles, it seems, accepted that the court reformers had no option but to align themselves with political realities. John Hooper wrote that Bainton, Butts and others 'truly favoured the Gospel', when he might have been expected to condemn them as temporisers.[37] Such circumstances were corrosive to any strict party or doctrinal loyalties. Rather than speak of a reformist 'faction' at court, we would do better to think of a series of shifting and overlapping cliques: tight knots of men and women with like minds and shared interests. A sense of religious affinity was one of the bonds that might tie such cliques together, especially during the periodic crises in religious politics; but it was never the only one, nor could religious disagreements be allowed to become unbridgeable. The result was a court evangelicalism which was more than a source of patronage for the wider movement. It was a source of fluidity. At court, the evangelical movement's different doctrinal elements were able (or were compelled) to coexist. The political identity of evangelicalism would in the event be decisive for shaping English Protestantism: and in the last years of Henry VIII, that identity remained remarkably unformed.

'A MADDING TYME': POETS AND REFORMERS

Many of the faces of court evangelicalism are already familiar from the wider movement. The world of moderate reformism as preached and printed within

[37] *ET*, 23 (cf. *OL* 36–7).

the law, and the world of scholarly evangelicalism, both had their analogues at court. Some of the court groupings, however, show us aspects of late Henrician religious reform not easily glimpsed elsewhere. The remainder of this chapter will examine two of those groupings in more detail: the passionate yet elusive reformism of a circle of young nobles and poets, and the alternative meanings of reform pursued by a group of high-flying clergy and bishops.

The presiding genius of the poets' circle was Sir Thomas Wyatt the elder. Wyatt's convoluted and dangerous career is well known, and the debates about how his poems can be woven into that career are well worn.[38] His life story does not suggest particularly strong religious convictions. He was born to the courtly life, and in 1536 it was also nearly his death, when he was imprisoned following the fall of his patron (and perhaps lover), Anne Boleyn. He was married to Elizabeth Broke, the sister of George Broke, Lord Cobham, but the marriage quickly became a sham. To the fury of the Broke family, in the late 1530s Wyatt was openly living with Elizabeth Darrell. He freely conceded, 'I graunte I do not professe chastite' – although he denied rumours that he had seduced nuns while on a diplomatic mission to Spain. He also admitted that he had a reputation for using the strong language which evangelicals so deplored: 'I am wonte some tyme to rappe owte an othe in an erneste tawlke.' And he had a talent for making enemies. The duke of Suffolk had an 'immortall hate' for him. Edmund Bonner, the future bishop of London, united with Simon Heynes, the evangelical dean of Exeter, to lay capital charges of treason against Wyatt, which led to his being imprisoned in the Tower for a second time in 1541. Although he was released it was on the condition – bitter to Wyatt – that he should be reconciled to his wife. A year and a half later, in October 1542, he died of a fever.[39]

However, there is no doubting Wyatt's commitment to the reformist cause. In Spain in 1538, his outspoken defence of Henry VIII's actions landed him in trouble with the Inquisition, and Charles V apparently had to intervene personally to resolve the matter. He admitted that he was 'suspecte of a Lutherane', adding that he could not easily clear himself of that charge. Evangelicals saw him as a champion of their cause. Like his estranged brother-in-law Lord Cobham, he probably acted as a patron for Thomas Becon in the early 1540s.[40] For once, however, we can glimpse something of

---

[38] The best summary of Wyatt's life remains Kenneth Muir, *Life and Letters of Sir Thomas Wyatt* (Liverpool, 1963); see also Susan Brigden, '"The shadow that you know": Sir Thomas Wyatt and Sir Francis Bryan at court and in embassy', *HJ* 39 (1996), 1–31. For his poetry, see *The Poems of Sir Thomas Wiat*, ed. A. K. Foxwell, 2 vols. (London, 1913).

[39] Alastair Fox, *Politics and Literature in the Reigns of Henry VII and Henry VIII* (Oxford, 1989), 259–60, 273; *LP* XVI 662; BL Harleian MS 78 fos. 11^r, 12^r, 13^v–14^r (*LP* XVI 641).

[40] BL Harleian MS 78 fo. 10^r (*LP* XVI 641); *ET*, 23 (cf. *OL*, 36–7); Becon, *New pollecye of warre*, sig. A2^r.

the texture of this court reformer's religion, from his surviving poetry. His clearest doctrinal statements come in his extended paraphrase of the seven penitential psalms, based loosely on the Italian version of Pietro Aretino. The understanding of penitence which Wyatt expounds in this poem depends on an evangelical view of justification. We read that God 'doth impute / No more his fawte' to the penitent: 'Clensid now the Lord doth hym reput, / As adder freshe, new stryppid from his skin.' He emphasises the insufficiency of human action: God matches 'mesureles marcys to mesureles fawte'. Works are explicitly denied any place in this scheme other than that of response:

> He takes all owtward dede in vayne,
> To bere the name off ryghtfull penitence,
> Wich is alone the hert retornd agayne;
> And sore contryt that doth his fawte bymone,
> And owtward dede the sygne or fruyt alone.

And one passage gives as elegant an exposition as one could wish of the evangelical understanding of how divine justice and mercy are reconciled in Christ.

> ... Pardon thow than,
> Wherby thou shalt kepe still thy word stable,
> Thy Justice pure and clene; by cawse that whan
> I pardon ame, then forth with justly able,
> Just, I ame jugd, by justice off thy grace.[41]

Wyatt might, perhaps, be one of the 'carnal gospellers' against whom evangelical polemicists inveighed, but that he was a gospeller of some kind is beyond dispute.

By the time of his death, Wyatt was at the centre of a circle of admirers at court: young men, many of them poets or would-be poets, and many of them at least dabbling in fashionable evangelicalism. The most significant of these was Henry Howard, the earl of Surrey. Surrey was a poet of comparable ability to Wyatt: he was also arrogant, mercurial and hot-tempered, and almost entirely lacking in political horse sense. It was a dangerous combination. Amid the hair-trigger political tensions of late 1546, his loose tongue and an implicit, heraldic claim to royal status brought about his execution on the (not quite baseless) charge that he was conspiring to seize the throne once the old king was dead.[42] He was only thirty-one. It was a shocking end, and Henry VIII's final spasm of bloodletting. But Surrey had a reputation as

---

[41] Wyatt, *Poems*, 218, 231, 236, 243 (Psalm 32, lines 16–19; Psalm 51, lines 25–9; 5th Prologue, line 18; 6th Prologue, lines 20–4).

[42] The events leading up to this, and Surrey's religious politics in general, are best summarised in Brigden, 'Henry Howard'. See also W. A. Sessions, *Henry Howard, the Poet Earl of Surrey: A Life* (Oxford, 1999).

a proud and quarrelsome man, and this was not the first time he had been in trouble. In 1539, John Barlow, the dean of Westbury-on-Trym and a man never short of an opinion, called Surrey 'the most folish prowde boye that ys in Englande'. When Surrey briefly won the military command he had longed for during the winter of 1545–6, at Boulogne, he was a flamboyant disaster. One commentator, the evangelical Welsh soldier Ellis Gruffyd, was unforgiving. Surrey's pride prevented him from calling for reinforcements, Gruffyd claimed, 'for he wanted the glory for himself alone'. He failed to win the respect of his soldiers, addressing them 'with vain contemptuous words'.[43] The failure at Boulogne was especially galling to Surrey, since his considerable family pride was grounded in his grandfather's victory at Flodden. With an *amour-propre* that seems pitiful with hindsight, he wrote of himself as 'a lyon of the race, / That with his pawes a crowned kinge devoured. . . . For my vaunte, I dare well say my blood is not untrew.' If this is what he committed to paper, it is no surprise that talk amongst servants was a good deal looser. In 1543, a maid in the Arundel household, where Surrey was a frequent guest, was arrested and interrogated for describing Surrey as a prince. She had added that 'if oughte other then good shuld become of the king, he is like to be king'. She claimed to have heard this from her mistress, which was hardly reassuring.[44] Simple arrogance was one thing: to permit this kind of talk, however, smacked of treason.

The personal tragedy of Surrey's failure as a military commander was foreshadowed by the farcical events of January 1543. On the night of 21 January, he and a gang of other young men – including Wyatt's son Thomas, later to lead the rebellion of 1554 – spent five hours out on the streets of London, armed with stone-bows (catapults). Some of them were dressed in soldiers' russet coats. 'The next daye after their was a greate clamour of the breaking of many glasse wyndowes bothe of houses & churches, and showting at men.' On the face of it this was little more than hooliganism, and at the time the only explanation which Surrey could offer for his behaviour was that 'we shal haue a madding tyme in our youghe'. The matter was taken sufficiently seriously for the Privy Council to intervene, and in April, Surrey was given a taste of the Fleet prison. In addition to this rampage, he and a number of his fellows were reprimanded for blatant disregard of the Lenten fast. Surrey himself had secured a dispensation from the fast, but 'he had not vsed it so secretly as he ought'. His gang had been ignoring the fast regulations all winter. An evangelical butcher had provisioned them, but this in itself is no indication of their religious views. When young

---

[43] Constantine, 'Memorial', 62; Gruffyd, 'Boulogne and Calais', 40–1.
[44] Henry Howard, *The Poems of Henry Howard Earl of Surrey*, ed. Frederick Morgan Padelford (Seattle, 1920), 74 ('Eache beeste can chuse his feere', lines 29–30, 34); PRO SP 1/175 fo. 85^r, 1/176 fo.151^r (*LP* XVIII (i) 73.1, 315).

noblemen choose to eat heartily they are not necessarily making a doctrinal statement.[45]

There was more to Henry Howard than this, however. In prison, he justified his night's troublemaking in a withering satire on London. He portrayed himself as 'a scourge for synn' against a corrupt city, and while this deserves some scepticism it should not be dismissed altogether. The targets of the rampage had certainly included some of London's leading political and financial figures. London evangelicals might not have approved of Surrey's methods, but they would not have shed many tears for his victims. Surrey claimed he was aiming to bring retribution to the city's sins in secret, and so set out 'with a reckles brest, / To wake thy sluggardes with my bowe.' The rap of pebbles on windows might awaken Londoners to the impending judgement, as thunder warned of lightning. His target was not the windows, but the 'prowd people that drede no fall' who sheltered behind them. He was a little vague about the faults he was reproaching, running through the whole list of the seven deadly sins, but his apocalyptic conclusion had a sharper edge. Addressing the city, he declaimed:

> Thy martyres blood, by swoord & fyre,
> In Heaven & earth for iustice call.
> The Lord shall here their iust desyre;
> The flame of wrath shall on the fall.
> With famyne and pest lamentablie
> Stricken shalbe thy lecheres all;
> Thy prowd towers and turretes hye,
> Enmyes to God, beat stone from stone;
> Thyne idolles burnt, that wrought iniquitie.

This moves beyond a simple commonwealth agenda. London's martyrs who died by fire can only refer to reformers such as Barnes, Garrett and Jerome; and the promise that London's iniquitous idols shall be destroyed is unmistakably evangelical.[46] This is not the language one expects from the duke of Norfolk's son, but in his religion, Surrey apparently came to follow his poetical mentor rather than his father.

How and when Surrey came to be friendly with Wyatt is unclear. The Boleyn connection provided a family link, and we might presume that a young poet with the noblest blood in the land and a more accomplished author whose position was less assured would find one another to be congenial

---

[45] The episode is discussed in Brigden, *London*, 340–4. PRO SP 1/175 fo. 87[r], 1/176 fo. 156[r] (*LP* XVIII (i) 73.3, 327); M. J. Crossley Evans, 'A portrait of a Tudor usurer: the life of Alderman Sir John Gresham (c. 1496–1556) and the foundation of his grammar school', *Norfolk Archaeology* 41 (1993), 412–13; *APC*, 104; Bodleian Library, Jesus MS 74 fo. 258[r].
[46] Howard, *Poems*, 70–2 ('London, hast thow accused me', lines 19–20, 22, 45, 56–64).

friends. It may be that Surrey helped to secure Wyatt's release from prison in 1541. All that is certain is that Surrey's first poetical venture into print was an epitaph for Wyatt, one of several he wrote, and that these praised more than his virtue and eloquence. Surrey specifically celebrated Wyatt's most religious work, the penitential psalms:

> Where he doth painte the lively fayth and pure,
> The stedfast hope, the sweet returne to grace,
> Of iust David, by perfect penitence.

Given Wyatt's firmly evangelical exposition of 'perfect penitence', Surrey's words imply that he had been persuaded to take a similar view.[47] Further hints emerge in the paraphrases of the psalms which he himself wrote, most likely during his final imprisonment. The themes of the psalms he chose were doctrinally uncontroversial: the bitterness of betrayal and the ruin of the godless. Yet he referred repeatedly to God's 'elect', a word heavily loaded with evangelical implications, and claimed that 'in thy worde [I] haue set my trust and ioye'. There is also more than a hint of penitence that he had not lived according to this faith as he should. He spoke of having had a 'secreat zeale to God', which he had confided only in a close friend. However, his resentment at his enemies had so consumed him that 'the faith did faynt that shold haue ben my guyde'.[48]

By the time of his death, Surrey's faith seems to have been much like Wyatt's. Neither man was a hero of the faith; neither lived up to any very impressive moral standards, or centred his life around his religion. Yet they did have religious convictions on which they could draw, and in both cases these leaned towards evangelical ideas. In this, they seem to have been representative of their whole circle. While none of the others were poets of comparable ability, some of them made their views rather plainer. Two of Surrey's psalm paraphrases were dedicated in intimate terms to two undoubted court evangelicals, Sir Anthony Denny and George Blage. Blage, who nearly burned for his sacramentarian views in 1546, was an important member of this group (and himself a rather stilted poet). He was a nephew of George Broke, Lord Cobham, and thus also a nephew of Wyatt's estranged wife. However, he was close to Wyatt, who during his imprisonment in 1541 named Blage as one who would vouch for him. According to John Leland, Wyatt 'took delight in Blage's subtle mind'. Blage had business links with the Denny family, and was also friendly with his fellow evangelical courtier William

---

[47] Henry Howard et al., *An excellent epitaffe of syr Thomas wyat, with two other dytties* (RSTC 26054: 1545?); Howard, *Poems*, 77 ('The great Macedon, that out of Persy chased', lines 7–9).
[48] Howard, *Poems*, 92–6 (Psalm 55, line 25; Psalm 73, lines 3, 24, 63; Psalm 88, line 22). All of the statements referred to are additions by Surrey to the original text.

Palmer. In 1542 he helped Palmer when his kinsman John Porter was imprisoned as a heretic. After Wyatt's death, Blage also remained friendly with Surrey, although he was not involved in the window-smashing of January 1543 and indeed rebuked the earl for it. Their friendship broke under the political strains of 1546: Blage feared that Surrey was indeed laying plans for a Howard regency in the event of the king's death, and claimed that he would rather kill his friend himself than see this happen. But the breach was apparently not irreparable, as Surrey dedicated a psalm paraphrase to Blage from his condemned cell.[49]

Others in the Wyatt–Surrey circle can also be associated with evangelicalism. Thomas Hussey, one of Surrey's gambling partners, was imprisoned in 1543 for breaking Lent with him; he was also a cousin to Anne Askew. Thomas Pickering, who had broken windows as well as Lent in Surrey's company, had supported the innovators over Greek pronunciation when at Cambridge and was later to support another of Surrey's rioters, Thomas Wyatt the younger, in his rebellion against Queen Mary.[50] The courtier and soldier William Blount will have known Surrey since his youth, when Surrey was an intimate friend of Blount's nephew, Henry Fitzroy, the duke of Richmond. But Blount also surfaces in 1542 assisting George Blage and William Palmer in defending John Porter. Another friend of Surrey's, Edward Warner, was a sewer in the king's privy chamber, and had a brother in the queen's chamber. He was later to marry into Lord Cobham's family. In May 1546 he was arrested together with Surrey's younger brother, Lord Thomas Howard. The two of them were charged with 'undiscrete medling in Scripture thinges' and with disparaging the conservative sermons preached at court that Lent. A still more outspoken reformer was Surrey's sister, Mary Fitzroy, the dowager duchess of Richmond. She continued the family habit of Lent-breaking after 1543, and may already have been acting as a surreptitious patron to radical reformers such as John Bale.[51]

A slightly different light is cast on this network by the case of Henry, Lord Neville, the son and heir of the earl of Westmorland. Neville was hardly a paragon of the noble virtues. His principal pastimes seem to have been gambling and whoring, and he was arrested in 1546 for conspiring to murder his wife and his father by sorcery. Yet his regular gambling partners included Sir Nicholas Poyntz, who had been a close friend of Wyatt's and who may

---

[49] Brigden, 'Henry Howard', 521; TCC MS R3.33 fo. 133v; PRO SP 1/176 fo. 156r (*LP* XVIII (i) 327); BL Harleian MS 78 fo. 12v (*LP* XVI 641); *LP* XV 942.98; Muir, *Life and Letters of Wyatt*, 264; Head, *Ebbs and Flows of Fortune*, 220–2.

[50] *APC*, 104, 106, 114, 125; PRO SP 1/176 fo. 156r (*LP* XVIII (i) 327); Bodleian Library, Jesus MS 74 fo. 258r; Brigden, 'Henry Howard', 517, 525; Fines, *Biographical Register* (Pickering).

[51] HPT (Blount, Warner); TCC MS R3.33 fo. 133v; *APC*, 114–15; 400, 408, 411; *LP* XX (ii) Appendix 2; CLRO Repertory 11 fo. 176r; King, *English Reformation Literature*, 71.

have been giving shelter to evangelical clergy since the early 1530s. Another of Neville's fellow-gamblers, Robert Thistlethwayt, had his house searched on the orders of the Privy Council during the heresy scare in the spring of 1546. And Neville himself, appealing for his life from prison, filled his letters to Sir William Paget with evangelical language. He proclaimed his conviction that 'thoro mye faythe that Y have yne hys blesyd blovd, wyche was oyns shed apon the crosse for the salvacyone of me and all manekynd, Y trovste mye sovyll shall be saved'. And like Surrey, he repented his failure to live up to that faith, as one who would 'profes hys word with my lyppes and lyve cleyne contrarye yne mye dedes' – the citing of the *word* of God again being an evangelical trademark. He also thanked Paget for sending him a friend who had often before exhorted him 'to lyve after the laues of god and to leyfe mye vycyous lyveynge'.[52] Neville was clearly not a model reformer, and he may only have been making the religious noises that he thought Paget would like to hear. Even if this is so, however, he knew how to make those noises fairly convincingly, especially given that his education was pretty basic. If he did not have evangelical inclinations himself, he had clearly had a certain amount of exposure to those who did.

Amongst the younger generation of courtiers, a smattering of evangelical ideas and language seems to have been thoroughly in fashion by the mid-1540s. Some, like George Blage and Mary Fitzroy, can be described as committed reformers. For others, such as Wyatt and Surrey themselves, evangelical ideas seem to have been a part of their mental world, but not necessarily a dominant theme. Still others, such as Neville, seem to have done little more than pick up on fragments of an intellectual fashion without letting it affect their lives too deeply. This is in some ways the most significant evidence of all. If these people do not show us a faith which would move mountains, they do demonstrate that the most important social circle in England – the nobility, the wealthier gentry and the functionaries of government – was coming to be infested with heterodoxy. If the convinced evangelicals remained a small minority, many more in these circles were adding some reformist ideas, slowly and piecemeal, to their mental furniture. For one thing, these beliefs were useful. Paying lip-service to the Gospel was the means by which one might justify abandoning irksome practices like the Lenten fast. In the Neville case, a confused and superficial understanding of justification by faith even seems to have been invoked to justify a murder. More importantly, however, scripturalism and evangelicalism were fashionable – intellectually fashionable in a world that respected scholarship, and politically fashionable

---

[52] PRO SP 1/226 fos. 120^r, 124^r, 126^{r-v} (*LP* XXI (ii) 417–19); *APC*, 385–6; K. G. Powell, 'The beginnings of Protestantism in Gloucestershire', *Bristol and Gloucestershire Archaeological Society (Transactions)* 90 (1971), 151; Muir, *Life and Letters of Wyatt*, 264. On the Neville case, see my 'A fool and his Wisdom', forthcoming.

as the king still praised Scripture and inveighed against papistry. The new ideas also gained glamour from association with men such as Wyatt and, especially, Surrey.

Fashions do not produce deep religious conversions, although they may facilitate them. They can, however, foster a gradual shift in patterns of thinking. At the least, evangelicalism would become a respectable stance taken by influential people, rather than a dangerous heresy pursued by disreputable fanatics. The intellectually or spiritually lazy, a breed well-represented at court, might fall into an easy reformism without too much thought. This mood was not unchallenged at court, and it was not, of its nature, able to be the vanguard of evangelicalism. It did, however, undermine the ability of court conservatives to rally the country against further religious change. Even England's leading lay conservative, the duke of Norfolk, was raising a nest of heretics. Under these circumstances, creating any real momentum at court in favour of the prosecution of heresy was almost impossible. If the court, gentry and nobility had remained firmly wedded to the old ways, Henry VIII's Reformation would have been strangled within hours of the old king's death. In the event, however, for many of those around the king, the path of least resistance was now to play along with the word of God.

THE ROAD BACK TO ROME

Amongst the higher clergy, the prospects for reform looked very different. There were certainly committed evangelicals amongst the bishops and other senior clergy, but they were few in number and scarcely holding their own. This was a marked change from the 1530s. Under Anne Boleyn's and, to a lesser extent, Cromwell's patronage, a substantial number of evangelicals had been given ecclesiastical preferment. Controversial men such as Edward Crome, Robert Barnes or Miles Coverdale never secured senior appointments, but Hugh Latimer, Nicholas Shaxton, Edward Foxe, John Hilsey, William Barlow and Thomas Goodricke were made bishops, in addition, of course, to Thomas Cranmer at Canterbury. Simon Heynes was made dean of Exeter. These appointments were real victories for the reformist cause. Bishops could have a marked impact on the religious life of their dioceses, and to a greater or lesser extent these men did. They also had a voice in national politics. During the 1540s, however, evangelicals were unable to hold onto these gains, much less consolidate them. Their ranks were thinned: Foxe died in 1538 and Hilsey in 1539, and in 1539 both Latimer and Shaxton chose to oppose the Act of Six Articles in such a way that they were compelled to resign. No comparably reliable friends of reform were appointed in their places.

Richard Rex has pointed out how few reformers were appointed to the episcopal bench after about 1536, and suggested that this reflects a renewed conservatism in royal policy.⁵³ In fact, however, most of the post-1536 appointments were ciphers, without discernible religious preferences of any kind. Of the twenty-one men made diocesan bishops between Anne Boleyn's fall and Henry VIII's death, only three can be called evangelicals – Henry Holbeach at Rochester, John Bird at Bangor and Chester, and Robert Holgate at Llandaff and York. The obscure Henry Man, bishop of Sodor and Man, may conceivably also belong in this group. But, of these men, only Holbeach was partisan about his reformism. However, during the same period there were also only three consistent religious conservatives appointed: Richard Sampson at Chichester and at Coventry and Lichfield, William Reppes at Norwich and John Bell at Worcester. Robert Aldrich at Carlisle might also be included in this group. The remaining bishops fell into two distinct groups, and the larger of these consisted of careerists and time-servers, many of whom were former monks or friars. John Wakeman, Robert King, John Chamber, Paul Bush, Robert Warton and Anthony Kitchen had all been heads of religious houses, and were made bishops of Gloucester, Oxford, Peterborough, Bristol, St Asaph and Llandaff respectively. Most of them moved their seats only a few miles, if at all. Such preferments both ensured a degree of continuity and, more importantly, spared the crown the burden of the substantial pensions which ex-abbots received. Bell was a similarly easy choice for Worcester, as the archdeacon of Gloucester. William Knight had been archdeacon of Richmond and of Chester; when the two archdeaconries were formed into the new diocese of Chester in 1541, some preferment was needed for Knight, and he was made bishop of Bath and Wells. Arthur Bulkeley was a similarly easy choice for bishop of Bangor in 1541, as a member of a prominent local family whose liberal collection of benefices had already made him a force in the region's ecclesiastical politics. Rex is right to discern a shift in episcopal appointments around 1536, but it is not from evangelicalism to conservatism. In the early years of his reign, Henry VIII had appointed a series of remarkably talented bishops, making England's episcopate a model of good practice.⁵⁴ In the last decade of his life, he mostly appointed lacklustre administrators. Of all these names, only Sampson had a significant impact on national religious politics.

The picture changes if we include the last five bishops appointed during this period, figures who might be thought to be conservatives: Edmund Bonner at Hereford (briefly) and London, John Skip at Hereford, Nicholas Heath at Rochester and Worcester, Thomas Thirlby at Westminster and George

---

⁵³ Rex, *Henry VIII*, 144–5.
⁵⁴ Andrew A. Chibi, 'The social and regional origins of the Henrician episcopacy', *Sixteenth Century Journal* 29 (1998), 955–73.

Day at Chichester. These men had backgrounds in top-flight scholarship and at court. They also shared a considerable religious ambiguity. In the 1530s all of them had been reputed to be reformers (Day less so than the others), and evangelicals welcomed their appointments. But by the end of Henry's reign, all of them had moved to decidedly conservative views – Skip, apparently, less so than the others. Bonner, Heath and Day were deprived of their bishoprics under Edward VI. All except Skip (who died in 1552) served as bishops under Queen Mary, and Bonner acquired a reputation as a particularly vindictive persecutor. The path which these men trod was an unusual one, and it is worth examining. If we still think of the Reformation as a process by which Catholics were made into Protestants, and if we observe the progress of fashionable evangelicalism through most of the court, it may be salutary to consider those who bucked the trend – especially when they were such prominent men as these.

There can be no doubt that in the 1530s these future bishops were firmly allied with evangelical reform. Nicholas Heath, archbishop of York under Queen Mary, had earlier been a chaplain to Archbishop Cranmer. As an ambassador to the German Lutherans in the 1530s, he impressed his hosts. Philip Melanchthon singled him out for his sound understanding of religion, declared that he 'excels in humanity and learning', and corresponded with him for some time. He also impressed Martin Bucer. In 1539, the London evangelical Alice Wethers left a bequest for sermons to be preached by named reformers; Heath was listed along with Robert Barnes and Edward Crome. In 1540 he was a member of the committee of theologians considering the doctrine of the sacraments (as were all of these five men), and when that committee split on the place of auricular confession in the Christian life, Heath came down on the side of the reformers. He also denied that there were seven sacraments; and he was willing to consider laymen being empowered to excommunicate and possibly, under exceptional circumstances, to ordain.[55] Thomas Thirlby was another close friend of Cranmer's, although Thirlby seems to have been an unusually affable character, with an enviable talent for remaining on friendly terms with almost everyone. This made him a valuable diplomat, but he was also a theologian. On the sacramental committee of 1540, he argued – like Heath – that auricular confession was merely 'the surest waye' to forgiveness, a convenience rather than a necessity. Like Heath,

---

[55] John Strype, *Ecclesiastical Memorials, Relating Chiefly to Religion and the Reformation of it*, 3 vols. (Oxford, 1822), vol. I, part i, 351; *LP* XIV (i) 667; *OL*, 530; PRO PCC Prob. 11/27 fos. 232^v–3^v; BL Cotton MS Cleopatra E.v fos. 43^v, 46^v (*LP* XV 826); Gilbert Burnet, *The History of the Reformation of the Church of England*, ed. Nicholas Pocock, vol. IV (1865), 452, 458, 491.

he cast doubt on the traditional number of seven sacraments. He was more sanguine than Heath about the possibility that laymen might ordain.[56]

George Day was somewhat more conservative. On the 1540 committee, he lined up with the traditionalists on auricular confession, although he emphasised that he thought the question finely balanced. Again, however, he denied the traditional number of seven sacraments, permitted lay excommunication and admitted that under some circumstances princes might ordain. Day might seem the odd man out from this group – he had written against Luther in his youth and was a protégé of John Fisher's. However, as provost of King's College, Cambridge, he was deeply and congenially involved in the world of Cambridge reformism. John Cheke and John Taylor were his friends, and Cranmer regarded him as an ally.[57] John Skip was another Cambridge man, the master of Gonville Hall, who became chaplain to Anne Boleyn and who brought Matthew Parker to the attention of the court. During the political turmoil which led up to Boleyn's arrest, Skip preached a passionate and foolhardy sermon in defence of his mistress. In the process, he attacked the planned dissolution of the monasteries as a programme of asset-stripping. He was not defending monasticism, but rather anticipating many later reformers by arguing that monastic wealth should pass to the universities, not the crown. In the 1540 committee, he toed the evangelical line on confession, the number of the sacraments and lay excommunication. According to John Foxe's admittedly questionable witness, as late as 1543 Skip was doing what he could to protect John Marbeck from the heresy charges laid against him, apparently on the grounds that he approved of Marbeck's project to compile an English concordance.[58]

Edmund Bonner, Foxe's 'Bloody Bonner', might be thought the unlikeliest reformer in this group. Bonner was a lawyer who had risen in Wolsey's service and been taken up by Cromwell. He wrote the preface for Stephen Gardiner's defence of the royal supremacy, *De vera obedientia*, but for several years he was on very bad terms with Gardiner. Indeed, Bonner seems to have been as short-tempered and quarrelsome as Thirlby was genial. His diplomatic career in the late 1530s was a series of disasters, which ended when he insulted Francis I to his face, and the outraged king flung him out. By then, he had made an enemy of Sir Thomas Wyatt, who was his colleague on an embassy to Spain in 1538. Wyatt has left us a memorably vicious

---

[56] T. F. Shirley, *Thomas Thirlby: Tudor Bishop* (1964); BL Cotton MS Cleopatra E.v fos. 43^v, 44^v, 46^r (*LP* XV 826).

[57] BL Cotton MS Cleopatra E.v fos. 43^v–4^v, 47^r (*LP* XV 826); Burnet, *History*, vol. IV, 486, 488; Rex, 'Early impact', 42; Mullinger, *University of Cambridge*, 37–9; Nichols (ed.), *Narratives*, 248–9.

[58] Mullinger, *University of Cambridge*, 48; Parker, *Correspondence*, 1–2; Ives, 'Anne Boleyn and the early Reformation', 397–8; *LP* X 615; BL Cotton MS Cleopatra E.v fos. 43^v, 44^v, 46^r (*LP* XV 826); *AM*, 1216–18.

description of 'the lyttell fatt prest' whose drinking and naive womanising on that trip provided unintended entertainment for their hosts. But Wyatt also depicted Bonner during that time as breezily evangelical, refusing to go to Mass in Spain, even though Wyatt urged him to do so for appearance's sake. Bonner admitted that he had acquired a reputation as a 'lutherane', and was also extremely warm about his fellow-ambassador Simon Heynes, an undoubted evangelical, whom he repeatedly praised to Cromwell. In Paris in the same year, Bonner was charged with overseeing the printing of the Great Bible, and he did so with some enthusiasm, spending long hours with the printers. He seems to have had a lifelong interest in the technology of printing and its applications. And according to Foxe, when he was translated to London in October 1539, London evangelicals were full of hopes for their new bishop. Richard Grafton, who knew him from Paris days, claimed that Bonner promised that he would further the cause of the English Bible as vigorously as his predecessor John Stokesley had opposed it, and that six copies would be made available for consultation in St Paul's Cathedral.[59]

The London reformers' relationship with their new bishop quickly turned sour, and Foxe was clear as to why.

So long as Cromwell remained in autoritie, so long was Boner at his beck and friend to his friends. . . . But so soone as Cromwell fel, immediatly Boner and [Gardiner, bishop of] Winchester pretended to be the greatest men that liued, and no good word could Boner speak of Cromwell . . . calling him the rankest heretike that euer liued.

Richard Grafton provided Foxe with a tale of having met Bonner the day after Cromwell's arrest. The two had previously been on excellent terms, but on this occasion, when Grafton lamented Cromwell's fate, Bonner replied: 'Are ye sory for that? . . . It had bene good that he had bene dispatched long ago. With that Grafton looked vpon hym and knew not what to say, but came no more to Boner.'[60] On this view Bonner was simply a fair-weather friend of reform. In the 1550s, Bale scornfully described Bonner and those like him as 'turnyng like wethercockes, ersy vercy, as the wynde bloweth'.[61] Yet this simple morality tale will not quite do. It is certainly true that Bonner did not shy away from enforcing the heresy laws. In 1541 he prosecuted Alexander Seton and William Tolwin, and he had Richard Mekins burned. These events put him beyond the pale for evangelicals, but it is perhaps not

---

[59] Redworth, *In Defence of the Church Catholic*, 83; BL Harleian MS 78 fos. 13ᵛ–14ʳ (*LP* XVI 641); Inner Temple Library, Petyt MS 47 fos. 1ʳ⁻ᵛ, 3ᵛ (*LP* XIII (ii) 59, 60); *LP* XV 121, 154, 168; *AM*, 1191; Arthur Joseph Slavin, 'The Tudor Revolution and the devil's art: Bishop Bonner's printed forms', in *Tudor Rule and Revolution*, ed. Delloyd J. Guth and John W. McKenna (Cambridge, 1982). See also Alexander, 'Life and career of Edmund Bonner'.
[60] *AM*, 1992.
[61] Stephen Gardiner, *De vera obedencia an Oration . . . Nowe translated into english*, ed. John Bale (RSTC 11585: London?, 1553), sig. A3ᵛ.

surprising that a man with so thorough a legal training would wish to enforce the law. Yet in the 1540s he was not the bloodthirsty persecutor of Protestant legend (if indeed he ever was). As we have seen, he went to some lengths to secure recantations, even ambiguous ones, from such high-profile evangelicals as Robert Wisdom and Anne Askew, and he was credited (together with Heath) with helping to secure Nicholas Shaxton's recantation in 1546.[62] The murkiest case of persecution in his diocese – the suspicious death of John Porter in prison – was not his doing. Bonner was abroad on diplomatic work; the case was the initiative of Henry Cole, the diocesan chancellor and a redoubtable conservative.[63] In 1546, the conservative William Peryn praised Bonner as 'a mooste charitable exhorter, reformer, & recouerer (wher is any hope of reformacyon) of suche, as are infected wyth these euyl errors and horryble heresyes', and this fits with what we know of him.[64]

Even so, by the end of Henry VIII's reign Bonner was plainly taking a traditionalist line with growing enthusiasm. He worked to secure recantations from Askew and Shaxton, but he was clearly appalled by their sacramentarian heresies. In May 1546, at the head of a Six Articles commission in Essex, he recommended leniency for two of the five suspects arrested, on the grounds that they were young and simple and had been led astray. However, he was firm in his pursuit of the death penalty for the other three, who had all explicitly denied Christ's presence in the Eucharist. He even asked the king if the executions might be held at different places across Essex, so that the public example might 'move your people of the same to be ware of the lycke offence'.[65] In the next reign, Bonner's opposition to the accelerating process of reform was manifest, leading to his deprivation in 1549. By this stage, other formerly evangelical bishops had joined him. In 1544, Heath and Day both opposed the relaxation of the penal code of the Act of Six Articles. During the crisis sparked by Edward Crome's preaching in 1546, Heath was trusted by the Privy Council as a key witness, interrogator and messenger. There were clearly no doubts about where his loyalties lay, although his lingering reputation as a reformer may have made him particularly valuable. Skip, too, was willing in 1543 to play an aggressive part in the prosecution of Robert Wisdom, who was hardly a dangerous radical. Thirlby was no persecutor, but his old friendship with Stephen Gardiner had strengthened sufficiently by 1546–7 that Henry VIII struck him from his will, claiming that 'he was scholed . . . by the bishoppe of Winchester'. Most strikingly of

---

[62] Bonner Register fo. 108^v; Gina Alexander, 'Bonner and the Marian persecutions', in *The English Reformation Revised*, ed. Christopher Haigh (Cambridge, 1987); and see above, pp. 83–4.
[63] See Appendix I.   [64] Peryn, *Thre godlye and notable sermons*, sig. *4^r.
[65] PRO SP 1/218 fos. 139^r–40^r (*LP* XXI (i) 836).

all, Thirlby, Heath and Day were the three senior members of the committee of six which drew up the section of the *King's Book* on justification – a document which firmly rejected the reformers' doctrines.[66]

Again, the reformers' accusation was that these men were simply careerists who had followed the prevailing political winds. For George Constantine, the bishops' willingness to accept the Six Articles merely demonstrated their 'cowardnes'.[67] Cranmer's secretary Ralph Morice later recalled that Thirlby, Heath and Day had been promoted by Cromwell, and that Cranmer 'toke [them] to be his frendes', but that after Cromwell's arrest they had 'revolted' to Gardiner's party.[68] George Joye and William Turner apparently thought that it was promotion to episcopal office, rather than Cromwell's fall, which had corrupted them. Both men made general attacks on those who had been wise enough when they were scholars in the universities, but who on promotion to bishoprics had shown themselves to be 'blynde & folisshe', 'slepyng dogges that dar not bark'.[69] Again, however, matters may not be so simple. It is perhaps a little unlikely that five such prominent figures should all have changed principles for cynical reasons at the same time. It is even more unlikely that, having done so, they should have stuck to those new-found principles after Henry VIII's death, at considerable cost to themselves. It may be that these men, rather than being trimmers, were in fact following a distinctive path away from the evangelicalism of Cromwell's Reformation.

We can only speculate as to why they did so, but one theme consistently emerges: the impact of holding episcopal office itself. Joye and Turner's implication was that power corrupts, but power also interacts with the conscience in other, more subtle and less blameworthy ways. Tudor bishops were obliged to concern themselves with order and obedience, and a bishop's-eye view of England's religious turmoil was necessarily very different from that of an ordinary preacher or theologian. The views and actions of lowly clerics were of no great consequence, and such men might sympathise with and even press for religious change. Bishops, however, had to control it. All bishops felt these responsibilities. Latimer, it seems, found them deeply distasteful. He refused to be yoked into the episcopate again under Edward VI, and his resignation in 1539 may have been rather more voluntary than we usually think.[70] Even Cranmer found himself having publicly to balance the needs to spur some on to further reform, and to bridle those who would run ahead

---

[66] MacCulloch, *Cranmer*, 328; *APC*, 414; PRO SP 1/218 fo. 90r (*LP* XXI (i) 811); BL Harleian MS 425 fo. 7ᵛ; *AM* (1563), *AM* (1563), 815; Gardiner, *Letters*, 365.
[67] Constantine, 'Memorial', 59.
[68] Nichols (ed.), *Narratives*, 248–9. Morice also included Nicholas Shaxton in this group.
[69] Joye, *Defence of the mariage of preistes*, sig. B1ʳ; Turner, *Huntyng and fyndyng out of the Romishe fox*, sig. E8ᵛ.
[70] *AM*, 1739.

too far and too fast.[71] Late in life, Heath commented to Queen Elizabeth that the bitter lesson his life had taught him was that 'great mischief accrues' to change in general and religious change in particular.[72] They are the words of a man who was unable to control change but nevertheless felt himself responsible for doing so.

These tensions were exacerbated by the reformers' understandable reluctance to make allowances for them. It is most likely true that, as Grafton reported, Bonner was unwilling to sympathise publicly with Cromwell the day after the minister's arrest, but this tells us little about Bonner's views. It would have been foolhardy for one of Cromwell's clients to defend him when it was still very possible that a full-scale purge might ensue; and it would have been disloyal (not to say seditious) to question the actions of his anointed sovereign. Yet what looks like simple political realism from Bonner's viewpoint seems malicious from Grafton's. A similar conflict lies at the centre of the most contentious issue of Bonner's early episcopate, the question of the Bibles in St Paul's. As Bonner had promised, he placed English Bibles in the cathedral for public consultation, but he quickly became alarmed by the manner in which they were being used. This, at least, is the impression given by two undated advertisements which are recorded in Bonner's episcopal register as having been displayed in the cathedral, and which were also apparently printed.[73] The first of these condemned 'the abuse, defaute and evill behavyour of a few' of those who used the Bibles. Through their rashness, these reformers 'rather hynder then set forwarde the thynge that ys good of yt self'. His specific concerns were that large numbers were congregating around the Bibles; that some readers were expounding the text rather than simply reading it; and that some were reading 'with noyse' during divine service. The English Bibles were becoming a focus of religious dissent, and the bishop could not allow this to continue. His calls for good order, however, seem to have gone unheeded, for there follows a second advertisement which almost pleads for better behaviour. In this, Bonner repeated that his aim was simply that 'the worde of god . . . might bothe bee duylye honoured and hadd in better estymacion then it hathe been and also the better goe forwarde'. Yet the disruption of services and even sermons by Bible-readers had continued. Eventually, he warned, he might be forced to remove the Bibles, but his strong preference was 'to amende the faulte and abuse of the thinge, suffering the good thinge well vsed to remayne and to contynewe'.

These requests seem moderate enough. Royal policy, after all, was that the grant of the English Bible to the people was conditional on their using

---

[71] MacCulloch, *Cranmer*, 259.
[72] Lacey Baldwin Smith, *Tudor Prelates and Politics, 1536–1558* (Princeton, 1953), 67.
[73] Bonner Register fos. 26^v–7^r; and see above, p. 101, n. 30.

it rightly, and few things could have been better calculated to convince the king that the condition had been breached than to see public dissension over Bibles in the most prominent church in the land. Yet for the majority of reformers who did not concern themselves with such political problems, the English Bible was non-negotiable, and Bonner's threats to remove it provoked outrage. John Bale's interpretation was that Bonner placed more value on matins, evensong and other 'Romyshe rablementes' than on Scripture. Indeed, Bale alleged that Bonner had set up the Bibles only as a trap, 'to knowe whych were the busy byble menne of London', so that he might murder them as he did John Porter. This dizzyingly malicious reading is perhaps what we might expect from Bale, but more moderate and politically astute reformers such as Sir Thomas Wyatt also attacked Bonner's willingness to contemplate removing the Bibles.[74] Even Becon believed that Bonner's men had been tearing pages out of the Bibles, although we know that evangelical readers were perfectly capable of doing this themselves.[75] In this case, a disagreement over public order quickly widened into a confessional gulf, with the bishop somewhat aggrieved to find himself on the conservative side. It is difficult to see how any bishop of London could have tolerated the activities of reformist *provocateurs* in St Paul's; it is difficult to see how any evangelicals could have tolerated the bishop's response.

These bishops were not, of course, the only people who had embraced reform in the 1530s but who grew cool to it in the 1540s. John Pylbarough, who in 1539 had written an unctuously reformist tract for Cromwell, was in 1546 working alongside Bonner on the Essex Six Articles commission.[76] Nicholas Shaxton recanted sacramentarian beliefs in 1546 and subsequently stood by his recantation. Indeed, even Gardiner's journey bears comparison to that of these bishops, despite the obvious differences. Before he had attained a bishopric he had been on good terms with many evangelicals, and in the 1540s he grounded his opposition to the evangelicals on the need to uphold authority in an uncertain world.[77] Yet Bonner, Heath and the others remain the most important examples, partly because they are well-documented, but also because their dilemmas illustrate the strains which the reformist coalition of the 1530s experienced after Cromwell's death. They were humanists and reformers, naturally in sympathy with Cromwell's projects and committed to the Royal Supremacy. They were clearly hostile

---

[74] Bale, *A dysclosynge or openynge of the Manne of synne*, fos. 9^r, $93^{r\text{-}v}$; BL Harleian MS 78 fo. 13^v (*LP* XVI 641).

[75] Becon, *New yeares gyfte*, sig. $F1^r$; cf. Anthony Gilby's sanguine admission that he had torn a leaf which interested him from a chained book in Lincoln Cathedral. Gilby, *Answer to the deuillish detection*, fo. 12^r.

[76] PRO SP 1/218 fo. 139^v (*LP* XXI (i) 836).

[77] Diarmaid MacCulloch, 'Two dons in politics: Thomas Cranmer and Stephen Gardiner, 1503–1533', *HJ* 37 (1994), 1–22; and see above, pp. 183–8.

to sacramentarian ideas, but as we have seen, in this they were joined by most prominent evangelicals. This position became increasingly untenable after 1540. In a newly hostile political environment, some reformers found themselves having to weigh their allegiance to the king against their understanding of the Gospel. Many succeeded in finding some kind of precarious balance; some came down decisively on the side of reform. It should be no surprise that others came down on the side of the king, including some of those closest to the centre of power. It was not a glorious path that they chose, but it was an important one. It demonstrates that there was more than one option available to reformers in the 1540s. Steady progress towards more radical views was neither inevitable nor universal. Moreover, it reminds us that Cromwell's intentions were neither to lay the foundations for Protestantism nor to preside over the first of England's Reformations. In their legal conservatism, their distrust of radical doctrines and public disorder and their stout adherence to royal authority, these bishops were the true heirs of Cromwell's Reformation. The impossibility of remaining faithful to the whole of that unravelling heritage was one of the main sources of political tension in Henry VIII's last years. Some were driven back into the safe harbours of traditionalism. Others were forced out into the uncharted and dangerous waters of further reform.

7

The evangelical underground

While we haue therfore time, let vs do good vnto all men, & specially vnto them whych are of the housbollde of fayth.   Galatians 6:10

THE UNACCEPTABLE FACE OF REFORMISM

Early evangelicals have never been easy people to find. Attempts to guess at their numbers are clearly futile, although tempting.[1] All our knowledge about the early modern world is fragmentary, but Henrician evangelicals took active steps to conceal themselves and their opinions. They bought their survival at the very reasonable price of historical anonymity. A few evangelicals became visible by virtue of their place in English society: the reformers at court, amongst the higher clergy or in the universities. Others chose to make themselves visible: preachers, authors and printers. While of enormous significance to the movement, naturally none of these groups were representative of the rank and file. A third group had visibility thrust upon them. The sporadic enforcement of heresy laws has left us with a few glimpses of late Henrician heresy as it existed behind closed doors, in parishes across the country. This private face of reformism is qualitatively different from the aspects of the movement which we have seen so far. However, it is also intimately related to the more visible evangelical movement. The connections between the private and the public worlds can help us understand the nature of both.

Single heretics crop up unevenly across the country during this period, but more useful than such individual cases are those in which groups were detected. Six such cases from this period deserve attention. In 1540, Bishop Bell of Worcester discovered a group of reformers who had been holding secret meetings in northern Gloucestershire for two years;[2] in 1541, a conventicle in Salisbury was uncovered by Bishop Salcot;[3] in 1542, several reformers

---

[1] Ryrie, 'Counting sheep', 85–7.   [2] WCRO MS BA 2764/802, pp. 107–10, 115, 171–2.
[3] PRO STAC 2/34/28 fos. 5ʳ–8ᵛ.

Table 7.1 *Accusations of heresy against Kentish clergy, 1543*

	No. of offenders
Sacramentarianism	1
'Dispised' the Mass on his death-bed	1
Iconoclasm	9
Opposing the Mass without denying the Real Presence	4
Preaching justification by faith	2
Opposing auricular confession	2
Opposing traditional ceremonial, prayer for the dead, etc.	5
Total	24

from Coventry were accused by their enemies in the town of violating the Six Articles;[4] and in 1545, an artisan conventicle was discovered in London.[5] The last two groups are more extensive. In 1543, the conservative plotters against Archbishop Cranmer accused him of maintaining heretics in his diocese, and in his investigations into the plot Cranmer recorded these charges of heresy, sometimes in considerable detail. His deposition book is one of only two of these sources to describe heresy in a rural area. It is also the only one to include significant numbers of clergy. Seventy-three individuals were accused of reformist heresy, of whom twenty-four were clergy and eight were women.[6] The charges against them are made individually and are circumstantial, but their numbers are sufficient that division into categories makes a certain amount of sense. A numerical breakdown of these figures is shown in tables 7.1 and 7.2. The final and largest group consists of some two hundred London reformers whom John Foxe recorded as having been arrested and whose troubles can be dated to July 1540. This list is the broadest single snapshot of heresy which we have from these years, but it has to be approached with some caution. Foxe's source, a document amongst the London diocesan records, is now lost; and since Foxe himself will have worked from a transcript prepared by one of his research assistants, the document we now have is at best a third-hand report. During this process some comments were clearly added to the document; it may be that other, less obvious additions were made or (which is more likely) that other material was omitted. The list is known to be incomplete. The level of detail is also limited.[7] The last fifteen names on the list have clearly been appended to it

---

[4] PRO KB 9/129 (*LP* XVII 537); cf. Elton, *Policy and Police*, 133.
[5] CLRO Repertory 11 fos. 158^r–60^r, 179^r.   [6] CCCC MS 128 (*LP* XVIII (ii) 546).
[7] *AM*, 1202–6; cf. John Foxe, *The ecclesiasticall history contaynyng the Actes and monuments. Newly recognised and inlarged* (RSTC 11223: 1570), 1376–80, where the suspects are allocated to their parishes somewhat more clearly. See above, pp. 17 and 40–41. One of the problems of using documents such as these is that the evidence is often merely of accusation. Although we usually have no alternative but to accept these charges at face value, it is worth

Table 7.2 *Accusations of heresy against Kentish laity, 1543*

	No. of offenders
Sacramentarianism	5
Iconoclasm	10
Other public protest, such as disrupting services	4
Holding 'unorthodox' reformist views*	3
Opposing the Mass without denying the Real Presence	1
Impersonating a priest	1
Opposing traditional ceremonial, prayer for the dead, etc.	16
Membership of a conventicle or other support for reformers	5
Unspecified heresies	4
Total	49

* 'Unorthodox' views include Anabaptist, Christological or other heresies which went beyond magisterial Protestantism.

Table 7.3 *Accusations of heresy against London laity, July 1540*

	No. of offenders
Overt or apparent sacramentarianism	16
Opposing the Mass without apparently denying the Real Presence	24
Holding 'unorthodox' reformist views	7
Disrupting services or other public protest	10
Membership of a conventicle or other support for reformers	39
Opposing traditional ceremonial, prayer for the dead, etc.*	32
Refusal to attend church or participate in services	63
Reading the English Bible	2
Marrying a nun	1
Total	194

* 27 reformers are actually listed as having committed such offences, but Foxe also comments, having listed nine members of the conventicle at St Botolph without Aldgate, that 'many of their wiues' despised holy bread and processions; that is here taken to mean five people. *AM*, 1205.

from other sources, but the body of the list records 196 offenders, of whom 189 are laypeople. A breakdown of these figures will be found in table 7.3.

Of these groups, it is the Canterbury diocesan clergy who present us with the most familiar face. Their offences are reminiscent of the moderate

remembering that not all those charged with heresy were guilty, and that some accusations were certainly malicious.

evangelicalism which preachers and domestic authors had been spreading during the period 1541–3.[8] Only one of these clergy is accused of explicit denial of the Real Presence: Anthony Pearsone, who had been burnt as a sacramentary by the time this document was drawn up. Others expressed their views with such caution that they could scarcely be called heretical. The Canterbury Cathedral preacher John Scory was clearly uneasy about aspects of the Mass, but he couched his worries in the same language of opposition to abuses which Bonner employed to deal with the controversies over the English Bible:

> Those thynges that be good of theymselfes may not vtterly be put away, although they be abused. For than the holy sacrament of the aultare sholde be set aside, which is dayly bought and solde.

He went on to assert justification by faith in strong terms.[9] Nevertheless, the mood amongst these clergy is subtly different from that of the moderate evangelical press. Neither their words nor their actions carry the same sense of willingness to compromise. A third of these clergy were noted as image-breakers, and while some simply enforced the official iconoclasm programmes of 1538 and 1541 over-zealously, others went much further. Edmund Cranmer, archdeacon of Canterbury and the archbishop's brother, removed a rood and other goods from St Andrews, Canterbury, '& dyd violently breake the armes & legges of the roode'.[10] In some cases, iconoclasm was merely the most serious of a string of offences. Thomas Dawby, the parson of Wychling, removed no less than eight images which had not been abused from his church. He also preached against clerical celibacy, and, allegedly, 'he said our Ladie was no better than an other woman and said she was but a sacke to put christe in'.[11] John Bland, the vicar of Adisham, was accused of a range of heresies, some mundane (deploring prayer to saints and auricular confession) and some less so (denying the sacrifice of the Mass and claiming that 'in the masse book is plaine detestable heresies'). He is even alleged to have said that 'he cannot fynd Trinitas thorought scripture, but that Athanasius put it in his symbolum' – although it is easy to see how an innocent comment to this effect might be misrepresented as heretical.[12] Yet neither of these men is recorded as attacking the Real Presence, although we may be sure that their opponents would have seized on any such attack. The charges against Dawby, indeed, include no mention of the Mass at all.

These clergy, then, were different from the evangelicals of London's pulpits and printshops, but not wholly different. Their doctrines were similar but their mood was fiercer. Much of this may be due to the circumstances in which

---

[8] See chapter 4. [9] CCCC MS 128 pp. 34, 42 (*LP* XVIII (ii) 546 pp. 302, 304).
[10] *Ibid.*, p. 30 (*LP* XVIII (ii) 546 p. 300). [11] *Ibid.*, p. 82 (*LP* XVIII (ii) 546 p. 315).
[12] *Ibid.*, pp. 67–71 (*LP* XVIII (ii) 546 pp. 311–12).

we meet them. Instead of their own works, we are relying on selections made by their enemies, who would certainly pull the most sensational phrases out of context and distort them as much as they could.[13] We are also often hearing words spoken several years previously, before Cromwell's fall had made reformers more circumspect. Bland's remark about the Trinity was made in 1539. Nevertheless, the strain of evangelicalism prevalent in the parishes of Kent seems a good deal more robust and combative than that to be found in the book market at St Paul's.

When we examine the laity, both in Kent and in London, these differences become unmistakable. Many in Kent trod the same path as their clergy, opposing ceremonies or assisting in the orderly removal of images. Amongst the laity, however, violent and desacralising iconoclasm was more widespread. John Toftes not only removed an image of the Virgin from St Mary Northgate in Canterbury, but took it home '& ther did hew her all in peces'. George Wyborne 'did hedde and quarter S. Stephen and also burned him', symbolically executing an idol as heretic and traitor.[14] Others publicly disrupted worship by ostentatious refusal to join in processions or by open denunciations of traditional devotions. Those Kentish lay people who mentioned the Mass took an unmistakably harder line. Five of the six were accused of explicitly rejecting the Real Presence. The evidence from London is less clear, owing to the brevity of the summaries of offences, but sixteen of those arrested were accused explicitly or implicitly of sacramentarian beliefs. A further twenty-four impugned the sacrament in some way, but it is impossible to know whether, for example, the 'common syngars against the sacraments and ceremonies' were actually sacramentaries.[15]

Some of these lay offenders ventured beyond the bounds of any mainstream Christian orthodoxy. A Kentish couple, John and Joyce Benson, argued that the Virgin had no choice whether or not to bear Christ. John Toftes' daughter Margaret added that 'it cannot be redde in scripture that our Ladie shoulde be in heaven'. Nicholas Newell, a Frenchman living in London, was also 'a great iester . . . at our Lady'. The London parish of St Michael Queenhithe was apparently a hotbed of heterodoxy. Three men there were accused, to Foxe's embarrassment, of denying all sacraments outright, and two others seem to have veered towards the spiritualism characteristic of some Anabaptists: they were allegedly 'great reasoners in Scripture, sayeng that they had it of the spirite'. The Kentishman Thomas Hasylden made the equally unorthodox claim that if 'he could lyve without synne he wer as good

---

[13] Cranmer's investigators discovered that the conservative JP Sir Thomas Moyle had systematically added phrases to the indictments so as to bring borderline cases under the remit of the Act of Six Articles. CCCC MS 128 pp. 105–8, 135 ff. (*LP* XVIII (ii) 546 pp. 320–1, 323–4).

[14] *Ibid.*, pp. 31, 55 (*LP* XVIII (ii) 546 p. 300, 308).   [15] *AM*, 1204.

as god'. In addition to their doctrinal adventures, some of these reformers were marked out from more moderate types by the crudity of their language. Margaret Toftes claimed that 'her dowghter dyd pysse as good holy water as the priest could make', but she was outdone by Raynold Buckemer:

He said that the sacrament of the alter was bread as other brede was. And that the knave preistes did receyve hym before none, and did pisse and shitt hym at hooreys arses in the after none.

Thomas Hasylden matched a similar crudity with a willingness to place himself in open opposition to the king and to the Henrician settlement. He 'spake contemptuously againste the kinges Iniunctions saying a farte for theym'. Likewise, two lawyers of St Andrew's, Holborn, were arrested for shouting down their curate's attempts to read the royal Injunctions and the *Bishops' Book* in church. We cannot know how representative such feelings were, but it seems likely enough that a good many London and Kentish reformers were stepping beyond the bounds of respectability.[16]

The London and Kent lists are the fullest portraits of evangelicalism in the parishes which we have for these years, but the more limited records of other conventicles tell a similar story. The Salisbury group was led by two evangelical clerics, and, in keeping with what we have seen in Kent, they were apparently fairly cautious in their reformism. Our only record of their doctrines comes from an account of a sermon by one of those clergy, John Forsett, which fully reflects the moderate reformers' agenda. Forsett preached justification, praised Luther and played down the importance of confession without actually denying it. However, he also labelled the preacher who had spoken before him a traitor and heretic.[17] The accusations against the Coventry reformers must be even more doubtful than usual, since the accused managed to have the charges dismissed as malicious. If there was any truth in them, however, this was a more outspoken group. Twelve laypeople were accused of heresies ranging from the denial of purgatory and the cult of saints to more dangerous ideas such as the advocacy of clerical marriage. Heresy was leavened with anticlericalism. Alice Banwell allegedly stated that 'I had asleve be shriven at a poost as at a preist, for all preistes be knaves'. John Pynnynge went beyond this to deny the necessity even of church buildings:

I wolde, that the parishe Churche of seynt Michell in Couentre were dissolued . . . and that ther were neuer a parishe Churche in Englond. For I could take my rightes vpon a hill in the feild aswell as in a Churche, for the parishe Churches do no good but meyntaign a meny of knave preistes to spend mennes goodes.

---

[16] CCCC MS 128 pp. 52–3, 62 (*LP* XVIII (ii) 546 p. 307, 310); *AM*, 1203–4.
[17] PRO STAC 2/34/28 fo. 7ʳ.

Seven of the twelve were accused of holding sacramentarian opinions or of supporting those who did. Pynnynge expressed his views in pungent terms: 'Maisters what make you of the Sacrament of the Alter, or how take yowe it. I do take it but as a floure, And I hadd as leivre turne my Arse to it as my face.'[18]

The beliefs and manners of the Gloucestershire group seem to have been very similar. Nine reformers in this group are named. Most met monthly in a mill at Upleadon in 1538–40. Several of them spoke against the sacraments; one was accused of denying all seven. Their leader, Matthew Price, denounced the Mass in uncompromising terms: 'The saide sacrament of thalter was . . . bredde & wyne, and not made by god, but by mannes hande, for Christe toke his owne bodye with hym vp in to heven, and left it not behynde hym.' Once again, there is the accusation that this group went beyond any respectable evangelicalism, and claimed 'that our sauyour Christ Ihesus receaued not flesshe & blode of the virgyne marie, And that he was neuer fleshe & blode presente vpon the erthe.' Since this last accusation is only recorded in the episcopal injunctions against the offenders and not in the depositions, this may be suspect. There are, however, two separate accounts of another equally shocking incident. When in Upleadon church with one William Baker, Price

> toke in his hande tholy water dassell sayinge to the saide william baker, remembre thy baptym, and thean & there the saide baker in contempte of the saide holywater turned his ars towardes the saide mathew, And the same mathew thean & there vilipendiously spryncled & cast holy water vpon the saide william Bakers ars.[19]

In neither of these groups is there any mention of issues such as justification by faith. We are a long way from the respectable world of fashionable reformism.

These fragments of evidence, then, suggest a divergence between views of the visible leadership of the evangelical movement in the early 1540s and those of at least a portion of the mass movement. Where the clergy had a leading role, this seems to have been reduced but not eliminated. It is hardly surprising that there should be a degree of divergence. Those reformers who were in the public eye – as, to an extent, all clergy were – needed to watch their step. Those who believed that their views would remain hidden could be more frank. However, there is more to the contrast between the caution of the clergy and the more forthright views of the rank and file than simple prudence. A further examination of these clandestine groups of reformers suggests two plausible reasons for this difference, and also helps us to rule out a third possibility.

[18] PRO KB 9/129 fos. 5ʳ–8ʳ, 10ʳ, 11ʳ (*LP* XVII 537); PRO STAC 2/3 fo. 61ʳ.
[19] WCRO MS BA 2764/802 pp. 107–10, 171–2.

To take the blind alley first, there is no evidence that the radicalism of these groups is connected to the comparable views being expressed by evangelical exiles. The only group to have owned exile publications was the London set unearthed in 1545. We might expect books to attract particular attention from heresy-hunters, as they are more visible than beliefs, and since charges relating to books had a legal simplicity rare in heresy cases. Yet the records from Kent make no mention of heretical books, and the only one of Foxe's London offenders to be noted as involved with illegal literature was Thomas Lancaster, a cleric.[20] This is particularly striking, as the four leading evangelical printers – John Gough, John Mayler, Richard Grafton and Edward Whitchurch – were all arrested in the 1540 purge. All, however, were arrested for offences unrelated to their work (although Gough was also noted to have been involved with Lancaster). There is no information as to what books, if any, the Coventry or Gloucestershire groups might have owned. The Salisbury conventicle not only owned heretical books but belonged to a network which traded them across the country. The books themselves, however, appear to be thoroughly moderate, and this would fit with our picture of the Salisbury group as the mildest of these conventicles.[21] None of this should be a great surprise. The moderate evangelical publications of the early 1540s were far more readily available than were those of the exiles, even after 1543. Some copies of exile publications do surface in London in the mid-1540s. At the same time, however, we find that a gentleman in deepest Derbyshire had managed to acquire an evangelical library which does not seem to have included any recent exile publications, but did include a complete set of Thomas Becon's books.[22] These and other moderate texts were the books conventicles would be most likely to buy, especially those outside London. Moreover, in those areas where reformism had taken strongest hold, books were no longer critical to its spread. Print's unique power was to reach into virgin territory, to travel where preachers could not. Under most circumstances the word preached remained more powerful than the word printed.[23] This is, of course, an argument from silence, and clearly some exile works were circulating, especially in London. Nevertheless, while these reformers may seem close to the exiles in mood and even in doctrine, there is very little evidence of direct influence.

More positively, a striking peculiarity of the Kent evidence is the prevalence of charges of iconoclasm and the rejection of images. In our other sources, there is much less concentration on the subject of images. The exiles, of course, disapproved of them. Authors and preachers in England were

[20] Cf. CLRO Journal 14 fo. 210^r (cited in Brigden, *London*, 320).
[21] See above, p. 228.   [22] Becon, *Iewell of ioye*, sig. C1^v.
[23] See Alexandra Walsham's article in *The Uses of Script and Print 1300–1700*, ed. Julia Crick and Alexandra Walsham (Cambridge, forthcoming).

more cautious, but were quick to praise the king's activities on this front. However, actual acts of iconoclasm were rarely recorded in the 1540s. The two most prominent examples both involved soldiers; and while their actions seem to have been deliberate and ritualised enough to be counted real iconoclasm rather than simple hooliganism, soldiers are perhaps always more likely than most to use violence to express their convictions.[24] That Kent should be an exception is hardly mysterious. Iconoclasm was possible in Kent because it was an activity usually either performed or authorised by the clergy. Would-be iconoclasts in Kent had the active support of the local ecclesiastical hierarchy, especially Cranmer's aggressive commissary, Christopher Nevinson. Behind this local phenomenon, however, lies a point of wider importance. Henry VIII's regime was more unequivocally evangelical in its attitude towards images than in almost any other area, and most even of the Kentish iconoclasts were doing no more than pushing at the limits of royal policy. That policy went beyond the Lutheran tendency to tolerate most images and to treat idolatry as a low-order problem. At times the king seemed to veer towards the Reformed suspicion of images as inherently dangerous. His zeal for reform in this area, as expressed after the northern progress of 1541, seems to have been genuine. Richard Rex has argued that Henry's peculiar policy of destroying images, but only those that had been venerated, can be understood in terms of his developing self-image as an Old Testament king.[25] Be that as it may, the policy introduced an uncharacteristically radical element into the Henrician settlement.

This is most visible in the matter of the numbering of the Ten Commandments. Renumbering the Commandments in order to treat the prohibition of graven images as a Commandment in its own right was symbolic of the Reformed tradition's profound suspicion towards any religious use of material objects. This renumbering, first explicitly used in Zurich in 1534, was introduced into England in the following year and was adopted for the *Bishops' Book* in 1537. By 1539 even the conservative Cuthbert Tunstall had accepted this numbering, and in the 1540s it was all but universal. Those such as Becon who held quasi-Lutheran views nevertheless retained this numbering. The *King's Book* also retained it, although it adopted the bizarre expedient of rewriting the second commandment to fit official policy more closely.[26] Only two English-language printed texts surviving from the 1540s retain the traditional numbering; both are works with a Continental Lutheran

---

[24] PRO SP 1/177 fo. 64ʳ (*LP* XVIII (i) 420); Gardiner, *Letters*, 153–4.
[25] Rex, *Henry VIII*, 98–9, 173–4.
[26] Margaret Aston, *England's Iconoclasts*, vol. I (Oxford, 1988), 371–92; Cuthbert Tunstall, *A sermon of Cuthbert byshop of Duresme, made vpon Palme sondaye laste past* (RSTC 24322a: 1539), sig. E5ʳ⁻ᵛ; Becon, *Inuectyue agenst swearing*, fo. 14ᵛ; *King's Book*, fos. 45ʳ–69ᵛ; MacCulloch, *Cranmer*, 192.

provenance.[27] The radical attitude towards images which the renumbered Commandments represented introduced a destabilising element into English evangelicalism. To view images as idols, as blasphemous offences before God rather than as a distraction and an irrelevance, was to stand at the top of a slippery theological slope. The distinction between images which were abused and those which were not was difficult to define and enforce on the ground, and evangelicals were quick to exploit this. Nevinson used this ambiguity to pursue a ruthless iconoclastic campaign. More importantly, however, any evangelical who learned that showing reverence in the presence of physical objects was dangerous was quickly confronted with the most widespread form of such reverence, namely adoration of the Host during the Mass. For conservatives, of course, such adoration was qualitatively different from the *dulia* shown towards images, but for all its theological clarity this distinction was hard to maintain in practice. The exiles exploited this problem with gusto, while evangelical publicists in England avoided the subject as best they could. The regime's suspicion of images gave a rare shot of legitimacy to radical reformers, and opened up a high road to more extreme ideas, including, critically, sacramentarianism. This may be one of the reasons for the comparative radicalism of at least the Kentish reformers. It may also have had a wider impact on the moderate consensus.

Another possible explanation for the radicalism of the conventicles picks up an old historiographical chestnut: the place of Lollardy, the 'fifth business' of the English Reformation. The debate over Lollardy's impact on the Reformation, if any, has been lively and, as all sides admit, made possible largely by lack of evidence. The work of Anne Hudson and others has at least made it clear that the movement was neither extinct nor merely 'sub-Christian paganism'.[28] Equally, there can be no doubt that Lollardy was rapidly subsumed into English Protestantism, and that while a kind of continuity between Lollards and later nonconformists is certainly conceivable, it makes no sense to speak of Lollardy after about 1550. Most recently, Richard Rex has taken a more sceptical view still, dismissing any causal relationship between Lollardy and the rise of English Protestantism. Rex argues that the connections which can be established between Lollards and evangelicals are 'statistically insignificant', and that claims for geographical continuity dissolve if they are examined at all closely. More importantly, perhaps, he stresses the different moods of the two movements, with Lollards characterised by 'a reclusive quietism hidden beneath outward conformity' while evangelicals pursued 'a new heaven and a new earth'. To move from one tradition to the other, he argues, was tantamount to a major religious

---

[27] These were the *Lytle treatyse of the instruction of chyldren*, sigs. A1^v–5^v, on which see above, p. 127; and Legate, *Breife Catechisme*, sig. A8^r, on which see above, pp. 157–8.

[28] Hudson, *Premature Reformation*; Scarisbrick, *Reformation and the English People*, 46.

conversion. Finally, he points out that the evangelical leadership owed almost nothing to Lollardy. The old heresy had had very few adherents amongst the clergy and gentry, while those groups both dominated English evangelicalism and made its eventual successes possible.[29] It is a strong case, as far as it goes. Yet while Lollardy clearly neither caused the English Reformation nor provided the majority of evangelical converts, its presence may nevertheless have contributed to the early history of evangelicalism in other ways.

Part of the problem for any consideration of Lollardy's role in the Reformation is that, as R. D. Kendall puts it, 'smelling a Lollard in the wind was not always a precise art'.[30] If Henrician evangelicalism was vague, late Lollardy was vaguer, without creed or boundaries. Its doctrinal priorities, broadly speaking, were the authority of English Scripture and the rejection of any claims that objects, places or people might be sacred. As such, images, church buildings, pilgrimages, most traditional ceremonial and the cult of saints were rejected. Most importantly, of course, most Lollards rejected the Mass, abandoning Wyclif's subtle Eucharistic theology for forthright and often crude rejections of the Real Presence. The theological underpinning of these beliefs had withered by the early sixteenth century, but the passionate advocacy of vernacular Scripture and a certain blunt commonsense rationalism ensured that Lollardy remained more than a series of rejections.[31] The movement is, however, perhaps not best understood through its doctrines, but through its social shape. These were retiring, secretive heretics, scattered through both rural and urban communities in some parts of England, living in varying degrees of conformity with the lawful Church, meeting in small groups with no plans to convert the nation.

It is impossible to know how far this movement became enmeshed with evangelicalism. Nevertheless, our scraps of evidence suggest that any boundaries between the two quickly dissolved. The new printed Bibles were particularly attractive to Lollards. The tale of Robert Barnes providing two Lollards from Steeple Bumpstead in Essex with a Tyndale New Testament has passed into historiographical folklore, but the Lollards of Colchester and Braintree were also using printed New Testaments by 1527.[32] As Rex points out, that dissidents long committed to vernacular Scripture took advantage of a new and much improved English text is no surprise, and 'hardly entails any theological relationship'.[33] Yet it does indicate a social relationship between the established Lollard book-trading networks and the nascent evangelical

---

[29] Rex, *Lollards*, 115–42.
[30] R. D. Kendall, *The Drama of Dissent: The Radical Poetics of Nonconformity, 1380–1590* (Chapel Hill, NC and London, 1986), 14.
[31] Dickens, *Lollards and Protestants*, 9, 244–5; Hudson, *Premature Reformation*, 469; Thomson, *Later Lollards*, 244.
[32] Strype, *Ecclesiastical Memorials*, vol. I, part ii, 54–5; Oxley, *Reformation in Essex*, 8–9.
[33] Rex, *Lollards*, 118.

ones, and such relationships could be a conduit for more than Bibles. Indeed, Lollard groups seem to have taken to evangelical ideas enthusiastically. Even in the 1520s Lollard conventicles were showing an interest in the Continental Reformation.[34] Old Lollards can be found picking up novel doctrines such as justification by faith, and doing so in the company of such prominent evangelicals as Simon Heynes.[35] In 1532, one Buckinghamshire Lollard whose heretical career stretched back over twenty years was accused of heresy for the fourth time; this time he was found to own a number of printed books including an English New Testament and Tyndale's *Obedience of a christen man*.[36] The Lollards, however, were not merely passive recipients of evangelical ideas. They adapted them to their own purposes. The Scottish Lollards of Ayrshire, for example, owned a Scots manuscript of the Wycliffite New Testament which bears, in a later hand, a series of marginal notes. These prove to have been copied almost verbatim from Miles Coverdale's New Testament of 1538. However, this evangelical source was not adopted uncritically. The Lollard scribe omitted Coverdale's marginal notes on Matthew 5 which emphasised the legitimacy of lawful oaths – a doctrine about which, as we have seen, Lollards were thoroughly uneasy.[37] While we may be struck by the contrast between conformist Lollardy and fiery evangelicalism, it appears that the Lollards themselves saw matters differently. Their quietism can be overstated. Some Lollard texts do betray a continuing urge cautiously to spread their message, fired by anticlericalism.[38] More importantly, however, they were happy to embrace the new books and the doctrines that came with them without abandoning either their own beliefs or their habits of conformity. When Lollards became evangelicals – and sooner or later almost all of them did – they do not seem to have seen themselves as undergoing any kind of conversion, but simply to have incorporated some new ideas into their existing framework. Perhaps this made their evangelicalism less courageous than the preachers' ideal. As we have seen, however, evangelicals too could be discreet and conformist – which may itself show Lollard influence at work.[39]

If Lollards readily embraced evangelical ideas, evangelicals were equally eager to adopt the Lollard tradition for themselves. Just as Luther had

---

[34] AM, 985.
[35] Derek Plumb, 'The social and economic status of the later Lollards', in *The World of Rural Dissenters*, ed. Margaret Spufford (Cambridge, 1995), 122–3.
[36] Bowker, *Henrician Reformation*, 145–6.
[37] BL Egerton MS 2880; cf. Miles Coverdale (tr. and ed.), *The new testament of oure sauyour Jesu Christ. Faythfully translated, & lately correcte* (RSTC 2836: Antwerp, 1538). I owe this reference, the analysis of the marginalia and the detection of the inconsistency to Martin Dotterweich. On oaths, see above, pp. 76–9.
[38] For example, see Cambridge University Library, MS Ff. VI.2 fo. 84^{r-v}.
[39] See above, pp. 78–81; Rex, *Lollards*, 131–2.

claimed Wyclif as one of his predecessors, English evangelicals were keen to appropriate the legitimacy which Lollardy's history could give them. A series of Lollard texts were put into print by evangelical editors.[40] These editors readily amended their texts to fit evangelical doctrinal sensitivities. For example, when John Gough printed an edition of the prologue to the Wycliffite Bible in 1540, he replaced a reference to salvation being 'for oure goode deedis' with the assertion that it was 'onely by the precyous bloud of Iesu chryst, and not by oure synfull workes'.[41] Nevertheless, evangelicals did more with the Lollard tradition than plunder it. As Diarmaid MacCulloch has speculated, it may be more than a coincidence that in 1540, Cranmer singled out the tombs and chantries of Archbishop Arundel and Bishop Buckingham of Lincoln for destruction. Both had been bitter persecutors of Lollardy.[42] Wyclif himself was described by Tyndale as England's Jonah, whose message, had it been believed, might have averted the calamities of the fifteenth century. Bale saw Wyclif as 'a true Apostle of Christ' and considered writing a book about him. Cataloguing Wyclif's works was apparently one of Bale's earliest bibliographical projects.[43] Nor was this simply lip-service. Bale's *Image of bothe churches* drew deeply on Lollard ideas, such as the *ecclesia malignantium* ('Church of malignants') and the view that the millennium had already ended.[44] The evangelicals' fondness for cycles of homilies on the liturgical readings possibly owes something to the tradition of the Lollard sermon-cycle. George Joye and the court reformer John Lassells both made use of a Lollard reading of the book of Daniel, which identified the god worshipped by Antichrist, 'Maosym', with the Mass.[45]

However, evangelicals seem to have been most interested in and influenced by Lollard sacramentarianism. The racy polemic on the subject in the pseudonymous tract *Wyclif's Wicket* was adopted eagerly by evangelicals. In his 1540 treatise *The Lordis flayle*, the former Augustinian Thomas Solme praised Zwingli in the course of a thoroughly Swiss exposition of the Ten

---

[40] Firth, *Apocalyptic Tradition*, 12; Margaret Aston, 'Lollardy and the Reformation', *History* 49 (1964), 156–7; Ryrie, 'Problem of legitimacy', 79–80.
[41] Rex, *Lollards*, 139; D. S. Dunnan, 'A note on John Gough's *The dore of holy scripture*', *Notes and Queries* 234 (1989), 309–10.
[42] MacCulloch, *Cranmer*, 266.
[43] Aston, 'Lollardy and the Reformation', 152; Bale, *Mysterye of inyquyte*, fo. 10[r–v]; Askew, *The first examinacyon*, fo. 6[r].
[44] Richard Bauckham, *Tudor Apocalypse: Sixteenth Century Apocalypticism, Millenarianism and the English Reformation* (Oxford, 1978), 28, 57–8.
[45] Andrew Hope, 'The lady and the bailiff: Lollardy among the gentry in Yorkist and early Tudor England', in *Lollardy and the Gentry in the Later Middle Ages*, ed. Margaret Aston and Colin Richmond (Stroud and New York, 1997), 261; Joye, *Daniel*, fo. 225[v]; John Lassells, William Tracy et al. *Uvicklieffes wicket. Faythfully ouerseene and corrected. . . . With the protestation of J. Lassels late burned in Smythfelde* (RSTC 25591: 1548?), sigs. A3[r], C1[v]. Cf. Daniel 11:38.

Commandments, but also plagiarised sections of the *Wicket*. Joye echoed the *Wicket*'s language, and even one author who wished to defend the Real Presence borrowed the *Wicket*'s terminology for an attack on transubstantiation. The conservative Richard Smith saw the *Wicket*'s arguments as part of the standard reformist armoury.[46] The *Wicket* itself was finally printed in 1546, in two editions. Even the mere business of establishing a precedent could give Lollard texts real authority in a society which ascribed such authority to the past, but the use of Lollard texts went beyond this. Evangelicals became thoroughly familiar with them, both in print and in manuscript, and drew on them to form their own arguments. It is true that none of the leading evangelical clergy can be shown to have had a Lollard background, but they appropriated the Lollard tradition, and they made Lollard texts and ideas available much more widely than they would otherwise have been.

By 1540 the Lollard and evangelical traditions had become thoroughly mixed up together. Clearly the evangelicals were the dominant partner – numerically, in their social status and in the coherence and dynamism of their beliefs. Yet Lollardy's impact on the small world of early evangelicalism is not therefore to be dismissed. Former Lollards were neither the leaders nor the martyrs of the reformist movement. They were, however, amongst its foot-soldiers, and when we examine the records of conventicles and other clandestine reformers, a Lollard flavour lingers around them. Anne Askew's evangelical credentials are beyond dispute, but when she attempted to equivocate her beliefs under examination, by meeting questions with questions or by simply quoting biblical texts and refusing to elaborate on them, she was using well-established Lollard techniques. Hudson has commented that some of the exchanges which Askew records could have occurred a century before.[47] The same mixture can be seen in the conventicles we have been examining. Is Thomas Dawby to be called an evangelical because he preached justification by faith? Or is he a Lollard because he deprecated the Virgin, and did so in such strong terms that he wound up distorting his Christology?[48] Neither Askew nor Dawby is likely to have had Lollard roots; however, they are very likely to have come across former Lollards or

---

[46] Solme, *The Lordis flayle*, sigs.C2^r, 5^v; Joye, *Daniel*, fo. 104^v; BL Cotton MS Cleopatra E.v fos. 180^r, 182^r (*LP* XIV (i) 1067); Richard Smith, *Assertion and defence*, fos. 122^v, 164 [1]^v; 'John Wyclif' (a pseudonym), *Wycklyffes wycket: whyche he made in Kyng Rycards dayes the second* (RSTC 25590: London?, 1546), sigs. A6^v, 8^{r-v}.

[47] Hudson, *Premature Reformation*, 157–60, 502.

[48] See above, p. 226. Christological speculation was, of course, linked to Anabaptism as well as Lollardy, and indeed it is no surprise that England's most famous Anabaptist, Joan Bocher, seems to have started her heretical career as a Lollard. However, Lollards seem to have begun with deprecation of the Virgin and allowed that to dictate their Christology, while Anabaptists had more serious theological reservations about traditional understandings of the Incarnation.

their books. For others of these heretics, the position is clearer. There is a strong case for believing that the Coventry and Gloucestershire conventicles were predominantly Lollard in origin. They display several of the tell-tale characteristics – a rejectionist doctrinal agenda, including sacramentarianism, expressed in crude and violent terms; an apparent lack of interest in the theological issues surrounding justification by faith; and a tendency to make vigorous attacks on the Virgin which veered into Christological speculation. Moreover, both areas had well-established histories of Lollard activity.[49] In Kent and London, the case is less clear-cut; but these, too, were Lollard strongholds of old, and many of the layfolk arrested show some of the same distinctive characteristics. Lollard influence on early 1540s heresy cannot be proven, of its nature, but it is the most plausible explanation for much of what we can see.

Lollardy neither 'caused' the English Reformation nor dictated its social or geographical shape. Yet former Lollards and their books did pervade parts of the world of clandestine reformism. Where Lollard networks already existed, evangelicals seem to have attached themselves to them without difficulties. One consequence of this can be seen in the conventicles we have examined: a mood and a set of doctrinal priorities strongly reminiscent of Lollardy and quite opposed to the more moderate messages being preached and printed by the domestic leadership of the evangelical movement. Whether Lollard influence in these circles was of any lasting importance is another issue. Arguably, the doctrinal shift towards a more aggressive brand of reformism in the late 1540s owed much to changes of heart amongst leading evangelicals and little to grass-roots reformers. However, those grass-roots reformers remain important, both (of course) for their own sake, and also because during these difficult years, the links of patronage, friendship and mutual protection which tied the evangelical movement together embraced them too.

RADICAL CONVENTICLES AND RESPECTABLE PATRONS

The reformers in these groups did not, of course, come to the attention of the authorities because they held heterodox beliefs, but because they acted on them. While the penumbra of vague, partial or uncommitted sympathy with reformist ideas may have been sizeable, the reformist cadres, the most important groups, are the ones who translated belief into action. Yet if the beliefs of clandestine evangelicals are tolerably clear, it is much less obvious

---

[49] Two of the Coventry group shared surnames with individuals prosecuted for Lollardy there at the turn of the century. Shannon McSheffrey, *Gender and Heresy: Women and Men in Lollard Communities, 1420–1530* (Philadelphia, 1995), 164.

how they put them into practice. We do not know what it meant, in the early Reformation, to live an evangelical life.

Leaving aside the private prayer and devotional practices of early reformers (an important subject which awaits its historian), we can find several examples of evangelicals gathering in secret for religious purposes. Most of those groups of which we know met in private houses, and seem essentially to have been small gatherings of like-minded friends. The Kent depositions describe two such conventicles in the city of Canterbury.[50] In 1539, reports of a similar group in Calais alarmed Lord Lisle, the king's deputy. 'The Commissary here, with sundry persons of the Retinue, viij or ix, do keep daily a congregation secretly in a priest's house . . . and whosoever knocketh, no man shall come in but such as please them.'[51] The greatest concentration of such groups was, of course, in London, and it is here that we have the most information about them. During the arrests of July 1540, several conventicles were rounded up *en masse*. Groups ranging from six to eleven people were accused of meeting secretly in the parishes of St Matthew Friday Street, St Michael Wood Street, St Magnus and St Botolph without Aldgate. There are also indications that similar groupings existed in other parishes, such as St Giles Cripplegate and St Bride Fleet Street. In the autumn of 1540, a conservative pamphleteer vilified those who try to 'hyde your secte' and 'brotherly sorte', holding meetings to which only a select few were welcome. John Huntingdon wrote with contempt of such gatherings, describing how the reformers

> . . . kepe in store
> Full close and pryuelye
> Their cankered heresye.

In 1546 another conservative, William Peryn, was also alarmed by the manner in which sacramentaries 'go a bought craftely, to breath, and to blow theyr venomus contagion (where they may and dare) in to the bosome, of such that wyll secreatly receaue, and abyde theyr smoky communycacyon.'[52]

What such 'smoky communycacyon' might consist of remains unclear. There is no evidence to suggest that these clandestine groups engaged in any sacramental celebrations, although these would of course be the activities that would be most carefully concealed. Perhaps the most important activity was simply to meet and talk: to share ideas, to ask questions and to support one another. This seems to have been all that the north Gloucestershire conventicle did. Evangelicals were always keen to encourage godly and edifying

---

[50] CCCC MS 128 pp. 7, 72 (*LP* XVIII (ii) 546 pp. 291, 312).
[51] Byrne, *Lisle Letters*, vol. V, 599.
[52] *AM*, 1203–5; Thomas Smith, *An Enuoye from Thomas Smith*; Bale, *Mysterye of inyquyte*, fo. 76^r; Peryn, *Thre godlye and notable sermons*, sig. *3^r.

conversation, in the home and elsewhere. While the regime was concerned that no one should teach except those in positions of authority, reformers saw exhortation as a mutual obligation.[53] A former friar from Essex, Robert Ward, was made to recant in around 1540 for presuming to teach. His offence was the more serious because he had been explaining his views of Scripture 'in alehouses, and other vncomelie, and vnmeate places'. Robert Wisdom likewise found himself in trouble for urging his Essex parishioners 'to take the Scripture in their handes when thei meate to gither on the sondays and holydays at the ale house and to talke and commune and reson of ytt'.[54] If they did not actually meet in the alehouse, evangelical meetings might nevertheless often be occasions for meat and drink, especially during Lent and other traditional fasts. Fast-breaking was of course an activity with a wide appeal, but some of the numerous fast-breaking groups do seem to have had links to religious dissidence. We have already seen how such a group in Oxford was attracting known reformers in 1539, and how the earl of Surrey's circle was implicated in Lent-breaking in 1543. In 1540, Sir George Carew, the evangelicals' most reliable friend on the Calais Council, admitted to having eaten flesh in Lent the year before along with several others.[55] At least two of the London butchers troubled in the 1540s for supplying meat during Lent were known reformers.[56] There are even hints that evangelical households would use the lure of a well-stocked table to draw in outsiders and introduce them to further heresies.[57] Breaking Lent was an easy way in to evangelicalism.

For other groups, the central activity seems to have been the reading of heretical texts – following an old Lollard pattern.[58] Manuscripts of Robert Barnes' *Protestation* were circulating in London conventicles shortly after his death.[59] Books played an important part in the Salisbury conventicle, and the evidence against the London conventicle discovered in 1545 is dominated by records of the heretical books which they read aloud to one another. Henry Brinklow, who was intimately involved with the world of the London conventicles, seems to have aimed his books at this market, noting that he addressed both readers and hearers.[60] Equally, the discussions held by some of these groups seem sometimes to have shaded into impromptu

---

[53] The king and Cranmer had quarrelled over this point: Cranmer, *Letters*, 102–3. Cf. *A boke of prayers called ye ordynary fasshyon of a good lyuynge*, sig. A7^r.
[54] Bonner Register fo. 62^v; BL Harleian MS 425 fo. 6^r.
[55] PRO SP 1/146 fo. 252^v, 1/158 fo. 189^v (*LP* XIV (i) 684, XV 460).
[56] PRO SP 1/175 fo. 87^r (*LP* XVIII (i) 73.3); Brigden, *London*, 343–4; *AM*, 1203; CLRO Repertory 11 fo. 176^r.
[57] This is what William Holmes of Salisbury was accused of doing by his debtor Sir Anthony Willoughbye. PRO STAC 2/17/261, 2/24/189.
[58] Thomson, *Later Lollards*, 6. [59] Smith, *A lytell treatyse agaynst sedicyous persons*.
[60] CLRO Repertory 11 fo. 158^{r-v}; Brinklow, *Lamentacion of a Christian*, sig. B7^r.

sermons. This is the pattern suggested by Thomas Becon's books. Four of his books published in 1542–3 are dialogues between a host and his three guests. They take place in the host's house, where he expounds some portion of Scripture; the guests interrupt with questions or chip in with additional observations and suggestions.[61] As well as teaching doctrine through these books, Becon was providing a model of how evangelicals should conduct themselves and learn from one another. How far this model was followed is unclear, but we do know of genuine clandestine sermons being preached to some conventicles. The Whitechapel bricklayer John Harrydance was arrested in 1539 for preaching from his window into the street, but during the case it emerged that he had repeatedly 'declared . . . the worde of god' before some half-dozen of his neighbours in private.[62] In 1540, William and Margaret Ettis of the St Matthew Friday Street conventicle were accused of procuring 'one Tauerner being no Priest' to preach, presumably in secret. This was Richard Taverner, compiler of the popular set of evangelical homilies. In the same year John Willock was arrested not merely for 'doubtfull' preaching, but also for 'calling of suspecte persons to hys Sermons by a bedle, without ryngyng of any bell' – in other words, for preaching to secretly gathered congregations.[63] Such clandestine sermons had an unmistakable air of sedition to them, whatever their contents might be. Even Luther was thoroughly suspicious of assemblies of this kind. In 1531 he had forbidden Dutch Lutherans to celebrate the Eucharist in secret, and in 1544 he denounced secret preaching as the work of 'rats and sects', urging conventicles to restrict themselves to the use of printed books.[64]

Events such as these were certainly worrying to the regime, but they do not represent the limit of the conventicles' activity. As well as arranging clandestine sermons for themselves, the conventicles worked to provide reformist preaching for the community at large. This, at least, is the implication of the statements that all four of the conventicles referred to in the London arrests of 1540 were 'bringing ill preachers . . . amongst the people', 'mainteyning . . . certayne preachers, as then it was called, of the newe learning', 'maynteyning . . . Barnes & such other preachers', 'procurers of heretikes to preache'.[65] Some of London's parish churches seem to have functioned as gathered reformist congregations. We know that reformers such as William Tolwin and Edward Crome opened their pulpits to other evangelical preachers, and the

---

[61] The *Christmas bankette*; the *Potacion for lent*; the *Pleasaunt newe Nosegay*; and the *New yeares gyfte*. Together, these four books went through eight editions in 1542–3.
[62] PRO E 36/120 fo. 135ᵛ (*LP* XIV (ii) 42); Wriothesley, 82–3.
[63] *AM*, 1204.
[64] Guido Marnef, *Antwerp in the Age of Reformation*, tr. J. C. Grayson (Baltimore and London, 1996), 80–1.
[65] *AM*, 1203–5.

most plausible explanation for the high numbers of people charged with non-attendance in the 1540 purge is that they were choosing to attend other, more amenable churches. In 1542 Bishop Bonner issued injunctions against the practice of crossing parish boundaries, but as Mark Byford has noted, even in moderately sized towns the clustering of parish churches within yards of one another was inimical to a strong sense of parochial identity and 'must have predisposed people towards gadding to sermons'.[66]

In addition to such semi-legitimate activities, enough evidence survives to show that the conventicles' members pursued their reformism in several different arenas, and that they were connected by a complex web of relationships to one another and to parts of the evangelical movement that might seem to have nothing to do with them. For example, Richard Downes was a London clothworker who seems to have been a typically moderate, quasi-Lutheran evangelical. His will, made in December 1542, expressed lengthy and vigorous commitment to justification by faith, but this definitely did not extend to sacramentarian views, since his first bequest was for a wax taper to burn before the sacrament at St Michael Cornhill for tithes forgotten. Downes was a man with a wide range of evangelical contacts. One of the key documents which Bishop Salcot discovered during his investigation of the Salisbury conventicle was a letter written by one of that group's clerics to Downes and another London evangelical. It also seems Downes had links with the reformers at court, for after his death his widow Joan married Edward Underhill, a member of the royal bodyguard later famed as a 'hot-gospeller'. More importantly, Downes was apparently involved with a conventicle closer to home. In his will he bequeathed gold rings, inscribed with 'some proverbe as shalbe thought mete, as Christe died for our synnes, or christe is rysen for our Iustificacion, or suche other', to several friends and relatives. One of these was his brother-in-law and former business partner, John Merifield. Merifield is listed by Foxe as being one of nine members of the conventicle at St Matthew Friday Street arrested in 1540. Although Downes lived half a mile away, he seems to have had considerable involvement with that conventicle, for his apprentice was Alexander Ettis, the son of William and Margaret, also of Friday Street, whom we have already met.[67] Margaret Ettis may have been a well-established heretic, if she is the Mrs Etyes who was living at the sign of the Ball in Friday Street who was denounced in January 1528. Her husband was a girdler and one of the wealthiest men in the parish. In 1541–2 he was churchwarden, and he and his fellow-warden

---

[66] Seton and Tolwin, *Declaracion made at Poules Crosse*, sig. A2ʳ; PRO SP 1/244 fo. 9ʳ (*LP* Addenda 1548); Bonner Register fo. 40ʳ; Mark Byford, 'The price of Protestantism: assessing the impact of religious change on Elizabethan Essex' (DPhil. thesis, Oxford, 1989), 149–50.
[67] PRO PCC Prob. 11/29 fos. 113ᵛ–14ᵛ; STAC 2/34/28 fo. 6ʳ; Nichols (ed.), *Narratives* 133, 147–8; HPT.

were involved in a dispute with their predecessors, who had attempted to oust 'a pore Chauntery pryste' named William Smith from his post. It was a common enough name, but this is likely to be the same William Smith whose radical preaching in Calais had led to an abjuration and his banishment from the town in 1539; and who in 1540 was being supported by another London conventicle, that at St Magnus. On this occasion Ettis and his fellow-warden, Henry Coldewell, succeeded, but Ettis' combative style was not always so successful. When there was another dispute over the election of wardens at St Matthew's in 1544, the Court of Aldermen identified Ettis as the main troublemaker.[68] Coldewell, Ettis' fellow-warden, was a goldsmith; in 1541, he stood surety for a fellow-goldsmith called William Callaway when Callaway (another of those listed by Foxe as belonging to the Friday Street conventicle) had been imprisoned on an apparently malicious charge of handling stolen goods.[69]

The Friday Street conventicle's support of evangelicals such as Taverner and Smith was if anything surpassed by that at St Magnus. Foxe gives us the names of some of the preachers whom that conventicle promoted. Amongst them is Robert Wisdom. Wisdom was no radical, but he had extensive contacts within the evangelical underground. When he fell foul of the regime and was imprisoned in 1543, his sureties included the fiery polemicist Henry Brinklow and the scrivener William Carkke. With Carkke, we find ourselves in another evangelical network. His wife was hauled before the Court of Aldermen in February 1541 for comparing a recently deceased alderman to the rich fool in Luke's gospel, and saying 'that he dyed more lyke abest then a man'. A sympathetic scrivener, however, was useful to a wide range of evangelicals when they came to make their wills. His connections extend our web to include figures such as Philip Bale, curate of St Michael Queenhithe, a royal chaplain and an apparently moderate reformist; Thomas Parnell, an old London reformer who twice sheltered Robert Barnes; and the preacher Edward Crome. Carkke witnessed wills together with all of these men.[70] Nor was Carkke's contribution to the evangelical cause limited to writing wills. From 1541 the Court of First-Fruits and Tenths kept systematic records of those clergy who were unable to pay first-fruits when they entered on a benefice, and also recorded the names of the sureties who compounded with them to guarantee that the payment would eventually be forthcoming. The

---

[68] R. G. Lang (ed.), *Two Tudor Subsidy Assessment Rolls for the City of London: 1541 and 1582* (London Record Society, 1993), 99; PRO C 1/981 fo. 85^r; Byrne, *Lisle Letters*, vol. V, 588; AM, 1203–4; CLRO Repertory 11 fo. 33^v; Fines, *Biographical Register*.

[69] AM, 1204, 1230; P&O, 155; Bonner Register fo. 32^v; Hall, *The vnion . . . of Lancastre & Yorke*, fo. 257^r.

[70] AM, 1192–3, 1203; Bonner Register fo. 45^r; CLRO Repertory 10 fo. 194^r; PRO PCC Prob. 11/27 fos. 32^r, 93ff., 233^v; Brigden, *London*, 399; ET, 400 (OL, 617).

resulting documents give an unrivalled wealth of information about lay patronage of the clergy.[71] Carkke stood surety for six clerics' first-fruits after 1541 – twice as many as any other scrivener. One of those clerics was John Taylor, the master of St John's College, Cambridge. Taylor was clearly evangelical and in the 1530s had had a reputation as one of the best preachers in London, but his opposition to radical doctrines was plain: he had been responsible for bringing John Lambert to trial (and thus to the stake) for sacramentarian heresy in 1538. Those who stood surety alongside Carkke included the courtier William Gray, whose forthright reformism landed him in prison in 1541 and again in 1546.[72] Impressive as such connections might seem, they would not have been out of place in the St Magnus conventicle itself. Its eleven recorded members included two MPs: John Sturgeon, a merchant friend of Hugh Latimer's who represented the City in 1542, and John Starkey, a former mayor of Canterbury. Starkey, indeed, seems to have hosted the conventicle in his London house, for in April 1541 the Court of Aldermen noted with displeasure that

Iohn Starky ... who hath before this tyme had warnyng by the constable where he dwellyth & comaundement meny tymes to avoyde suche naughty & evyll disposed persones, as were wont to haunt & resorte to hys howse, hath not onely disobeyed that comaundement, butt also resorted & meynteyned within his howse & yet doth within his howse att this present tyme more evyll rule & lewde persones then ever he dyd before.[73]

He was committed to ward, but was not dissuaded from his heretical activities. In the 1543 Kent depositions, Starkey reappears as a leading figure in Canterbury's most heretical parish, St Mary Northgate.[74]

It is perhaps less surprising that a similar story can be told in the diocese of Canterbury itself, where the systematic promotion of reformers by Cranmer's administration has long been recognised. The evidence of the first-fruits composition books reinforces this picture, showing how Cranmer regularly used members of his household to stand surety for protégés of his such as John Joseph, Richard Astall, John Vyall, John Ponet and Rowland Taylor.[75] However, this evidence also underlines the extent to which links of patronage and friendship crossed doctrinal lines. Edmund Farley, for example, was a trusted agent of Cranmer's in the diocese, but when he compounded for his first-fruits as rector of Great Mongeham in October 1544, one of his sureties

---

[71] On these records, see Patrick Carter, 'The records of the Court of First Fruits and Tenths', *Archives* 21 (1994), 57–66.
[72] PRO E 334/2 fo. 166^v, E 334/3 fo. 68^v; Strype, *Ecclesiastical Memorials*, vol. I, part ii, 369; TCC MS R3.33 fo. 36^r; *AM*, 1121; HPT.
[73] *AM*, 1203; CLRO Repertory 10 fo. 204^v.
[74] CCCC MS 128 pp. 58, 171 (*LP* XVIII (ii) 546 pp. 309, 334).
[75] PRO E 334/2 fos. 24^v, 93^v, 151^v; E 334/3 fos. 11^r, 48^r.

was William Kinderdaye, a different sort of character altogether. As a soldier in Calais in the late 1530s, Kinderdaye had supported the sacramentarian priest Adam Damplip, and was charged with saying that 'yf a knave preste cowde make god, then he wold hyre oone suche god maker, for a yere, and gyve hym twentye poundes to make ffysshes and ffowles'. Kinderdaye also attacked the *Bishops' Book*, saying

> that the oone part of the boke cowlde not be amendyd. And the other part of the same boke, yf all the devyls of hell had byn at the makyng therof, they cowld not haue made it so evyll.

He was expelled from the garrison and the town as a result, and apparently settled in Great Mongeham, where he appears in the 1543 depositions as a witness against several of the conservative clergy who had plotted against Cranmer.[76] In this case, a radical patron was supporting a moderate cleric, but the opposite situation can also be found. John Bland, who was far more aggressive in his evangelicalism than the archbishop, was collated to a prebend in Wingham College in March 1543. His sureties were Cranmer's agent Rowland Taylor, and Cranmer's secretary.[77]

With Taylor, we once again find ourselves in a complex and high-powered network of reformers. He was an old university friend of the exiled polemicist William Turner. In 1544, Cranmer appointed him to the rectory of Hadleigh in Suffolk, where Nicholas Shaxton, the former bishop of Salisbury, served him as an informal curate. When Taylor won a prebend in Hereford Cathedral in 1542, his sureties were the printer William Bonham (an associate of John Mayler's with a history of involvement in heretical printing) and the grocer John Blage.[78] Blage was a well-connected and committed reformer. He was arrested in the London purge of July 1540, and was involved in circulating Melanchthon's letter against the Six Articles in the same year. George Blage, the court reformer who was nearly burned in 1546, may have been his brother.[79] One of John Blage's most significant contributions to the reformist cause, however, was his patronage of reformist clergy, which extended well beyond Rowland Taylor. In 1542, for example, he stood surety for George Parker's first-fruits at Clewer in Berkshire; Parker was a veteran of the underground book trade of the 1520s who was still involved with illegal books into the 1540s.[80] Blage also acted as a surety for Henry Man,

---

[76] PRO E 36/120 fo. 126ʳ (*LP* XV Appendix 3); E 334/3 fo. 31ʳ; SP 1/158 fo. 189ᵛ (*LP* XV 460); MacCulloch, *Cranmer*, 370; Byrne, *Lisle Letters*, vol. VI, 71; CCCC MS 128 pp. 29, 91 (*LP* XVIII (ii) 546 pp. 299, 317).
[77] PRO E 334/2 fo. 139ʳ.
[78] Whitney R. D. Jones, *William Turner*, 8; MacCulloch, *Suffolk and the Tudors*, 163–5; PRO E 334/2 fo. 114ᵛ; Duff, *Century of the English Book Trade*; RSTC.
[79] See above, pp. 56, 201–2, 210–11.
[80] PRO E 334/2 fo. 112ʳ; *AM*, 1205; Fines, *Biographical Register*.

dean of Chester and later bishop of Sodor and Man. Little is known of Man's religious views, but the link with Blage, and the fact that he was preferred to his bishopric by Sir Anthony Denny, suggest an evangelical inclination.[81] Man is only one of a number of figures who were tight-lipped about their religious inclinations, but whose connections suggest that they were more deeply involved at least in the social circle of religious radicalism than we might otherwise think. For example, Anthony Husee, Cranmer's registrar, acted as surety for clerics ranging from John Butler, the controversial former commissary of Calais, through John Barlow, brother of the bishop of St David's and a known reformer, to more ambiguous figures such as Anthony Bellasis, the archdeacon of Colchester, whose religious views can be inferred only from the company he kept.[82]

Even the conventiclers themselves may be found exercising patronage of this kind. John Sturgeon and William Ettis both stood surety for the first-fruits of Kentish clerics in these years.[83] Another conventicler, the plumber Christopher Dray of St Bride Fleet Street, was both radical and incautious. He was arrested in 1540 for his sacramentarian views ('the body of god was not there, but it was a representacion & siegnificacion of the thing') and in 1544 stood surety for a fellow parishioner who had publicly mocked the Mass. Yet in 1543 he also guaranteed the first-fruits of his new vicar, John Cardmaker, whose views were equally colourful but less radical. His fellow surety was Robert Huick, an evangelical physician well advanced in royal service.[84] The fragmentary nature of the evidence which has come down to us makes all this no more than suggestive. What is clear, however, is how tightly woven together these different worlds of reformism were – Kent and London, lay and clerical, moderate and radical, conventicles and courtiers.

It is unfortunate that our best evidence for these networks all comes from the same corner of England, but there are hints that a similar pattern held good elsewhere. The most tantalising evidence comes from the Welsh diocese of St David's. William Barlow, bishop from 1536 to 1548, was Cranmer's least unreliable episcopal ally after 1539. The dearth of ecclesiastical records from the diocese means that we know far less about Barlow's activities than we do about Cranmer's, despite Glanmor Williams' invaluable work on his episcopate. However, the first-fruits composition books enable us to see a little more of how reform was being promoted in west Wales. Tracing those who stood surety for, or alongside, known evangelicals opens up a complex web of patronage. George Constantine, Barlow's registrar, is one of those

---

[81] PRO E 334/2 fo. 147^r; Swensen, 'Noble hunters of the Romish fox', 177.
[82] PRO E 334/2 fos. 115^r, 145^r, 163^r; MacCulloch, *Cranmer*, 316.
[83] PRO E 334/2 fo. 103^r; E 334/3 fo. 51^v.
[84] PRO SP 1/243 fo. 75^r (*LP Addenda* 1463), cf. *AM*, 1204; Brigden, *London*, 404; PRO E 334/2 fo. 79^r; *DNB*. On Cardmaker, see above, p. 141.

who can be found acting as a surety, as we might expect.[85] Other cases are more intriguing. Thomas Young, the future archbishop of York, was given a Welsh rectory in May 1541; Thomas Talley, who had been accused of heresy as early as 1537 and who produced a series of translations of biblical texts into Welsh during the 1540s, became vicar of Llansantffraid in Brecknock in 1545. Both men had amongst their sureties one Nicholas Dixson.[86] Dixson was, like other supporters of heresy whom we have already met, a goldsmith of St Matthew Friday Street, London, who seems likely to have been connected to the conventicle there. The first-fruits composition books make it clear that he was a major patron of reformers, with a strong connection to south-western Wales. Although not particularly wealthy, between 1541 and 1546 he stood surety for thirteen clerics, an extraordinarily high number. Apparently only one of these thirteen did not hold a benefice in the diocese of St David's, and that one, William Lancaster, who became rector of Pluckley in Kent, was a thoroughgoing evangelical who rejected a swathe of traditional ceremonial.[87] It seems reasonable to suggest that Dixson's other clients also inclined towards reformism. Dixson, moreover, is only the most visible member of what seems to have been an active network of lay supporters of evangelical clergy in the diocese of St David's. Some of these were also Londoners. John Knevet was a grocer in the parish of All Hallows Lombard Street who stood surety for Welsh clerics, including Bishop Barlow's brother John, alongside such evangelical stalwarts as George Constantine and Anthony Husee.[88] Martin Pollard, a haberdasher of St Clement Eastcheap, was another regular patron of Welsh clergy, standing surety for four during the period, again including John Barlow. This was not simply a matter of Londoners imposing their clients onto Wales, however. The network also included a number of Welsh clergy and their associates. One of Pollard's co-sureties was Stephen Grene, the master of St Mary's College within St David's Cathedral and another regular patron of evangelical clergy.[89] Likewise, one of those for whom Dixson stood surety was a Thomas Huic, who had won a prebend in the collegiate church of Abergwili. On six separate occasions, when Dixson stood surety for other clergy – including Talley – his co-surety was a Thomas Huick, a gentleman from Abergwili and presumably a relative of his namesake.[90]

---

[85] PRO E 334/3 fo. 28^v.
[86] Williams, *Welsh Reformation Essays*, 121, 125, 147; BL Cotton MS Cleopatra E.v fo. 415^r; PRO E 334/2 fo. 37^r; E 334/3 fos. 65^v–6^r.
[87] CCCC MS 128 p. 50 (*LP* XVIII (ii) 546 pp. 306–7); PRO E 334/2 fos. 37^r, 87^v, 109^v, 112^r; E 334/3 fos. 22^r, 52^r, 65^v–6^r, 78^r, 80^r, 88^v, 102^v; Lang, *Two Tudor Subsidy Assessment Rolls*, 99.
[88] PRO E 334/2 fo. 115^v; E 334/3 fo. 28^v.
[89] PRO E 334/2 fos. 29^r, 33^v, 111^r, 116^r, 120^v.   [90] PRO E 334/3 fo. 53^r.

The Welsh evidence, therefore, confirms the pattern which the London and Kentish material suggests: that is, that late Henrician evangelicalism was supported by overlapping networks of patronage and friendship which produced some unlikely bedfellows. Urban radicals, sacramentarian clergy, moderate preachers, cautious officials, reformers in royal service, reformers in rural areas, reformers in the book trade – despite the real differences between them all these were linked by layers of patronage and friendship. This picture is an important corrective to the doctrine-heavy portrait of evangelicalism which can be derived from the reformers' writings. The reformers' club was small and intimate. Its internal politics were mostly conducted between people who knew one another well, who shared the same friends and feared the same enemies. Doctrinal divisions, which were in any case ill-defined, did not necessarily result in open breaches. The exiles made a virtue of necessity and rejected any association with those tainted with compromise. Few in England could afford the same purity, had they even wanted it. The consequence was an extremely fluid religious situation, in which reformers of all kinds usually rubbed along together and in which there were no sharp boundaries. This had its advantages, but if no divisions existed with which evangelicals could insulate themselves from one another's views, any doctrinal consensus which emerged – such as the moderate, quasi-Lutheran consensus which held precarious sway until 1543 – was bound to be extremely fragile. This eclectic state of affairs may have been an agreeable situation for English reformers. It was also highly unstable.

Conclusion

In the reign of Edward VI, the Church of England found itself being governed by an evangelical clique with a startlingly aggressive agenda. From the beginning of the new reign, this clique pursued a vision of Reformation which went well beyond anything that had been attempted under Thomas Cromwell in the 1530s. It did so under the influence of the Reformed theologians of Switzerland and southern Germany. The purists of the Reformed camp may have felt that Cranmer and his allies were permitting too many relics of papistry to remain, but it was clear that they had left the Lutherans behind them.[1] In six and a half years, England's religious life was torn down and rebuilt. In the process, the reformers created what was to become the English Protestant tradition. It was a tradition with a radical edge, informed by the restlessness of Reformed theology; a tradition that was to colonise the New World and fight the Civil War. That tradition, however, was itself built on the evangelicalism that was inherited from the last years of Henry VIII.

This book has examined the fortunes of evangelicals during those years, politically and in their varied social settings. Thomas Cromwell's Reformation left behind it an evangelical movement which had a considerable presence in some of the most influential circles of English society and government, and which also tended towards both political and doctrinal moderation. After Cromwell's fall, these reformers continued to hope that the king would favour their cause – and in this they were not wholly disappointed. The radical minority who were forced into exile took a dim view of the regime, but as exiles their influence was limited. The leading propagandists of evangelicalism within England picked up the traditions laid down under Cromwell. They preached justification by faith alone while not meddling with more extreme doctrines, and they retained a non-confrontational style of preaching which arose from the assumption that the regime was, in the end, on their side. However, there was more to late Henrician evangelicalism

---

[1] MacCulloch, *Cranmer*, 387–92.

than political conciliation. Even those who preached relatively mild doctrines were becoming alienated from the regime over a range of social questions, in particular the regime's disastrous failure to provide education with the support which reformers of all stripes agreed it needed. Within the universities themselves, this suspicion fed into a somewhat different atmosphere. The reformers had attained a degree of intellectual dominance, particularly in Cambridge, and while they were no less moderate in their doctrines they were a good deal less willing to appease conservatives. The resulting intellectual drift towards evangelical ideas can also be seen at work in the court, where the well-entrenched reformist minority found itself being reinforced by scholars and nobles caught by the allure of fashionable doctrines. All of these evangelicals, what is more, were connected by webs of patronage and friendship to a rather different grass-roots reformism: a movement without political or other sensitivities and with a fondness for more radical doctrines, perhaps reflecting Lollard influence. Their political disappointments, the intellectual implications (or drift) of their own stance and their radical friends all conspired to pull conformist evangelicals in a more confrontational direction.

Some resisted this pull. We have seen how several prominent evangelical clergy whose episcopal appointments put them in a dangerously public position found it impossible to continue to be allied to grass-roots evangelicals. They were not alone in this, for some others who remained clearly in the reformist camp also worked to disassociate themselves from their more radical brethren. Another bishop, Goodricke of Ely, supported the evangelical cause in Parliament and Convocation, but was no great patron of reform in his diocese. The first-fruits composition books do not reveal any sustained attempt by him or his household to promote reformers, in striking contrast to the efforts of Cranmer and Barlow.[2] Some in the universities, too, were distinctly uneasy about the emergence of a more confrontational evangelicalism. In May 1546, Edward Crome was finally browbeaten into recanting, not by a religious conservative, but by a university evangelical, Richard Cox.[3] There is little reason to believe that Cox's and Crome's doctrinal views differed markedly, but for Cox, it seems, doctrinal principle was secondary to the overwhelming need to defuse confrontation with the regime. If a division was emerging in late Henrician evangelicalism, it was not between 'moderates' and 'radicals'. It was between the majority who were willing, with widely varying degrees of reluctance, to recognise that it

---

[2] In only one case do members of Goodricke's household appear as sureties, and in this case neither they nor the cleric on whose behalf they acted have any identifiable evangelical connections. PRO E 334/2 fo. 38^v.
[3] PRO SP 1/218 fo. 44^v (*LP* XXI (i) 790.1).

might be necessary to defy Henry VIII for the sake of the Gospel; and the rump of conformist evangelicals who were not, in the end, willing to separate their allegiance to the Gospel from their allegiance to Henry VIII.

By the time of the old king's death, England's well-placed minority of evangelicals had acquired sufficient social, intellectual and political momentum to become a leading contender for the country's future religious identity, the rising star which other hopefuls had to defeat. In the same way, the more plain-spoken, confrontational and doctrinally assertive of the evangelicals had acquired sufficient momentum to seize the reins of the movement. The last great religious crisis of Henry's reign was sparked by the carefully balanced preaching of Edward Crome in 1546. The substance of Crome's preaching, as we have seen, was moderate enough: he refused to move beyond an essentially Lutheran view of the sacrament. However, the ferment which he provoked quickly ran beyond his control, to be dominated by the issue of the Real Presence. Crome recanted his denial of the sacrifice of the Mass, but Anne Askew and John Lassells burned for denying the Real Presence, and Askew's account of her examinations suggests that other issues were scarcely mentioned. Dozens of other evangelicals faced prosecution as sacramentaries that summer, while only a handful apparently followed Crome's line. In the heat of the crisis, we find some who had previously affirmed the Real Presence joining the ranks of the sacramentaries. Nicholas Shaxton left his unofficial cure in Suffolk for London, apparently with the deliberate intention publicly to denounce the regime. He preached of the Eucharist that 'his natural body is not therein, but it is a sign and a memorial of his body crucified for us'.[4] English conservatives certainly detected a shift within reformism in 1546, to which they responded with an unprecedented level of vernacular printed polemic. Four tracts in defence of the Mass appeared in print in 1546. Three of these were chiefly or solely concerned with the Real Presence, and went through five editions between them in the year.[5] However, away from the storm of public debate, a potentially more important shift was taking place. During 1546 or early 1547, while Gardiner was publicly confronting the sacramentaries, Nicholas Ridley privately persuaded Archbishop Cranmer to adopt sacramentarian views himself.[6] Cranmer's conversion is symbolic of a fundamental shift in evangelicalism's centre of gravity. In the last year of Henry VIII's life, conformist evangelicals stopped conforming, and the loyal opposition reached the limits of its loyalty.

For evangelicals' trust in their king, while considerable, was not unshakeable. Their continued confidence in the regime after 1540 was underpinned by one central part of the Henrician settlement: whatever else remained

---

[4] *LP* XXI (i) 1383.49; cf. Bonner Register fo. 108ᵛ. [5] See Appendix II.
[6] MacCulloch, *Cranmer*, 354–5; Jasper Ridley, *Nicholas Ridley* (1957), 94–6.

to be reformed, the English Bible was set forth freely. This was the token which demonstrated that Henry's Church remained committed, however half-heartedly, to the evangelical cause. Thomas Becon could scarcely mention the provision of vernacular Scripture without acclaiming the king's 'moost noble fame & immortal glory'.[7] When Becon claimed that 'all false Religion is exterped', his evidence was that 'the moost sacred Byble is freely permytted to be red of euery man in the Englysh tonge'. Becon still had Tyndale's faith in the power of unvarnished Scripture to transform the common people, and so, like Tyndale, he was willing to see almost every other issue as secondary if vernacular Scripture was made freely available. For with the Bible open, the accomplishment of a true reformation could only be a matter of time. 'Euen the very ydiot', Becon rejoiced, 'maye nowe become learned in the kyngdom of God.' Robert Wisdom joined Becon in seeing vernacular Scripture as a solvent which, if left to work unhindered, would itself be enough to bring down the whole edifice of papistry. Richard Morison called Scripture the 'one thyng . . . that we neede to our lyfe, to our iustification, to Christen freedom'.[8] Cranmer himself was moved to a rare expression of unmitigated delight by the royal grant of permission to publish an English Bible, seeing it as the greatest achievement of Henry's Reformation. Similarly, in his continuation of Hardyng's chronicle, Richard Grafton singled out the provision of 'the whole Scripture in our English tongue' as a particular reason to praise the king. Richard Tracy's 1544 *Supplication* argued that it was only through suppressing vernacular Scripture that the Roman Church had ever been able to stand.[9] The moderate reformers' commitment to the centrality of the English Bible is as visible in the structure of their books as in their expressed beliefs. Most of Becon's works, and Tracy's 1543 tract on justification, were simply strings of organised biblical quotations. And the Bible was obviously central to the sets of postils on the liturgical epistles and gospels. Grafton's set made this scripturalism explicit in its exposition of the tale of the rich man and Lazarus, emphasising the story's concluding point that the Scriptures are all-sufficient for salvation. Richard Taverner spoke for many when he stated that

---

[7] Becon, *Christmas bankette*, sig. G3ᵛ; cf. Becon, *Newes out of heauen*, sig. A5ᵛ, and Becon, *Pathway vnto praier*, sigs. B1ᵛ–2ʳ.

[8] Becon, *Potacion for lent*, sig. E6ʳ (cf. Becon, *Pathway vnto praier*, sigs. R5ʳ, 7ʳ, and Becon, *Pleasaunt newe Nosegay*, sigs. A2ʳ–3ᵛ); ECL MS 261 fo. 100ʳ; BL Royal MS 17.B.xxxv fo. 6ʳ; Harleian MS 423 fo. 14ʳ. This was no doubt an over-optimistic view, but there are occasional signs of the effect that the reformers predicted. The conservative parish clerk of Hastings was so disturbed by his discovery that some of the apostles had been married that he demanded that the Bible be burned. PRO E 36/120 fo. 8ʳ⁻ᵛ (*LP* XIV (ii) 301).

[9] BL Cotton MS Cleopatra E.v fo. 348ʳ (Cranmer, *Letters*, 345–6; *LP* XII (ii) 512); Hardyng, *Chronicle*, vol. II, fo. 160ʳ. This phrase was omitted from the second edition of the Chronicle, printed after May 1543; Tracy, *Supplycacion to Henry the eyght*, sig. A3ᵛ.

your highnes neuer did thing more acceptable to god, more profitable to the aduauncement of true christianitie . . . then when your maiestie lycenced and wylled the moost sacred Byble conteynyng the vnspotted and lyuely worde of God to be in the Englysh tong set forth.[10]

It followed that attempts to keep Scripture from the people roused fierce opposition even from otherwise pacific reformers. Those who did so, preached Cranmer's protégé Michael Drum, 'did even so goo about to pluck Christes wourds and the holy gost from the people'. This was one of the few subjects that could provoke real anger in Becon. Denial of Scripture, he argued, was the sin against the Holy Spirit. The case of John Porter, who died in suspicious circumstances in prison after reading aloud from the Bible in St Paul's Cathedral, roused Becon to denounce the malice and guile of those who believed that 'menne shulde haue no knoledge of Goddes word'. To Bonner and others in authority, reading the Bible in this way was an issue of public order, but few evangelicals agreed. Thomas Dawby even tried to organise a rota of evangelicals in his own and, apparently, other parishes to read from the Bible in a low voice throughout every service. Moreover, Bonner's perceived heavy-handedness over this issue provoked genuine outrage. The normally measured London Commonwealthman wrote, 'If any one light or frantik persone by preachyng or reding the bible disturbed at any time any one litle parish church in london, it was so exaggerat as thowgh the hole realme had bene in an hurly burleye.' Lord Lisle's ban on reading the Bible during divine service in Calais was felt by the reformers there as one of his most provocative actions. Becon denounced as 'Antechristes' and 'wicked Papistes' those who would 'to the vttermoost of theyr power plucke men from redynge the moost sacred Byble'.[11] The English Bible was the point at which willingness to compromise stopped.

This put even the most cautious of reformers on a collision course with Henry VIII's regime. The king's own view was that the English Bible was a royal gift, given principally in order to inculcate good order and obedience, and if it failed to do that it would be restricted or withdrawn.[12] But royal warnings to that effect were ignored, and in 1543 the Act for the Advancement of True Religion barred all but the social elite from access to vernacular Scripture. Although apparently scarcely enforced,[13] the Act provoked fury from every part of the spectrum of evangelical opinion. The exiles' reaction is

---

[10] *Brefe Postyl, vpon the Epystles and Gospelles*, fo. 207^v (cf. Luke 16:29–31); Richard Taverner (ed.), *The most sacred Bible, whiche is the holy scripture, conteynyng the old and new testament* (RSTC 2067: 1539), fo. ii^r.
[11] CCCC MS 128 pp. 49, 82 (*LP* XVIII (ii) 546 pp. 306, 315); Becon, *Pathway vnto praier*, sig. R7^v; Becon, *Pleasaunt newe Nosegay*, sig. A6^{r-v}; Becon, *New yeares gyfte*, sig. F1^r; BL Royal MS 17.B.xxxv fo. 8^r; PRO SP 1/151 fo. 226^r (*LP* XIV (i) 1009).
[12] Rex, 'The crisis of obedience'. [13] See above, pp. 49–50.

predictable. George Joye wrote that the bishops were 'very theues and cruell murtherers of the chirche of Chryst, takinge awaye hir beste garments, euen the holy Bybles'. William Turner was one of several authors whose outrage was sharpened by his views on the reform of the commonwealth. Bad enough to have partially withdrawn the Bible, but the Act implied that God's Word was fit for gentlemen but not for ordinary folk. There were, Turner stated bluntly, 'mo[re] gentle fooles then yemen fooles'. The author of *A supplication of the poore Commons* asked if the king would deny physical bread, as well as the bread of life, to all but the wealthy. 'Hath God put immortall soules in none other but in such as be possessioners of this world?' Most of the authors of Scripture, he observed, would have been banned by the Act from reading their own books. Bale took a different tack, suggesting that Bible-reading would soon be outlawed even amongst the gentry – a view which was not entirely without foundation.[14]

The exiles' anger, however, was equalled by that of their co-religionists at home. Robert Crowley noted gloomily that the prediction that the Gospel would be taken from the people if they did not repent had been proved right. He also argued that the poor were the only people who could truly benefit from reading Scripture, since the rich habitually read it merely as an entertainment and did not amend their lives as a consequence.[15] The London Commonwealthman felt it as a betrayal that the restriction had been enacted 'vnder colour of obedience'. He urged his readers not to be deceived by the conservative bishops again, and 'whatsoeuer colour, face or simplicite they shew vtwardly, neuerthelesse to drede their inward imaginations and practices'.[16] George Blage, awaiting execution (as he thought) in 1546, likewise lamented that 'the liueinge wourd the bred of lyffe' had been taken from the people, and had been replaced with 'byshopes bren' – the *King's Book*, which the people had been given in place of Scripture.[17] That substitution also riled Robert Wisdom, who denounced the Act at some length.

Dyd not Christe dye for pore men, as well as for gentellmen? . . . But thei will saye. Ther is a boke sett owte of mooste Christen doctrine for the people. To that I answer. The boke of moost Christen doctrine ys the holie Testament of Iesu Christe. . . . If their were ten thousande bokes sett oute, yet oughte not that to be taken aweye from the people.

Indeed, Wisdom argued that kings had no authority to remove Scripture, comparing such an attempt to Ahab's seizure of Naboth's vineyard. In tones

---

[14] Joye, *Present consolation*, sig. A5^v; Turner, *The huntyng and fyndyng out of the Romishe fox*, sigs. F3^r–4^r; Brinklow?, *Supplication of the poore Commons*, sig. A4^{r-v}; Bale, *Epistle exhortatorye*, fo. 15^{r-v}; see above, p. 47.
[15] Crowley, *The opening of the woordes of the prophet Joell*, sigs. A7^v–8^v.
[16] BL Royal MS 17.B.xxxv fos. 6^r, 8^r.   [17] Muir, *Life and Letters of Wyatt*, 273–4.

reminiscent of the exiles, he denounced the bishops as 'very antichristes, and wolfes devouringe the shepe of Christe'. He clearly felt that his eyes had been opened by the Act:

Men shall never more be deceyved by you, nor studye who ys Antichriste nor who are his membares, but when so ever thei loke vpon this horrible facte thei shall see yt more clearer then light.

He ended with a ringing declaration of the authority of Scripture. In doing so, he denounced those who argued that, 'The bishops haue decreed this ergo noman maye saye ageinst it. The olde fathers taught this, ergo it is trewe.' This much he might have said in an incautious moment before 1543, but now he added a third, far starker, rejection of those who believed that 'this is the kinges boke, ergo he is an heritike that saith ageinst it'.[18]

This evangelicalism can no longer be described as moderate or conformist. The impact of the Act for the Advancement of True Religion was reinforced by that of the *King's Book* itself, which, by explicitly rejecting justification by faith alone, made it obtuse for reformers to continue to pretend that the Six Articles' silence on this subject betokened any actual ambiguity on the regime's part. Many reformers had been willing to accept a slow pace of reform, if necessary a glacially slow pace, in the name of good order. However, the reversal of reform, which was what happened for the first time in May 1543, was another matter entirely. The fragility of the alliance between moderate reformers and the state was pitilessly exposed.

The reformers were not, of course, merely disillusioned. They were also silenced by the clampdown on heretical printing. The vacuum thus created was filled by the works of the exiles, who now at last began to find something of an audience in England. However, the exiles were filling not only a publishing vacuum, but a theological one. The dominant foreign influence on English evangelicalism during the 1530s had come from Lutheran Germany, but after 1540 many of the contacts which had nurtured this influence were cut. Perhaps the only Englishman of the period with a clear and direct allegiance to the Wittenberg theologians was Robert Barnes, who was put to death in 1540. The other main voice of Lutheranism in England, the Scot Alexander Alesius, had fled to Germany the year before. After the disaster of the Cleves marriage, Henry VIII and the Schmalkaldic League withdrew from attempts to ally with one another in mutual disgust, and the king's admiration for Philip Melanchthon was severely dented after Melanchthon wrote against the Six Articles. Many of the exiles, by contrast, made their way to the centres of Reformed Protestantism, and it was that influence which was reflected in their writings. If the political territory which the moderate evangelicals had

---

[18] BL Harleian MS 425 fo. 4^r; ECL MS 261 fos. 111^v–13^v, 127^r; I Kings 21:1–14.

occupied was disappearing from beneath their feet, the theological rationale that had held their position together was also being eaten away.

As a result, when the next crisis came in 1546, the remnants of the reformist coalition which Thomas Cromwell had assembled finally unravelled, and new battle-lines formed. During the crisis provoked by Edward Crome, Bishop Bonner conducted a full-scale heresy-hunt; Bishop Heath and Richard Cox interrogated Crome himself. Many others who had previously held to more or less moderate positions found themselves siding with the persecuted evangelicals. This was partly the perennial, polarising effect of persecution and (especially) martyrdom. When men and women are being killed, neutrality or moderation become very difficult. However, it also reflected deeper shifts within the hopes and fears of English evangelicals.

The events of 1543 had forced many previously conformist evangelicals into varying degrees of open opposition to the regime. However, opposing Henry VIII's regime from a moderate evangelical position after 1543 was harder than it looked. As we have seen, reformers quickly regained much of the ground that had been lost during that year, and during 1544–5 even won some political victories.[19] This political ambiguity made a degree of coexistence with the regime possible, but it also made opposition tricky. The reformers' grievances were clear enough. All evangelicals lamented the regime's disastrous failure to look to the state of the commonwealth, its rejection of justification by faith alone and, above all, the restrictions on the English Bible. But the matter of the commonwealth was a question of degree, and the restrictions on the Bible were not being enforced. The rejection of justification by faith was clear enough, but this was too abstract a doctrine to serve as a rallying-cry. In the 1530s, evangelical partisans had usually pursued the issue of justification through attacking those traditional practices which were seen as detracting from the sufficiency of Christ's sacrifice: pilgrimages, auricular confession, prayer for the dead, the use of images. It made excellent polemical sense to focus in this way on the points at which the clash of theologies was made tangible, which made the question altogether more concrete. By 1546, however, these targets had become distinctly evasive. While most of the doctrine of the old faith remained in place, serious inroads had been made into many of the practices to which evangelicals objected most strenuously. Pardons and indulgences had disappeared with papal jurisdiction. Auricular confession had been rendered less objectionable by the Six Articles. The *King's Book* had emasculated the practice of prayer for the dead. Even the monopoly on Latin in worship had been broken. Clerical celibacy remained unreformed but, by its nature, was a practice which could rouse little ire amongst the laity. Monasticism was gone; pilgrimages had

[19] See above, pp. 41–53.

been prohibited; official iconoclasm was steadily eroding the use of images. The official orthodoxy on the cult of the saints was visibly moving. Evangelicals demanded further reformation of all these matters, of course, but they were no longer questions of black and white, with which the rhetoric of opposition could fully engage.[20] Their ambiguous status only served to emphasise the one flagship issue which remained wholly unreformed, a conservative salient deep in territory which the evangelicals were beginning to regard as their own: the Mass.

Of course, a loathing of the Mass was common to all reformers, whether their theological leanings were Lutheran, Reformed or Lollard. However, the quasi-Lutheran position, which deplored the sacrifice of the Mass but maintained a belief in the Real Presence, was a far more subtle and carefully balanced argument than the blunt Reformed denial of Christ's presence. The vulnerability of the moderate position became clear in April 1546, when Edward Crome chose publicly to confront the regime by denouncing the sacrifice of the Mass. Crome himself was able to tread the narrow Lutheran line in his attack. However, as a doctor of theology said to be one of the best preachers in London, he was hardly representative. During the more general confrontation that followed, the point at issue quickly became the Eucharistic presence. Crome's own carefully balanced argument was less important than his tacit acknowledgement that, willy-nilly, the Mass had become the battleground. It was a battleground on which those radicals who rejected the Real Presence had a distinct advantage. Reformers found themselves forced to choose between Heath and Bonner's path of submission to the regime and Askew and Lassells' path of defiance. Crome tried to steer the middle course of doctrinal moderation and political resolution, and he failed. He broke, and recanted, and this time his fellow reformers did not forgive him.[21] Instead, they deserted the centre ground which had given way beneath him. Wisdom fled to exile. Cranmer abandoned the Real Presence. Even Cox, perhaps, felt the need to atone for his role in Crome's persecution. When the old king died six months later, his evangelical subjects had moved far closer to embracing the sacramentarian doctrines that had always horrified him. The identity of the evangelicalism that would drive the religious revolution in the new king's reign had been decided.

The last years of Henry VIII's reign were the crucible of English Protestantism – or perhaps, to borrow Thomas Wylley's term, its purgatory. Evangelicals had inherited from Thomas Cromwell the presumption that the cause of the Gospel was most likely to be furthered by the hand of the king. It was

---

[20] John Cheke stated in 1545–6 that the reform of the Church was 'for the most part...effected'. McDiarmid, 'John Cheke's preface to "De Superstitione"', 118.
[21] Henry Ellis (ed.), *Original Letters, Illustrative of English History*, 2nd series, vol. II (1827), 177.

an agreeable presumption, allowing as it did two loyalties to exist side by side. The strength of those loyalties made the task of holding them together urgent; the comparative mildness of royal policy and of many reformers' doctrines made it possible. If the king was neglecting God's Word in some areas, the religious situation remained reasonably open. Most reformers were able to find enough space both to serve their king and to salve their consciences – whether by carefully balancing their public pronouncements, taking shelter in the relative calm of court or university, or through simple discretion. That space, however, came under increasing pressure. Royal action tested evangelicals' loyalty to the king, as their Bibles were banned and ecclesiastical endowments were plundered. Those reformers who had trusted the regime now felt themselves betrayed. George Blage wrote, bitterly,

> Our gides haue erd and walkd out of the wey
> and we bi them full crafftely ar trapt.
> Whom thei swold lede they driue out of arey.[22]

At the same time, the reformers' Gospel demanded steadily more from them, buoyed up by the radicalism of the conventicles and by its own internal logic. The two pressures reinforced one another. As reformers were forced into opposition, they were driven to more radical stances, spurred on by the newly audible exiles and the relentless consequences of persecution.

This was not, perhaps, inevitable. If the reformers' fears had not come to outweigh their hopes, a more Cromwellian understanding of reformation might have endured. In the event, however, confessional historians of all stripes combined to smooth out the diversity and the compromises of late Henrician evangelicalism. It is worth recalling the contingency of some of the pressures which forced English evangelicals in the early 1540s to rebalance their twin loyalties, to the Gospel and to Henry VIII. Some contrived to evade the choice, although this was not easy. For others, political loyalties either trumped or embraced religious duties. Yet in the event, the dominant response was to embrace a more aggressive reformism. These evangelicals certainly continued to hope for, and to use, political favour, but they were no longer willing to tarry for the magistrate indefinitely. Increasingly, they did not look for the reform of the Church to be completed, but for a religious revolution to be begun. The fire of faith had done its work.

[22] Muir, *Life and Letters of Wyatt*, 273.

Appendixes

Appendix I: Reformers executed or exiled between the passage of the Act of Six Articles and the death of Henry VIII

The Act of Six Articles came into force on 12 July 1539. Henry VIII died on 27 January 1547.

BURNED FOR HERESY

1. *After 18 March 1540: Valentine Freez.* A Dutch evangelical of long standing, resident in York. He was convicted of sacramentarian heresy by the Council in the North shortly before 18 March 1540, and was burned outside York soon afterwards, together with his wife. PRO SP 1/158 fo. 72^r (*LP* XV 362); *AM*, 1027; Dickens, *Lollards and Protestants*, 30–2.
2. *After 18 March 1540: Mrs Freez.* Wife of Valentine Freez (above) and burned with him as a sacramentary.
3. *3 May 1540: John.* An Italian painter, and one of three burned at Southwark for 'heresie against the sacrament of the aulter'. Presumably also one of the three who Richard Hilles states were burned in Southwark after Easter 1540 for denying transubstantiation. Foxe dates the burning to 'about' 1539 and places it in St Giles in the Fields. Wriothesley, 118; Bale, *Epistle exhortatorye*, fos. 14^v–15^r; *ET*, 133 (*OL*, 200); *AM*, 1279.
4. *3 May 1540: Giles Germaine.* A joiner burned with John the painter. Wriothesley, 118; Bale, *Epistle exhortatorye*, fos. 14^v–15^r; *AM*, 1279.
5. *3 May 1540: Maundevild or Lancelot.* A French groom to the queen, burned with John the Italian painter. Foxe claims he was a royal servant present at the examination of John and Germaine, who 'seemed by his countenaunce & gesture to fauour both the cause & the poore men his frends'. He was arrested and condemned with them. Wriothesley, 118; Bale, *Epistle exhortatorye*, fos. 14^v–15^r; *AM*, 1279.
6. *7 July 1540: William Collins.* A lawyer and an outspoken reformist who is variously described as 'a crazed man' or 'madde and distract of his perfect wittes'. He was imprisoned in 1536, apparently for shooting an arrow at a crucifix. He also reportedly mocked the elevation at Mass by elevating a dog over his own head. In 1538 he was imprisoned again,

apparently for heretical writings, and was eventually burned in London for 'heresie against the sacrament of the aulter'. Wriothesley, 119; *ET*, 133 (*OL*, 200–1); *AM*, 1131; PRO SP 1/144 fos. 221^v–2^r, 1/242 fo. 229^r (*LP* XIV (i) 647, *LP* Addenda 1407); Brigden, 'Popular disturbance and the fall of Thomas Cromwell', 259, 272–3.

7. *30 July 1540: Robert Barnes*. Former Augustinian friar and leading reformer, attainted for heresy and burned in the wake of Thomas Cromwell's fall. Lusardi, 'The career of Robert Barnes'.

8. *30 July 1540: Thomas Garrett*. Veteran of the underground book trade of the late 1520s, attainted and burned with Barnes. Fines, *Biographical Register*; *DNB*.

9. *30 July 1540: William Jerome*. Vicar of Stepney, accused in March 1540 of seditious preaching. Attainted and burned with Barnes. PRO SP 1/158 fo. 50^r (*LP* XV 354.1); Fines, *Biographical Register*; *DNB*.

10. *? Early 1541: A Calais labourer*. Only recorded by Foxe, who tried unsuccessfully to learn his name. He had been converted to sacramentarian views by the preaching of Adam Damplip, and was executed by order of Robert Harvey, the commissary of Calais. Foxe claims that this was 'within halfe a yeare' of Harvey's own death on 30 July 1541. *AM*, 1229.

11. *30 July 1541: Richard Mekins*. A boy aged, according to various reports, between 14 and 18, who was convicted at Bishop Bonner's behest of denying transubstantiation (although not the Real Presence). A first jury refused to convict him. Bale, *Epistle exhortatorye*, fo. 8^v; Bale, *A dysclosyng or openynge of the Manne of synne*, fo. 24^{r-v}; Hall, *The vnion of . . . Lancastre & Yorke*, fo. 244^r; Wriothesley, 126; TCC MS R3.33 fo. 127^r; *ET*, 147 (*OL*, 221).

12. *1541–2: Richard Spenser*. A priest who married and earned his living 'with the sweate of hys browes and labours of hys handes'; he is also said to have become 'a player in enterludes'. He was burned in Salisbury for his opinions on the sacrament. Bale dated the execution to 1542: Foxe, initially working from a separate source, believed it was in the same year as Mekins' death. *AM* (1563), 613; *AM*, 1202; Bale, *Epistle exhortatorye*, fo. 13^v; Bale, *Catalogus*, vol. I, 666.

13. *1541–2: John Ramsey*. Named by Bale as having been burned at Salisbury with Spenser. Foxe eventually added this name to his own account. Bale, *Epistle exhortatorye*, fo. 13^v; Bale, *Catalogus*, vol. I, 666; *AM*, 1202.

14. *1541–2: Andrew Hewet*. Foxe gave this name for the man burned at Salisbury with Spenser. Although Foxe eventually concluded that three men died, it is more likely that this name is a mistake for Ramsey. Another Andrew Hewet had been burned in July 1533. *AM* (1563), 613; *AM*, 1202.

15. *1542: Thomas Capper*. Convicted of heresy in Cardiff and burned there after being imprisoned for 130 days. J. Gwynfor Jones, *Wales and the Tudor State: Government, Religious Change and the Social Order, 1534–1603* (Cardiff, 1989), 86; Williams, *Wales and the Reformation*, 143.
16. *9 September 1542: Dennis Tod*. A Yorkshireman and perhaps a former friar whose unorthodox reformist beliefs caused him to flee to Germany, c. 1535. He believed, amongst other things, that all sacraments were merely outward signs. In June 1542 his travels took him to Neuchâtel, where he was arrested. A month later the French authorities handed him over to the English. He was burned at Calais. PRO SP 1/171 fos. 53^r–5^r (*LP* XVII 427); *LP* XVII 431, 507, 829.
17. *28 July 1543: Anthony Pearsone*. Sacramentarian priest burned at Windsor. He was also linked to reformist circles in Canterbury diocese and to evangelicals at court. Hall, *The vnion of . . . Lancastre & Yorke* fo. 256^v; *AM*, 1210–20; CCCC MS 128 pp. 77, 81 (*LP* XVIII (ii) 546 pp. 313, 315); *APC*, 97; MacCulloch, *Cranmer*, 302.
18. *28 July 1543: Henry Filmer*. A tailor from Windsor, where he was burned with Pearsone. He had been convicted of calling the Eucharist 'nothyng but a similitude and a Ceremony', although this was only on his brother's evidence, and he denied the charge. Hall, *The vnion of . . . Lancastre & Yorke*, fo. 256^v; *AM*, 1210–20.
19. *28 July 1543: Robert Testwood*. A singing-man in St George's chapel, Windsor, and a notoriously disruptive evangelical. In 1543 he was convicted of mocking the elevation at Mass, saying, 'what, wilte thou lifte hym vp so high, what yet higher, take hede, let hym not fall'. He denied it, but was burned at Windsor with Pearsone. Hall, *The vnion of . . . Lancastre & Yorke*, fo. 256^v; *AM*, 1210–20.
20. *1545: Henry*. Burned at Colchester with his servant. *AM*, 1231.
21. *1545: Henry's servant*. Burned at Colchester with his master. *AM*, 1231.
22. *After 16 May 1546: John Camper*. From Essex. He was convicted with four others of sacramentarian views before Six Articles commissioners in May 1546. They wrote that 'he lytle regardeth to dye but yet seameth to be repentante'. On 16 May the Privy Council ordered that he and two of the others be burned in Essex, one of them at Colchester. PRO SP 1/218 fo. *139^{r-v} (*LP* XXI (i) 836); *APC*, 418.
23. *After 16 May 1546: Joan Bette*. An articulate Essex sacramentary convicted with Camper. She was 'moche perplexed to suffer sayeng that her flesshe woold not burne being vntruyly condempned'. PRO SP 1/218 fos. *139^v–40^r (*LP* XXI (i) 836); *APC*, 418.

24. *After 16 May 1546: Thomas Skygges*. From Essex. He was convicted alongside Camper and Bette of holding and spreading sacramentarian heresies. PRO SP 1/218 fo. 140^r (*LP* XXI (i) 836); *APC*, 418.
25. *16 July 1546: Anne Askew*. Lincolnshire gentlewoman who left her husband and moved to London following a conversion, and who was in contact with prominent court reformers. After an ambiguous recantation, she was rearrested, and burned as a sacramentary, following torture. *DNB*.
26. *16 July 1546: John Lassells*. Nottinghamshire gentleman in the king's privy chamber, and a committed and passably learned evangelical. His vehement support for Edward Crome in May 1546 led to his arrest: he was convicted of holding extreme and idiosyncratic Eucharistic beliefs. A friend and perhaps an instructor of Anne Askew, with whom he was burned. Nichols (ed.), *Chronicle of the Grey Friars*, 51; PRO SP 1/218 fo. 45^v (*LP* XXI (i) 790.1); Askew, *The lattre examinacyon*, fo. 67^r; Lassells et al., *Uvicklieffes wicket . . . with the protestation of J. Lassels*; Susan Brigden and Nigel Wilson, 'New learning and broken friendship', *English Historical Review* 112 (1997), 396–411.
27. *16 July 1546: John Hadlam*. A Colchester tailor arraigned as a sacramentary in London in June 1546. Examined by the Privy Council, he remained obstinate. He was burned at Smithfield with Askew and Lassells. Wriothesley, 167; *APC*, 464; Askew, *The first examinacyon*, fo. 7^v; *AM*, 1240–1.
28. *16 July 1546: John Hemsley*. A former Observant friar from Richmond or, alternatively, a priest from Essex. He was arraigned for heresy on 12 July 1546 and burned with Askew, Lassells and Hadlam. Nichols (ed.), *Chronicle of the Grey Friars*, 51; Wriothesley, 169–70.
29. *?? 16 July 1546: Nicholas Belenian*. A Shropshire priest whom Foxe names as the fourth man burned with Askew, Lassells and Hadlam, instead of Hemsley. No other source mentions him, and this is likely to be an error. *AM*, 1241.
30. *Summer or autumn 1546: Rogers*. A Norfolk man burned at Smithfield 'for the vj. articles' some six months before Henry VIII's death. *AM*, 1242.
31. *November 1546: John Kerby*. From Mendlesham, Suffolk. He, his wife and Roger Clarke were arrested at Ipswich on 8 May 1546 for sacramentarian beliefs. His wife was apparently spared, but he was burned at Ipswich. *APC*, 417; *AM*, 1231–3.
32. *November 1546: Roger Clarke*. Also from Mendlesham. He was burned at Bury St Edmunds. *AM*, 1231–3.
33. *? c. 1546: Oliver Richardine*. Only mentioned by Foxe, whose full account is: 'One Olyuer Richardyne of the Parish of Whitchurch was

burned in Hartford weste, Syr John Ygone being Sheriffe the same time. Whiche seemeth to be about the latter yeare of king Henry viij.' *AM*, 1715.

EXECUTED FOR TREASON

1. *28 July 1540: Thomas Cromwell*. Henry VIII's chief minister and supporter of evangelicals. *DNB*.
2. *2 May 1543: Adam Damplip, als. George Bucker*. An evangelical former servant to Reginald Pole. His sacramentarian preaching in Calais in 1538 led to his arrest. He was released, but as fresh evidence emerged he was rearrested in 1541, and eventually executed in Calais on charges deriving from his contact with Pole. Byrne, *Lisle Letters*, vol. V, 530, 567, vol. VI, 108–9; *APC*, 117; PRO SP 1/158 fo. 188^r (*LP* XV 460); *AM*, 1228–9.
3. *7 March 1544: Robert Singleton*. Lancashire-born cleric and protégé of Anne Boleyn's. Combative, evangelical and ostentatiously learned. He was brought to recant his preaching and writing in 1543, and was executed for treason at Tyburn eight months later. This may have been for treasonous writings, but there are hints he was engaged in murkier conspiracies. Gardiner, *Letters*, 244; Christopher Haigh, 'The Reformation in Lancashire to 1558' (PhD thesis, Manchester, 1969), 253; CCCC MS 128 pp. 153, 267 (*LP* XVIII (ii) 546 pp. 329, 359); Bonner Register fo. 45^r.

DIED IN CUSTODY

1. *12 April 1540: Thomas Saxy*. A priest who apparently hanged himself at the bishop of Winchester's porter's lodge in Southwark. Two coroners gave a verdict of suicide, but evangelicals assumed he had been murdered. PRO STAC 2/1 fo. 103^r; Wriothesley, 115; Brinklow, *Complaynt of Roderyck Mors*, sig. C8^v; Bale, *Epistle exhortatorye*, fo. 13^v; *AM*, 1231.
2. *July 1540 or soon after: Robert Ward*. A London shoemaker arrested in July 1540 'for holding against the Sacrament of the aulter'. He died in Bread Street prison. Bale, *A dysclosyng or openynge of the Manne of synne* fo. 41^v; *AM*, 1204.
3. *1542: John Porter*. Layman who fled Calais having been troubled for his sacramentarian views. Once in London, he regularly preached from the Bible in St Paul's Cathedral. In 1542 he was arrested for sacramentarianism, allegedly on false evidence. He died in Newgate gaol. He had apparently been kept in grim conditions and denied food, and the gaolkeeper's reported comment – 'what matter ys it, how an heretyke dothe

die' – lends credence to the repeated assertion that he was deliberately starved, if not to the allegation that he was tortured to death. PRO SP 1/153 fos. 21^v–2^r (*LP* XIV (ii) 30.2); TCC MS R3.33 fos. 130^r–5^v; Bale, *A dysclosyng or openynge of the Manne of synne*, fos. 41^{r-v}, 66^r; *AM*, 1206–7.

REFORMIST EXILES, 1539–47

1. *John Abel*. Reformist English merchant settled at Strassburg from the early 1540s. C. H. Smyth, *Cranmer and the Reformation under Edward VI* (Cambridge, 1926), 89.
2. *Alexander Alane, als. Alesius*. A Scottish reformer who from 1535 was in England as an emissary of the German Lutherans. On 2 July 1539 Cranmer warned him to leave before the Six Articles came into force. He was in Wittenberg by 9 July. He remained in Germany until his death in 1565. Alane, *Of the auctorite of the word of god agaynst the bisshop of london* (RSTC 292: Strassburg, 1541), sigs. A2^v–B1^r; MacCulloch, *Cranmer*, 251; *LP* XIV (i) 353; Fines, *Biographical Register*.
3. *Jane Alder*. Daughter of a Cambridge alderwoman who married William Turner (below) in December 1540. She was in exile with him soon after February 1541. Whitney R. D. Jones, *William Turner*, 12; Eric Josef Carlson, 'The marriage of William Turner', *Historical Research* 65 (1992), 336–9.
4. *Edmund Allen*. Evangelical fellow of Corpus Christi College, Cambridge, who shortly after 1539 took leave from the college to go to Germany. He managed to have this leave extended despite reports of unpriestlike behaviour while abroad. He may have married during this period. Masters, *History of the College of Corpus Christi*, 213–15.
5. *Dorothy Bale*. John Bale's wife, who fled into exile with him. In 1545 she returned briefly to Norwich to visit her son. She was arrested but soon released. McClendon, *The Quiet Reformation*, 85.
6. *John Bale*. Suffolk Carmelite turned leading evangelical publicist. He and his wife Dorothy fled abroad in about 1540, and seem to have spent most of the next eight years based in Antwerp. Fairfield, *John Bale*, 71–2.
7. *John Burcher*. Reformer who left England in 1538, spending the next eight years in Strassburg, Basel and Zurich. He belonged to the circle of exiles around Heinrich Bullinger. *ET*, 25, 133, 156–63, 413 (*OL*, 40, 201, 236–47, 637).
8. *John Butler*. An English reformer who moved to Zurich as early as 1536. He also visited Geneva and Strassburg. For a time he contemplated returning, but in 1542 he sold his remaining property in England and

settled permanently in Switzerland. *ET*, 131–2, 145, 150, 393–406 (*OL*, 197–9, 218, 225, 605–26).

9. *Miles Coverdale*. Biblical translator in exile in Antwerp from c. 1529 to 1535. By the end of 1540 he had returned to the Continent with his wife Elizabeth Macheson. He was based in Strassburg but took a doctorate at Tübingen and also visited Denmark. From 1543 he was minister of a small town near Strassburg. He returned to England in 1548. J. F. Mozley, *Coverdale and his Bibles* (1953), 7–13.

10. *John Dodman*. An English reformer in exile in Strassburg in the mid-1540s. Coverdale recommended him as a pastor. Mozley, *Coverdale*, 12.

11. *Christopher Hales*. A nephew and namesake of the attorney-general. He graduated MA from Cambridge in 1541 and went to Strassburg to study in 1543. He remained there until at least 1550 and helped to negotiate the passage of continental reformers to England early in Edward's reign. Fines, *Biographical Register*.

12. *Richard Hilles*. Opinionated young London Zwinglian who fled into exile in 1540, escaping arrest by a whisker. He settled at Strassburg, continuing to work as a merchant tailor. *ET*, 24, 131–2, 153–4, 414 (*OL*, 38, 198–9, 230–2, 639).

13. *Richard Hilles' servant*. Hilles judged him to be 'truly pious' and brought him to Strassburg in 1540, but faced with material hardship, isolation and 'the simplicity of the religious worship in this country' he decided by September 1541 to return home. Hilles permitted this, despite worries that he might fall away. *ET*, 144 (*OL*, 217).

14. *John Hooper*. Zealous reformer arrested in 1539. He escaped to Paris and, after an abortive attempt to return to England, settled in Strassburg, where he fell seriously ill and was cared for by Hilles. He travelled to England in the summer of 1546. It was clearly a harrowing journey, and he claimed that he was twice imprisoned during it. By 1547 he was in Zurich. *ET*, 21–2, 26, 166–9 (*OL*, 33–5, 41, 251–4); Fines, *Biographical Register*.

15. *George Joye*. Biblical translator in exile 1527–35; he had returned to exile by 1541. He apparently lived in or near Antwerp, but may have travelled as far as Augsburg. He was apparently married during both his periods in exile, but his wife's (or wives') name and nationality are unknown. Butterworth, *George Joye*, esp. 86; Joye, *Present consolation*, sigs. F2^v–3^r.

16. *Thomas Knight*. An English bookseller who by January 1547 was working in Venice and corresponding with Bullinger. He was acquainted with others in Bullinger's circle. *ET*, 237 (*OL*, 357–8); Duff, *Century of the English Book Trade*.

17. *Robert Legate*. Translator of a pair of Lutheran catechetical dialogues into English. The book was printed at Wesel in November 1545. Legate, *Breife Catechisme and Dialogue*, sig. A2^r.
18. *John MacAlpine, als. Maccabeus*. Scottish evangelical, in England from 1534. He married his fellow Scottish exile Agnes Macheson. By October 1540 they had fled to Bremen. The following month he matriculated at Wittenberg University. In 1542 he became professor at Copenhagen, where he remained until his death. *DNB*; Mozley, *Coverdale*, 8.
19. *Agnes Macheson, als. Sutherland*. Scottish noblewoman in English exile from the early 1530s. She married her fellow exile John MacAlpine and fled to Germany with him. Mozley, *Coverdale*, 8.
20. *Elizabeth Macheson*. Agnes' sister, also in England from the early 1530s. She married Miles Coverdale and went into Continental exile with him. Mozley, *Coverdale*, 8.
21. *George Marshall*. A London priest with a long evangelical pedigree. By 1546 he had left the country without licence and moved to Danzig, where he married and practised as a physician. Although he had reportedly written against the king, the Privy Council hoped he could provide useful information about Poland and encouraged him to return. *APC*, 417; Brigden, *London*, 125, 253, 389; MacCulloch, *Cranmer*, 171.
22. *Edward More*. Scholar at New College, Oxford, who by November 1538 was in Wittenberg as a pupil of Luther's. Emden.
23. *William Peterson*. One of the group of English reformers who moved to Zurich in 1536. His attempt to support himself there by selling bowstaves failed, and by September 1541 he had returned to England. *ET*, 144, 392–6, 407–8 (*OL*, 217, 604–10, 628–9); Smyth, *Cranmer and the Reformation*, 81.
24. *John Philpot*. Scholar at New College, Oxford. He had gone abroad by May 1541, when he forfeited his fellowship due to prolonged absence. He travelled to Italy, 'and places thereabouts', visiting Venice, Padua and Rome, and perhaps taking a degree. He returned to England in Edward's reign. *AM*, 1795; Emden; Bodleian Library, MS Jones 3.
25. *John Rogers*. Bible translator in Antwerp from 1534 to 1540, during which time he married a Dutch woman. In November 1540 he matriculated at Wittenberg. He remained in Germany until 1548, becoming sufficiently proficient in German that he was given charge of a German congregation. *AM*, 1485; Mozley, *Coverdale*, 131–4.
26. *Thomas Rose*. A fiery reformist preacher who fled abroad, apparently in 1539, after the duke of Norfolk ordered his arrest. He visited Zurich and Basel, returned briefly to England in 1540, and then settled in Aarau with his wife. They remained there for three years. Eventually they decided

to return home. After a shipwreck and a month in a French prison, they were taken in by Henry Radcliffe, earl of Sussex. MacCulloch, *Suffolk and the Tudors*, 155–61; AM, 1202–3, 2083.
27. *Anthony Scoloker*. An evangelical printer and translator, apparently in German exile in the last years of Henry's reign. *DNB*.
28. *Thomas Solme*. A former Augustinian canon whose book, *The Lordis flayle*, was printed in Antwerp in c. 1540. From this he may be presumed to have spent at least some time in exile. *The Lordis flayle*; Fines, *Biographical Register*.
29. *William Swerder*. Former master of a Canterbury hospital who, by 1545, was in exile in Strassburg and in touch with the circle around Bullinger. *ET*, 163 (*OL*, 247).
30. *William Thomas*. A lawyer in the household of the privy councillor Sir Anthony Browne. In 1545 he fled England, going to Germany and thence to Venice. His supposedly evangelical opinions may have contributed to his decision to leave, but the more immediate problem was that he had embezzled money from his master to cover gambling debts. E. R. Adair, 'William Thomas: a forgotten clerk of the Privy Council', in *Tudor Studies*, ed. R. W. Seton-Watson (1924).
31. *Dennis Tod*. See above, p. 263.
32. *Bartholomew Traheron*. One of the circle of English reformers in Zurich in the 1530s. He remained in England from 1540 until at least 1543, working as a translator and schoolteacher. By 1546 he was in Geneva. He returned to England the following year. Johannes de Vigo, tr. Bartholomew Traheron, *The most excellent workes of chirurgerye* (RSTC 24720: 1543); *ET*, 150, 209–11, 404–6 (*OL*, 226, 316–19, 623–6); HPT.
33. *William Turner*. Cleric, botanist, physician and evangelical publicist who married Jane Alder in November 1540. By April 1541 they had fled the country. He seems to have gone first to Italy, and thereafter to Zurich, Basel, Bonn, Cologne and Strassburg. From 1544 he was physician to the duke of Emden. He returned to England in 1547. Whitney R. D. Jones, *William Turner*, 6–19; Carlson, 'The marriage of William Turner'.
34. *Francis Warner*. English evangelical living in Strassburg in 1543. He was in contact with Bullinger's circle. *ET*, 235–6 (*OL* 355–7).
35. *Oliver Whitehead*. In August 1546 he was one of sixty English evangelicals who fled to Bremen 'for feare of deathe ... [and] of the grat persecucion which ys done by the byschopes'. PRO SP 1/223 fo. 152^r (*LP* XXI (i) 1491).
36. *Robert Wisdom*. Popular reformist preacher who was forced to recant in 1543. In May 1546, the Privy Council ordered his arrest, but he

escaped, and by August he was in Bremen. *DNB*; PRO SP 1/223 fo. 152^r (*LP* XXI (i) 1491); Becon, *Iewell of ioye*, sigs. C5^v–6^v; Bonner Register fos. 44^r–5^r; *APC*, 424.

37. *William Woodroffe*. One of the first group of English evangelicals to travel to Switzerland. He arrived in Zurich in 1536. From there he travelled to Geneva and Frankfurt, but never returned to England. *OL* 81–2, 610; Fines, *Biographical Register*.

Appendix II: Controversial religious printing in English, 1541–6

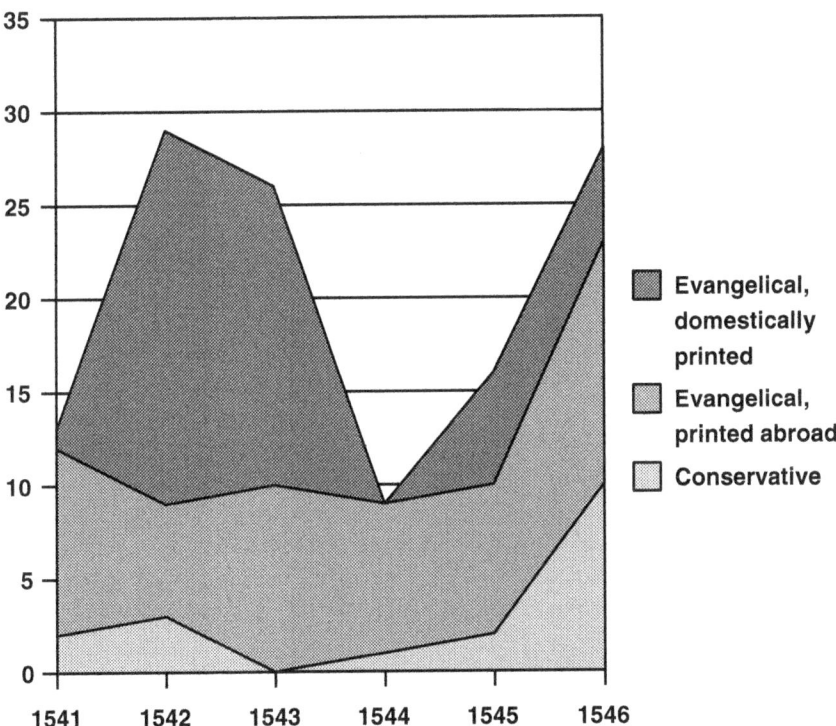

Fig. A.1 Controversial religious imprints in English, 1541–6

As far as possible, this figure includes all known imprints which contained controversial religious material, even if such material was a small part of the work in question.

Domestic evangelical imprints: RSTC 977.5, 1713, 1714, 1715, 1717, 1730.5, 1731, 1734, 1734.5, 1735, 1738, 1739, 1740, 1742, 1743, 1749, 1750, 1775, 1776, 2967.3, 2967.5, 2968.3, 2968.5, 2969.3, 2969.5, 2970, 2970.3, 2972.7, 3326.5, 4045.5, 4047, 4048, 5069, 5070, 10460, 11917, 12766.7, 13910, 14106.2, 14919, 17760.5, 19187, 20197.3, 24164, 24216a; and the following imprints now lost: Thomas Becon, *A new Cathechisme* (1542?);[1] Thomas Becon, *Christmasse carols very new and godly* (1542?).[2]

Foreign evangelical imprints: RSTC 292, 848, 1270, 1276, 1280, 1291, 1291.5, 1291a, 1296.5, 1303, 1309, 1462.9, 3047, 3759.5, 3764, 3765, 4045, 4046, 4070.5, 4079.5, 4797.3, 5014, 5888, 5889, 10808, 10884, 11382, 13612, 14717, 14823, 14826, 14828, 14828.5, 14830, 16984, 17793, 17798, 21804, 23435.5, 24165, 24165.5, 24217, 24353, 24354, 24355, 24468, 25590, 25590.5, 26138; and the following imprints now lost: John Bale, *Adversus impostorem Standicium* in English (1541?);[3] John Bale, *Apologiam pro Barnes* in English (1541?);[4] John Bale, *Pro Grayo Contra Smithum* in English (1541?);[5] Henry Brinklow, *Expostulationem ad clerum* in English (1542?);[6] John Bale, *The image of both churches* (lost edition of all three parts, 1546?).[7] Four imprints included here are assigned to London, 1546 by the RSTC (10884, 14828.5, 25590 and 25590.5), but if such blatantly illegal works were indeed printed in London, it must have been after Henry VIII's death.

Conservative imprints: RSTC 5106.5, 11588, 11589, 11591, 11591.3, 14126.5, 19785.5, 19786, 22249.5, 22815, 22820, 22820a, 22821; and the following imprints now lost: John Huntingdon's *The genealogy of heresye* (two imprints in 1541?);[8] a first edition of RSTC 22249.5 (1542); Edmund Bonner, *Two declarations*, apparently on the availability of the Bible (1542?);[9] Stephen Gardiner, *The examinacyon of the hunter* (1544).[10]

---

[1] Bonner Register fo. 44ᵛ.   [2] Bonner Register fo. 92ʳ.
[3] Bale, *A dysclosyng or openynge of the Manne of synne*, fo. 87ʳ; Bale, *Catalogus*, vol. I, 704.
[4] Bale, *Catalogus*, vol. I, 704.   [5] Bale, *Catalogus*, vol. I, 704.
[6] Bale, *Catalogus*, vol. II, 105.   [7] See chapter 3, n. 58.
[8] Bale, *Mysterye of inyquyte*, sig. A2ʳ, fo. 84ʳ.
[9] Bale, *A dysclosyng or openynge of the Manne of synne*, fo. 97ᵛ; see above, p. 220.
[10] Reprinted in Turner, *Rescuynge of the romishe fox*, and datable from Bale, *Epistle exhortatorye*, fo. 29ʳ.

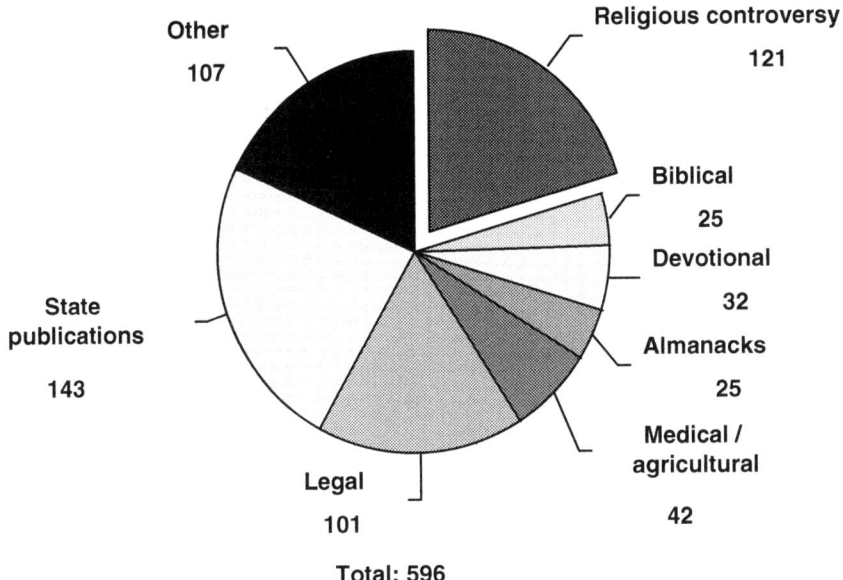

Fig. A.2 English-language imprints by type, 1541–6

'Other' works include chronicles, news pamphlets and classical, humanist and literary works, including the works of Erasmus – but excluding any works which contain any controversial religious material.

BIBLIOGRAPHY

Manuscripts and individual early printed books

BURY ST EDMUNDS: SUFFOLK RECORD OFFICE

IC 500 / 5 / 1 – Archdeaconry of Sudbury act and admonition book 1544–7[1]

CAMBRIDGE: CAMBRIDGE UNIVERSITY LIBRARY

MS Ff. VI.2

CORPUS CHRISTI COLLEGE

MS 106
MS 108
MS 109
MS 128 – "Prebendaries' Plot" papers

EMMANUEL COLLEGE

MS 261 – Robert Wisdom papers

TRINITY COLLEGE

MS R3.33 – William Palmer's poem on Stephen Gardiner

EXETER: DEVON RECORD OFFICE

ECA Book 51 – John Hooker's commonplace book

DEAN AND CHAPTER LIBRARY

Chapter Act Book 3552 (1537–66)

---

[1] I am grateful to Diarmaid MacCulloch for the use of his microfilm of this MS.

GLOUCESTER: GLOUCESTER COUNTY RECORD OFFICE

GDR 2 – Diocesan visitation book 1542–47

LONDON: BRITISH LIBRARY

Additional MSS 12483, 19400, 32650, 46367
Cotton MSS Cleopatra E.iv, v, vi, F.ii; Faustina C.ii; Nero B.vi; Titus B.i
Egerton MS 2880
Harleian MSS 78, 283, 353, 367, 416, 419, 421, 423, 425, 540, 604, 1197, 2252
Lansdowne MSS 2, 97
Royal MSS 7.C.vi, 7.F.xiv, 17.A.xlvi, 17.B.xxxv, 17.B.xl, 17.C.xxx, 18.A.xl
Appendix. 78
C.25.b.4 (2). The psalter of Dauid in English (1544?), *tr.* G. Joye (Henry VIII's copy)

CORPORATION OF LONDON RECORD OFFICE

Court of Aldermen Repertory Books 9–11
Court of Common Council Journal 14

GUILDHALL LIBRARY

MS 9531/12 – Register of Bishops Bonner and Thirlby

INNER TEMPLE LIBRARY

Petyt MS 47

LAMBETH PALACE LIBRARY

Register of Thomas Cranmer
MS 113
MS 306

PUBLIC RECORD OFFICE

C 1 – Early Chancery proceedings
E 36 / 120 – Exchequer miscellaneous: a volume of depositions on treasonable matters, temp. Henry VIII
E 334 / 2, 3 – First-fruits composition books
KB 9 / 129 – indictments for heresy in Coventry
PCC Prob. 11 – Prerogative Court of Canterbury Wills
SP 1 – State Papers of Henry VIII: main series
SP 6 – State Papers of Henry VIII: theological tracts
STAC 2 – Star Chamber papers, Henry VIII

NORTHAMPTON: NORTHAMPTONSHIRE COUNTY RECORD OFFICE

MS Fitzwilliam (Milton) Correspondence 21 – Letterbook of William Paget

NORWICH: NORFOLK RECORD OFFICE
NCR 16a / 5 – Mayoral court book

OXFORD: BODLEIAN LIBRARY
MS Jones 3 – John Philpot on royal and ecclesiastical power
Jesus College MS 74
4° Rawlinson 245 – Henry VIII's annotated copy of the *Bishops' Book*

TROWBRIDGE: WILTSHIRE COUNTY RECORD OFFICE
Sarum Archdeaconry Register Book I

WORCESTER: WORCESTERSHIRE COUNTY RECORD OFFICE
BA 2764 / 802 – Bishop Bell's visitation book
Wills 1538

Printed primary sources

ANONYMOUS EARLY PRINTED MATERIAL

The byble in Englyshe, that is to saye the content of all the holy scrypture [the 'Great Bible'] (RSTC 2068: Paris and London, 1539)
A boke of prayers called ye ordynary fasshyon of a good lyuynge (RSTC 3326.5: 1546?)
A brefe apologye or answere to a certen craftye cloynar, or popyshe parasye, called Thomas Smythe (RSTC 22880.7: Antwerp, 1540)
A compendyous treatyse of sclaundre, declarynge what sclaundre is (RSTC 24216a: 1545?)
[Ends:] *The ende of this brefe Postyl, vpon the Epystles and Gospelles of all the Sondayes in the yeare* [title page missing on only surviving copy] (RSTC 2972.7: 1543)
An exhortation vnto prayer . . . to be read to the people in euery church afore processyons (RSTC 10620: 1544)
[Free will and predestination: fragmentary verses on the verso of an anatomical fugitive sheet] (RSTC 11366.3: c. 1540?)
A generall free Pardon or Charter of heuyn blys (RSTC 19187: 1542)
A glasse for housholders, wherin thei maye se, bothe howe to rule them selfes & ordre their housholde (RSTC 11917: 1542)
Here after foloweth twoo fruitfull and godly praiers, the one in laude and praise of the trinitie, and the other desiryng grace to with stande the feare of death (RSTC 20197.3: 1545)
Here beginneth a good lesson for yonge men (RSTC 15525: 1540)
[Ends:] *Here ends thys lytle treatyse of the instruction of chyldren* [title page missing on only surviving copy] (RSTC 14106.2: 1543)
The institution of a christen man [the 'Bishops' Book'] (RSTC 5163: 1537)
An inuectiue ageinst glotony and dronkennes (RSTC 14126.5: 1545)
A meane to die well [= headline, sig. B1ʳ] (RSTC 17760.5: c. 1545)

A necessary doctrine and ervdition for any christen man, sette furthe by the kynges maiestie [the 'King's Book'] (RSTC 5168: 1543)
A paumflet compyled by G. C. / To master Smyth and Wyllyam G. (RSTC 4628.5: 1540)
Praiers of holi fathers, Patryarches, Prophetes, Iudges, Kynges, and renowmed men and women of eyther testamente (RSTC 20200: 1544)
This lytle treatyse declareth the study and frutes of Barnes borned in west smyth felde (RSTC 1473.5: 1540)
A very declaracyon of the bond and free wyll of man (RSTC 6456.5: St. Albans?, 1539)

OTHER PRINTED PRIMARY SOURCES

Alane als. Alesius, Alexander, *Of the auctorite of the word of god agaynst the bisshop of london* (RSTC 292: Strassburg, 1541)
Ascham, Roger, *The Whole Works of Roger Ascham . . . With a life of the author*, ed. J. A. Giles, 3 vols. (1864–5)
Askew, Anne, *The first examinacyon of Anne Askew, latelye martyred in Smythfelde*, ed. John Bale (RSTC 848: Wesel, 1546)
The lattre examinacyon of Anne Askewe, latelye martyred in Smythfelde, ed. John Bale (RSTC 850: Wesel, 1547)
Bale, John, *A Christen exhortacion vnto customable swearers. What a ryght & lawfull othe is: whan, and before whom, it owght to be* (RSTC 1280: Antwerp, 1543?)
(ps. John Harryson), *A dysclosynge or openynge of the Manne of synne* (RSTC 1309: Antwerp, 1543)
A brefe chronycle concernynge the Examinacyon and death of the blessed martyr of Christ syr Iohan Oldecastell the lorde Cobham (RSTC 1276: Antwerp, 1544)
(ps. Henry Stalbrydge), *The epistle exhortatorye of an Englyshe Christiane unto his derely beloued contraye of Englande* (RSTC 1291: Antwerp, 1544)
A mysterye of inyquyte contayned within the heretycall Genealogye of Ponce Pantolabus (RSTC 1303: Antwerp, 1545)
The actes of Englysh votaryes, comprehendynge their vnchast practyses and examples by all ages (RSTC 1270: Antwerp, 1546)
The Image of bothe churches after the moste wonderfull and heauenly Reuelacion of Sainct Iohn the Euangelist (RSTC 1297: Antwerp?, 1548?)
Scriptorum illustrium maioris Brytanniae, quam nunc Angliam & Scotiam uocant: Catalogus, 2 vols. (Basel, 1557, 1559)
John Bale's King Johan, ed. Barry B. Adams (San Marino, CA, 1969)
Bateson, Mary (ed.), *Grace Book B: Containing the Proctors' Accounts and Other Records of the University of Cambridge for the Years 1488–1544*, 2 vols. (Cambridge, 1903, 1905)
Becon, Thomas, *The Gouernans of vertue, teachyng a Christen man, howe he oughte dayely to lede his life* (RSTC 1724.5: 1538)
(ps. Theodore Basille), *Newes out of heauen* (RSTC 1740: 1541)
(ps. Theodore Basille), *A Christmas bankett garnyshed with many pleasaunt and deynty disshes* (RSTC 1715: 1542)
(ps. Theodore Basille), *A Potacion or drinkynge for this holi time of lent* (RSTC 1749: 1542)

(ps. Theodore Basille), *A newe pathway vnto praier, ful of much godly frute and christen knowledge* (RSTC 1734: 1542)
(ps. Theodore Basille), *A pleasaunt newe Nosegay, full of many godly and swete floures* (RSTC 1742: 1542)
(ps. Theodore Basille), *Dauids Harpe ful of moost delectable armony, newely strynged and set in tune* (RSTC 1717: 1542)
(ps. Theodore Basille), *The new pollecye of warre, wherin is declared not only how ye mooste cruell Tyraunt the great Turke may be ouer come, but also all other enemies of the Christen publique weale* (RSTC 1735: 1542)
(ps. Theodore Basille), *A new yeares gyfte more precious than golde, worthy to be embrased no lesse ioyfully than thankfully* (RSTC 1738: 1543)
(ps. Theodore Basille), *An Inuectyue agenst the moste wicked & detestable vice of swearing* (RSTC 1731: 1543)
The iewell of ioye (RSTC 1763: 1550)
The worckes of Thomas Becon, 3 vols. (RSTC 1710: 1560–4)
The Early Works of Thomas Becon, ed. John Ayre (Cambridge: Parker Society, 1843)
Brinklow, Henry (ps. Roderick Mors), *The complaynt of Roderyck Mors . . . vnto the parliament howse of Ingland* (RSTC 3759.5: Strasburg, 1542)
The Lamentacion of a Christian, against the Citie of London (RSTC 3764: Bonn, 1542)
(?), *A supplication of the poore Commons* (RSTC 10884: London or Antwerp, 1546)
Bullinger, Heinrich, *The christen state of Matrimonye*, tr. Miles Coverdale (RSTC 4045: Antwerp, 1541)
The christen state of Matrimonye, wherin housbandes and wyfes maye lerne to kepe house together with loue, tr. Miles Coverdale (RSTC 4046: 1543)[2]
The golden boke of christen matrimonye, moost necessary and profitable for all them, that entend to liue quietly and godlye in the Christen state of holy wedlock, ed. and ascribed to Thomas Becon (ps. Theodore Basille) (RSTC 4047: 1543)
Bullinger, Heinrich, and Jean Calvin, *Two Epystles . . . whether it be lawfull for a Chrysten man to communycate or be pertaker of the Masse of the Papystes* (RSTC 4079.5: Antwerp, 1544)
Burnet, Gilbert, *The History of the Reformation of the Church of England*, ed. Nicholas Pocock, vol. IV (1865)
Byrne, Muriel St Clare (ed.), *The Lisle Letters*, 6 vols. (Chicago, 1981)
Camden, William, *Annales rerum Anglicarum et Hibernicarum regnante Elizabetha*, ed. Thomas Hearne, 3 vols. (1717)
Charles V, *The answere of Carolus the fyfte . . . vnto the letters conuocatorye of Paule the thyrd Bysshope of Rome concerninge A Generall Concell to be celebrated at Trident* (RSTC 5014: Antwerp, 1543)
The answer of Charles the fyft . . . vnto the letters conuocatorye of Paule the thyrde bishop of Rome, concernyng a generall councell to be held at Trident (RSTC 5015: 1543)
Chaucer, Geoffrey, *The workes of Geffray Chaucer newly printed with dyuers workes whiche were neuer in print before* (RSTC 5070: 1542)
Chedsay, William, and C. Scott, *Two notable sermones lately preached at Pauls crosse. Anno 1544* (RSTC 5106.5: 1545)

---

[2] This is a version printed in England which omits the most controversial chapters.

Chrysostom, John, *A compendious Treatise of saynte John Chrysostom prouinge that no man is hurte but of him selfe* (RSTC 14640: 1542)
tr. Thomas Lupset, *A Sermon of Saint Chrysostom* (RSTC 14639: 1542)
Constantine, George, 'A memorial from George Constantine to Thomas Lord Cromwell', *Archaeologia* 23 (1831)
Coverdale, Miles, *A confutacion of that treatise, which one Iohn Standish made agaynst the protestacion of D. Barnes* (RSTC 5888: Zurich, 1541)
(tr.), *The actes of the disputacion in the councell of the empyre holden at Regenspurg: concernyng the christen relygion* (RSTC 13612: Antwerp, 1542)
Coverdale, Miles (tr. and ed.), *The new testament of oure sauyour Jesu Christ. Faythfully translated, & lately correcte* (RSTC 2836: Antwerp, 1538)
Cramer, J. A. (ed. and tr.), *The Second Book of the Travels of Nicander Nucius of Corcyra*, Camden Society old series 17 (1841)
Cranmer, Thomas, *Miscellaneous Writings and Letters of Thomas Cranmer*, ed. John Edmund Cox (Cambridge: Parker Society, 1846)
Crowley, Robert, [fragment on the prophet Joel] (RSTC 6088.9: 1547?)
 The confutation of .xiii. Articles, wherunto Nicolas Shaxton, late byshop of Salisburye subscribed and caused to be set forthe (RSTC 6083: 1548)
 The opening of the woordes of the prophet Joell, in his second and third chapters, concerning the signes of the last day. Compiled M.D. XLVI (RSTC 6089: 1566)
D'Avalos, Alfonso, *A ioyfull new tidynges of the goodly victory that was sent to the Emperour*, tr. John Mayler (RSTC 977.5: 1543)
Dasent, John R. (ed.), *Acts of the Privy Council of England*, vol. I (1890)
Edgeworth, Roger, *Sermons very fruitfull, godly and learned: preaching in the Reformation c. 1535–c. 1553*, ed. Janet Wilson (Cambridge, 1993)
Ellis, Henry (ed.), *Original Letters, Illustrative of English History*, 2nd series, vol. II (1827)
Epistolae Tigurinae de rebus potissimum ad ecclesiae Anglicanae reformationem (Cambridge: Parker Society, 1848)
Erasmus, Desiderius, *A Dialoge or communication of two persons . . . intitled the pilgremage of pure deuotyon* (RSTC 10454: c. 1540?)
 tr. Philip Gerrard, *A very pleasaunt and fruitful Diologe called the Epicure* (RSTC 10460: 1545)
 The first tome or volume of the Paraphrase of Erasmus vpon the newe testamente (RSTC 2854: 1548)
Fabyan, Robert, *The chronicle of Fabyan, whiche he hym selfe nameth the concordance of historyes* (RSTC 10661: 1542)
Flanley, Ralph (ed.), *Six Town Chronicles of England* (Oxford, 1911)
Foxe, John, *Actes and Monuments of these latter and perillous dayes* (RSTC 11222: 1563)
 The ecclesiasticall history contaynyng the Actes and monuments. Newly recognised and inlarged (RSTC 11223: 1570)
 Actes and monuments of matters most speciall in the church (RSTC 11225: 1583)
Frere, Walter, and William Kennedy, *Visitation Articles and Injunctions of the Period of the Reformation*, 3 vols., Alcuin Club Collections 14–16 (1910)
Gairdner, James, and R. H. Brodie (eds.), *Letters & Papers, Foreign & Domestic, of the Reign of Henry VIII*, 21 vols. (1862–1932)
Gardiner, Stephen, *A declaration of such true articles as George Ioye hath gone about to confute as false* (RSTC 11588: 1546)

A detection of the Deuils Sophistrie, wherwith he robbeth the vnlearned people, of the true byleef, in the most blessed Sacrament of the aulter (RSTC 11591: 1546)

De vera obedencia an Oration . . . Nowe translated into english, ed. John Bale (RSTC 11585: London?, 1553)

The Letters of Stephen Gardiner, ed. James Arthur Muller (Cambridge, 1933)

Geoffroy, Antoine (?), *The order of the great Turckes courte* (RSTC 24334: 1542)

Gilby, Anthony, *An answer to the deuillish detection of S. Gardiner* (RSTC 11884: London?, 1548)

'An admonition to England and Scotland, to call them to repentance', in *The Works of John Knox*, ed. David Laing, vol. IV (Edinburgh, 1895)

Gough, John (ed.), *The dore of holy scripture* (RSTC 22587.5: 1540)

Gray, William, *A balade agaynst malycyous Sclaunderers* (RSTC 1323.5: 1540)

An answere to maister Smyth (RSTC 12206a.3: 1540)

The returne of M. Smythes enuoy (RSTC 12206a.7: 1540)

Gruffyd, Elis, 'Boulogne and Calais from 1545 to 1550', ed. and tr. M. Bryn Davies, *Bulletin of the Faculty of Arts, Fouad I University*, Cairo 12 (1950)

Hall, Edward, and Richard Grafton, *The vnion of the two noble and illustrate famelies of Lancastre & Yorke* (RSTC 12721: 1548)

Hardyng, John, and Richard Grafton, *The chronicle of Jhon Hardyng in metre, from the first begynnyng of Englande*, 2 vols. (RSTC 12766.7: 1543)

The chronicle of Jhon Hardyng in metre, from the first beginning of Englande, 2 vols. (RSTC 12767: 1543)

Hooper, John, *An answer vnto my lord of wynchesters booke* (RSTC 13741: Zurich, 1547)

Howard, Henry, earl of Surrey, *The Poems of Henry Howard Earl of Surrey*, ed. Frederick Morgan Padelford (Seattle, 1920)

Howard, Henry, et al., *An excellent epitaffe of syr Thomas wyat, with two other dytties* (RSTC 26054: 1545?)

Huggarde, Miles, *The displaying of the protestantes, with a description of diuers their abuses* (RSTC 13557: 1556)

Hughe, William, *The troubled mans medicine*, 2 vols. (RSTC 13910: 1546)

Hughes, Paul L., and James F. Larkin (eds.), *Tudor Royal Proclamations 1485–1553* (New Haven and London, 1964)

Journals of the House of Lords, vol. I

Joye, George (ps. James Sawtry), *The defence of the mariage of preistes: agenst Steuen Gardiner* (RSTC 21804: Antwerp, 1541)

A frutefull treatis of Baptyme and the Lordis Souper (RSTC 24217: Antwerp, 1541)

George Ioye confuteth, Winchesters false Articles (RSTC 14826: Antwerp, 1543)

Our sauiour Iesus Christ hath not ouercharged his chirche with many ceremonies (RSTC 14556: Antwerp, 1543)

The vnite and Scisme of the olde chirche (RSTC 14830: Antwerp, 1543)

A present consolation for the sufferers of persecucion for ryghtwysenes (RSTC 14828: Antwerp, 1544)

The exposicion of Daniel the Prophete (RSTC 14823: Antwerp, 1545)

The refutation of the byshop of Winchesters derke declaration of his false articles, once before confuted (RSTC 14828.5: London?, 1546)

Kaulek, Jean (ed.), *Correspondance Politique de MM. de Castillon et de Marillac* (Paris, 1885)

Kelton, Arthur, *A commendacion / Of welshmen* (RSTC 14919: 1546)

Lang, R. G. (ed.), *Two Tudor Subsidy Assessment Rolls for the City of London: 1541 and 1582* (London Record Society, 1993)
Lassells, John, Wilham Tracy et al., *Uvicklieffes wicket. Faythfully ouerseene and corrected . . . With the protestation of J. Lassels late burned in Smythfelde* (RSTC 25591: 1548?)
Latimer, Hugh, *Sermons and Remains of Hugh Latimer*, ed. George Elwes Corrie (Cambridge: Parker Society, 1845)
Legate, Robert (tr.), *A Breife Catechisme and Dialogue betwene the Husbande and his Wyfe. . . . Item dyuerse other Dialogues betwene the Truthe and the Unlearned man* (RSTC 4979.3: Antwerp, 1545)
Longland, John, *A sermond made be for the kynge at Grene wich* (RSTC 16796: 1538)
Luther, Martin, *Luther's Works Vol. 53: Letters III*, ed. and tr. Gottfried G. Krodel (Philadelphia, 1975)
Marbeck, John, *A concordance, that is to saie, a worke wherein ye maie finde any worde conteigned in the whole Bible* (RSTC 17300: 1550)
Melanchthon, Philip, *The epistle of the famous and great Clerke Philip Melancton made vnto oure late Souereyne Lorde Kynge Henry the eight, for the reuokinge and abolishing of the six articles* (RSTC 17789: Antwerp, 1547)
Moone, Peter, *A short treatise of certayne thinges abused* (RSTC 18056: 1548)
Morison, Richard, *An exhortation to styrre all Englyshe men to the defence of theyr countreye* (RSTC 18110: 1539)
An invective ayenste the great and detestable vice, treason (RSTC 18111: 1539)
Nichols, John Gough (ed.), *Chronicle of the Grey Friars of London*, Camden Society old series 53 (1852)
Narratives of the Days of the Reformation, Camden Society old series 77 (1859)
Nicolas, Harris (ed.), *Proceedings and Ordinances of the Privy Council of England*, vol. VII (1837)
Oliver, George, *Lives of the Bishops of Exeter and a History of the Cathedral* (Exeter, 1861)
Parker, Matthew, *Correspondence of Matthew Parker, D.D., Archbishop of Canterbury*, ed. John Bruce (Cambridge: Parker Society, 1853)
Parr, Katherine, *Prayers or meditacions, wherin the mynde is styrred paciently to suffre all afflictions here* (RSTC 4818.5: 1545)
The lamentacion of a sinner, bewayling the ignoraunce of her blind life (RSTC 4827: 1547)
Peryn, William, *Thre godlye and notable sermons, of the sacrament of the aulter* (RSTC 19786: 1546)
Proctor, John, *The fal of the late Arrian* (RSTC 20406: 1549)
Pylbarough, John, *A commemoration of the inestimable graces and benefites of God* (RSTC 20521: 1540)
Robinson, Hastings (ed.), *Original Letters Relative to the English Reformation* (Cambridge: Parker Society, 1846)
Salomon the Jew, *A wounderfull Prophecie or pronostication . . . to the lawde and prayse of the moost victoryous Emperowre Charles the fyfthe* (RSTC 21629: Antwerp, 1543)
Seton, Alexander and William Tolwin, *The declaracion made at Poules Crosse in the Cytye of London, the fourth sonday of Aduent* (RSTC 22249.5: 1542)
Smith, Richard, *A defence of the blessed masse, and the sacrifice therof* (RSTC 22820: 1546)

The assertion and defence of the sacramente of the aulter (RSTC 22815: 1546)

A godly and faythfull Retraction made and published at Paules crosse in London (RSTC 22822: 1547)

Smith, Thomas, *A lytell treatyse agaynst sedicyous persons* (RSTC 22880.4: 1540)

A treatyse declarynge the despyte of a secrete sedycyous person, that dareth not shewe hym selfe (RSTC 22880.6: 1540)

An Enuoye from Thomas Smith vpon thaunswer of one WG (1540, RSTC 22880.2: 1540)

Smyth P., R. (a pseudonym), *An artificiall apologie, articulerlye answerynge to the obstreperous Obgannynges of one WG* (RSTC 22877.6: 1540)

Solme, Thomas, *Here begynnyth a traetys callyde the Lordis flayle* (RSTC 22897: Antwerp, 1540)

Standish, John, *A lytle treatise composyd by Iohan Standysshe . . . against the protestacion of Robert Barnes at the tyme of his death* (RSTC 23209: 1540)

Statutes of the Realm, printed by command of his majesty King George III (1817)

Taverner, Richard (tr.), *The confessyon of the faythe of the Germaynes. To which is added the apologie of Melancthon* (RSTC 908: 1536)

A Catechisme or institution of the Christen Religion (RSTC 23709: 1539)

The Epistles and Gospelles with a brief Postyl vpon the same from Aduent tyll Lowe sonday (RSTC 2967.3: 1542)

The epistles and gospelles with a brief postil . . . from after Easter tyll Aduent, . . . the Somer parte (RSTC 2968: 1540)

The epistles and gospelles with a brief postyll . . . from Trinitie sonday tyll Aduent (RSTC 2969: 1540?)

The gospels with brief sermons vpon them for al the holy dayes in ye yere (RSTC 2970, 1542?)

(ed.), *The most sacred Bible, whiche is the holy scripture, conteyning the old and new testament* (RSTC 2067: 1539)

Tracy, Richard, *The profe and declaration of thys proposition: Fayth only iustifieth* (RSTC 24164: 1543)

A supplycacion to our moste soueraigne lorde Kynge Henry the eyght (RSTC 24165: Antwerp, 1544)

A bryef & short declaracyon made, wherby eue[ry] chrysten man maye knowe, what is a sacrament (RSTC 24162: 1548)

Tunstall, Cuthbert, *A sermon of Cuthbert byshop of Duresme, made vpon Palme sondaye laste past* (RSTC 24322a: 1539)

Turner, William (ps. William Wraghton), *The huntyng and fyndyng out of the Romishe fox* (RSTC 24353: Bonn, 1543)

The huntyng and fyndyng out of the Romyshe foxe (RSTC 24354: Antwerp, 1544?)

The rescuynge of the romishe fox . . . The seconde course of the hunter at the romishe fox (RSTC 24355: Bonn, 1545)

The huntyng of the romyshe vuolfe (RSTC 24356: Emden, 1555)

Tyndale, William, *The obedience of a Christen man and how Christen rulers ought to governe* (RSTC 24446: Antwerp, 1528)

Vergil, Polydore, *An abridgement of the notable woorke of Polidore Vergile conteignyng the deuisers and firste finders out aswell of Artes, Ministeries, Feactes and ciuill ordinaunces, as of Rites, and Ceremonies*, ed. T. Langley (RSTC 24656: 1546)

Vigo, Joannes de, *The most excellent workes of chirurgerye*, tr. Bartholomew Traheron (RSTC 24720: 1543)
Whitford, Richard, *Here foloweth dyuers holy instrucyons and teachynges very necessarye for the helth of mannes soule* (RSTC 25420: c. 1541)
Wilkins, David (ed.), *Concilia Magnae Brittaniae et Hiberniae*, vol. III (1737)
Wriothesley, Charles, *A Chronicle of England during the Reigns of the Tudors*, ed. William D. Hamilton, vol. I, Camden Society new series 11 (1875)
Wyatt, Sir Thomas, *The Poems of Sir Thomas Wiat*, ed. A. K. Foxwell, 2 vols. (1913)
Wyclif, John (a pseudonym), *Wycklyffes wycket: whyche he made in Kyng Rycards dayes the second* (RSTC 25590: London?, 1546)
Zwingli, Huldrych, *The Rekening and declaracion of the faith and beleif of Huldrik Zwingly, bisshoppe of Zijryk*, tr. John Bale (RSTC 26138: Antwerp, 1543)

SECONDARY SOURCES

Adair, E. R., 'William Thomas: a forgotten clerk of the Privy Council', in *Tudor Studies*, ed. R. W. Seton-Watson (1924)
Alexander, Gina, 'The life and career of Edmund Bonner, bishop of London, until his deprivation in 1549' (PhD thesis, London, 1960)
  'Bonner and the Marian persecutions', in *The English Reformation Revised*, ed. Christopher Haigh (Cambridge, 1987)
Archer, Ian, 'The burden of taxation in sixteenth-century London', *HJ* 44 (2001), 599–627
Aston, Margaret, 'Lollardy and the Reformation', *History* 49 (1964), 149–70
  Lollards and Reformers: Images and Literacy in Late Medieval Religion (1984)
  England's Iconoclasts, vol. I (Oxford, 1988)
Bailey, Derrick Sherwin, 'Robert Wisdom under persecution 1541–43', *JEH* 2 (1951), 180–9
  Thomas Becon and the Reformation of the Church in England (Edinburgh, 1952)
  'Thomas Becon: some additional biographical notes', *Notes and Queries* 227 (1982), 402–4
Batley, J. Y., *On a Reformer's Latin Bible: Being an Essay on the Adversaria in the Vulgate of Thomas Bilney* (Cambridge, 1940)
Bauckham, Richard, *Tudor Apocalypse: Sixteenth Century Apocalypticism, Millenarianism and the English Reformation* (Oxford, 1978)
Bindoff, S. T. (ed.), *The House of Commons 1509–58*, 3 vols. (History of Parliament Trust, 1982)
Blackburn, Ruth H., *Biblical Drama under the Tudors* (The Hague, 1971)
Bowker, Margaret, *The Henrician Reformation: The Diocese of Lincoln under John Longland 1521–47* (Cambridge, 1981)
Bradshaw, Christopher, 'David or Josiah? Old Testament kings as exemplars in Edwardian religious polemic', in *Protestant History and Identity in Sixteenth-Century Europe*, ed. Bruce Gordon, vol. II (1996)
Brigden, Susan, 'Popular disturbance and the fall of Thomas Cromwell and the reformers, 1539–40', *HJ* 24 (1981), 257–78
  'Youth and the English Reformation', *Past and Present* 95 (1982), 37–67
  London and the Reformation (Oxford, 1989)

'Henry Howard, earl of Surrey, and the "Conjured League"', HJ 37 (1994), 507–37
'"The shadow that you know": Sir Thomas Wyatt and Sir Francis Bryan at court and in embassy', HJ 39 (1996), 1–31
Brigden, Susan, and Nigel Wilson, 'New learning and broken friendship', *English Historical Review* 112 (1997), 396–411
Britnell, Jennifer, 'John Gough and the "Traite de la difference des schismes et des conciles" of Jean Lemaire de Belges', *JEH* 46 (1995), 62–74
Brown, Andrew J., *Robert Ferrar: Yorkshire Monk, Reformation Bishop and Martyr in Wales (c. 1500–1555)* (1997)
Burne, R. V. H., 'The founding of Chester Cathedral', *Journal of the Chester and North Wales Archaeological and Historic Society* ns 37 (1948), 37–68
Butterworth, Charles C., *The English Primers (1529–1545): Their Publication and Connection with the English Bible and the Reformation in England* (Philadelphia, 1953)
Butterworth, Charles C., and Allan G. Chester, *George Joye 1495?–1553: A Chapter in the History of the English Bible and the English Reformation* (Philadelphia, 1962)
Byford, Mark, 'The price of Protestantism: assessing the impact of religious change on Elizabethan Essex' (DPhil thesis, Oxford, 1989)
Cameron, Euan, *The Reformation of the Heretics: The Waldenses of the Alps, 1480–1580* (Oxford, 1984)
'Medieval heretics as Protestant martyrs', *Martyrs and Martyrologies*, ed. Diana Wood, *Studies in Church History* 30 (Oxford, 1993), 185–207
Carleton, Kenneth, *Bishops and Reform in the English Church 1520–1559* (Woodbridge, Suffolk, 2001)
Carlson, Eric Josef, 'Clerical marriage and the English Reformation', *Journal of British Studies* 31 (1992), 1–31
'The marriage of William Turner', *Historical Research* 65 (1992), 336–9
Carter, Patrick, 'The records of the Court of First Fruits and Tenths', *Archives* 21 (1994), 57–66
Chibi, Andrew A., 'The social and regional origins of the Henrician episcopacy', *Sixteenth Century Journal* 29 (1998), 955–73
Clark, Peter, *English Provincial Society from the Reformation to the Revolution: Religion, Politics and Society in Kent 1500–1640* (Hassocks, Surrey, 1977)
Clebsch, William A., *England's Earliest Protestants 1520–1535* (New Haven and London, 1964)
Collinson, Patrick, *Godly People: Essays on English Protestantism and Puritanism* (1983)
'England', in *The Reformation in National Context*, ed. Bob Scribner, Roy Porter and Mikuláš Teich (Cambridge, 1994)
'Comment on Eamon Duffy's Neale Lecture and the Colloquium', in *England's Long Reformation 1500–1800*, ed. Nicholas Tyacke (1998)
Copeman, W. S. C., *Doctors and Disease in Tudor Times* (1960)
Coulton, Barbara, 'The establishment of Protestantism in a provincial town: a study of Shrewsbury in the sixteenth century', *Sixteenth Century Journal* 27 (1996), 307–35
Craig, John, *Reformation, Politics and Polemics: The Growth of Protestantism in East Anglian Market Towns, 1500–1610* (Aldershot, Hants., 2001)
Craig, John, and Caroline Litzenberger, 'Wills as religious propaganda: the testament of William Tracy', *JEH* 44 (1993), 415–31

Crawford, Patricia, *Women and Religion in England 1500–1720* (1993)
Davies, Catharine, *A Religion of the Word: The Defence of the Reformation in the Reign of Edward VI* (Manchester, 2002)
Davis, John F., 'Joan of Kent, Lollardy and the English Reformation', *JEH* 23 (1982), 225–33
  'Lollardy and the Reformation in England', *Archiv für Reformationsgeschichte* 73 (1982), 217–37
Dawson, Jane, 'The foundation of Christ Church, Oxford and Trinity College, Cambridge in 1546', *Bulletin of the Institute of Historical Research* 57 (1984), 208–15
Devereux, E. J., 'Empty tuns and unfruitful grafts: Richard Grafton's historical publications', *Sixteenth Century Journal* 21 (1990), 33–56
Dewar, Mary, *Sir Thomas Smith: A Tudor Intellectual in Office* (1964)
Dickens, A. G., *Robert Holgate, Archbishop of York and President of the King's Council in the North* (1955)
  Lollards and Protestants in the Diocese of York 1509–58 (Oxford, 1959)
  The English Reformation (1964)
  Late Monasticism and the Reformation (1994)
Dictionary of National Biography
Disley, Emma, 'Degrees of glory: Protestant doctrine and the concept of rewards hereafter', *Journal of Theological Studies* ns 42 (1991), 77–105
Dormer, Ernest W., *Gray of Reading: Sixteenth-Century Controversialist and Ballad-Writer* (Reading, 1923)
Dowling, Maria, 'The Gospel and the court: Reformation under Henry VIII', in *Protestantism and the National Church in Sixteenth-Century England*, ed. Peter Lake and Maria Dowling (1987)
Duff, E. Gordon, *A Century of the English Book Trade* (1905)
Duffy, Eamon, *The Stripping of the Altars* (New Haven and London, 1992)
Duke, Alastair, *Reformation and Revolt in the Low Countries* (1990)
Duncan, G. D., 'The heads of houses and religious change in Tudor Oxford 1547–58', *Oxoniensia* 45 (1980), 226–34
Dunnan, D. S., 'A note on John Gough's *The dore of holy scripture*', *Notes and Queries* 234 (1989), 309–10
Durston, C. G., '"Wild as Colts Untamed"; radicalism in the Newbury area during the early modern period', *Southern History* 6 (1984), 36–52
Edwards, Arthur John, 'The sede vacante administration of Archbishop Thomas Cranmer, 1533–53' (MPhil thesis, London, 1968)
Eire, Carlos M., 'Prelude to sedition? Calvin's attack on Nicodemism and religious compromise', *Archiv für Reformationsgeschichte* 76 (1985), 120–45
Eisenstein, Elizabeth L., *The Printing Press as an Agent of Change*, 2 vols. (Cambridge, 1979)
Elton, G. R., *The Tudor Revolution in Government* (Cambridge, 1953)
  Policy and Police: The Enforcement of the Reformation in the Age of Thomas Cromwell (Cambridge, 1972)
  'Tudor government: the points of contact. III: the court', *Transactions of the Royal Historical Society*, series v. 26 (1976), 211–28
  Reform and Reformation (1977)
  'Reform and the "commonwealth-men" of Edward VI's reign', in *The English Commonwealth*, ed. P. Clark, A. Smith and N. Tyacke (Leicester, 1979)
Emden, A. B., *A Biographical Register of the University of Oxford A.D. 1501 to 1540* (Oxford, 1974)

Evans, M. J. Crossley, 'A portrait of a Tudor usurer: the life of Alderman Sir John Gresham (c. 1496–1556) and the foundation of his grammar school', *Norfolk Archaeology* 41 (1993), 410–26

Fairfield, Leslie P., 'John Bale and Protestant hagiography in England', *JEH* 24 (1973), 145–60

John Bale, Mythmaker for the English Reformation (West Lafayette, IN, 1976)

Fehrenbach, R. J., and Elisabeth Leedham-Green, *Private Libraries in Renaissance England: A Collection and Catalogue of Tudor and Early Stuart Book-Lists*, vol. II (Binghamton, NY, 1993)

Fines, John, *A Biographical Register of Early English Protestants and Others Opposed to the Roman Catholic Church 1525–58* (part I: Sutton Courtenay Press, 1985; part II: unpublished)

Firth, Katharine R., *The Apocalyptic Tradition in Reformation Britain 1530–1645* (Oxford, 1979)

Fisher, R. M., 'The Reformation of clergy at the Inns of Court 1530–1580', *Sixteenth Century Journal* 12 (1981), 69–91

'The Reformation in microcosm? Benchers at the Inns of Court, 1530–1580', *Parergon* ns 6 (1988), 33–62

Fox, Alastair, *Politics and Literature in the Reigns of Henry VII and Henry VIII* (Oxford, 1989)

Fox, Alastair and John Guy, *Reassessing the Henrician Age: Humanism, Politics and Reform 1500–1550* (1986)

Garrett, Christina Hallowell, *The Marian Exiles: A Study in the Origins of Elizabethan Puritanism* (Cambridge, 1938)

Gordon, Bruce, 'Malevolent ghosts and ministering angels: apparitions and pastoral care in the Swiss Reformation', in *The Place of the Dead*, ed. Bruce Gordon and Peter Marshall (Cambridge, 2000)

Gordon, Bruce (ed.), *Protestant History and Identity in Sixteenth-Century Europe*, 2 vols. (Aldershot, Hants., 1996)

Green, Ian, *Print and Protestantism in Early Modern England* (Oxford, 2000)

Greengrass, Mark, *The French Reformation* (Oxford, 1987)

Gregory, Brad S., *Salvation at Stake: Christian Martyrdom in Early Modern Europe* (Cambridge, MA, 1999)

Grell, Ole Peter, *Calvinist Exiles in Elizabethan and Stuart England* (Aldershot, Hants., 1996)

Gunn, S. J., *Charles Brandon, Duke of Suffolk c. 1484–1545* (Oxford, 1988)

Haigh, Christopher, 'The Reformation in Lancashire to 1558' (PhD thesis, Manchester, 1969)

Reformation and Resistance in Tudor Lancashire (Cambridge, 1975)

English Reformations (Oxford, 1993)

1546, Before and After: The Making of Christ Church (Oxford, 1996)

(ed.), *The English Reformation Revised* (Cambridge, 1987)

Hall, Basil, 'The early rise and gradual decline of English Lutheranism (1520–1660)', *Reform and Reformation: England and the Continent c. 1500–1750*, ed. Derek Baker, *Studies in Church History: Subsidia* 2 (1979), 103–31

Hamann, Edmund G., 'The clarification of some obscurities surrounding the imprisonment of Richard Grafton in 1541 and in 1543', *Papers of the Bibliographical Society of America* 52 (1958), 262–82

Happé, Peter, *John Bale* (New York, 1996)

Head, David M., *The Ebbs and Flows of Fortune: The Life of Thomas Howard, Third Duke of Norfolk* (Athens, GA, 1995)

Heal, Felicity, 'The parish clergy and the Reformation in the diocese of Ely', *Proceedings of the Cambridge Antiquarian Society* 66 (1977), 141–63
  Of Prelates and Princes: A Study of the Economic and Social Position of the Tudor Episcopate (Cambridge, 1980)
Heal, Felicity, and Rosemary O'Day (eds.), *Church and Society in England: Henry VIII to James I* (1977)
Heijting, Willem, 'Early Reformation literature from the printing shop of Mattheus Crom and Steven Mierdmans', *Nederlands archief voor kerkgeschiedenis* 74 (1994), 143–61
Herford, Charles H., *Studies in the Literary Relations of England and Germany in the Sixteenth Century* (Cambridge, 1886)
Hildebrandt, Esther F. M., 'A Study of the English Protestant Exiles in Northern Switzerland and Strasbourg 1539–47, and their Role in the English Reformation' (PhD thesis, University of Durham, 1982)
Hope, Andrew, 'Lollardy: the stone the builders rejected?', in *Protestantism and the National Church in Sixteenth-Century England*, ed. Peter Lake and Maria Dowling (1987)
  'The lady and the bailiff: Lollardy among the gentry in Yorkist and early Tudor England', in *Lollardy and the Gentry in the Later Middle Ages*, ed. Margaret Aston and Colin Richmond (Stroud and New York, 1997)
Horst, Irvin Buckwalter, *The Radical Brethren: Anabaptism and the English Reformation to 1558* (The Hague, 1972)
Houlbrooke, Ralph, 'Persecution of heresy and Protestantism in the diocese of Norwich under Henry VIII', *Norfolk Archaeology* 35 (1972), 308–26
  Church Courts and People during the English Reformation (Oxford, 1979)
  'Henry VIII's wills: a comment', *HJ* 37 (1994), 891–9
Hoyle, R. W., 'Petitioning as popular politics in early sixteenth-century England', *Historical Research* 75 (2002), 365–89
Hudson, Anne, *The Premature Reformation* (Oxford, 1988)
  'The mouse in the pyx: popular heresy and the Eucharist', *Trivium* 26 (1991), 40–53
Hudson, Winthrop S., *The Cambridge Connection and the Elizabethan Settlement of 1559* (Durham, NC, 1980)
Hutton, Ronald, 'The local impact of the Tudor Reformations', in *The English Reformation Revised*, ed. Christopher Haigh (Cambridge, 1987)
Ives, Eric W., *Faction in Tudor England* (Historical Association: Appreciations in History 6, 1979)
  'Henry VIII's will: a forensic conundrum', *HJ* 35 (1992), 779–804
  'Henry VIII's will: the protectorate provisions of 1546–47', *HJ* 37 (1994), 901–14
  'Anne Boleyn and the early Reformation in England: the contemporary evidence', *HJ* 37 (1994), 389–400
Jackson, W. A., J. F. Ferguson, and K. F. Pantzer, *A Short-Title Catalogue of Books Printed . . . 1475–1640. Revised* (1986)
James, Susan E., *Kateryn Parr: The Making of a Queen* (Aldershot, Hants., 1999)
Jones, J. Gwynfor, *Wales and the Tudor State: Government, Religious Change and the Social Order, 1534–1603* (Cardiff, 1989)
Jones, Whitney R. D., *William Turner: Tudor Naturalist, Physician and Divine* (1988)
Keeling, Susan M., 'The Reformation in the Anglo-Scottish border counties', *Northern History* 15 (1979), 24–42

Kendall, R. D., *The Drama of Dissent: The Radical Poetics of Nonconformity, 1380–1590* (Chapel Hill, NC and London, 1986)
King, John N., *English Reformation Literature: The Tudor Origins of the Protestant Tradition* (Princeton, 1982)
Kingdon, R. M., *Geneva and the Coming of the Wars of Religion in France, 1555–1563* (Geneva, 1956)
Kitch, M. J., 'The Reformation in Sussex', in *Studies in Sussex Church History*, ed. Kitch (1981)
Knappen, M. M., *Tudor Puritanism: A Chapter in the History of Idealism* (Chicago and London, 1939)
Kreider, Alan, *English Chantries: The Road to Dissolution* (Cambridge, MA, and London, 1979)
Lake, Peter and Maria Dowling (eds.), *Protestantism and the National Church in Sixteenth-Century England* (1987)
Le Neve, John, revised Joyce M. Horn et al., *Fasti Ecclesiæ Anglicanæ 1541–1857*, 8 vols. (1969–96)
Leedham-Green, Elisabeth, *Books in Cambridge Inventories*, 2 vols. (Cambridge, 1986)
  A Concise History of the University of Cambridge (Cambridge, 1996)
Lehmberg, Stanford E., *The Later Parliaments of Henry VIII 1536–1547* (Cambridge, 1977)
Lewis, C. S., *English Literature in the Sixteenth Century Excluding Drama* (Oxford, 1954)
Litzenberger, Caroline, *The English Reformation and the Laity: Gloucestershire 1540–1580* (Cambridge, 1997)
Logan, F. Donald, 'The origins of the so-called Regius Professorships: an aspect of the renaissance in Oxford and Cambridge', *Renaissance and Renewal in Christian History*, ed. Derek Baker, *Studies in Church History* 14 (Oxford, 1977), 271–8
Lusardi, James P., 'The career of Robert Barnes', in *The Complete Works of St Thomas More*, vol. VIII part III (Yale, 1973), 1365–1415
McClendon, Muriel, *The Quiet Reformation: Magistrates and the Emergence of Protestantism in Tudor Norwich* (Stanford, 1999)
McConica, James K., *English Humanists and Reformation Politics* (Oxford, 1965)
MacCulloch, Diarmaid, *Suffolk and the Tudors: Politics and Religion in an English County 1500–1600* (Oxford, 1986)
  'Two dons in politics: Thomas Cranmer and Stephen Gardiner, 1503–1533', *HJ* 37 (1994), 1–22
  'Henry VIII and the reform of the Church', in *The Reign of Henry VIII: Politics, Policy and Piety*, ed. MacCulloch (Basingstoke, 1995)
  Thomas Cranmer: A Life (New Haven and London, 1996)
  Tudor Church Militant (1999)
McDiarmid, John F., 'John Cheke's preface to "De Superstitione"', *JEH* 48 (1997), 100–20
McEntegart, Rory, *Henry VIII, the League of Schmalkalden and the English Reformation* (Woodbridge, Suffolk, 2002)
McSheffrey, Shannon, *Gender and Heresy: Women and Men in Lollard Communities, 1420–1530* (Philadelphia, 1995)
Marcombe, David (ed.), *The Last Principality: Politics, Religion and Society in the Bishopric of Durham, 1494–1660* (Nottingham, 1987)

Marnef, Guido, *Antwerp in the Age of Reformation*, tr. J. C. Grayson (Baltimore and London, 1996)
Marsh, Christopher, *Popular Religion in Sixteenth-Century England* (Basingstoke, Hants., 1998)
Marshall, Peter, 'Papist as heretic: the burning of John Forest, 1538', *HJ* 41 (1998), 351–74
  'Evangelical conversion in the reign of Henry VIII', in *The Beginnings of English Protestantism*, ed. Peter Marshall and Alec Ryrie (Cambridge, 2002)
  Reformation England 1480–1642 (2003)
Marshall, Peter, and Alec Ryrie (eds.), *The Beginnings of English Protestantism* (Cambridge, 2002)
Masters, Robert, *The History of the College of Corpus Christi . . . in the University of Cambridge* (Cambridge, 1753)
Monter, William, 'Heresy executions in Reformation Europe, 1520–65', in *Tolerance and Intolerance in the European Reformation*, ed. Ole Peter Grell and Bob Scribner (Cambridge, 1996)
Mozley, J. F., *Coverdale and his Bibles* (1953)
Muir, Kenneth, *Life and Letters of Sir Thomas Wyatt* (Liverpool, 1963)
Muller, James Arthur, *Stephen Gardiner and the Tudor Reaction* (1926)
Mullinger, James Bass, *The University of Cambridge from the Royal Injunctions of 1535 to the Accession of Charles the First* (Cambridge, 1884)
Neville-Singleton, Pamela, 'Press, politics and religion', in *The Cambridge History of the Book in Britain, Vol. III: 1400–1557*, ed. Lotte Hellinga and J. B. Trapp (Cambridge, 1999)
Nichols, Ann Eljenholm, 'Books-for-laymen: the demise of a commonplace', *Church History* 56 (1987), 457–73
Oxley, James E., *The Reformation in Essex to the Death of Mary* (Manchester, 1965)
Parish, Helen, *Clerical Marriage and the English Reformation: Precedent, Policy and Practice* (Aldershot, Hants., 2000)
Patterson, Annabel, *Censorship and Interpretation: The Conditions of Writing and Reading in Early Modern England* (Madison, WI, 1984)
Peters, Robert, 'Who compiled the sixteenth-century patristic handbook Unio Dissidentium?', G. J. Cuming (ed.), *Studies in Church History* 2 (1965), 237–50
Pettegree, Andrew, *Foreign Protestant Communities in Sixteenth-Century London* (Oxford, 1986)
  Marian Protestantism: Six Studies (Aldershot, Hants., 1996)
Phillimore, Robert, *The Ecclesiastical Law of the Church of England*, 3 vols. (1873)
Phillips, John, *The Reformation of the Images: Destruction of Art in England 1535–1660* (Berkeley and Los Angeles, 1973)
Pineas, Rainer, 'John Bale's nondramatic works of religious controversy', *Studies in the Renaissance* 9 (1962), 218–33
  'Polemical technique in the works of Thomas Becon', *Moreana* 5 (1968), 49–55
  'George Joye's *Exposicion of Daniel*', *Renaissance Quarterly* 28 (1975), 332–42
Plant, Marjorie, *The English Book Trade: An Economic History of the Making and Sale of Books* (1939)
Plumb, Derek, 'The social and economic status of the later Lollards', in *The World of Rural Dissenters*, ed. Margaret Spufford (Cambridge, 1995)
Pogson, Rex, 'God's law and man's: Stephen Gardiner and the problem of loyalty', in *Law and Government under the Tudors*, ed. Claire Cross, David Loades and J. J. Scarisbrick (Cambridge, 1988)

Porter, H. C., *Reformation and Reaction in Tudor Cambridge* (Cambridge, 1958)
Powell, K. G., 'The beginnings of Protestantism in Gloucestershire', *Bristol and Gloucestershire Archaeological Society (Transactions)* 90 (1971), 141–57
Redworth, Glyn, 'A study in the formulation of policy: the genesis and evolution of the Act of Six Articles', *JEH* 37 (1986), 42–67
  In Defence of the Church Catholic: The Life of Stephen Gardiner (Oxford, 1990)
Rex, Richard, *The Theology of John Fisher* (Cambridge, 1991)
  'The new learning', *JEH* 44 (1993), 26–44
  Henry VIII and the English Reformation (Basingstoke, 1993)
  'The crisis of obedience: God's Word and Henry's Reformation', *HJ* 39 (1996), 863–94
  'The role of English humanists in the Reformation up to 1559', in *The Education of a Christian Society: Humanism and the Reformation in Britain and the Netherlands*, ed. N. Scott Amos, Andrew Pettegree and Henk van Nierop (Aldershot, Hants., 1999)
  'The early impact of Reformation theology at Cambridge University, 1521–1547', *Reformation and Renaissance Review* 2 (1999), 38–71
  The Lollards (Basingstoke, 2002)
Rex, Richard and C. D. C. Armstrong, 'Henry VIII's ecclesiastical and collegiate foundations', *Historical Research* 75 (2002), 390–407
Ridley, Jasper, *Nicholas Ridley* (1957)
  Thomas Cranmer (Oxford, 1962)
Riordan, Michael, 'Gospellers at court during the conservative reaction, 1539–47' (MA dissertation, St Andrews, 1998)
Riordan, Michael, and Alec Ryrie, 'Stephen Gardiner and the making of a Protestant villain', *Sixteenth Century Journal* 35 (forthcoming)
Russell, Henry G., 'Lollard opposition to oaths by creatures', *The American Historical Review* 51 (1946), 668–84
Ryan, Laurence V., *Roger Ascham* (Stanford, 1963)
Ryrie, Alec, 'The problem of legitimacy and precedent in English Protestantism, 1539–47', in *Protestant History and Identity in Sixteenth-Century Europe*, ed. Bruce Gordon, vol. I (Aldershot, Hants., 1996)
  'The unsteady beginnings of English Protestant martyrology', in *John Foxe: An Historical Perspective*, ed. David Loades (Aldershot, Hants., 1999)
  'English evangelical reformers in the last years of Henry VIII' (D.Phil. thesis, Oxford 2000)
  'The strange death of Lutheran England', *JEH* 53 (2002), 64–92
  'Counting sheep, counting shepherds: the problem of numerical allegiance in the English Reformation', in *The Beginnings of English Protestantism*, ed. Peter Marshall and Alec Ryrie (Cambridge, 2002)
  'Divine kingship and royal theology in Henry VIII's Reformation', *Reformation* 7 (2002), 49–77
Sander, F., 'John Bird, D.D., Bishop of Chester 1541–54', *Journal of the Chester and North Wales Archaeological and Historic Society* ns 13 (1907), 110–26
Scarisbrick, J. J., *Henry VIII* (1968)
  The Reformation and the English People (Oxford, 1984)
Sessions, W. A., *Henry Howard, the Poet Earl of Surrey: A Life* (Oxford, 1999)
Shagan, Ethan, 'Protector Somerset and the 1549 rebellions: new sources and new perspectives', *English Historical Review* 114 (1999), 34–63
  Popular Politics and the English Reformation (Cambridge, 2002)

Shephard, Robert, 'Court factions in early modern England', *Journal of Modern History* 64 (1992), 721–45
Sheppard, Elaine M., 'The Reformation and the citizens of Norwich', *Norfolk Archaeology* 38 (1983), 44–58
Shirley, T. F., *Thomas Thirlby: Tudor Bishop* (1964)
Skeeters, Martha C., *Community and Clergy: Bristol and the Reformation c. 1530–c. 1570* (Oxford, 1993)
Slavin, Arthur Joseph, *Politics and Profit: A Study of Sir Ralph Sadler 1507–47* (Cambridge, 1966)
  'The Tudor revolution and the devil's art: Bishop Bonner's printed forms', in *Tudor Rule and Revolution*, ed. Delloyd J. Guth and John W. McKenna (Cambridge, 1982)
Smith, Lacey Baldwin, *Tudor Prelates and Politics, 1536–1558* (Princeton, 1953)
  'Henry VIII and the Protestant triumph', *American Historical Review* 71 (1966), 1237–64
  'Englishmen at Wittenberg in the sixteenth century', *English Historical Review* 36 (1921), 422–33
Smyth, C. H., *Cranmer and the Reformation under Edward VI* (Cambridge, 1926)
Somerville, Johann P., 'The "new art of lying": equivocation, mental reservation and casuistry', in *Conscience and Casuistry in Early Modern Europe*, ed. Edmund Leites (Cambridge, 1988)
Spufford, Margaret, *Contrasting Communities: English Villagers in the Sixteenth and Seventeenth Centuries* (Cambridge, 1974)
Starkey, David, 'Intimacy and innovation: the rise of the Privy Chamber, 1485–1547', in *The English Court: From the Wars of the Roses to the Civil War*, ed. David Starkey (1987)
Stone, Darwell, *A History of the Doctrine of the Holy Eucharist*, 2 vols. (1909)
Strype, John, *The Life of the Learned Sir Thomas Smith* (Oxford, 1820)
  Ecclesiastical Memorials, Relating Chiefly to Religion and the Reformation of it, 3 vols. (Oxford, 1822)
Swensen, Patricia Cole, 'Noble hunters of the Romish fox: religious reform at the Tudor court, 1543–1564' (PhD thesis, University of California at Berkeley, 1981)
Taylor, Larissa, *Soldiers of Christ: Preaching in Late Medieval and Reformation France* (Oxford, 1992)
Thompson, Stephen, 'The pastoral work of the English and Welsh bishops, 1500–1558' (DPhil thesis, Oxford, 1984)
Thomson, John A. F., *The Later Lollards 1414–1520* (Oxford, 1965)
Took, Patricia M., 'Government and the printing trade, 1540–1560' (PhD thesis, London, 1979)
Trueman, Carl R., *Luther's Legacy: Salvation and English Reformers, 1525–1556* (Oxford, 1994)
Tudor Craig, Pamela, 'Henry VIII and King David', in *Early Tudor England*, ed. Daniel Williams (Woodbridge, Suffolk, 1989)
Tyacke, Nicholas (ed.), *England's Long Reformation 1500–1800* (1998)
Wabuda, Susan, 'The provision of preaching during the early English Reformation: with special reference to itineration, c. 1530 to 1547' (PhD thesis, Cambridge, 1991)
  'Equivocation and recantation during the English Reformation: the "subtle shadows" of Dr. Edward Crome', *JEH* 44 (1993), 224–42

'The woman with the rock: the controversy on women and Bible reading', in *Belief and Practice in Reformation England*, ed. Susan Wabuda and Caroline Litzenberger (Aldershot, Hants., 1998)

Walker, Greg, 'Saint or schemer? The 1527 heresy trial of Thomas Bilney', *JEH* 40 (1989), 219–38

Persuasive Fictions: Faction, Faith and Popular Culture in the Reign of Henry VIII (Aldershot, Hants., 1996)

Walsham, Alexandra, *Providence in Early Modern England* (Oxford, 1999)

Wansborough, Henry, and Anthony Marett-Crosby (eds.), *Benedictines in Oxford* (1997)

Ward, Jennifer C., 'The Reformation in Colchester, 1528–1558', *Essex Archaeology and History* 3rd series, 15 (1983), 84–95

Watt, Tessa, *Cheap Print and Popular Piety* (Cambridge, 1991)

Wawn, Andrew, 'The genesis of *The Plowman's Tale*', *Yearbook of English Studies* 2 (1972), 21–40

'Chaucer, *The Plowman's Tale* and Reformation propaganda', *Bulletin of the John Rylands Library* 56 (1973), 174–92

White, Paul Whitfield, *Theatre and Reformation: Protestantism, Patronage and Playing in Tudor England* (Cambridge, 1993)

Whiting, Robert, 'Abominable idols: images and image-breaking under Henry VIII', *JEH* 33 (1982), 30–47

The Blind Devotion of the People: Popular Devotion and the English Reformation (Cambridge, 1989)

Williams, Glanmor, *The Welsh Church from Conquest to Reformation* (Cardiff, 1962)

Welsh Reformation Essays (Cardiff, 1967)

Recovery, Reform and Reorientation: Wales c. 1415–1642 (Oxford, 1987)

The Welsh and their Religion (Cardiff, 1991)

Wales and the Reformation (Cardiff, 1997)

Wilson, F. P., *The English Drama 1485–1585* (Oxford, 1969)

Winchester, Barbara, *Tudor Family Portrait* (1955)

Wooding, Lucy, *Rethinking Catholicism in Reformation England* (Oxford, 2000)

Yost, John K., 'German Protestant humanism and the early English Reformation: Richard Taverner and official translation', *Bibliothèque d'Humanisme et Renaissance* 32 (1970), 613–25

Zagorin, Peres, *Ways of Lying: Dissimulation, Persecution and Conformity in Early Modern Europe* (Cambridge, MA, 1990)

INDEX

Aarau 268
Abel, John 266
Abergwili 246
Act for the Advancement of True Religion (1543) 15, 18
　contents of 46, 47, 128
　enforcement of 49–50
　reactions to 103, 252–4
Act of Six Articles (1539) 15, 16, 26–39, 46, 143, 150
　ambiguities of 33–4
　amendments to in parliament 31–2, 36
　commissions issued under the Act 40, 42, 218, 263
　contents of 27–8
　diplomatic background to 29–31
　evangelical responses to 19–21, 38, 254
　opposition to 36–7
　penal code of 27
　penal code of relaxed 18, 51, 218
　purposes of 35–6, 38–9
adiaphora 131; *see* Nicodemism, obedience
Adisham, Kent 226
Adrian, Friar 102
adultery 151
Ainsworth, Oliver 172
Alder, Jane 266, 269
Aldrich, Robert, bishop of Carlisle 214
Alesius, Alexander 93, 254, 266
Allen, Edmund 96–7, 203, 266
Anabaptism, Anabaptists 38, 105, 120, 140, 227, 236
　on oaths 76
　prohibition of 15, 34
Anne of Cleves 16
Antichrist 2, 109
anticlericalism 141, 228, 234
antinomianism *see under* justification

Antwerp 95
　English exiles in 110, 266, 267, 268
　printing in 108, 110, 115, 269
apocalypticism 108–10, 125–6, 149, 209
Aquinas, Thomas 74
Aretino, Pietro 207
Arran, earl of *see* Hamilton, James
Arthur, Thomas 88
Arundel, Thomas 208
Ascham, Roger 197
Ashford, Kent 140
Askew, Anne 5, 26, 50, 54–6, 211, 264
　arrest and interrogations 25
　beliefs 204, 250
　Examinations of 100–1
　execution 82, 202
　recantation 76, 133, 218, 236
　torture 5, 82–3
assurance 132, 190–1
Astall, Richard 243
Athanasius 226
Audley, Thomas, lord chancellor 30, 40, 99, 160, 199
Augmentations, Court of 150, 167
Augsburg 267
Augsburg Confession 105, 133, 172
Augustine of Hippo 74, 75
auricular confession *see* penance
Ayre, John 138
Ayrshire 234

Bainham, James 73
Bainton, Edward 99, 199
Baker, John 55
Baker, William 229
Bale, Dorothy 100, 266
Bale, John 96–7, 107
　apocalyptic views 109–10, 180, 235
　as bibliographer and historian 59, 97, 105, 173, 235

293

Bale, John (*cont.*)
  as martyrologist 178
  exile 95, 100–3, 110, 266
  mentioned 38, 96, 211
  on auricular confession 32
  on the 'commonwealth' 77, 150, 153, 160, 163
  on the English Bible 253
  on moderation 126, 132–3, 217
  on recantation 69, 75, 87–8
  on the Six Articles 20
  political comment by 48, 62, 67, 69, 221
  publications and writings of 97, 105, 107, 189
    Anne Askew's *Examinations* 100–1
    Christen exhortation vnto customable swearers 77, 104
    Disclosynge or openynge of the Manne of synne, A 104, 106, 107
    Epistle exhortatorye of an Englyshe Christiane 104, 107, 121
    Image of both churches 105, 107, 180, 235
    plays 62, 128, 179–80
  reputation 105, 107
  theological views 97, 98, 123, 135
  violence of language 122, 192
Bale, Philip 242
ballads 113–14
Bangor, bishop of *see* Bird, John; Bulkeley, Arthur; Salcot, John
Bankes, Richard 114, 119
Banwell, Alice 228
baptism 229
Barlow, John 208, 245, 246
Barlow, William, bishop of St David's 44, 128, 161, 171, 199, 213
  as patron of reformers 176, 245–7
  theological views of 29, 31
Barnes, Robert 215, 240
  career of 21, 40, 170, 213, 233
  execution of 21, 25, 85, 262
  on royal authority 71–2
  Protestation of 95, 239
  recantation 88
  views of 39, 139, 147, 163, 191, 254
Basel 255, 268, 269
Basille, Theodore 115, 119; *see* Becon, Thomas
Bath and Wells, bishop of *see* Knight, William
Beaufort, Margaret 161
Becket, Thomas 73, 128
Becon, Thomas 115, 192, 204, 206, 221, 231, 240
  apocalyptic views 149
  arrest and recantation 47–8, 75–6, 117, 140, 191
  as conformist 120
  internal exile 111
  on auricular confession 32
  on ceremonies 130, 131
  on clerical marriage 131
  on conservatives 130
  on the 'commonwealth' 147, 148, 149, 150, 152, 153, 159–60
  on the English Bible 251–2
  on the Eucharist 131, 138, 140, 142
  on justification 134, 136, 137
  on oaths and swearing 76–7, 78, 149
  on prayer to saints 128, 129
  on proselytisation 123–4, 125
  on recantation 72, 75–6
  on the royal supremacy 66, 68
  publications of 104, 106, 115, 126, 133, 152, 172, 230, 251–2
Bedford, earl of *see* Russell, Francis
Belenian, Nicholas 23, 264
Bell, John, bishop of Worcester 86, 214, 223
Bellasis, Anthony 245
Benett, Robert 48
Benson, John and Joyce 227
Benson, William, abbot of Westminster 31
Berkeley, Gilbert 175
Berthelet, Thomas 45, 61, 116, 198
Best, John 177
Bette, Joan 263
Bible 28
  interpretations of 190–1
  Welsh translations of 246
Bible, English 44, 54, 172, 225, 233, 252
  Coverdale's Bible 234
  'Great Bible' 43, 44, 117, 133, 217
  importance of for evangelicals 118, 145, 221, 250–2
  official support for 15, 40, 42–3, 44
  restrictions on use of 15, 28–9, 44, 47, 49–50, 220–1, 252–4
  Tyndale's Bible 47, 50, 117, 233, 234
  Wycliffite Bible 105, 234, 235
Bickley, Thomas 175
Bilney, Thomas 74, 84, 88, 127, 158
Bird, John, bishop of Bangor and Chester 171, 214
bishops 213–22; *see also under individual bishops*
  episcopacy linked to conservatism 219–20
  episcopal appointments (1536–47) 214–15
  new bishoprics created (1540–2) 25, 43

Bishops' Book (1537) 45, 132, 173, 197, 228, 244
  revision of 31–2, 45
Blage, George 210–11, 212, 244, 253, 257
  arrested and reprieved (1546) 56, 201
Blage, John 114, 204, 244–5
  arrested for heresy (1540) 41
Bland, John 226, 227, 244
Blount, William 211
Bocher, Joan 236
Bois, Thomas 35
Boleyn, Anne 22, 199, 213
Bonham, William 244
Bonn 108, 269
Bonner, Edmund, bishop of Hereford and London 41, 45, 151, 206, 216–18, 220–1, 241
  and the English Bible 44, 101, 217, 220–1, 226, 251–2
  as persecutor of heresy 24–5, 54, 82, 104, 217–18, 255
  as religious moderate 25, 54, 83–4, 132, 214–15
  evangelicals' views of 122, 218
books and book trade 21, 229–30, 239
  censorship 18, 46–7, 54, 104–5, 117
  export of books 95, 101
  impact of the Six Articles on 27
  limits of censorship 51, 100, 117, 128
  underground trade 103–5, 107, 108, 114, 120, 230, 233, 244
Boughton, Thomas 80
Boulogne 99, 208
Bowker, Margaret 7
Braintree 233
Brandon, Charles, duke of Suffolk 99, 195, 206
Brandon, Katherine *see* Willoughby, Katherine
Brecon 161
Bremen 48, 94, 268, 269, 270
Bretton, Edward 49–50
Brinklow, Henry 87, 110, 111, 201, 239, 242
  on the 'commonwealth' 146–7, 149–50, 153, 155, 160, 163
  on the royal supremacy 63–4
  on the Six Articles 20
  publications of 110, 121, 152
Brinklow, Margery 201
Bristol 191
  bishop of *see* Bush, Paul
Broke, Elizabeth 206

Broke, George, Lord Cobham 200, 204, 206, 210
Broke, William 204
Browne, Anthony 269
Brunfels, Otto 74, 172
Bucer, Martin 72, 74, 93, 172, 215
  on the Six Articles 21, 37
Buckemer, Raynold 228
Bucler, Walter 100, 204, 205
Bugenhagen, Johannes 172
Bulkeley, Arthur 214
Bullinger, Heinrich 74, 77, 84, 97
  English contacts of 21, 72, 85, 99, 266, 267, 269
  publications of 105, 115, 126, 133, 148, 172
Bullyngham, Nicholas 175
Burcher, John 266
Bury St Edmunds 264
Bush, Paul, bishop of Bristol 214
Butler, John, archbishop's commissary in Calais 238, 245
Butler, John, correspondent of Heinrich Bullinger 21, 266
Butts, William 99, 195, 202
Byford, Mark 241

Calais 96, 99, 100, 200, 204, 263
  evangelicals in 40, 100, 238, 239, 241–2, 244, 251–2, 265
Callaway, William 242
Calvin, Jean xvi, 74, 84, 105, 172, 174
Calvinism *see* Reformed Protestantism
Cambridge University 102; *see also* universities
  colleges and halls of
    Buckingham College 160
    Christ's College 172, 179–82
    Corpus Christi College 166, 266
    Gonville Hall 216
    King's College 216
    King's Hall 166, 169
    Magdalene College 160
    Queens' College 166, 190
    St John's College 178
    Trinity College 166, 168
    Trinity Hall 179
  early evangelicalism in 170
  impact of the dissolution of the monasteries on 162
  strength of evangelicalism in 171–4, 178–87, 193, 249
  White Horse Inn 170
Cameron, Euan 81
Camper, John 263

Canterbury 25, 41
  archbishop of *see* Cranmer, Thomas
  Cathedral 171, 176, 226
  diocese of, evangelicals in 243–5
  evangelical conventicles in 238
  St Andrew 226
  St Mary Northgate 227, 243
Capito, Wolfgang 172
Capon, John *see* Salcot, John
Capper, Thomas 23, 263
Cardiff 23, 263
Cardmaker, John 141, 245
Carew, George 99–100, 202, 239
Carew, Peter 204
Carkke, William 242–3
Carlisle, bishop of *see* Aldrich, Robert
Cartwright, Nicholas 175
cathedrals 154; *see also under individual cities*
Catholicism *see also* conservatism
  medieval Catholicism 7
Cawarden, Thomas 202
celibacy 72, 111, 150, 226, 228, 255, 266
  and oaths and vows 76–8
  and the Six Articles 27, 28, 37–8
  evangelical ambiguity on 37–8, 131
censorship *see* books and book trade
Chamber, John, bishop of Peterborough 214
chantries 33
Chantries Act (1545) 51, 164–5
Charles V, Holy Roman Emperor xv, 46, 96, 106, 204, 206
Chaucer, Geoffrey 127
Chedsay, William 131, 151, 158–9, 189
Cheke, John 166, 183, 185, 197, 198, 216, 256
Chester, bishop of *see* Bird, John
Chichester, bishop of *see* Day, George; Sampson, Richard
Chilterns 24
Christology, heretical 225, 226, 227, 229, 236
Chrysostom, John 74, 116
church buildings 228, 233
Churden, Humphrey 135
Clarke, Roger 264
clerical celibacy *see* celibacy
Clewer, Berkshire 244
clothing 148
Cobbe, Stephen 117, 201, 204
Cobham, Lord *see* Broke, George
Cochlæus, Johannes 172
Cockes, William 171
Colchester 26, 233, 263, 264
Coldewell, Henry 242

Cole, Henry 103, 218
Colet, John 158
Collins, William 261
Collinson, Patrick 8–9, 13–14
Cologne 269
'commonwealth' ideas 60, 145–56, 159–64, 209, 253–4
communion *see* Eucharist
confession *see* penance
conformism 113–34, 144–5
conservatism, conservatives
  definitions xv
  moderation amongst 131–2
  on the 'commonwealth' 151
  on education 158
  publications of 250
Constantine, George 37, 68, 139, 154, 219, 245, 246
conventicles 105, 107, 169, 223–43
  activities of 237–43
  patronage of reformers 240–3
  preaching in 239–40
  use of evangelical books in 229–30, 239
conversion 157–8, 213
Convocation 36, 44, 45, 249
Copenhagen 268
Cotes, George 175
Coventry
  Lollards in 24, 237
  reformers in 26, 143, 224, 228–9, 237
  St Michael 228
Coventry and Lichfield, bishop of *see* Sampson, Richard
Coverdale, Miles 77, 96, 213, 267, 268
  later career 96–7
  on the royal supremacy 67
  on recantation 82
  publications of 103, 104, 105, 106, 123, 133, 148, 234
Cowbridge, William 177
Cox, Richard 169, 204
  on the 'commonwealth' 149, 154, 169
  religious views of 197, 205, 249, 255, 256
  university career of 168, 176
Coyte, John 50
Cranmer, Edmund 226
Cranmer, Thomas, archbishop of Canterbury 18, 21, 171, 213
  archiepiscopal role of 43, 235
  impact on religious policy 14, 43, 44, 45, 51–2, 203
  on the Eucharist 39, 139, 250, 256
  on justification 135, 136, 198
  on the royal supremacy 63

patronage and protection of reformers 197, 215, 243–5, 251–2, 266
plots against 48, 49, 194, 200, 224
religious views of 29, 31, 44, 45–6, 152, 219
Croft, Robert 174
Crome, Edward 119, 199, 203, 213, 215, 240, 242
  on 'private Masses' (1541) 34, 41–2, 51, 113
  on the sacrifice of the Mass (1546) 53, 142, 205, 218, 250, 255, 256, 264
  recants (1541) 82, 84
  recants (1546) 54, 72, 88, 200, 249, 256
Cromwell, Thomas, Lord Privy Seal, earl of Essex 1, 14, 16, 20, 61, 248
  and the royal supremacy 60–1
  as patron of evangelicals 119, 199–202, 213
  fall and execution of 15, 21, 40, 265
  legacy of 221–2, 256
  religious policy of 30, 139
Crowley, Robert 82, 122, 136, 144
  on the 'commonwealth' 147, 149, 150, 154, 253
  publications of 147

Dallison, Richard 102
Damplip, Adam 244, 262, 265
Daniel 65–6, 70
Danzig 94, 95, 268
Darrell, Elizabeth 206
Dawby, Thomas 226, 236, 251–2
Dawson, Jane 167
Day, George, bishop of Chichester 103, 214–15, 216, 218–19
Denmark 103, 267
Denny, Anthony 197, 201, 203, 210, 245
Denny, Joan 54, 118, 176
Dickens, A. G. 6, 7, 13–14
Disley, Emma 137
dissimulation *see under* recantation
Dixson, Nicholas 246
Dodman, John 267
Dotterweich, Martin 234
Downes, Richard 241
drama *see* plays
Dray, Christopher 245
Drum, Michael 176, 251–2
Dudley, John, Lord Lisle 100, 182
Duffy, Eamon 13–14
Duns Scotus 173, 174, 187
Durham, bishop of *see* Tunstall, Cuthbert
Dymocke, John 94, 200–1, 204

East Bergholt, Norfolk 49–50
Eck, Johannes 172–3, 174
economics, evangelical views of 149–50
Edgeworth, Roger 132, 191
Edmunds, John 183
education 148, 157–70
Edward VI 3, 6, 146, 248
  as prince 68, 109, 118, 197–9
Eglesfylde, Miles 172
Elizabeth I 17, 69, 220
Elton, G. R. 146
Ely, bishop of *see* Goodricke, Thomas
Emerson, John 177
Erasmus, Desiderius 116, 118, 173, 183, 187, 272
  Paraphrases 196
Erasmus, Sarcerius 133
Erley, John 22
Essex, earl of *see* Cromwell, Thomas; Parr, William
Eton College 196
Eton, Hugh 50, 245
Ettis, Alexander 241
Ettis, Margaret 240, 241
Ettis, William 240, 241–2, 245
Eucharist and Eucharistic theology 138–44, 180, 256; *see also* sacramentarians
  ambiguity on 131, 227
  and authority 187–8, 189
  and idolatry 232
  communion in both kinds 28, 29
  Eucharistic presence 256
    evangelicals accepting the Real Presence 30, 119, 138–42, 224, 225, 226
    non-standard formulations of 142–3, 226, 264
    Six Articles on 27–8, 34–6
    transubstantiation xvi, 36, 38, 139, 190
  exile views of 98
  Lollard views of 80
  'private Masses' 28, 29, 33–4
  sacrifice of the Mass 33–4, 53, 73, 130, 136, 138, 141–2, 226, 250
evangelicals
  numerical strength 6–7
Everat, George 95
exile and exiles 4, 54, 93–112, 125, 126, 135–6, 164, 205, 252–3, 266–70
  clerical celibacy and 111
  impact on events in England 106–10, 229–30
  internal exile 111
  isolation of 98–103
  legitimacy of 75

exile and exiles (*cont.*)
  publications by 97–9, 103–8, 230
  scale of the 1540s exile 94–5

faction and factional conflict 16, 23, 39–40
Fairfield, Leslie 101
Farley, Edmund 243
Faukener, John 176
Feckenham, John 151
Fehrenbach, R. J. 171
Ferrar, Robert 111, 162, 177
Filmer, Henry 48, 263
first-fruits, clerical 150, 151, 155, 242–6, 249
Fish, Simon 172
Fisher, John, bishop of Rochester 45, 158, 172, 174, 189, 216
Fitzroy, Henry, duke of Richmond 211
Fitzroy, Mary, née Howard, duchess of Richmond 100, 211, 212
Flodden 208
Folkestone, Kent 139
Ford, William 176
Forrest, John 79
Forsett, John 228
Forsett, Richard 34
Foster, John 27
Foxe, Edward, bishop of Hereford 171, 199, 213
Foxe, John 38, 48, 139, 158, 178, 185, 217
  Acts and Monuments 2, 15, 16, 97, 224–5
  doubtful accounts of martyrs in 23
  interpretation of the Reformation 2, 7, 13–14, 15–18
  on recantation 88
France 93
  persecution of evangelicals in 24
Francis I, king of France 127, 216
Frankfurt 270
Freeman, Thomas 16
Freez, Mrs 261
Freez, Valentine 261
Frith, John 98, 105, 107, 141, 172

Gardiner, Germain 49, 202
Gardiner, Stephen, bishop of Winchester 16, 18, 25, 40, 63, 81, 101, 197, 203
  as vice-chancellor of Cambridge 174, 175, 179–87, 193
  and the Six Articles 31
  and the revision of the *Bishops' Book* 32
  as conservative leader 44, 49, 52, 65
  evangelicals' views of 16, 17, 22, 56, 64, 101, 153, 184, 192
  on authority 185–8

  on the Eucharist 187–8, 250
  on evangelicals 64, 87, 96, 99, 107, 110, 144
  on prosecution of heresy 25
  publications of 106, 108, 122, 179, 187–8, 216
  theological views of 32, 45, 72, 221
Garrett, Thomas 21, 85, 88, 171, 262
Geffrye, John 107
Geneva 266, 269, 270
Germaine, Giles 261
Germany 254; *see also* Lutherans
  English evangelicals in 94
Gerrard, Philip 118, 130, 199
Gilby, Anthony 111, 122, 155, 157, 221
Gloucester, abbot of *see* Malvern, William
  bishop of *see* Wakeman, John
  diocese of 25
Gloucestershire, conventicle in (1540) 223, 229, 237
Goderick, Henry 139–40
Goodrich, Matthew 177
Goodricke, Thomas, bishop of Ely 44, 114, 166, 171
  and Cambridge University 178
  patronage of reformers 197, 249
  theological views of 31
Gough, John 46, 114–15, 117, 120
  arrest 117, 230
  publications of 105, 114, 115, 116, 127, 130, 235
Grafton, Richard 16, 38, 114–15, 149, 217, 220, 251–2
  arrests 47, 114, 117, 119, 230
  as chronicler 19
  as printer to Prince Edward 198–9
  publications of 114, 119, 133
    A glasse for housholders 126–7, 131, 134, 147, 148
    The order of the greate Turckes courte 127
    Postils 117, 124, 126, 130, 134, 137, 150, 251
    Praiers of holi fathers 117
Gray, William 101, 113–14, 119, 139, 200, 204, 243
Great Mongeham, Kent 244
Gregory, Brad 70, 73, 81
Grene, Stephen 246
Gruffyd, Ellis 208

Hadlam, John 264
Hadleigh, Suffolk 158, 244
Haigh, Christopher 5, 7, 13–14, 15, 166
Hales, Christopher 94, 96–7, 267

Hall, Basil 139
Hall, Edward 19
Hamburg 95
Hamilton, James, earl of Arran 162
Hancock, Thomas 142
Hardyng, John 127, 251–2
Harley, John 175
Harman, Edmund 202
Harrison, Giles 41
Harrydance, John 240
Harvey, Robert 262
Hastings 251
Hasylden, Thomas 227, 228
Hatley, John
Haverfordwest 265
Heath, Nicholas, bishop of Rochester and Worcester 215, 218–19, 220, 255
  religious position of 161, 214–15, 219
Hemsley, John 264
'Henry', evangelical martyr 23, 263
  servant of 263
Henry VIII 47, 51, 53, 56, 169; see also royal supremacy
  and prosecution of heresy 15, 56
  and religious conservatives 42, 56
  as Old Testament king 23, 60–1, 62, 64, 68, 231
  Assertio Septem Sacramentorum 173
  evangelicals' views of 17–18, 21, 59, 65–6, 71, 97, 106, 118, 155, 228, 250–2
  on the Bible 28–9, 36, 252
  on the 'commonwealth' 152, 161
  relations with German Lutherans 30–1, 254
  religious opinions 34, 39, 50, 135, 136
  religious policies 14, 17–18, 36, 43–4, 51–2, 56, 161, 231–2
Herbert, Lord William 118, 203
Hereford, bishop of see Bonner, Edmund; Foxe, Edward; Skip, John
  Cathedral 244
heresy prosecutions 16–17, 19, 47–8
  purposes of 48
  recantations and 81–4
  resistance to 25–6
  scale of 23–4, 50
Hertford, earl of see Seymour, Edward
Hewet, Andrew 23, 262
Heynes, Simon 48, 72, 160–1, 190, 206, 213, 217, 234
Hillenius, Michael 173
Hilles, Richard 34, 84, 85, 94, 100, 143, 205, 267
  Hilles' servant 94, 267

Hilsey, John, bishop of Rochester 171, 213
  theological views of 31
Hoby, Philip 48, 202
Holbeach, Henry 171, 214
Holgate, Robert, bishop of Llandaff and archbishop of York 161, 171, 214
  theological views of 31
Holmes, William 239
holy days 43
homilies see preaching
Hooper, John 72, 96–7, 122, 205
  and exile 99–100, 267
Hothfield, Kent 139
House of Commons, House of Lords see Parliament
Howard, Henry, earl of Surrey 55, 206–10
  religious views 209–10
  social circle of 210–11
Howard, Katherine 202
Howard, Mary see Fitzroy, Mary
Howard, Lord Thomas 211
Howard, Thomas, duke of Norfolk 27, 197, 213
  as opponent of evangelicals 22, 30, 65, 268
Hubmeir, Balthasar 105
Hudson, Anne 79, 159, 232, 236
Hughe, William 118, 129, 134, 176
Huic, Thomas, cleric 246
Huick, Thomas, gentleman 246
Huick, William als. Robert 86, 245
Huntingdon, John 75, 101, 108, 123, 238
  career 102
Hus, Jan 172
Husee, Anthony 245, 246
Husee, John 35
Hussey, Thomas 55, 211
Hussites 29
Huyck, William 177

images 28, 230–2, 233, 256
  evangelical views of 15, 126–7, 130
  iconoclasm 224, 225, 226, 227, 231
  official restrictions on (1541) 18, 43–4, 226, 231
injunctions, royal 228
intellectualism and anti-intellectualism 157–9, 187–8, 189–90, 192–3
Ipswich 26, 264
Italy
  English evangelicals in 94

Jerome, William 20, 21, 74, 85, 88, 171, 262
Jewel, John 175

John, Italian painter and martyr 261
Jonas, Justus 97
Joseph, John 86, 176, 243
Joye, George 95, 96, 97, 107, 219, 235, 236
　apocalyptic views 109
　exile 96, 267
　on celibacy and vows 77, 78, 150
　on the 'commonwealth' 150, 153, 160,
　　163–4
　on justification 135–6
　on moderation 133
　on recantation and martyrdom 70, 71, 87
　on the English Bible 253
　on the royal supremacy 61, 64, 65–6
　publications 97, 103, 104, 106, 107, 108,
　　123
　violence of language 122
justification 28, 125, 134–8, 224, 228, 234,
　　255
　and antinomianism 136–8
　evangelical views of 118
　exiles' view of 135–6
　King's Book on 45–6, 135, 166, 219, 254
　popularity of 143–4

Kelton, Arthur 118, 203
Kendall, R. D. 233
Kent, heresy charges in (1543) 135, 224,
　　225–8; *see also* Canterbury,
　　diocese of
Kerby, John 264
Key, Thomas 196
Kinderdaye, William 244
King, John 100
King, Robert, bishop of Oxford 214
King's Book (1543) 15, 46, 47, 49, 173, 231,
　　253, 254
　and diplomacy 46
　on the Eucharist 189
　on justification 45–6, 135, 166, 219, 254
　on purgatory 50–1, 255
King's Primer (1545) 51–2, 54
Kirchmeyer, Thomas *see Pammachius*
Kitchen, Anthony, bishop of Llandaff 214
Knappen, M. M. 94, 97
Knevet, Anthony 55–6
Knevet, John 246
Knight, Thomas 267
Knight, William, bishop of Bath and Wells
　　214
Knyvet, William 202–3
Kreider, Alan 165, 166

Lambert, John 15, 34, 39, 141, 243
Lancaster, Thomas 230

Lancaster, William 246
Lancelot *see* Maundevild
Langley, T. 116
Lant, Richard 115, 124, 137
Lassells, John 22–3, 54, 86, 202, 204, 235,
　　250, 264
Latimer, Hugh, bishop of Worcester 146,
　　171, 172, 175, 203, 213
　arrest (1546) 54, 85–6, 88
　and episcopacy 219
　on martyrdom and recantation 73, 74
　resignation 199, 213, 219
　theological views of 29, 31, 33
law and jurisprudence
　as an analogy for religious authority
　　186
　legal problems of heresy prosecutions
　　24–5
　legal reform 149–50
Le Roux, Jean 127, 134
Lee, Edward, archbishop of York 43,
　　197
　theological views of 31, 32
Leedham-Green, Elisabeth 165, 171
Legate, Robert 268
Legh, Thomas 200
Leland, John 210
Lent 179–80, 197
　fast-breaking 86, 99–100, 177, 208, 211,
　　212, 239
　Lenten ceremonial 130
　official relaxation of 18
Lewes, Robert, mayor of Canterbury 25
Lewis, C. S. 97
Lincoln, bishop of *see* Longland, John
　Cathedral 221
　diocese of 7, 17
Lisle, Lord *see* Dudley, John; Plantaganet,
　　Arthur
litany, English 51–2, 173
Llandaff, bishop of *see* Holgate, Robert;
　　Kitchen, Anthony
Llansantffraid, Brecknock 246
local studies 7–8
Lollardy, Lollards xvi, 17, 40, 232–7
　and books 105, 115, 127, 131, 235
　and education 159
　and recantation 79–81
　definitions 233
　links to evangelicals 80–1, 233–7,
　　239
　on oaths 78–9, 234
　persecution of 24
　Scottish 234
　theology of 29, 80, 126–7

London 121
  aldermen of 25, 87, 242
  bishop of see Bonner, Edmund; Stokesley, John
  conventicle in (1545) 224, 230, 239
  heresy arrests in (July 1540) 17, 19, 38, 40–1, 224–5, 244
  livery companies 25
  parishes:
    All Hallows Lombard Street 246
    St Andrew Holborn 228
    St Antholin 135
    St Botolph without Aldgate 225, 238
    St Bride Fleet Street 238, 245
    St Clement Eastcheap 246
    St Giles Cripplegate 238
    St Magnus 238, 242–3
    St Mary le Bow 176
    St Matthew Friday Street 238, 240, 241–2, 246
    St Michael Cornhill 241
    St Michael Queenhithe 227, 242
    St Michael Wood Street 238
  Paul's Cross 47, 54, 104, 135, 191
  St Paul's Cathedral 26, 44, 217, 220–1, 251–2, 265
  Whittington College 102
  'London Commonwealthman' 147, 148, 152, 163
    quoted 49, 83, 129, 154–5, 158, 159, 251–2, 253
    reform programme of 149–50, 160
London, John 49, 103, 177
Longland, John, bishop of Lincoln 80, 177
Lübeck 95
Lucy, William 176
Lupset, Thomas 116
Luther, Martin xv, xvi, 97, 137, 234, 240
  publications of 59, 105, 128, 172
  reputation of 97, 179, 228
  views on English affairs 21
Lutherans, Lutheranism 127, 145, 157, 231, 248, 254
  sacramental theology xvi, 29, 138
  Schmalkaldic League 29–31, 254, 266
lying see under recantation

MacAlpine, John 268
Maccabeus, John see MacAlpine, John
McClendon, Muriel 25
MacCulloch, Diarmaid 48, 139, 235
McEntegart, Rory 29–30, 36, 139
Macheson, Agnes 268
Macheson, Elizabeth 267, 268

Malet, Francis 196
Malet, Henry 27
Malvern, William, abbot of Gloucester 31
Man, Henry, bishop of Sodor and Man 214, 244
Man, John 177
Marbeck, John 48, 81, 196–7, 216
Marillac 42
marriage, clerical see celibacy
Marsh, Christopher 6
Marshall, George 94, 268
Martyr, Peter 175
martyrs and martyrdom 69, 70, 255, 266
  courting martyrdom 73–4
Mary, Virgin 2, 226, 227, 229, 236
Mary I 8–9
  as princess 196
  exiles under 93, 95
  persecution of Protestants under 24, 71
Mary Rose 100
Mass see Eucharist
Maundevild, groom to the queen 261
May, William 166
Mayler, John 115, 116, 117, 120, 127, 230, 244
Mekins, Richard 16, 24–5, 42, 143, 217, 262
Melanchthon, Philip 97, 137, 172, 174, 187, 215
  on Henry VIII 65
  on the Six Articles 21, 33, 37, 38, 114, 244, 254
Men, Horman 177
Mendlesham, Suffolk 264
Merifield, John 241
Middleton, William 115, 117, 134, 140
misprision 26
moderation, religious 113–34, 144–5, 213–22, 225–8, 249
monasticism and monasteries 15, 51
  dissolution of 21, 40, 42, 155, 161–4, 170, 216
Mont, Christopher 37, 204
Moone, Peter 20, 83
More, Edward 268
More, Thomas, lord chancellor 37, 40, 63, 84, 158, 172
Mores, Thomas 87
Morice, Ralph 17, 219
Morison, Richard 60, 69, 135, 136, 150, 200, 251–2
Mors, Roderyck see Brinklow, Henry
Moyle, Thomas 227n.
Mullins, John 175
Mychell, William 87

Nero 63
Netherlands 93, 107
  English exiles in 54, 94, 96, 201
  persecution of evangelicals in 24
Neville, Lord Henry 211–12
Neville-Singleton, Pamela 198
Nevinson, Christopher 231, 232
Nevinson, Stephen 139
Newell, Nicholas 227
Nicodemites, Nicodemism 70, 74, 79, 84–5, 87, 110; *see also* recantation
Norfolk, duke of *see* Howard, Thomas
Norwich 25, 266
  bishop of *see* Reppes, William
  Norwich Cathedral 49–50

oaths 76–9, 149, 206
obedience 4, 58–69, 71, 119–21
  and Nicodemism 71–2
Ochino, Bernardo 93
Œcolampadius, Johannes 97, 107, 172
Oglethorpe, Owen 175
Oldcastle, John 107
Osiander, Andreas 172
Osney Cathedral 168, 177
Owen, George 196
Oxford 149
  bishop of *see* King, Robert
  evangelicals in 86, 177
  St Frideswide's 168
Oxford University 162; *see also* universities
  colleges and halls of
    All Souls College 175, 177
    Balliol College 175
    Broadgates Hall 176
    Canterbury College 177
    Cardinal College 168, 170, 176, 177
    Christ Church 166, 168, 176
    Corpus Christi College 158, 175, 176, 177
    King Henry VIII College 168, 177
    Magdalen College 175–6, 178
    Merton College 175
    New College 174, 176, 177, 178, 268
    Oriel College 177
  limited impact of evangelicalism on 174–8

Padua 268
Paget, William 100, 149, 154, 168, 212
  as patron of reformers 197, 203–4
Palmer, William 47, 82–3, 106, 111, 150, 192, 211
Pammachius 179–82
Parish, Helen 111

parishes
  parish religion 6
Parker, George 244
Parker, Matthew 166, 167–8, 180–2, 199, 216
  elected vice-chancellor of Cambridge 102, 178
Parkhurst, John 175
Parliament 47, 110, 150
  House of Commons 20, 121, 164
  House of Lords 27
Parnell, Thomas 242
Parr, Anne 203
Parr, Katherine 15, 195
  as a patron of reformers 100, 166, 167, 196–7, 203
  attacked for heresy (1546) 56, 194
  evangelical views of 55, 137
  publications of 119, 129, 204
Parr, William, earl of Essex 55, 100, 182
Partridge, Nicholas 21
Patterson, Annabel 120
Paul III, Pope 106
Pearsone, Anthony 48, 73–4, 202, 226, 263
Pellican, Conrad 172
penance 32, 144, 224, 228, 255
  evangelical views of 31–2, 117
  Six Articles on 28, 31–2
Pepwall, Henry 173
Peryn, William 101, 107, 189, 218, 238
Peterborough, bishop of *see* Chamber, John
Peterson, William 94, 268
Pettegree, Andrew 88
Philpot, John 94, 96–7, 268
Pickering, Thomas 211
pilgrimage 15, 233, 255
Plantaganet, Arthur, Lord Lisle 34–5, 238, 251–2
Plantaganet, Honor, Lady Lisle 35
plays, evangelical 1, 2, 3–4, 179–82, 262; *see also* Bale, John
Pluckley, Kent 246
Pokysfene, John 117, 126, 134
Pole, Reginald 49, 203, 265
polemic 4, 97
  moderate styles of 126
  purposes of 121–5
Pollard, Martin 246
Ponet, John 243
Popes and the papacy
  English defenders of martyred 24
  evangelical opposition to papal supremacy 19
Porter, John 17, 23, 26, 211, 218, 251–2, 265

poverty, attitudes towards 147–8, 152
Poynings, Thomas 99
Poyntz, Nicholas 211
preaching 230
  clandestine 239–40
  evangelical postils 116–17, 124–5, 126, 130, 134, 137, 235
  official homilies to be issued 44
predestination 28, 123, 135
Price, John 203
Price, Matthew 229
pride, accusations of against evangelicals 190–2
primer *see King's Primer*
printing *see also* books and book trade
  limited effectiveness of for communication 103–4
  technical aspects 108
privy chamber 201–3
  attacks on evangelicals in 48–9
probate inventories 171–5
processional *see* litany
proclamations 18, 40, 43, 51, 54, 151, 178
Proctor, John 132, 190
proselytisation 121–8, 136
prostitution 151
Protestantism: *see also* evangelicals
  definitions xv–xvi
Prowet, Steven 102
purgatory and prayer for the dead 3–4, 28, 73, 164
  and 'private Masses' 33
  evangelical views of 15, 128, 224, 225, 228, 255
  official downplaying of 50–1
Purvey, John 79, 159
Pylbarough, John 60–1, 152, 221
Pynnynge, John 228, 229

Quarrye the pardoner 102

Radcliffe, Henry, earl of Sussex 269
Ramsey, John 262
Rastell, John 172
rebellions
  South-Western rebellion (1549) 6
recantation 41–2, 53, 69–89; *see also* Nicodemites, oaths
  exiles on 97, 133
  evasion and conformity 75–6, 79, 80
  legitimacy of lies 74–5
  Lollardy and 79–81, 236
  official collusion with 81–4
  propaganda use of 82–3

Redman, John 166, 168
Redworth, Glyn 35, 36
Reformed Protestantism 173, 248
  amongst exiles 97–8, 119, 254
  definitions xvi
  on the Ten Commandments 231
  sacramental theology xvi
Regensburg, colloquy of (1541) 203
Reppes, William, bishop of Norwich 214
  theological views of 31
resistance, illegitimacy of 59, 66
'revisionism' 2, 6, 7, 14, 16
Rex, Richard 29, 80, 170, 213, 214, 231, 232–3
Rhegius, Urbanus 70
rhetoric *see* polemic
Rich, Richard 55, 167
Richardine, Oliver 23, 264
Richmond 264
Richmond, duchess of *see* Fitzroy, Mary
Ridley, Lancelot 105
Ridley, Nicholas 178, 197, 250
Rochester, bishop of *see* Fisher, John; Heath, Nicholas; Hilsey, John; Holbeach, Henry
Rogers, John 97, 268
Rogers, martyr 264
Rome 268
Rose, Thomas 96, 97, 268
royal supremacy 14
  and authority 71
  evangelical views of 58–69
Rugge, William *see* Reppes, William
Russell, Francis, earl of Bedford 17

sacramentarians, sacramentarianism 224, 225, 226, 227, 228, 229, 245, 263, 265
  definitions xvi
  growth of 250
  hostility to 15, 34–5, 38, 140, 144
  Lollardy and 233, 235–6
  persecution of 23
sacraments 31, 227, 263; *see also* baptism, Eucharist, penance
Sadler, Ralph 42, 162, 200, 202
saints, veneration of 28, 228, 233; *see also* holy days
  evangelical views of 15, 128–9, 226
  official policy towards 43, 52, 256
St Asaph, bishop of *see* Warton, Robert
St David's, bishop of *see* Barlow, William
  Cathedral 246
  diocese of 245–7
St Paul's Cathedral *see under* London

Salcot, John, bishop of Bangor and Salisbury 105, 223, 241
    theological views of 31
Salisbury 17, 22, 239, 262
    bishop of *see* Salcot, John; Shaxton, Nicholas
    conventicle in 105, 223, 228, 230, 239, 241
Sampson, Richard, bishop of Chichester and of Coventry and Lichfield 51, 103, 214–15
Sampson, Thomas 72
Sandys, Edwin, Lord 35
Saxy, Thomas 23, 265
Scarisbrick, J. J. 2
Schmalkaldic League *see under* Lutherans
Scoloker, Anthony 269
Scory, John 226
Scotland 162
    Scottish evangelicals in England 93, 94
    Scottish Lollards 234
Scott, Cuthbert 131, 180, 181, 191
Seton, Alexander 17, 82, 88, 101, 135, 217
sexual conduct, evangelical views of 150–1
Seymour, Anne, countess of Hertford 54
Seymour, Edward, earl of Hertford, duke of Somerset 6, 100, 146, 195
    patronage of reformers 203
Shagan, Ethan 6
Sharington, William 203
Shaxton, Nicholas, bishop of Salisbury 54, 86, 158, 171, 199, 213, 219, 244
    theological views of 29, 31, 33, 250
    recantation and conversion 54, 82, 88, 218, 221
Singleton, Robert 50, 88, 265
Skip, John, bishop of Hereford 163, 214–15, 216, 218
Skygges, Thomas 264
Sleidanus, Johannes 172
Smethwick, William 22
Smith, Richard 26, 103, 121, 132, 151, 152, 236
Smith, Thomas, clerk of the queen's council 101, 113–14, 119
Smith, Thomas, scholar and royal tutor 166, 167, 183, 185, 187
Smith, William 133, 241–2
Sodor and Man, bishop of *see* Man, Henry
Solme, Thomas 67, 235, 269
Solway Moss 127
Somerset, duke of *see* Seymour, Edward
Southwark 151, 261, 265
Spenser, Richard 262
Spicer, Henry 177

Standish, John 143, 178
    career 102
    Lytle treatise . . . against . . . Robert Barnes 101, 103
Starkey, John 41, 243
Starkey, Thomas 161
statutes *see under names of specific Acts*
Stawme, William 102
Steeple Bumpstead, Essex 233
Stepney 262
Sternhold, Thomas 202
Stokesley, John, bishop of London 40, 173, 217
Strassburg, English exiles in 94, 95, 99, 100, 266, 267, 269
Sturgeon, John 243, 245
Sudbury, archdeaconry of 50
Suffolk, duchess of *see* Willoughby, Katherine
Suffolk, duke of *see* Brandon, Charles
supremacy *see* royal supremacy
Surrey, earl of *see* Howard, Henry
Sussex, earl of *see* Radcliffe, Henry
swearing *see* oaths
Swerder, William 269
Switzerland
    English evangelicals in 94

Talley, Thomas 128, 246
Taverner, Richard 85, 167, 169, 171, 200, 240, 251
    Postils 116–17, 119, 134
    publications of 105, 116, 133
Taylor, John *see* Cardmaker, John
Taylor, John, master of St John's College, Cambridge 178, 216, 243
Taylor, Rowland 54, 86, 243, 244
taxation 53, 60, 63
Ten Articles (1536) 50
Testwood, Robert 48, 263
Thirlby, Thomas, bishop of Westminster 214–16, 218–19
Thistlethwayt, Robert 212
Thomas, William 94, 269
Thompkyns, Thomas 87
Thomson, John A. F. 80, 81
Throckmorton, Nicholas 55
tithes 151, 152, 154
Tod, Dennis 96, 263
Toftes, John 227
Toftes, Margaret 227, 228
Tolwin, William 67, 105, 178, 217, 240
    recantation (1541) 67, 82, 87, 88, 101, 105
Tonge, John 199

Tracy, Richard 67, 111
  commitment to proselytisation 124
  on the Church 120
  on the 'commonwealth' 148, 153–4, 163
  on the English Bible 251–2
  on the Eucharist 141
  on justification 134, 136, 137
  on obedience 120
  publications of 110, 115, 120, 147, 152, 251–2
Traheron, Bartholomew 269
transubstantiation *see* Eucharist
Trentham, Thomas 143
Trinity, doctrine of the 226, 227
Tunstall, Cuthbert, bishop of Durham 84, 231
  on the Six Articles 31
  theological views of 32
Turner, William 52, 87, 88, 96, 107, 108, 109, 219, 244, 266
  exile 95, 103, 269
  later career 96–7, 155
  on the English Bible 253
  on the royal supremacy 62–3, 67, 69, 155
  on the universities 170
  publications of 104, 106, 107, 121
  theological views 97
Tyacke, Nicholas 94
Tyndale, William 47, 155, 163, 172, 201, 235, 251; *see also* Bible, English
  Obedience of a Christen man 59–60, 234
  on lies and dissimulation 74–5, 76

Udall, Nicholas 196
Underhill, Edward 203, 241
Unio dissidentium 172
universities 37, 44, 159, 160–93; *see also* Cambridge, Oxford
  attempted dissolution of (1546) 164–9
  evangelicalism's roots in 170
Upleadon, Gloucestershire 229

Vadianus, Joachim 174
Vaughan, Stephen 200, 201, 204
Venice 267, 268, 269
Vergil, Polydore 49, 116
vestments 72
violent and profane language used by evangelicals 122, 192, 228, 229
Vyall, John 243

Wabuda, Susan 85
Wakeman, John, bishop of Gloucester 214

Waldensians 24, 81
Wales
  evangelical efforts aimed at 203
  evangelical networks in 245–7
Ward, Robert, former friar 239
Ward, Robert, shoemaker 23, 265
Warner, Edward 211
Warner, Francis 269
Warton, Robert, bishop of St Asaph 31, 214
Wattes, William 102
Wesel 268
Westminster, abbot of *see* Benson, William
  bishop of *see* Thirlby, Thomas
Whitchurch, Edward 47
  arrest 117, 230
  publications of 115
Whitechapel 240
Whitehead, Oliver 269
Whitford, Richard 128
Williams, Glanmor 245
Williams, Robert 49, 116
Willock, John 41, 85, 86, 240
Willoughby, Katherine, duchess of Suffolk 54, 99, 195, 203
Willoughbye, Anthony 239
Wilson, Nicholas 34, 103, 113
Winchester, bishop of *see* Gardiner, Stephen
Winchester College 176
Windsor 48, 263
Wingham College 244
Wisdom, Robert 17, 148–9, 171, 239, 242
  arrest and recantation 47–8, 82, 83, 86, 88, 110, 218
  as preacher 119
  exile 54, 94, 256, 269
  on the 'commonwealth' 147, 148–9
  on the English Bible 251–2, 253–4
  on the Eucharist 141
  on Henry VIII 67
  on justification 135
  on prayer to saints 128
Wishart, George 93
Wittenberg 266, 268
Wolsey, Thomas 161, 168, 199
Wooding, Lucy 36, 131
Woodroffe, William 270
Worcester, bishop of *see* Bell, John; Heath, Nicholas; Latimer, Hugh
Worley, William 202, 205
Wriothesley, Charles 143
Wriothesley, Thomas, lord chancellor 55, 56, 133

Wyatt, Thomas, the elder 199, 203, 206–7, 209–10, 216, 221
  arrest (1541) 42, 206
  religious convictions 99, 206–7
Wyatt, Thomas, the younger 208, 211
Wyborne, George 227
Wyche, Richard 79, 82
Wychling, Kent 226
Wyclif, John 143, 175, 233, 235
Wyclif's Wicket 235–6
Wylley, Thomas 1–2, 3–4, 256

Young, Thomas 176, 246
York, archbishop of *see* Holgate, Robert; Lee, Edward
  evangelicals in 111, 261
Yoxford, Suffolk 1

Zurich 94, 231, 266, 267, 268, 269, 270
Zwingli, Huldrych xvi, 107, 144
  publications of 97, 172
  reputation of 97, 107, 235

Titles in the series

*The Common Peace: Participation and the Criminal Law in Seventeenth-Century England**
CYNTHIA B. HERRUP

*Politics, Society and Civil War in Warwickshire, 1620–1660**
ANN HUGHES

*London Crowds in the Reign of Charles II: Propaganda and Politics from the Restoration to the Exclusion Crisis**
TIM HARRIS

*Criticism and Compliment: The Politics of Literature in the England of Charles I**
KEVIN SHARPE

*Central Government and the Localities: Hampshire, 1649–1689**
ANDREW COLEBY

*John Skelton and the Politics of the 1520s**
GREG WALKER

Algernon Sidney and the English Republic, 1623–1677
JONATHAN SCOTT

*Thomas Starkey and the Commonweal: Humanist Politics and Religion in the Reign of Henry VIII**
THOMAS F. MAYER

*The Blind Devotion of the People: Popular Religion and the English Reformation**
ROBERT WHITING

*The Cavalier Parliament and the Reconstruction of the Old Regime, 1661–1667**
PAUL SEAWARD

The Blessed Revolution: English Politics and the Coming of War, 1621–1624
THOMAS COGSWELL

*Charles I and the Road to Personal Rule**
L. J. REEVE

George Lawson's 'Politica' and the English Revolution
CONAL CONDREN

Puritans and Roundheads: The Harleys of Brampton Bryan and the Outbreak of the Civil War
JACQUELINE EALES

*An Uncounselled King: Charles I and the Scottish Troubles, 1637–1641**
PETER DONALD

*Cheap Print and Popular Piety, 1550–1640**
TESSA WATT

*The Pursuit of Stability: Social Relations in Elizabethan London**
IAN W. ARCHER

Prosecution and Punishment: Petty Crime and the Law in London and Rural Middlesex, c. 1660–1725
ROBERT B. SHOEMAKER

Algernon Sidney and the Restoration Crisis, 1677–1683*
JONATHAN SCOTT

Exile and Kingdom: History and Apocalypse in the Puritan Migration to America*
AVIHU ZAKAI

The Pillars of Priestcraft Shaken: The Church of England and its Enemies, 1660–1730
J. A. I. CHAMPION

Steward, Lords and People: The Estate Steward and his World in Later Stuart England
D. R. HAINSWORTH

Civil War and Restoration in the Three Stuart Kingdoms: The Career of Randal MacDonnell, Marquis of Antrim, 1609–1683*
JANE H. OHLMEYER

The Family of Love in English Society, 1550–1630
CRISTOPHER W. MARSH

The Bishops' Wars: Charles I's Campaign against Scotland, 1638–1640*
MARK FISSEL

John Locke: Resistance, Religion and Responsibility
JOHN MARSHALL

Constitutional Royalism and the Search for Settlement, c. 1640–1649*
DAVID L. SMITH

Intelligence and Espionage in the Reign of Charles II, 1660–1685*
ALAN MARSHALL

The Chief Governors: The Rise and Fall of Reform Government in Tudor Ireland, 1536–1588*
CIARAN BRADY

Politics and Opinion in Crisis, 1678–1681
MARK KNIGHTS

The House of Lords in the Reign of Charles II
ANDREW SWATLAND

Catholic and Reformed: The Roman and Protestant Churches in English Protestant Thought, 1604–1640*
ANTHONY MILTON

Sir Matthew Hale, 1609–1676: Law, Religion and Natural Philosophy*
ALAN CROMARTIE

Henry Parker and the English Civil War: The Political Thought of the Public's 'Privado'*
MICHAEL MENDLE

Protestantism and Patriotism: Ideologies and the Making of English Foreign Policy, 1650–1668*
STEVEN C. A. PINCUS

Gender in Mystical and Occult Thought: Behmenism and its Development in England
B. J. GIBBONS

William III and the Godly Revolution
TONY CLAYDON

Law-Making and Society in Late Elizabethan England: The Parliament of England, 1584–1601
DAVID DEAN

Conversion, Politics and Religion in England, 1580–1625
MICHAEL C. QUESTIER

Politics, Religion and the British Revolutions: The Mind of Samuel Rutherford*
JOHN COFFEY

King James VI and I and the Reunion of Christendom*
W. B. PATTERSON

The English Reformation and the Laity: Gloucestershire, 1540–1580*
CAROLINE LITZENBERGER

Godly Clergy in Early England: The Caroline Puritan Movement, c. 1620–1643*
TOM WEBSTER

Prayer Book and People in Elizabethan and Early Stuart England*
JUDITH MALTBY

Sermons at Court, 1559–1629: Religion and Politics in Elizabethan and Jacobean Preaching
PETER E. MCCULLOUGH

Dismembering the Body Politic: Partisan Politics in England's Towns, 1650–1730
PAUL D. HALLIDAY

Women Waging Law in Elizabethan England
TIMOTHY STRETTON

The Early Elizabethan Polity: William Cecil and the British Succession Crisis, 1558–1569*
STEPHEN ALFORD

The Polarisation of Elizabethan Politics: The Political Career of Robert Devereux, 2nd Earl of Essex
PAUL J. HAMMER

The Politics of Social Conflict: The Peak Country, 1520–1770
ANDY WOOD

Crime and Mentalities in Early Modern England*
MALCOLM GASKILL

The Church in an Age of Danger: Parsons and Parishioners, 1660–1740
DONALD A. SPAETH

Reading History in Early Modern England
D. R. WOOLF

The Politics of Court Scandal in Early Modern England: News Culture and the Overbury Affair, 1603–1660
ALASTAIR BELLANY

The Politics of Religion in the Age of Mary, Queen of Scots: The Earl of Argyll and the Struggle for Britain and Ireland
JANE E. A. DAWSON

Treason and the State: Law, Politics and Ideology in the English Civil War
D. ALAN ORR

Preaching during the English Reformation
SUSAN WABUDA

Pamphlets and Pamphleteering in Early Modern Britain
JOAD RAYMOND

Popular Politics and the English Reformation*
ETHAN H. SHAGAN

Patterns of Piety: Women, Gender and Religion in Late Medieval and Reformation England
CHRISTINE PETERS

Crime, Gender and Social Order in Early Modern England
GARTHINE WALKER

Mercy and Authority in the Tudor State
K. J. KESSELRING

Unquiet Lives: Marriage and Marriage Breakdown in England, 1660–1800
CHRISTINE PETERS

The Gospel and Henry VIII: Evangelicals in the Early English Reformation
ALEC RYRIE

**Also published as a paperback*

Printed by Libri Plureos GmbH in Hamburg, Germany